PERFORMANCE OF THE U.S. RAILROADS SINCE WORLD WAR II

A Quarter Century of Private Operation

Kent T. Healy

VANTAGE PRESS
New York / Washington / Atlanta
Los Angeles / Chicago

Copyright © 1985 by Kent T. Healy

Published by Vantage Press, Inc.
516 West 34th Street, New York, New York 10001

Manufactured in the United States of America
ISBN: 0-533-06561-5

Library of Congress Catalog Card No.: 83-90465

Contents

Preface

The railroads of the United States almost uniquely provide the materials for an industry economic history more comprehensive than would be possible for any other industry, public utilities excepted. Government and corporations and various associations make available an almost limitless amount and variety of data covering every aspect of railroading—labor, finance, operation, and marketing. The only gap is the absence of measures of the qualities of service, which limit is of course associated with all primarily service-producing industries.

The challenge, then, of this historical analysis is to take advantage of this situation, aiming for an integrated understanding of all major factors involved in twenty-five years of postwar railroading. Among other things, this calls for a difficult balance between the vast extent of detail in all the available material and the amount that can be tolerated by the reader. This requires passing over many of the details, making hard decisions as to what are of sufficient significance to be included.

Valuable help and criticism for which I express deep thanks have come from three sources. Several former railroad officials have reviewed sections of the manuscript that lie in their respective fields: J. L. Barngrove, W. J. Dixon, G. M. Leilich, and R. W. Talbot. Academic colleagues reviewed a broader selection of chapters: Ed Morelock, J. C. Nelson, M. J. Peck, R. Ruggles, and H. C. Mansfield. Finally my wife, Ruth, has read most all pages from a broader point of view. Thanks is also due D. Howard for her patience in translating my handwriting and corrections.

1

Introduction

This historical analysis of the performance of the railroads of the United States during the twenty-five years following World War II deals with a significant chapter of the country's economic history and an important segment of the country's industry. The railroad industry was a major one, with sales of $7½ billion in 1947 and $13½ billion in 1972, and employment just after the war of some 1,400,000 and at the end of the period of somewhat under 600,000.

The railroads comprised a mature industry during a period of drastic change. Demands for their services were greatly reduced by the rapid development of other transport modes—pipeline, highway, waterway, and air. There were major locational shifts in the country's economic activity and in the geographic distribution of the population. There were broad changes in the mix of the commodities to be transported. The supply and character of the various railroad services were much changed. The inputs to produce them were altered as a result of technological advances in railroading, large investment in new facilities, and changes in the parameters of labor, material, and management inputs.

The publicized picture of the railroads was of an industry encumbered with a succession of crises and a persistent basic problem. The latter was the continuing loss of business to other transport modes, epitomized in the disappearance of express traffic, near to total loss of mail and less-than-carload freight, and almost 90 percent reduction of intercity passenger travel. Of the crises there was a succession of critical labor demands, first in 1950 leading to the president of the United States having to order army takeover of the railroads. Finally, in 1971 Congress had to enter the picture by prescribing labor contract terms to prevent shutdown of the railroads. The bankruptcy of the country's largest railroad, the Penn-Central, in 1969 created a major financial crisis for the country. Less apparent to the public but critical for shippers were major car shortages in the 1950s and again after 1966. Industry, political, and academic discussion of all these accounted for a large share of the printed words dealing with the postwar railroad industry.

The economic historian has the broader responsibility of covering all, rather than just the critical, publicized, aspects of the year-to-year problems of the railroad industry. This brings in the industry's little-hailed accomplishments and the just plain everyday operations, which are the broad base of its performance. The perspective of this study is then a systematic, balanced coverage of all major components of railroading without emphasis on special or single issues, in order

1

to properly weigh all the factors involved in the industry—and to explain its performance.

General and popular consideration of the postwar performance of the railroads has been characterized by much, and at times bitter, controversy between competing transport modes, between management and both labor and government regulatory agencies, and between exponents of the older ways versus promoters of the new. To counter and avoid any of the associated exaggeration and bias, this analysis so far as possible rests on that which can be measured quantitatively and for which statistics and demonstrable facts have been compiled over the twenty-five years surveyed. A noted limitation on this is that the outputs of the railroad industry are services that have numerically measurable aspects, such as ton-miles or passenger-miles, but also have quality aspects, which for the most part do not lend themselves to measurement.

The various commodities comprising rail traffic differ widely as to service qualities required with their handling. Thus a ton-mile of one can require very different resources and costs from that of another. For instance, the transport of oranges from country packing house to city auction purchaser calls for speedy train movement scheduled to meet destination auction market requirements with high degree of reliability. There is also special provision for rerouting to allow the shipper to take advantage of sudden changes in market prices city to city. The railroad must also be able from a wide range of car types to provide the particular type favored and ordered by the shipper. Further, the cars, once loaded, must be made available en route for checking of refrigeration and satisfactory condition of the oranges. A contrasting freight movement is of gravel, in a simple open-top hopper car moving in a tonnage freight train without need for fast movement or precisely scheduled elasped times and without protection against deterioration. These two services are measured in the common quantitative unit, the ton-mile, but are without numerical measures of the different service qualities. This lack introduces substantial uncertainty in analysis of comparative costs and values of the two services.

Because of these limitations the terms of this historical analysis are tied primarily to the functional elements of the goings-on of the railroads for which the numerical data are generally available. In respect to inputs, the identifiable elements are train and car movements and terminal handlings, and the installation and repair of locomotives, cars, track, structures, and supplementary facilities. In respect to outputs, the elements are the distinct identifiable items of service, the quantity, haul, and prices of each of which are the only numerical data available.

Some of these data are available for individual railroad systems, all are for regions and for the country as a whole. Some factors affecting performance are uniform over the country, such as basic wage rates and federal regulatory provisions. On the other hand, there are important regionally differentiated factors such as topography, economic growth rates and waterway developments. Thus regional performance and differences therein are emphasized.

The overall pattern of the analysis is guided to some extent by what price, market, and firm theories suggest are the basic elements in industry behavior that explain performance. In addition, considerable weight is given to the institutional aspects of the industry because of their great influence in much of railroad decision making. Further, in accounting for the position of a mature industry like the railroads, consideration of each aspect is prefaced with brief review of pertinent pre–World War II key developments.

The choice of period covered by this analysis, the roughly twenty-five years following World War II, is because it covers the last years of solely private ownership and operation of the railroads. In 1971 almost all intercity passenger operations were taken over by a federal government controlled and subsidized corporation, the National Railroad Passenger Corporation (Amtrak). Further, local governments had largely become involved in commuter operations in metropolitan areas. Then after 1972 the Penn-Central and other eastern roads posed such critical federal problems as to lead to their takeover by two government corporations.

This analysis then is of the United States railroads' performance, including innovation, investment, productivity, labor relations, pricing, and, to the extent possible, quality of services over a quarter of a century of private ownership and operation. The aim is to track the performance and both identify and appraise all the factors accounting for it in an integrated whole.

2

The Organization of the Railroad Industry

Changes in the overall organization of the railroad industry are of basic importance in the railroads' performance. Primary ones are the changes in the numbers, scale, and strategic relationships of the industry's individual decision-making units, the independent railroad systems. Other aspects of the industry's organization are its trade associations for review of pricing, for standardization of physical facilities and accounting, and for other practices and general advisory and oversight purposes. The industry organization also involves the structure of its relations with financial markets, with labor and its organization, the unions. Finally, there is the arrangement of the interface with government economic regulation.[1]

NUMBER AND SCALE OF RAILROAD SYSTEMS

At the end of World War II the railroad industry of the United States comprised a vast array, some 1,100, of privately owned, some large but mostly very small, railroad corporations. A few, 52, were in the special state of being in the hands of the courts under trusteeship or receivership, rather than the usual unencumbered private ownership. Some 250 were switching and terminal companies rather than line-haul. Exceptions to the private pattern were 5 terminal ones, municipally or state controlled. Otherwise, the switching and terminal roads were mostly controlled by line-haul railroads or shippers. The essentially universal private railroad control in the U.S. was contrary to the government controlled industry pattern in the rest of the world. The notable exception to this was neighboring Canada, with one of its two country-wide rail system nationalized and one private and with its new ore carriers private.[2]

Of the many U.S. railroad corporations only some 70 had over $10 million annual operating revenue in 1946. Of them, only 47 were independent decision-making units, that is, not subject to control of other railroads. The biggest was the Pennsylvania with $822 million revenue, and the smallest, the Bangor and Aroostook, with $10 million. By 1972 the industry total count had been reduced by acquisition and dissolution to 680. Taking inflation into account, by considering an increase in the minimum size counted as major system scale to be $20 million annual revenue, there were 31 large independent systems. The biggest, the Penn-Central, had $1,862 million annual revenue, more than twice that of its predecessor constituents, and a Maine road was again the smallest.

4

Map of the Three Primary Regions or Districts of the U.S. and One Subregion for Grouping of Railroads

Class I Line-Haul RR Operating Revenues
(Billions)

	East (Excl. Poc.)	Pocahontas	South	West	U.S.
1946	$3.0	$0.37	$1.1	$3.2	$7.6
1950	3.6	0.55	1.3	4.0	9.5
1960	3.3	0.61	1.4	4.2	9.5
1972	4.8		2.3	6.3	13.6

(The ICC gross E region statistical grouping for 1966 and thereafter includes the Pocahontas subregion.)

CONCENTRATION TRENDS

The effect of the reduction in numbers on industry structure was a major reduction in competition, critically so in large areas of the United States. A measure of this is the change in proportion of revenue accruing to the largest system in each of the major regions. In 1946 the largest system in the East, the Pennsylvania, accounted for 27 percent of the eastern revenue. By 1972 something over 50 percent of the equivalent region's (that is, the East, with estimates of the earlier Pocahontas roads deducted) revenue went to the Penn-Central system. In the South for 1946 the largest system, the Atlantic Coast Line and its stock controlled partner, the Louisville and Nashville, accounted for 30 percent of the region's revenue. By 1972, following merger with the Seaboard Airline, the new share rose to 46 percent. For the West the concentration of traffic occurred in the Northwest subregion and can only be measured in terms of number of independent direct through transcontinental routes, not revenue. From 1946 with three such routes, the 1967 Burlington-northern merger cut the number to just two, one being so weak as to soon withdraw as a transcontinental. On the other hand, there were no significant mergers in the Southwest, and no concentration of control. The details and other basic aspects of mergers and unifications involved in this restructuring are analyzed in subsequent chapters.

Another measure of concentration is the proportions of revenue going to the largest four systems. In 1946 the maximum concentration was in the Pocahontas and southern regions, with the two largest systems accounting for 88 percent of freight revenue in the former, and the four largest, 89 percent in the South. On the other hand, for the West for four it was only 49 percent, and the East, 61 percent. By 1972 the eastern district included the Pocahontas, and for the combined two regions the largest four systems got 84 percent of the revenue. In the West, four received only 63 percent, but in the South three got 91 percent.

Overall, by 1972 there was minimum concentration in the West, as there always had been. The great increase came in the East, and it was accompanied by the formation of the largest-scale company. The South throughout the years had the highest degree of concentration.

GOVERNMENT ENTRANCE INTO OPERATION AND OWNERSHIP

A key organizational characteristic of a quite different type evolved in latter years covered by this study. As losses from passenger operations became excessive, a number of systems, rather than choosing or being allowed to withdraw from service as demand declined, put increasing pressure on government to provide subsidies. The users of these services contributed importantly to the pressure. This, in some cases, led to actual government takeover of operation. Commuter services, being those with the highest proportionate losses, were the first to be proposed for aid and obtained local, state, or metro-area authority subsidies and finally takeover. In 1967 many years' negotiations with the Pennsylvania culminated in the complete public authority takeover of the Long Island, including freight as well as its passenger operation. This was notable for putting all aspects of railroading in one organization as it had been under private ownership. In subsequent years several major metropolitan regions in the country created a variety of arrangements of public and private ownership, operation, leasing, and other terms for provision of commuter services.

By the 1970s intercity passenger losses had loomed large enough to persuade Congress of the need to relieve the railroads of the associated burdens. A federal authority with its own governing board and ties to the Department of Transportation was created and federal funds were made available. The National Railroad Passenger Corporation (Amtrak) started operation in 1971. It was the primary owner of equipment but depended in most parts of the country on trackage rights over the existing privately owned and operated track and other facilities. However, the heavy traffic Boston-Washington corridor and some adjoining lines became largely the property and responsibility of Amtrak because of its dominating involvement with passenger traffic in the corridor facilities.

Following the merger and then collapse of the two principal systems in the East, and the bankruptcies of the merged system and several other eastern systems from 1970 through 1972, the federal government had to take over the total operations, including freight, of a major share of the eastern roads. The operations were consolidated under two federal public authorities, the U.S. Railroad Association and the Consolidated Railroad Corporation (Conrail). In much of the East this left eastern shippers with but one railroad with which to deal. This new operating railroad, Conrail, as an organization was hard to interpret as to its public versus private aspects, with the close relations to the Department of Transportation and strong congressional involvement in funding but a mixture of government and private directors. Despite the legislative hopes that the private aspect might turn out to be the overall ultimate character, the path to that looked rocky.[3]

THE INTRODUCTION OF CONGLOMERATES

The organization of railroad systems traditionally included subsidiaries involved in use of the land they might·own in excess of that needed just for transport operations. Some of this land was in metropolitan centers adjacent to major passenger terminals. With growing city populations and increasing station traffic the land increased greatly in value as it was developed and produced significant rental income. This became an important item in connection with calculations and disputes with respect to commuter fares—whether such income should be credited against expenses of commuter service and thus lower passenger fare revenue needs. Other land, most land acquired by the nineteenth-century land grants, brought in mining, oil, and timber sales, and royalty income. Several larger western roads profited substantially from these sources, the Union Pacific the outstanding example with its oil related income.

In the postwar years these various sources of income were developed more fully and combined with new nonrail transport activities to develop increasingly large, diversified organizations headed up by a holding company or a parent railroad with various types of enterprise operating with separate profit centers, each with its own chief officer reporting to a chairman. Most of this development was initiated by a parent railroad—the UP, ATSF, SP, and GN—but in one case, the Mississippi River Corporation, the initiator was a nonrail combination of gas pipelines and cement manufacturers.

With the development of general industry conglomerates, another type of conglomerate pattern was introduced to railroading. A railroad system could be used as a base for a wide range of enterprise either to get the advantage of past years' railroad losses to provide tax shelter for income from a variety of other activities or to generate cash flow that could be used for acquisition of other activities. The first move in this new direction was the formation in 1960 of a holding company by the small Bangor and Aroostook (BA), which in 1964 merged with a sugar company leading to the conglomerate ultimately named Bangor Punta. In the end, the railroad was severed from the conglomerate, being sold in 1969.

The two largest-scale rail systems changed to broad conglomerate form were the Chicago and Northwestern and the Illinois Central. The former had initiated growth with acquisition of smaller midwestern railroads without achieving particular success. In 1967 a chemical company was acquired by a CNW subsidiary, which in turn was converted to an overall holding company. It undertook acquisition of a wide variety of manufacturing and other operations whose sales revenues by 1972 became three times that of the railroad. With several years of failing to meet expenses, the railroad was finally sold to its employees in 1972, leaving the tax shelter of its deficits to the conglomerate, but also the continuing responsibility for certain of the railroad's financial obligations.

The other big case was the Illinois Central, initiated in 1962 with incorporation of IC Industries. First steps involved major land use developments in the Chicago area, then came nonrail industry acquisitions. By 1972 total general sales revenue was three times that of the railroad. IC Industries was reported to have been interested in selling the latter but could not find a buyer.[4]

Several small railroad systems, the MKT, KCS, BM, and WP, established conglomerates with varying degrees of success. In the case of the largest-scale merger of all, the Penn-Central, the holding company started out to expand into land development and other hoped-for growth enterprizes, but the PC railroad collapse led, after bankruptcy, to their separation from the railroad operations.

WIDENED ACCESS OF SHIPPERS TO INDIVIDUAL SYSTEMS

In a different way a very important change in the effective pattern of the railroad industry came with the postwar initiation of piggyback services. This enabled shippers to load and unload many types of carload freight on their premises without the necessity of having a private siding connected to an adjacent rail line or to a spur extended from one. Local roads and streets enabled a shipper to deal with his choice of railroads within an extensive range of his premises. For those commodities that could be handled in piggyback equipment this opened the opportunity for bargaining with more railroad systems than before as to carload rates and service. Previously, a shipper had a siding connected to an adjacent rail line, which had a monopoly position with respect to that shipper unless reciprocal switching with nearby railroads was the practice or there were joint terminal operation arrangements between competing systems or neutral terminal operating units.

ENTRANCE AND EXIT OF RAILROADS

Another key aspect in industry organization is the matter of entrance of new firms and exit of old ones. In the case of railroads, since the war there have been no new system entrants. This has not been because of regulatory constraints but because of the maturity of the industry, complete coverage of major centers of economic activity, and the lack in growth of demand for rail services. The problems of starting up a new system in an industry where coverage of most of the country's needs are more than complete seemed insurmountable. Interconnection with the existing network of the rest of the country would be critical to the viability of a new system and such interconnection would not be likely to be granted by existing systems. Thus the limited route miles added in the few developing areas or local situations came as extensions of existing systems.

The abandonment of existing independent systems in their entirety has been rare. In twenty-five years only four roads with annual revenue of over $1 million, have been liquidated: the New York Ontario and Western in New York State, the Rutland in Vermont, the Lehigh and New England in the anthracite region, and the Tennessee Central. In each case, viable segments of their lines have been taken over by connecting systems or, in Vermont, by the state. Overall abandonment has been primarily of branches. From 1946 to 1972 there was little change in the mileage of road in operation in the U.S., from 240,000 to 218,000 miles, only minus 9 percent. It was possible for freight operation to be reduced to as little as one train a week without reaching the state of abandonment as number of freight trains was not subject to regulatory control.

Clearly for the railroads, in contrast to a growing industry, new entry has not been a source of significant industry growth or added competition. Nor has abandonment of independent systems reduced freight competition or basic route capacity significantly. It has been the acquisitions, mergers, and unifications just mentioned and later reviewed in chapter 12 that have impacted the industry's balance of monopolistic and competitive elements.

The extent and way that the resultant changes in competition have taken effect requires knowledge of basic elements. For freight service, they are price, supply of cars for loading, and quality of terminal handling and road movement. The pricing in the first instance involves negotiating with the traffic and marketing representatives of the railroad on whose rails a shipper is located, that is, to which his private siding is connected (except as noted since piggyback has entered part of the picture). If the shipper is locating anew, his bargaining power is enhanced by the possibility of a choice between different locations and railroad systems. In this connection the reduction over the years in number of systems has greatly reduced the shipper's bargaining strength with fewer chances of finding different attitudes toward price adjustment and service among which to choose. The fewer the railroad system alternatives, the greater the incentive to go to other modes of transportation.

Because of merger and unification, the shipper increasingly must rely entirely on the one railroad to which he now has access. For long-distance movements the shipper also has the possibility of negotiation with railroads beyond that one, with the longer hauls being completed over joint routes. The added systems' marketing representatives involved may provide added influence over pricing, car supply, and service. The traditional practice has been that in the case of joint long hauls the originating railroad has the prerogative of handling shipments as far as possible on its own line, before turning them over to a connecting railroad. This establishes an increased monopoly power with the originating railroad. With end-to-end mergers or acquisitions and thus lengthening of the controlled haul, this power would be expected to be increased. The ICC in connection mergers, to prevent this, has required that all the premerger interconnections be continued. In practice, however, this has been difficult if not impossible to enforce so that in reality there has been significant reduction in effective alternative long-haul joint routes available to shippers.[5]

RATE ASSOCIATIONS

A key and nearly unique aspect, among industries in general, of the railroad industry's organization has been the regional rate associations. They are comprised of a permanent staff with a titular chief and an executive committee composed of the top traffic officers of the member railroads. The associations have provided a joint forum of regional railway systems for review of proposed changes in rates, fares, and conditions of transport. Proposals have been pubicly docketed; shippers and carriers can express their views. Each association through its staff and committees expresses approval or the reverse. The right of action independent of approval and the elimination of various means of, in effect, requiring approval were demanded by the courts before the turn of the century as necessary to meet the requirements of antitrust laws.[6] With these restrictions the associations operated for some half a century as private review groups and a critical element in the pricing process. They were without recognition in the industry's government regulatory structure. The associations were also involved in the publication of rates, fares, requirements for packing, etc., and in the policing of rail service and shipper behavior to see that the published requirements were adhered to.

Any effect the associations may have had by way of restraint on competition was officially only rarely questioned. It was felt that the group review and opinions were desirable as a means of preventing rate wars and stabilizing rates. The common publication of rates facilitated making them uniform as between competitors, and gaining publication economies. In the early 1920s there was a complaint followed by ICC investigation as to possible repression of independent action. There was evidence of pressure on those taking independent action to cooperate with the other carriers in an association so revenues would be "reasonably protected." Sixty-five percent of the proposals were voted against in a sample two-year period of that era.[7]

The next questioning came during the 1940s with the South worrying about its economic backwardness and Georgia in particular alleging that southern rail class rates were adverse to southern development and that the rate associations were a restraining factor. In addition, in the West there were allegations that railroad associations had restrained competition in respect to freight service. Antitrust proceedings were initiated against the associations. This focused attention on the fact that the rate associations had never been formally recognized in the regulatory statutes. The response by the railroads, regulatory agencies, and others was to get Congress to draw up and pass a federal statute that would legitimatize the associations, provided independent action was insured. With this proviso this statute gave railroad protection against antitrust constraints. The Reed-Bulwinkle bill, doing all this and placing the associations under ICC supervision, was passed in June 1948. President Truman vetoed the bill but the congressional support was so broad as to give quick passage over the veto. The president argued that even though rates were subject to regulation, the public interest demanded that competition needed to be maintained. Under the new statute the ICC promptly approved the rail association agreements. The associations continued their operations as before with the addition of supervision and potential controls by the ICC.

OTHER ASSOCIATIONS

The railroad industry has been characterized with a degree of association of both its top executives and of its specialized staff personnel not practiced in most industry. The primary association for the postwar period was the Association of American Railroads (AAR). There was also a corresponding association for smaller roads, the American Short Line Railroad Association. The AAR had been created in 1934 to replace the loosely organized American Railway Association with the aim of providing a more forceful organization to act as a general staff for the railroads as a whole.[8] The directorate was a representative group of presidents chosen from major railroads. The organization considered a wide range of industry problems from price policies, to competition of other modes, to government regulation. Suggestions were promulgated. There was room for system independence but also the possibility of group pressure toward conformity, or nonaction. The association was involved in lobbying and public relations for the industry. The AAR in its numerous technically oriented divisions did have the power to pass on and set industry standards in respect to accounting and operating practices, physical characteristics of equipment and facilities, and operating practices. This was standardization necessary for member railroads to engage in interchange and use of each other's facilities. The requirements of standardization imposed significant restriction on change, and on innovation.

There were also regional associations of top executives for consideration of local problems and dealing with local public and government relations. There were numerous professional organizations ranging from those of superintendents to air brake experts to passenger traffic officers. Overall, there was an unusually close association of railroaders at a wide range of professional levels.

Where the absolute necessity for standardization was not required for the interchange of traffic and equipment, there remained the possibility for diversity. Diversity reflected presidential and other top officer personality differences between systems and the great variation in the environments in which different railroads operated. There was among the more aggressive systems a significant element of generalized interfirm competition taking pride in particular directions for innovations, types of policy, and service characteristics.

FINANCIAL RELATIONS

So far as finances have been concerned the railroad industry traditionally dealt with the same financial institutions as industry in general. Basically, this has continued in the postwar years except that alliances with particular banking groups have been reduced by the 1944 ICC requirement of competitive bidding for security issues. The pattern established during the Great Depression of government assistance for the ailing railroads was extended with the passage of legislation in 1958 making $500 million available for weak roads needing rehabilitation and new facilities and finally in the 1970s with establishment of Amtrak and Conrail. Congress and the Treasury became major financing agencies.

LABOR RELATIONS

A major difference in the basic pattern of organization for the railroad industry as compared to other industries has been in the relations with labor. The railroads were among the first to be confronted with strongly organized labor. Key unions along craft lines originated early in the last half of the nineteenth century. By the 1890s the engineers, firemen, conductors, trainmen, and switching personnel had each built up strong craft organizations. Other crafts followed, so that ultimately the railroads have had to deal with over twenty nationwide unions.

The unions possessed greater strength than with industry in general because of their ability to strike to shut down the commerce of the country. The effects of this could be more disastrous than the cutting off of the production of any mine or manufactured product. Protection of the public interest in maintenance of rail service led to the early entrance of the government into the labor-railroad negotiations process. Government agencies were established to mediate and otherwise deal with disputes. The basic institutions involved were established in the 1920s, and they were to continue through the years. In addition to the so-called eight-hour law, Congress in 1916 established the precedent of itself determining settlement terms that would be binding on both the private railroads and their employees. In the postwar period the role of top government, the president and Congress, grew to levels not experienced in railroad industry labor relations earlier.

The railroads in turn have joined in regional and then national groupings to establish bargaining units matching the geographical scope of union ones. In the years of this study the emphasis has been on national-level bargaining. Since 1963 there has been a National Railway Labor Conference whose chairman has generally been the chief negotiator for the railroads. However, on several occasions the unions have been able to break down the unity that the conference implied and bargain individually with particular railroad executives in the East and the South. In recent years another element in the railway cooperation has been mutual assistance agreements whereby during the strikes the revenue accruing to railroads remaining in operation is shared with those strikebound.

* * *

By twenty-five years after World War II several important changes in the railroad industry had taken place. The railroads came out of the war after an excellent wartime performance in private hands. There was only such government supervision as was needed to take care of the extreme irregularities of wartime traffic and the shortage of various input items. After the war the problems that had loomed large before the war continued, and basically were the cause of modification of the all-private organizational base. Government involvement entered the passenger service picture, in the late sixties to early seventies. Takeover was by local authorities for commuter, and federal Amtrak for intercity service.

The industry competitive pattern saw major changes. Acquisition and merger mainly after 1960 reduced the number of firms and increased concentration in the East, South, and Northwest. The scale of systems was greatly increased and in the extreme case, the PC, contributed critically to the failure of private railroad operation in one region, the East. It led to government entrance into freight operation with Conrail in addition to the passenger operations involving Amtrak and local authorities.

A further structural change was the coming of conglomerates of a broader type than the one traditional to railroads, i.e., with development of land adjacent to the railroad or acquired via land grants. The new developments were based on not-so-successful railroad operations proving valuable as a source of tax shelters and of cash flow for acquiring nontransport enterprises.

3

Environment Surrounding the Railroads

The environment in which the railroads found themselves during the quarter of a century following World War II had three aspects of significance for their performance. One was the patter of the increase in the country's economic activity, with important shifts in its location and differences in particular industry and region rates of growth. Another was the tremendous expansion of other modes of transport as their technology improved, capital investment was attracted, and their networks and operations grew in response to increased demands. A third involved the government regulation of transport with its modification from time to time.

GROWTH OF ECONOMIC ACTIVITY[1]

The consequences of difference in rates of region growth is made difficult to gauge because relevant measures of activity region by region and industry by industry are not directly available. Gross regional product corresponding to gross national product (GNP) is not possible to calculate. However, it has been demonstrated that the personal earnings, a component of personal income, are a usable substitute because of their demonstrated "close and comparatively constant relationship to GNP," which holds true at the regional as well as the national level.[2] Fortunately these earnings data are available industry by industry and state by state. Initially for the year 1950, and then for latter years of this study, the last being 1971, these data are published in terms of constant dollars, providing rough adjustment for inflation and a useful base for this analysis.

From the point of view of intercity goods transport, it is necessary to separate growth of service activities from those of goods-producing industries. Services comprise utilities, finance, insurance, trade (particularly retail), professions, and government. Foods-producing industries include agriculture, forestry, fisheries, mining, construction, and manufacturing, mainly producing goods for intercity transport and therefore their activity level is a rough measure of potential demand for other than local goods transport.

In terms of growth of all economic activity, services that are basically not intercity transport demanding have grown more rapidly, 158 percent from 1950 to 1971, than the six transport demanding ones, only 81 percent.

Growth rates for the latter industries, measured by earnings, have regionally varied widely, particularly as between states. From 1950 to 1971 Arizona, Florida,

14

TABLE 1

*Changes in Goods-Producing Industry Personal Earnings by Regions
As Percent of U.S. Overall Change, 1950–1971*

Least		**Most**	
New England	−22%	South (Ohio-Mississippi-Gulf)	+53%
East (Atlantic Coast-St. Louis, Chicago)	−14%	Southwest "transcontinental"	
Northwest (Chicago-Seattle)	−24%	(Louisiana-California)	+57%

and California show the greatest gains, 273, 197, and 144 percent respectively, compared to 81 percent for the country as a whole. The two least were 6 and 18 percent, North and South Dakota. From the point of view of transport demand, particularly rail, the relevant differences were between grouping of states within which particular railroad systems tended to lie.

In Table 1 the southern region and southwestern "transcontinental" route rail systems stand out with more than half again as great increases as the national average. This was a very significant advantage over the New England, eastern, and northwestern "transcontinental" route regions' increases with a seventh to a quarter under the average. The effects of these differences are analyzed in relation to individual systems in chapter 11.

COMPETITION OF OTHER TRANSPORT MODES

Highway and Motor Vehicle[3]

After rapid growth following World War I highway development came to a sharp halt during World War II with the rationing of gasoline and curtailment of private motor vehicle manufacture and highway construction. After the war pent-up demand brought a burst in further growth without any reinforcement from major technological breakthroughs.

Eleven years after the war's end auto registrations had doubled and in fourteen years truck and tractor registrations had too. By 1972 autos in use had increased almost fourfold and trucks three-and-a-half-fold, the unit capacity of the latter increasing substantially. On the other hand, the number of intercity buses remained nearly constant.

The investment in autos was largely financed by individual households and by businesses in line with their use of mobility offered by the auto. That in trucks was largely by business and farms for their own use. Companies and individuals performing for-hire freight motor-carrier operations were also investing large sums from private sources. Class I and II motor carriers of property reported 238,000 trucks and tractors in intercity service in 1972 compared to a total of some 60,000

TABLE 2

Growth of Motor Vehicle Transport Facilities

	Registrations: Auto, Trucks, and Tractors (Millions)		"High-Load-Bearing" Primary State Roads (Thousands)	Four- (or More) Lane, Limited-Access Private State Roads (Thousands)
1946	26	6	155 mi.	
1950	40	8½	208	('56) 1 mi.
1965	75	15	316	19
1972	97	21	340	37

("High-load-bearing" = mixed bituminous and bituminous penetration with a combined thickness of surface and base of 7" or more, and/or a high-load-bearing capacity, bituminous concrete and portland cement concrete.)

(Source: DOT, FHA, *Highway Statistics.*)

at the end of 1946. Estimated book value of the carriers' investment, primarily in equipment, rose to over $6 billion gross, $3 billion depreciated, book value by 1972.

The intercity highway network, which was built and operated by the states, was expanded and upgraded as indicated in Table 2 with the mileage of primary state roads with high-load-bearing standards doubled by 1965. Then in the late 1950s the era of four- (or more) lane, divided, and limited-access highways was inaugurated. Most of these were part of the "interstate and defense highway" system built by the states according to federal general standards. The funds for capital outlays for intercity highway networks came from user charges collected by the states and those collected by the federal government to be turned back to the states. The proportion funded from debt issues became minor, and none came from federal borrowing. The user charges were composed of taxes on fuel, tires, oil, new vehicles and parts, with charges based on truck use along with license and registration fees. Fuel consumption was used as a practical measure of use, but due to the much lower diesel oil consumption per unit of output than gasoline, the generally uniform taxes per gallon of fuel make diesel-operated truck charges seriously lower than gasoline-operated ones. Highway operating expenses also came from these sources. In 1946 the capital outlays for state systems were $½ billion, in 1950, $1½ billion and by 1972, $10 billion. During the years covered by this study the intercity highway use of general tax funds, federal or state, for either capital or current expenses were not significant; the diversion of the user charges to nonhighway uses gradually increased to $½ billion annually. Over the same years an increasing amount of the user charge receipts was channeled to local government roads and streets, almost $3 billion by 1972.

Because intercity highways are used in common by automobiles, buses, and all variety of trucks, attribution of costs to these various categories of vehicles has been a matter of heated debate over the years between the various competing interest groups involved: automobilists, truckers, railroads, etc. In addition, for some roads military requirements have accounted for weight capacity and route layout over and above that for civil use. Numerous studies involving calculation of costs as between the different uses of the highways have been undertaken, many reflecting the points of view of one or more of the conflicting interests. The varying nature of factors involved in attribution of common costs leaves room for a considerable range in conclusions. One of the few published studies stressing the possible range depending upon the underlying premises was a 1965 federal study. One basis for allocation was the so-called incremental method, "each higher cost broken down into the increments occasioned by vehicles of different types." Differences were in terms of incremental costs arising from increases in costs with various uses. The contrasting method was the "differential-benefit" basis, reflecting estimates of the relative strength of demands from the users of each of the various types of vehicles. It was calculated that in respect to the federally collected $3½ billion of costs incurred in 1964, under the incremental cost basis for allocation, cost attribution was 64 percent for automobiles and 34 percent for trucks of all kinds; under the differential-benefit basis, the proportions were 74 percent and 25 percent. In respect to the various types of trucks, the one felt to be particularly competitive by the railroad industry, the five-axle tractor semi-trailers, the proportions were 3.4 percent under the incremental basis and 2 percent for the differential benefit. Of the user charge funds actually collected by the federal government, it was estimated that passenger cars contributed 61 percent, trucks as a whole, 38 percent, and the five-axle type in particular, 2.5 percent. The five-axle truck contributions were estimated to be 36 percent short of the incrementally allocated costs and 25 percent over the differential-benefit ones.[4]

The growth of truck transport must be analyzed primarily in terms of one of two broad categories because of differences in data availability. Data for one have not been collected, this including the federally unregulated operations covering private trucking of operator owned commodities, the intrastate for-hire motor carriers, and the interstate for-hire carriers of unprocessed agricultural products (livestock and fish) particularly exempted from federal regulation. Thus for these types of truck transport only rough estimates of growth based on highway traffic counts and occasional special other counts are possible. The category with adequate data was the interstate for-hire transport of all other commodities, which has been subjected to ICC oversight since 1935, with increasingly complete measures of its growth available since the war. For this category, during the postwar upturn, estimated revenue ton-miles probably doubled in the four years to 1950.

They doubled again in twelve years by 1963 and increased 90 percent from then to 1972.

The ton-miles totals represented the combination of less-than-truck-load (ltl) traffic corresponding roughly to the rail less-than-carload (lcl) together with some types of express and mail business, together with truckload (tl) traffic corresponding to rail carload. Comparison of the regulated motor-carrier growth in these categories with the competitive modes is only possible from 1950 on because it was only then that ltl and tl revenues first began to be separately compiled. Detailed comparisons remained limited because there was no breakdown of ltl revenue to show that coming under lcl, express, and mail descriptions. In 1950 motor-carrier ltl revenue was $1 billion, rail lcl $0.35 billion, and Railway Express Agency domestic, $0.30 billion (which included some from carload shipments). By 1972 motor-carrier ltl revenue was some $5.5 billion, the rail lcl negligible, and the rail express nothing. Of the ltl $0.72 billion was the United Parcel Service revenue, which had been small shipments of the Railway Express Agency and parcels of the U.S. postal service. It may be noted that, as pointed out in chapter 7, the rail lcl business in the postwar years had been considered an unprofitable one.

Growth of the regulated motor-carrier truckload (tl) traffic is to be compared with the rail cl handling of manufactured and other processed goods, categories comprising almost the entire intercity motor carrier traffic. With the pre-1964 commodity classification used by the ICC this was the broad group of "manufactures and miscellaneous," plus the processed items of animal and forest products. In 1950 federally regulated truck tl revenue was $1.3 billion and rail cl revenues for the above items amounted to $4.3 billion. By 1957 the corresponding amounts were $2.6 billion and $5 billion, the motor carriers had doubled and rail were up a sixth. In the next fifteen years, by 1972, with all rates subject to inflationary increases this type of railroad freight revenue nearly doubled and the motor carrier more than trebled, to $8.6 billion. The two became almost equal for the same range of commodities. In the twenty-two years from 1950 to 1972 the rail cl revenue with the help of the inflation had increased just over twofold; the motor carrier, almost sevenfold. The private truck carriage gain over the same years was large. Measures of it are not available.

Not all of the lesser rail growth was attributable to trucks. Processed petroleum products were for the long hauls taken over by so-called "product" pipelines. Decentralization of manufacturing reduced the demand for the long hauls of manufactured goods. Nevertheless, trucking, in a major degree through its regulated motor-carrier segment, made major inroads on the considered categories of rail carload movements.

Pipelines

Beginning with the years covered by this study major developments in pipeline technology led to larger diameter pipe and use of higher pressures with resulting capacity increases and economies in pipeline transport. This together with the bringing in of new oil and gas supplies led to the greatest rate of increase by this mode of transport of all freight modes.[5]

Crude oil pipeline transport had been significant for many decades. From 1946 to 1972 trunk-line mileage remained practically constant at around 60,000 miles, but its capacity was increased substantially by added pipe capacity and pumping stations. Barrel-miles carried rose from 430 billion in 1946 to 1,526 billion in 1972, three-and-a-half-fold. At the same time, product (gasoline, diesel fuel, light fuel oil, etc.) pipeline transport spurted ahead, from a slow start in the two prewar decades to approaching the order of magnitude of crude. Product trunk-line miles increased from 11,000 miles in 1946 to 59,000 in 1972, and barrel-miles, from 59 to 1,167 billion, an increase of twentyfold.

The construction and operation of these pipelines was in the hands of corporate organizations largely controlled by oil companies and their affiliates. Financing was through ordinary corporate channels and operations were subject to usual corporate property and income taxation. By 1972 the gross investment was nearly $7 billion, which covered gathering lines, storage facilities, as well as the trunk pipelines. This was up from some $1 billion at the end of 1946.

Although transmission of natural gas is not ordinarily counted as transport, it has been an important competitor to railroads haulage of the coal used for fuel. In 1945 there were something over 60,000 miles of gas transmission trunk lines in the United States. By 1972 there were over 190,000 miles. Marketed production had increased almost fivefold from 1947 to 1972. There were no data continuously compiled for cubic-feet-miles. By 1972 the volume of marketed natural gas was the equivalent in BTUs of some billion tons of coal. In that year the railroads originated 375 million tons of coal, metalurgical and "steam." While data for cubic-feet-miles have not been compiled, there was a lengthening of haul as a result of the extension of the market areas for southwestern state gas to the Pacific northwest and the North Atlantic states, so that cubic-feet-miles increased even more than market production. The vast development of gas transmission facilities was done by corporate organizations with financing through normal private channels. The investment involved was of the order of $15 billion to $20 billion by 1972.

Inland Water

Inland water transport has been dependent upon the federal government's providing navigable waterways on major lakes and rivers and coastal channels. The basic pattern of the network has not greatly changed, but there have been extensions on several rivers. As of 1965 there were said to be 16,000 route miles in commercial use. Over the postwar years the channel depths and lock sizes have been gradually increased, allowing larger vessels and tows to be introduced by users with resulting economies. In total, inland water ton-miles have increased more than rail but not as much as pipe and highway modes.[6]

Domestic waterway improvement and extensions have been funded, except for local aids, entirely from the federal general treasury. Any form of user charges has been successfully opposed by those using the waterways.

The total expenditures for capital improvement and operation of the waterway system are difficult to ascertain because reported summary figures do not differentiate between those for harbors involving foreign trade and those for the inland system. A special study covering 1957 through 1971 estimated federal expenditures by the Corps of Engineers related to navigation to have been $232 million in 1957 increasing to $435 million in 1971. In addition, there was $427 million spent by the Coast Guard in 1971. How much of the two types could be allocated to commercial domestic use and how much to recreational was not considered. A special improvement in the country's waterway network was the joint Canadian-U.S. St. Lawrence Seaway brought into operation in 1959 at the cost for the U.S. of a $138-million bond issue to be carried by tolls. They were not sufficient and in 1970 Congress transferred the burden to the Treasury.[7]

Initially, just after World War II, a major portion of waterway traffic was within the Great Lakes, mainly iron ore, coal, other mineral items, and grains. The remainder was concentrated on the Mississippi basin system. From that point there have been major changes in the focus of the traffic.

Table 3 shows the domestic traffic of the Great Lakes has gradually declined, while the foreign originated or destined traffic has increased though not as much as hoped for with the advent of the St. Lawrence waterway. The traffic on the

TABLE 3

Inland Waterway Freight Traffic— Ton-Miles, 1946–1972
(Billions)

	1946	1950	1960	1972
Great Lakes				
Domestic	96–	100e	80	74
Foreign-Canada	n.a.	15	14	20
-Overseas	n.a.		51	15
Mississippi River System	18	34	69	159
Atlantic Coast Rivers	1½	6	28	29
Gulf Coast Channels		1	17	32

(Source: DOA, Corps. of Eng., *Ann. Rep., Chf. Eng.,* 1950, Pt. 2; ———, *Waterborne Commerce of the United States,* 1960, 1972.)

other systems rose spectacularly: ninefold for the Mississippi, twentyfold for the Atlantic, and even more for the Gulf coastal and river waterways. Thus the other-than-Great Lakes waterway traffic has increased at a rate exceeding that of highway and petroleum pipe traffic.

Domestic Air

The postwar development of air transport grew out of the wartime technical advances in airplanes and engines and military airport construction. The impact was to be primarily on rail passenger transport. The attraction of transport at a speed of a different order from rail or motor vehicle created a tremendous demand. Air carriers responded with vast investment in new equipment, business and private individuals bought planes for their own use.[8]

The gross investment in equipment and other property for domestic for-hire air carriers was financed in normal private corporate channels and increased from around $¼ billion at the end of 1946 to a billion in 1954 and $12 billion by 1972. The amount spent by corporate and private owners is not compiled, but extrapolating from just the 20,000 multiengine aircraft in use in 1972, investment of many billions was involved.

The outlays for civil airports have been by state and local governments and their related agencies, with the exception of federal funding of the Washington, D.C., area ones. But federal aid was granted to the states and local units. This was provided out of general treasury funds until the collection of user charges beginning in 1971. The aid has ranged from $30 million to $100 million annually. Summary data for the total state and local outlays are only available in general compilations of government expenditures, with airport ones being first identified for fiscal 1959/60, when the amounts were some $⅓ billion. By 1971/72 the outlays had risen to some $1⅓ billion. Associated revenues from user charges and general facility rent, etc., were annually around $⅐ billion and $⅔ billion respectively. In addition, outlays, all federal, for airway development and operation were some $400 million in 1960 and had risen to $1½ billion by 1972.

Since civil airports are used in common by air carriers, and corporate and other privately owned planes, and the airways by all these and the military in addition, a problem arises as with highways and waterways of allocation of costs between types of users, and the disputes as to proper sharing are just as acute for the latter as with highways. Recent studies of the federal costs have suggested that around a third are attributable to general aviation. Its recent years' user charges have covered only 5 percent of that. Air carriers in turn were responsible for a half, to which their recent level of contributions covered 94 percent. No satisfactory allocation estimates are available as to state and local airport costs and revenues.[9]

An overview of the development of these competitive modes of transport is provided by the increases in passenger-miles and ton-miles over the quarter century

Intercity Freight Ton-Miles

(Source: ICC, *St. #6103* (1961); ICC, *T.E.,* Jan. 1966, p. 6, and subsequent annual reporting.)

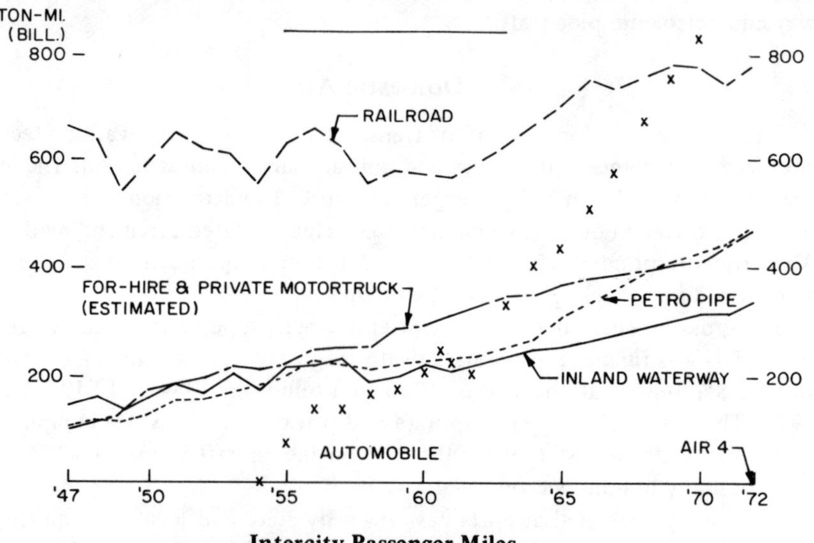

Intercity Passenger-Miles

(Source: ICC, *St. #580* (1958); ICC, *T.E.,* Feb., 1966, p. 1; Aug. 1962, revision #580, and subsequent annual reporting.)

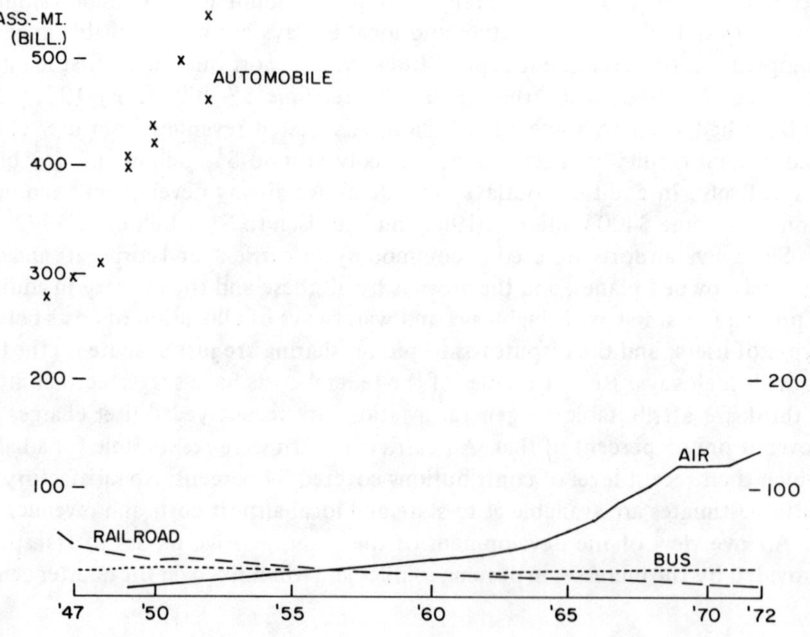

covered by this study. A limitation on inferences from their trends is that, as noted earlier, various types of passenger-miles and of ton-miles are not homogeneous. A ton-mile of oil in a pipeline and one in less-than-truckload shipments by truck represent services of greatly different values and very different resource inputs and thus are not comparable. For passenger transport two dominant features are apparent. First is the vast upsurge of automobile travel shortly after the war and continued growth throughout the following years. Second is the takeoff in air travel after the early 1960s (see chapter 4). The magnitude of growth in both cases is such that the predominant aspect has been the overwhelming really net addition to peoples' mobility, not the loss for a traditional mode of passenger transport. No such drastic growth occurred in the transport of goods by any mode. The greatest increase was that of energy in gas and liquid form by pipeline. Trucking growth essentially replaced rail lcl traffic and to a large extent was responsible for displacing rail express and a large segment of rail mail service. For other than raw commodities, trucking came to be of the same order as rail.

GOVERNMENT REGULATION

Historical Background[10]

A third element of the environment in which the railroads have operated has been that of government regulation. This has had a long history going back to legal underpinnings originating in the English common law applying to the then transport services with the object of insuring that they adequately fulfilled their role as a key factor in peoples' mobility and a country's economic activity. As regulation developed from these origins it was shifted to a statutory base, starting at the state level and, beginning with 1887, moving to a primarily federal one. The regulatory function spelled out in the evolving statutes was given to state commissions and to increasing degrees to the Interstate Commerce Commission (ICC), all subject to review by the courts. The scope of economic regulation was expanded detail by detail over the years. Twentieth-century federal regulation of physical aspects of rail facilities and operation also largely took over from earlier fragmented state regulation with increasingly significant economic effects.

The main early for-hire competitor of the railroads had been the coastal, Great Lakes, and river steamboats. A significant number of these had come under control of the railroads. In 1912 with the coming of the Panama Canal and in anticipation of expansion of such control over interocean steamship lines, regulation was extended by legislation prohibiting railroad control over water carriers generally. Several existing lines were, however, permitted to remain under railroad control.

A hiatus in regulatory developments occurred with World War I and the accompanying takeover of the railroads by the government. Afterwards, there was an expansion of regulation with the Transportation Act of 1920, adding constraints on construction or operation of new lines, on abandonment of existing operations, on acquisition of control of companies, on mergers, on issuance of securities, and, additionally, on rates by way of a so-called "rule of rate making" centered on the railroads' attaining a "fair return" on a "fair value" of the investment in their facilities. These additions, to a considerable extent, represented a combination of what the railroad interests wanted in order to improve their financial welfare but also what would further protect rail users against discrimination, excessive charges, and service inadequacies.

A decade later, with the depression of the 1930s, there were added financial provisions to facilitate the reorganization of the numerous failing roads and to better structure railroad finances for the future. In addition, the "rule of rate making" was reoriented to change the focus from rate of return, which had proved ineffective, to provision of sufficient revenue to provide adequate and efficient service. The depression and rapid development of highway transport led to railroad and to the then existing motor carriers combining to get legislation to limit new entry into trucking and to stabilize motor rates. In 1935 a full pattern of federal regulation was imposed on motor carriers. It carried with it prohibition of railroad entry into trucking except as it might be ancillary to railroad operations. Pressure from farmer and similar primary product interests got exemption from this motor carrier regulation for agricultural commodities, fish, and livestock.

In response to the change in the environment in which the railroads found themselves and the debate between rail, highway, and water interests. Congress in 1940 promulgated a national all-mode transport policy. It called for federal regulatory administration to "recognize and preserve the inherent advantages of each mode of transport," "promote safe, adequate economical and efficient service in transport," and "encourage reasonable charges without unfair or destructive competition" and "fair wages and equitable working conditions." It was all "to the end of developing, coordinating and preserving a national transportation system by all modes." At the same time the 1920 act promotion of railroad consolidation or merger in line with an ICC formulated plan was replaced by authorizing ICC approval of acquisition and merger if "consistent with the public interest" and subject to the protection of the interests of employees and of other roads and to the consideration of effects on adequacy of transport service.

In addition, the 1940 act reduced the original requirement that roads that had been promoted by grants of federal land must give reduced rates and fares to all government traffic to just reduction for military traffic. At the end of the war further reduction followed with the 1946 cancellation of the discount on fares and rates for military traffic as well. Because parallel unaided lines had given the same discount to be competitive for the traffic, the overall increase in revenue was more than that directly resulting from the reductions in exemptions called for directly by the 1940 and 1946 acts.

During the 1940s, as noted earlier, there was a southern and midwestern uprising against alleged discrimination at the hands of the railroads and their rate associations because of higher class rates in those regions than the eastern. The railroad response was to propose legal recognition of the associations accompanied with their specific exemption from antitrust requirements and submission of the associations to ICC regulatory control. Congress did this in 1948 over the president's veto, which was based on his feeling that the proposed legislation would confirm a significant restraint on interrailroad competition.

With sharp build-up of rail versus truck and waterway competition after the war the role of government regulation of rates had become highly controversial in the transport industry. The railroads' dissatisfaction grew in respect to what they felt was ICC denial of or tampering with their attempts to adjust their rates so as to obtain greater shares of traffic in the competition with trucks and water carriers and thus improve net income. The railroads aimed at changing the underlying terms of their general rate-making rule. In the middle 1950s three "shall nots" were advocated to apply in connection with the ICC passing on rail rate adjustments: it should not consider (1) their effects on another mode of traffic, (2) their competitive relation to rates of other modes, or (3) whether the rail rates might be lower than necessary to meet the competition of other modes.[11] The result was 1958 legislation that said that the ICC "in determining whether a rate is lower than a reasonable minimum rate shall consider the facts and circumstances attending the movement of the traffic by the carrier or carriers to which the rate is applicable. Rates...shall not be held up to a particular level to protect the traffic of any other mode—giving due consideration to the objectives of the National Transportation Policy" (Sec. 15a [3]). The revised statute became a new rate-making rule for the fourteen years to 1972. The courts' review and affirmation interpreted it as requiring the ICC to allow greater competitive opportunity for the railroads to counter water and truck transport. Later cases affirmed the courts' active role in shifting the ICC tendency to continue support of other-modes attempts to fend off adverse rail proposed adjustments.[12]

In another area the railroads had traditionally been free to use their managerial judgment as to what interstate passenger service to provide. In the latter 1950s the accelerated discontinuance of passenger trains prompted active public interest in restraining such loss of passenger service. In response, the 1958 legislation required ICC authorization for interstate discontinuance granted upon finding that it would be in the public interest. As compensation for this increased regulation, the new statute gave the ICC authority to review the traditional state control over intrastate passenger trains with a view to overriding state refusal of discontinuance, which could be shown to be an undue burden on interstate commerce.

The last new areas of regulation came in the field of safety and physical standards. Since the turn of the century, government standards for design of facilities and details of operation were set as excessive accidents occurred. Those traceable to particular causes led to adoption of specific remedial requirements. In the 1960s there was a drastic increase in derailments largely attributed to deteriorating levels of maintenance. This led to the 1970 Railroad Safety Act, providing for Department of Transportation promulgation of track standards and related train speed limits and a new pattern of government enforcement procedures. Maintenance standards had traditionally been the prerogative of railroad managements and a key area for controlling costs (see chapter 13) so that the new regulations imposed federal constraints on maintenance expenditures and operating practices with important overall economic consequences.[13]

ICC Regulatory Activity, 1947–1972

After World War II the railroads found themselves in a regulatory environment consisting of a wide range in vintage of constraints.[14] The regulatory process carried out by the ICC reflects the array of old and recent statutes. Much is essentially administrative by way of drawing up rules, policing carrier adherence to them, emergency ordering of freight car handling and distribution, collection of data, and the like. Then there are the substantive reviews and decisions, which can be divided into three general categories. First are major, once-in-a-lifetime, specially directed investigations. First in the period of this study were the "Class Rate" and "Consolidated Classification," broad decisions for investigation initiated before the war but decided in the 1950s. These are reviewed in chapter 7. Two other special cases involved defining the scope and rules for piggy back (TOFC) service.[15]

The role of costs in rate matters had been a persistent problem, intensifying in the intermodal context. The ICC finally initiated an in-depth study of costs in 1962 and produced a comprehensive report in 1970.[16] Then in 1970 a total review of all rates as to their reasonableness and fairness was ordered by Congress. It exceeded "in a scope and complexity of anything hitherto undertaken." It ended in a three-volume decision of 3,203 pages. Despite its magnitude, it fell far short of the coverage asked for. It dealt with the rate structures for only a few of the almost infinite number of commodities that made up the country's commerce.[17]

A second category of ICC decisions was broad coverage proceedings spaced at irregular intervals. From 1946 to 1972 it included a series of thirteen general rate increases along with decisions in a number of interregional division of rates disputes. These are reviewed in chapter 7. In the same class there were cases involving mergers and acquisitions, the lengthy larger-scale ones being a major burden on railroad legal staffs and the commission. They are reviewed in chapter 12.

A third category of proceedings includes the reviews of requests for new operations and abandonments and of protested rate adjustments. These involved various levels of the ICC organization, a few finally reviewed by the commission as a whole.

It is possible to assess the extent of basic regulatory constraints analyzing the findings of cases in this third group. One type in this category involved authority for on the one hand new operation or construction and on the other abandonment of rail operations.[18] Of the former requests brought to the final stage of consideration, only 12 percent were denied authority in the 1950s, 25 percent in the first half of the 1960s, and 16 percent thereafter. Of abandonments, 22 percent were not allowed in the first half of the 1950s, 9 percent in the second half, and 8 percent thereafter. With respect to the 1958 passenger train discontinuance provisions, from 1958 to 1969, excluding the 1966 wholesale requests of two roads, 78 percent were permitted and the rest required to be continued subject to reconsideration. The net effect is reviewed in chapter 4.

The third category also includes the numerous rate and fare proceedings involving protests of rail rate adjustments in the new and supplemental tariffs published every year. These proceedings display the regulatory constraints on railroad pricing but leave unmentioned the multitude adjustments never challenged. They are analyzed in typical settings in the history of three commodity rate structures in chapter 7.

There were 100,000 or more freight rate adjustments filed annually in the first several years of the postwar period, thereafter from 40 to 60,000. Data for rail adjustment protests and suspensions were first published in 1955. Out of the tens of thousands annually, there were around 600 protested each year from 1955 through 1958, 1,000 from 1959 through 1963, and only 700 the next two years. Thereafter, the number dropped to between 400 and 600. For most years of the protested adjustments after preliminary eliminations only around a quarter were suspended. The exceptions were a decline to a sixth from 1963 through 1967 and for 1970 and 1971, when most suspensions were involving increases, the proportion rose to over 40 percent. It is to be noted that the decline in proportions suspended after 1962 followed the Court decisions warning the ICC to allow greater opportunity for competitive rate adjustments.

Over the years there were several times as many protests for motor-carrier adjustments. Most of these involved decreases, with proceedings leading to a substantially greater proportion of suspensions than for the rail cases.

The substantive details of these proceedings provide a running review of the ICC interpretations of the statutory rate regulation guidelines. The variations in interpretation and in their acceptability in the view of the courts hearing appeals emphasize difficulties inherent in the wording of the statutory guidelines. The conflicting political pressures from the three competitive transport modes as well as the varied user interests had led to statutory wording that was all things to all interests. This together with the wide spread in vintage of the guidelines posed major problems of compromise and reconciliation for the commissioners and made room for considerable difference as between their individual conclusions. Beginning in the 1930s, at the beginning stages particularly of rail-truck competition, there was also conflict with the traditional regulatory point of view of protecting the public interest by resisting changes in the pattern of rates, which might harm the vested interests of industries and communities dependent upon the continuance of rate relationship.[19] Reduced rates of motor carriers and railroads made in the course of competition for shares of traffic were bound to raise cost consideration more than the traditional rates, since rate makers under these circumstances had to keep their eyes on out-of-pocket costs as a bottom limit. Then with regulation of motor carriers and a comprehensive national transportation policy, the ICC interpretation of their responsibilities for both "preserving" and "promoting" the various modes led to their settling rate competition by making a pragmatic assessment of rate differentials that would balance truck advantages over rail by way of, for instance, lower minimums, speedier services, and door-to-door service. The cents-per-100-pound difference to do this was frequently quite small. A few cents under or over could shift traffic. However, the wording of the newer rule of rate making required that the consideration of the effect of rates on movement of traffic be confined just to movement by the carriers for whom the rates were set. It was the 1958 amendment and its interpretation in 1961 and 1963 by the courts that led to a rejection of differentials to prevent takeover of traffic. "Simply because the rate would divert some or all the traffic from a competing mode" did not make the rate "unfair or destructive." Room was left, however, for a finding of "unfair" competition as grounds for limiting rate reductions.[20]

Consideration of costs was always in the background in intermodal rate considerations, but there was vacillating between out-of-pocket and related costs, fully distributed ones and ones somewhere in between, or otherwise defined. The conflicting possibilities were brought out in a key case in 1940. Again the 1961 and 1963 decisions spoke of the cost dilemmas.[21] The earlier one referred to "cost" as used by the ICC as "a term of art." In a 1968 Supreme Court decision a separate opinion relative to defining a possible cost standard opined that the Court had "simply postponed a difficult issue," perpetuating the long-expressed uncertainty associated with cost considerations.[22]

Running through early postwar years' consideration of both intra- and intermodal rate adjustments, the ICC had on its mind the need to maintain carrier revenues to insure adequate net incomes. It often specifically emphasized the objective of stabilizing rates to preserve revenues. The words of the National Transportation Policy to "foster sound economic conditions—among the several carriers" were quoted for support. Further, the commission on its own emphasized the need to maximize revenues from high-valued commodities like alcoholic liquors and cigarettes able to pay higher rates because they would not inhibit their transport. Thus cutting their rates for competitive reasons would be a wasteful depletion of both rail and motor-carrier revenues.[23]

After the 1958 statutory change in the rule of rate making and court interpretations thereof, the ICC shifted its philosophy as it revealed in its annual reports beginning with the 78th in 1964. It was more willing to conclude that proposed reduced rates were not "predatory" or "destructive." It emphasized greater latitude when they were against unregulated carriers. It supported reductions when they were tied to increased minimum loading or other means to increase railroad productivity. Further, it criticized a mandatory rate structure because it "discourages rates based mainly on cost of service or on competitive need" and "in essence prevents negotiation of rates to meet the needs of the shipping public."[24] Most importantly, decisions that had approved differentials which determined intermodal shares of traffic were reversed. In sum, there was significant change in the commission's attitude toward competition in favor of removing restraints on competitive rate adjustments.[25]

* * *

Those responsible for private railroad enterprise from its beginning have held a hostile position toward government regulation. An important aspect of this is that people, in general, do not like to be told what they may or may not do and this applies particularly to those having substantial responsibilities and power. On the other hand, the railroad industry has recognized bases for regulation and have guided many aspects of it toward their own objectives. In turn, society has demanded certain standards of railroad performance and experience has shown that, for some, regulation is the only way they can be insured.[26]

The key aspect of regulation until the 1930s emphasized price and service discrimination, level of prices, earnings and return. Subsequently, with the rapid growth of highway and water transport and their strong competitive gains *vis-a-vis* the railroads, the emphasis shifted to the regulatory role in respect to intermodal relations. This provided a new focus for railroad hostility.[27]

In the meantime, there was a shift in the approaches to general industry economic analysis from emphasis on the individual firm and industry by way of explanation of their performance to a broader prospective of society as a whole and what standards and policies should be established to optimize performance. A key tenet was that in principle it would come for the railroads as a private enterprise industry with a competitive market structure that meant prices set at marginal costs. Regulation of rates that fostered or permitted deviation from this would impose social losses. However, marginal pricing under certain conditions could produce less than enough revenue to provide for total costs that had to be paid for. This raised problems of cross subsidy or taxation to make good particular shortfalls. Dealing with them would involve retreat from optimality ideals and bring back long, traditional debate as to attribution of particular costs to particular services, how prices might be related to reduced anti-trust restraints, and undermine the premise of the optimum competitive markets.[28]

* * *

Between the three prime environmental factors influencing railroad performance, there have been significant differences as to their relative importance. By all odds, the most important were the technological advances in other than rail transport. Few bounds have applied to highway, pipe, and air advances. Water has been restricted locally by the requirement of major natural/water source routes, but they were scattered widely. Technical advances have provided improved service so appealing that capital for innovation diffusion universally was made available, the new services widely demanded, and resources committed to them. As a result, major segments of intercity rail transport were displaced regardless of region.

Government regulation was also, for the most part, uniform countrywide; state regulation in the total picture was minor. Only in connection with divisions of through rates did federal regulation get involved in possible regional differentiation and then, in practice, it was not major to any degree. Regulation was not powerful enough to significantly counteract the push of technological advances toward widespread diffusion of improved services; nor did it counter the effect of different regional economic growth rates. Differences in area economic growth rates had significant influence on relative regional performance, and maximum southwestern strong growth rates meant predominantly properous railroads; eastern minimal rates meant troubled railroads.

4

Passenger Service, Fares, and Operation

Analysis of railroad passenger service performance in the postwar dynamic environment of vastly increasing peoples' mobility is faced with some significant methodological limitations. As was noted initially, in respect to service-producing industries, such as transport, analysis requires accounting for more than just the simple raw units produced, for instance, in this case, just coach and first-class passenger-miles. The various qualities of service going with each type of passenger-mile are major determinants of both the demand for and the inputs needed to supply each type. The difficulty for analysis is that qualities cannot be quantitatively assessed. It is impossible to express in numerical terms physical comfort, privacy, sociability, or convenience. But these immeasurables are important, for example, in the choice for a trip between New York and Chicago, between a bedroom on the Broadway Limited, a seat in an express bus, a coach seat in a jet airplane, or one's own automobile. The only quantitative basic railroad data regularly available have been railroad by railroad—the number of people using each broadly identified type of service, their passenger-miles, what they paid, equipment inventory and capacities, miles run, train-miles, and service schedules. Passenger trip lengths have not been compiled since available data are by railroad, not by a combination of railroads that may have been involved in a long trip.

This analysis, then, will be based on the changes over time revealed in limited data supplemented by such qualitative evaluations as seem significant and reasonable. The analysis does not carry beyond 1970 because, as noted earlier, most all intercity traffic was subsequently taken over by the National Railroad Passenger Corporation (Amtrak) and much of suburban by local authorities or with government grants or subsidies. The consequent dispersion of control over service and operation destroys the comparability of data with reference to the previous years. Further, from 1970 to 1972, developments under the new patterns were transitional so that the results of analysis would not be meaningful.[1]

THE PRE–WORLD WAR II BACKGROUND

Before 1929

Going back in the past, the interurban electric railway coming around the turn of the century was the first technological advance in passenger transport to invade the railroads' traditional province. In turn, this was soon followed by the

31

automobile, improved highways, and the bus, which together spelled the end of the electric railway and encroached further on the railroads' passenger traffic. For them, excluding war-traffic related years, peak passenger traffic was reached in 1914 on a per capita basis and in 1923 on an absolute one. From 1923, when separate data for coach and first-class traffic first became available, to 1929, despite the growth of the country's population and national income, railroad, noncommutation, coach passenger-miles fell 42 percent; on a per capita basis, 47 percent. On the other hand, first-class travel increased 5 percent, suggesting that the bus and auto were not strong competitors for this type of service. By 1929 rail first-class travel was slightly greater than coach, and intercity bus was estimated to be as much as 60 percent of rail coach.

Railroad, Bus, and Passenger-Miles, 1923–1939

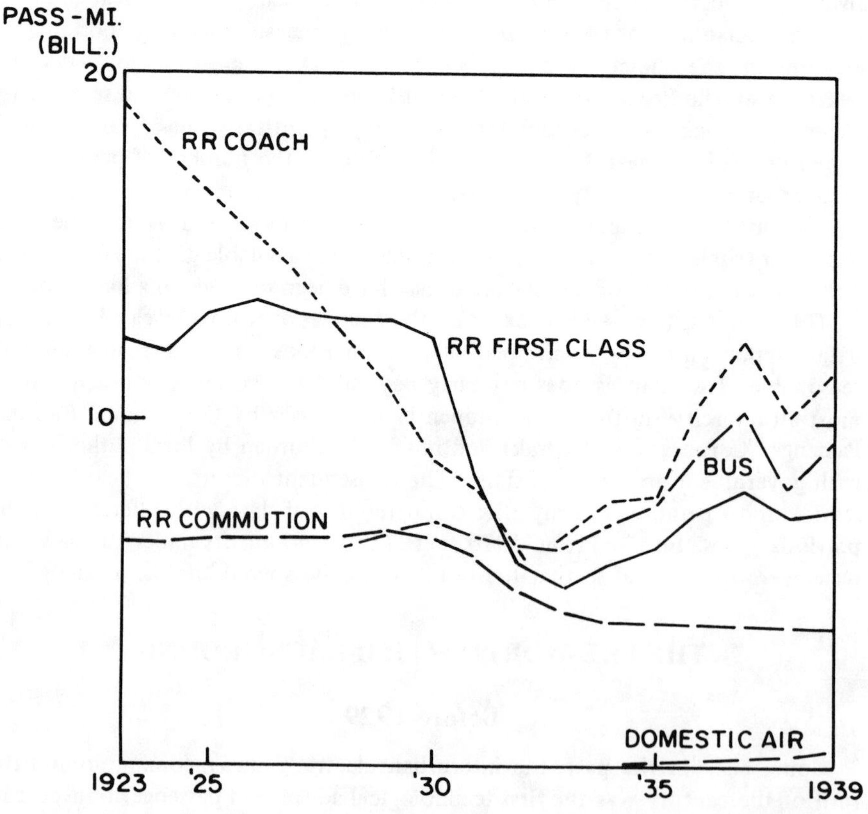

These losses of passenger, mail, express, and baggage traffic for the country as a whole led to a 54 percent decline in related rail revenues. Based on the ICC's expense allocation formula (validity of this is discussed later), prior to 1926 the passenger train service revenues exceeded directly related operating expenses. Thereafter the net declined sharply, becoming a deficit in the West by 1928, and the year after in the South.

The principal policies during these years in the several areas of railroad decision making are worth reviewing. Large investments were made in improved passenger train cars and the steam motive power to pull them. For reasons of economy, internal-combustion engine self-propelled cars were developed for and installed in branch-line service in lieu of locomotive trains. There was no change essentially in either the passenger train-miles run or the miles of line over which passenger services were offered. In 1920, following major postwar wage rate increases, the railroads with ICC approval established basic fares of 3.6 percent per mile, common to both coach and first-class, and a first-class surcharge averaging 0.3¢ a mile. These basic fares were not changed during the 1920s. The railroads, however, experimented with numerous special reduced fares so that the average coach fares declined from 1923 to 1929 by 5 percent and first-class by 4 percent.

During this period numerous railroads entered the bus business via subsidiaries and purchasing interests in passenger motor carriers operated by others. Largely at the suggestion of the railroads, a number of states had come to require certificates of public convenience and necessity for interstate bus operations in the late 1920s. There was no regularity constraint on entering the interstate business. It was estimated that in 1930 railroad interests in bus lines provided service over some 66,000 route miles. The peak involvement came in the mid-1930s. At the same time the ICC had no role in the extent or quality of the rail passenger service.[2]

1930–1939

After 1929 the general depression together with increased highway competition reduced rail passenger traffic still further. Despite the depression or perhaps because of it the railroads responded more aggressively. There was a wide range of experimentation with innovations such as the manufacture by aerospace equipment companies of lightweight cars, tire companies providing rubber-wheeled cars, and rail equipment manufacturers arranging diesel and steam propulsion directly on cars without locomotives. Investments, which were relatively large for depression times, were made in experimental new equipment and considerable amounts were spent on upgrading tracks of key routes in the West. Of the innovations finally put into general use, a significant but not high investment cost one was air-conditioning. Substantial sums were spent on cars of new designs providing improved decor and comfort, and major reduction, a third less, in car weight.

TABLE 4

Improvement in Key Intercity Schedules

	1929	1939	
New York-Chicago	20 hr.	16 hr.	−20%
New York-Miami	33⅓ hr.	26¼ hr.	−21%
Chicago-New Orleans	22½ hr.	20 hr.	−11%
Chicago-St. Paul	11 hr.	6¼ hr.	−43%
Chicago-Denver	25½ hr.	16 hr.	−37%
Chicago-Los Angeles	58 hr.	39¾ hr.	−42%

The major innovation was the high-speed diesel-electric locomotive propelled passenger train. By 1936 top speeds of 100 to 120 miles per hour were regularly maintained by these trains in the rural areas of the mid-part of the country. In the more densely settled metropolitan regions and in the more mountainous territory speeds were lower. All told schedules were drastically shortened for long hauls (see Table 4).[3]

The 1930s had started with regional average fares, coach and first-class (including its surcharge), as shown in Table 5. The differences between regions were largely a reflection of the varied use of special reduced fares and of the degree of competitive route circuity imposed by railroad network georgraphy. In 1932 and 1933 there was extensive experimentation with reduced coach fares in the South with some as low as 1¢ per mile. By December 1933 the southern roads established a 1½¢ round-trip basic coach fare and a two-level, 2¢ and 2¼¢, first-class one. The western roads started even earlier and in 1934 put in a basic 1.8¢ round-trip coach fare and a first-class one the same as the southern. Both regions dropped the surchage.

TABLE 5

Average Fares per Passenger-Mile

	East		South		West	
	Coach	First Class	Coach	First Class	Coach	First Class
1929	3.3¢	3.7¢	3.2¢	3.5¢	2.9¢	3.2¢
1939	2.1	2.7	1.5	2.4	1.5	2.0

(Source: ICC, *SRUS*, Table 52.)

In the East for several years the basic 3.6¢ a mile as in general retained for both classes along with the first-class surcharge, but a wide range of special reduced fares were offered. The major passenger-carrying roads in the East—the Pennsylvania, New York Central, and New York, New Haven, and Hartford—favored this pattern for marketing on the grounds that the basic demand in the East was pricewise less elastic than in the other regions and thus revenues and net would more likely be maximized by offering reduced fares tailored to special price-sensitive classes of traffic. On the other hand, the Baltimore and Ohio (BO), a lesser eastern carrier passengerwise, favored a reduction in basic fares to 2¢ coach and 3¢ without surcharge first class. The Norfolk and Western (NW), on the border with eastern territory, had reduced its fares to this level in 1934. In 1936 the ICC in an unprecedented incursion in passenger fare making required all railroads to establish the BO proposed levels, the main impact of this being on the prior mentioned eastern roads.[4]

Railroad Coach and First-Class Passenger-Miles, 1929–1939

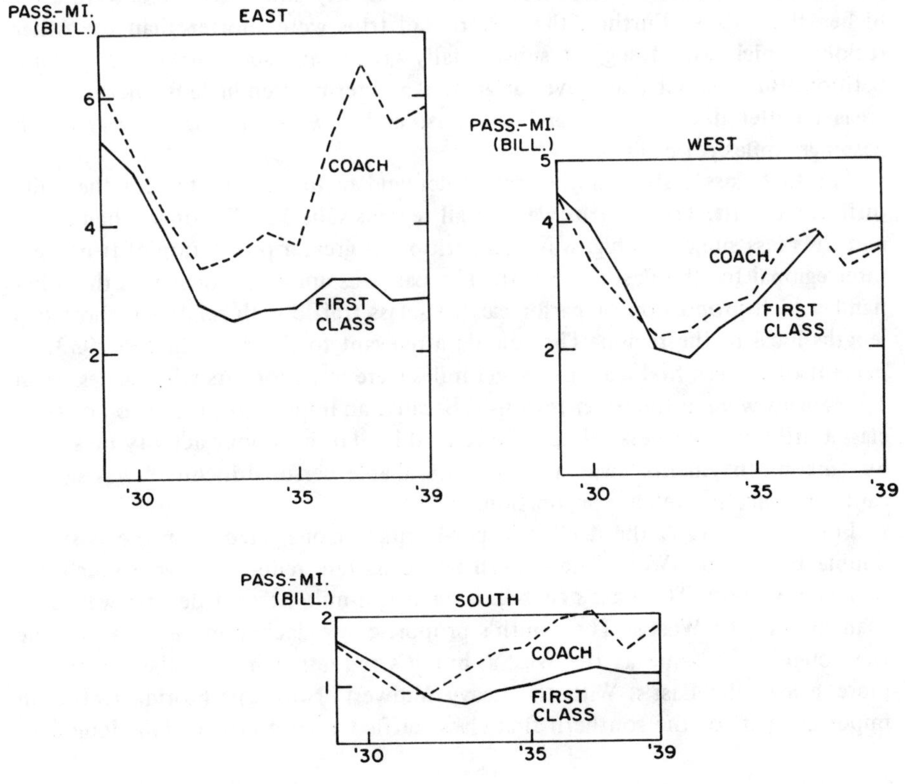

By 1939 the many adjustments resulted in average fare levels shown in Table 5. The corresponding 1939 country-wide average bus fare was $1\frac{1}{2}\cent$.

For the country as a whole from 1929 to 1939 coach traffic held its own but first-class declined 42 percent. In turn, the railroads reduced passenger train service around 30 percent in each of the regions. Only country-wide data, and these only by way of estimates, are available for highway traffic. Bus passenger-miles increased around 40 percent and automobile probably something over 50 percent.

Regional comparisons from 1929 to 1939 provide evidence of the factors in change. For coach traffic in the South, lowest level per capita "available" income, automobile ownership and gasoline consumption together with maximum reduction in fares led to no overall loss in passenger-miles and a noticeable gain over 1929 for the best year, 1937.

On the other hand, in the West high-level per capita available incomes together with maximum ownership and gasoline consumption were associated with significant decline in coach passenger-miles, despite both fare declines comparable to those in the South and the greatest improvement in service. In the case of the East, there were high car ownership and gas consumption along with least fare reduction, yet passenger-miles declined only slightly and 1937 levels were a bit higher than 1929. Further, the eastern rail trips were shorter than the other regions, which would suggest substantially greater impact from highway competition. But the fact that travel originated and terminated in dense metropolitan areas countered this factor and the East ended with the highest rail coach passenger-miles per capita.[5]

For first-class traffic another set of demand factors accounted for the quite different results. Trip lengths were in all regions substantially longer than coach and thus less subject to highway competition. A greater proportion of trips were interregional for the East and South. The East was unique in having on the other hand a high proportion of parlor car first-class traffic with relatively short trip lengths local to the region. The sole data relevant to this show that in 1933, 21 percent of eastern first-class passenger-miles were in parlor cars whereas less than $1\frac{1}{2}$ percent were in the other regions.[6] Because an important proportion of first-class traffic was business related the general level of economic activity measured by "income payments" was a factor. "Available personal income" was significant for a vacation related proportion.

For 1929 to 1939 the decline in per capita personal income in the East was double that of the West. The eastern first-class fare reductions were much less than the western. The East's first-class passenger-mile percent decline was more than double the West's. The South's proportionate decline in personal income was roughly the same as the West's, but it's reduction in first-class fares was more nearly the East's. With the heavy Midwest, Northeast-Florida traffic an important part of the southern first-class traffic tended to rise or fall along with the eastern region's. The southern passenger-mile decline was nearer the East's than the West's. The West's lowest rate of first-class passenger-mile decline was associated with its greatest reduction in fares, least decline in income, and a non-quantifiable factor—the greatest improvement in quality of rail service. It is notable that the western first-class traffic was the only case of substantial comeback by 1939 from its depression low, a 90 percent recovery compared to 52 percent for the southern and only 15 percent for the eastern.

Air competition did not play a significant role in respect to rail trends, even first-class. For the country as a whole there were only two-thirds of a billion air-passenger miles by 1939, only a small fraction of the 5 billion decline in rail first-class. From 1929 to 1939 there was some 50 percent decrease in passenger train service revenue in each of the four regions. The railroad response was reduction in passenger train-miles and route miles with passenger service. The eastern and southern roads both cut train-miles some 35 percent, but the former reduced the route miles 29 percent; the latter, only 15 percent. The western roads, although notably worse off financially than the other regions, reduced train-miles only 29 percent and route miles 26 percent. Relative to passenger-mile decline, the southern roads took the strongest position in eliminating train-miles.

Passenger Service Costing

Since the passenger and allied service associated expenses are in part incurred in common with freight services the problem arises of how to determine the extent of the passenger part, and in what terms to be associated with the former. What is appropriate has been a matter of continuous debate among those having varied views of, and interests in, passenger versus freight services.

At a basic level there are so-called "solely related" expenses unequivocally associated with production of passenger services. The ICC has required the railroads to account separately among operating expenses for these items. They comprise the expenses of crews and energy to operate passenger trains and switch passenger train cars; the direct expenditures for passenger equipment repairs (not the supervisory, machinery, and other overhead expenses of shops, etc.); the depreciation allowances for equipment used in passenger trains; and expenditures for terminal staff, buildings, sales force, etc., solely connected with passenger and allied services. The "solely related" categories exclude any expenses for labor, materials, etc., used in common with freight service. For instance, maintenance of way expenses for tracks used in common with freight trains are ignored in connection with "solely related" expenses. This excludes most all track and right-of-way expenses because there was insignificant mileage used just by passenger trains. This excludes added expenses for higher track and other standards needed for passenger train operations but not for freight, for the added wear caused by passenger trains, and for those tracks used at times for freight service but which would not have been built except to provide added capacity needed by the passenger service. These expense items do not include any capital costs including that arising from investment in facilities and equipment solely used in passenger and allied services. Finally, these "solely related" items do not cover that part of general expenses that has varied with changes in level of passenger and allied services. Despite these numerous shortfalls in accounting for the resources used in providing passenger and allied services, "solely related" expenses will be used in this study because they are the only ones not affected by arbitrary assignment methods and the only ones recorded continuously over the span of years covered by this analysis.[7]

By way of appraising the significance of these "solely related" expenses two other measures are of interest. The ICC has compiled an additional category, "assignable" expenses, which added to the "solely related" ones purport to give a more inclusive measure of resources involved. The bases for determining the assigned amounts are freight and passenger train gross ton-miles, fuel used, employee hours, etc.

The second approach has been to analyze by multiple regression techniques the detailed expenses of a cross section of individual railroads to estimate passenger and freight service cost functions. For Class I railroads in 1955 this latter method concluded that "avoidable" passenger costs if passenger service was to be eliminated would be $1,975 million. The comparable ICC "solely related" expenses were $1,351 million so that "avoidable" were 46 percent more than the "solely related." In turn, the ICC "assignable" plus "solely related" expenses combined were $1,743 million, the avoidable being 13 percent more than the combined two.

For the country as a whole, in 1929, revenues from passenger and allied services had been 41 percent in excess of the "solely related" expenses; by 1939 they were only 14 percent. In 1929 the excess was $541 million; in 1939, $87 million. That $87 million was the sole contribution of passenger service users toward the costs of right of way, structures, and track used in common with freight service, the common general expenses, and the interest and amortization of debt for passenger equipment and related fixed facilities. It was clear that the $87 million did not cover any of the wide range of possible estimates of the share of these latter items attributable to passenger train produced services.

WORLD WAR II

World War II produced a sharp reversal in 1930s picture. Greatly increased levels of economic activity, heavy troop movements, added private travel of military and related persons, and severe government restrictions on automobile we resulted in an over fourfold increase in passenger-miles by 1944. Further, there were severe government restrictions on increasing passenger train-miles to provide for increased civilian traffic. Supply was not allowed to respond upward, as normally, to demand. Quality of service declined well below acceptable peacetime standards. Lack of coach seats even for long trips was common, for instance. The ability to satisfy requests for reserved accommodations was greatly reduced. The average train-loading rose from 58 passenger-miles per train-mile in 1939 to a peak of 201 in 1944. Despite a slight decline in average intercity fare levels and no increase in mail rates, total passenger train revenue rose to a peak in 1944, which was two times the "solely related" expenses for the country as a whole and almost two-and-a-half times in the South and West.

POST-WORLD WAR II

Phases, 1946–1970

The post-World War II history of the United States railroad passenger and allied services has been complex and varied, falling into four well-differentiated phases. There were the immediate postwar years, 1946–1950, with return to normal peacetime conditions, with revived highway traffic, and the beginning of modern air transport. There were also sharply higher levels of input prices for labor, materials, supplies, and capital equipment. This phase also saw the beginning of a large-scale investment in modernized rail passenger equipment. Then from 1950 to 1955 was a period of settling in with the modern facilities and attempting to maintain traffic levels after the loss of the temporary upward lift in demand during the Korean War. The impact of an investment of over a billion dollars and of a higher level of fares was tested against advances in other forms of passenger transport. Then from 1955 to 1962 the railroads had to face up to the continuing rise in prices of inputs with little chance of improving the productivity of labor or capital. At the same time they were confronted with further declining demand for long-haul travel due to the introduction of the jet and vast expansion of the air network. There was also loss of intermediate-length travel due to the greater motor vehicle ownership and further improvements in highway trasnport. Finally, the period from 1962 on saw the full impact of the jet and all-out expansion of air transport. Increases in railroad input prices continued and productivity was eroded severely as use reached minimal density levels.

1946–1950

In the years immediately following the surrender of Japan there was a reduction in military related passenger traffic, the return to widespread use of automobile transport, and a resumption of peacetime service and load-factor conditions for the railroads. Comparing 1947 as the first postwar year reasonably free of demobilization traffic with 1939 as the last year before the influences of World War II traffic, railroad passenger-miles were double and bus were two-and-a-half-fold, but automobile were up only some 15 percent. Air traffic increase was of the order of ninefold, but air passenger-miles in 1947 were minor compared to rail. From 1939 to 1947 average intercity railroad coach fares had risen some 12 percent, and first-class, 18 percent. In 1947 average passenger-miles per train-mile were still well above those in 1939, 110 compared to 58. The coach trip length had increased by a half; first-class, only slightly. There had been wage increases of some 50 percent and prices of materials and equipment had risen almost as much. Together these factors produced a situation where passenger and allied revenues were not much above the "solely related" expenses. There was, however, the more promising prospective from the long-run point of view that despite highway competition, 1947 rail passenger-miles, all classes, were half again as many as in 1929, a seeming augur of the viability of rail passenger transport free of depression and war. Further, the greater volume was handled with 26 percent less train-miles than in 1929 and 29 percent less miles of line over which passenger service was operated. From 1929 to 1947 major increases in equipment and track productivity had been achieved.

Investment

1946 was the year of decision for the railroads in respect to postwar passenger train services. The background prospective just described provided the basis for the large orders placed then and several years thereafter for new passenger cars and locomotives, at an annual rate that exceeded any previous year. Although the precise amounts added to investment accounts for passenger service locomotives cannot be established because of the considerable use of the same locomotives for both passenger and freight service, the amounts for passenger train cars can be. Annual investment for cars rose from $49 million in 1946 to 79, 119, 134, and $140 million in consecutive years through 1950. During these years the railroads, as a result of antitrust rulings against the Pullman Company, were for the first time themselves purchasing the new parlor and sleeping cars for Pullman service and accounting for them as their own investment in equipment. An indirect indication of the extent of investment in motive power is the increase in proportion of diesel propelled passenger train-miles during those years, from 14 percent in 1946 to 54 percent in 1950. Another indication was that 20 percent of the inventory of locomotives earmarked as passenger at the end of 1950 had been purchased since January 1, 1947. There were no great innovations connected with these large capital expenditures. They were primarily to bring the inventory of equipment up to the standard of the innovations that had been decided upon as desirable just before or during the war. These large investments reflected the decisions of the railroads to go after the passenger business with their best efforts despite the universal and sharp decline in traffic that became visible as each year following the war came along.

**Railroad Coach and First-Class Basic and Annual Average
Regional Fares, 1946–1950**

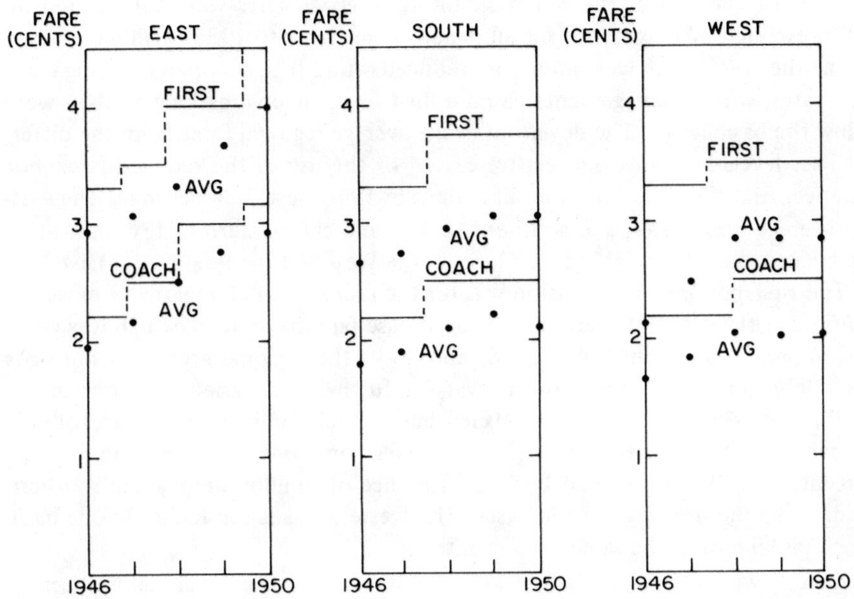

Competition

From 1947 through 1950 the other-than-rail modes of transport went through drastic postwar reconstitution. Private highway passenger transport came back into its own with the general availability of automobiles. An additional 2.2 million were produced in 1946 and three times that in 1950, an annual figure not to be reached again until 1960. Highway construction, stopped during the war, proceeded again. Estimated intercity auto passenger-miles from 1947 to 1950 increased some 120 billion, 205 percent. The public segment of passenger highway transport in buses after rapid growth during the war declined from 1947 to 1950, least in the West with 10 percent and most in the South, 23 percent.

The most dramatic changes, however, were in the air transport field. The introduction in 1946 and 1947 of a new generation of planes, the "Connie" and the DC-6's, along with the Convair and Martin two-engine planes, all pressurized, resulted in a major jump in both speed and comfort. There were rising costs for airlines, but they were countered by increasing productivity. Fares were increased with three consecutive 10 percent general increases from April 1947 to September 1948. However, 1948 was also the year in which the family plan and coach fares were initiated. The net result was only a 10 percent rise in average scheduled air carrier fares per mile from 1947 to 1950. Air passenger-miles increased almost 2 billion, 31 percent.

41

Fares

The pricing of passenger services was a critical area of rail management decision making. At the end of the war basic intercity coach fares were still limited by ICC prescribed 3¢ maximums for all regions going back to 1936, with an increase during the war. There were numerous reduced round-trip, excursion, sliding scale, etc., rates, which managements could adjust on their own as long as they were below the basic levels. The deviation in the average regional fares from the different base levels indicates the relative extent of the use of the reduced fares. For instance, first-class base fares in all regions in 1946 were 3.3¢ per mile. The eastern average was 2.95¢; the southern, 2.65¢; and the western, 2.13¢; indicating the greatest use of special reduced fares in the West and the least in the East.[8]

The first postwar fare decision was for the railroads of all regions to move for continuing the 1942 10 percent increased base fare maximums, which was given ICC approval. Then in 1947, 1948, and 1949 the regional groups of railroads separately petitioned and got approval for further and varied increases in the maximums. The eastern carriers pushed basic coach fares up each year, totaling 53 percent. The southern roads put into effect only one coach fare increase, 14 percent, in 1947. There had been a difference of opinion among the southern roads as to the urgency for increases. The western roads too had only one basic coach fare increase, the same 14 percent.

Policies with respect to first-class fares followed the same regional patterns as for coach fares. The eastern roads raised the basic fare each year, finally to 4½¢, overall 36 percent. Southern and western roads made only one increase in the basic first-class fare, 6 percent in 1947. Simultaneous restriction of special reduced fares led to average fares actually increasing by 15 percent in the South and 29 percent in the West. This meant that the first-class differences with the East were not as great as the contrasting basic level changes might suggest.[9]

The arguments in support of the various increases made it clear that the motive behind them was to try to increase revenues to keep up with the rapidly rising unit expenses. There seemed to be no choice but to hope that increased fares would not turn away passengers so much as to reduce revenue. But these hopes were not borne out by experience. From 1947 to 1950 regional revenue declines for coach ranged between 21 and 31 percent; first-class from between 4 and 16.

Intercity coach traffic declines from 1947 to 1950 did not vary greatly between regions. The East had by far the largest postwar coach fare increase, 50 percent to a 2.9¢ average in 1950. The West's was 23 percent to 2¢. The East's maximum contributed to its greatest traffic decline, 41 percent, and the West's, minimum, to the least decline, 30 percent. The South had a fare decrease less than the West's, 17 percent to 2.1¢, and a traffic decline of 36 percent. It had a substantially higher increase in auto registration than the West, a factor in the southern's greater than western decline.

Railroad (Coach and First-Class) and Bus Passenger-Miles,* and Annual Average Fares, 1946–1950

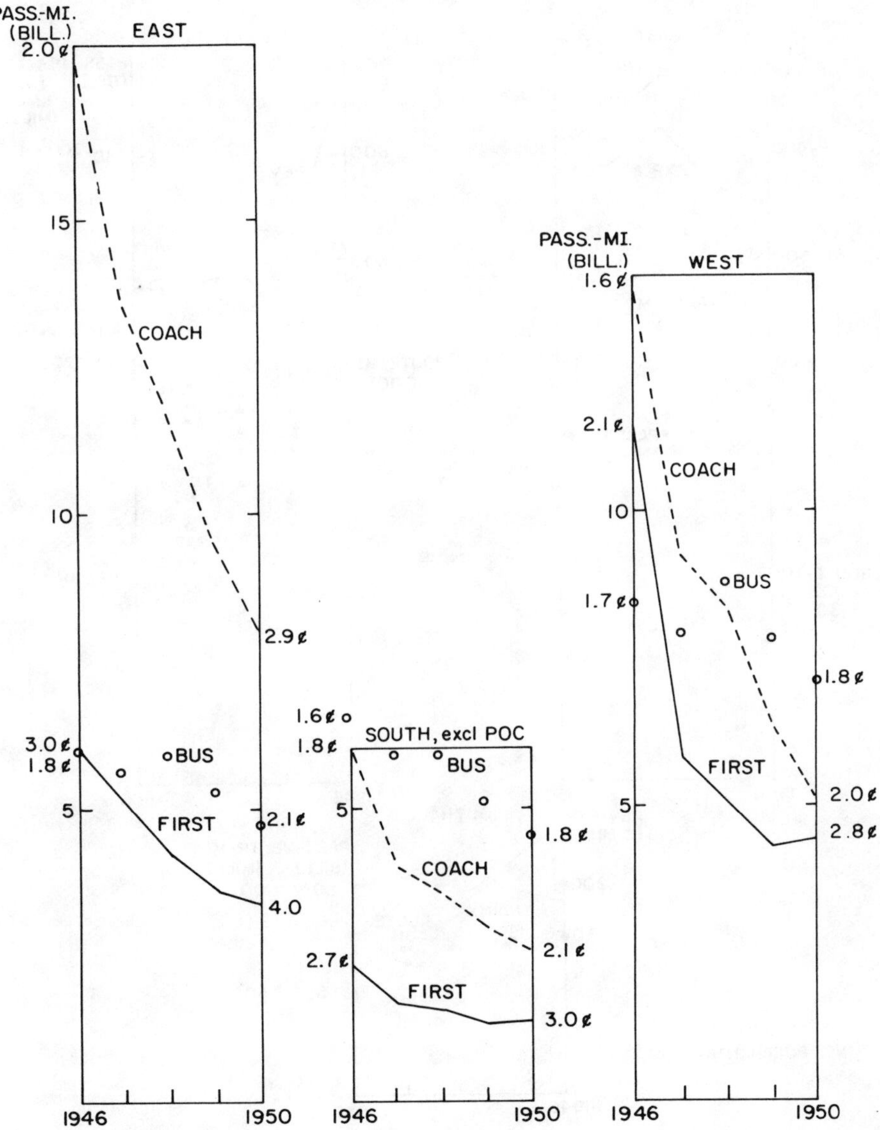

*Bus pass.-mi. understated by an estimated 3 percent for 1950 because of a change in definition of Class I carriers.

Passenger and Allied Services Revenues, "Solely Related" Expenses, Train-Miles, Route-Miles, and Passenger Miles, 1946–1950

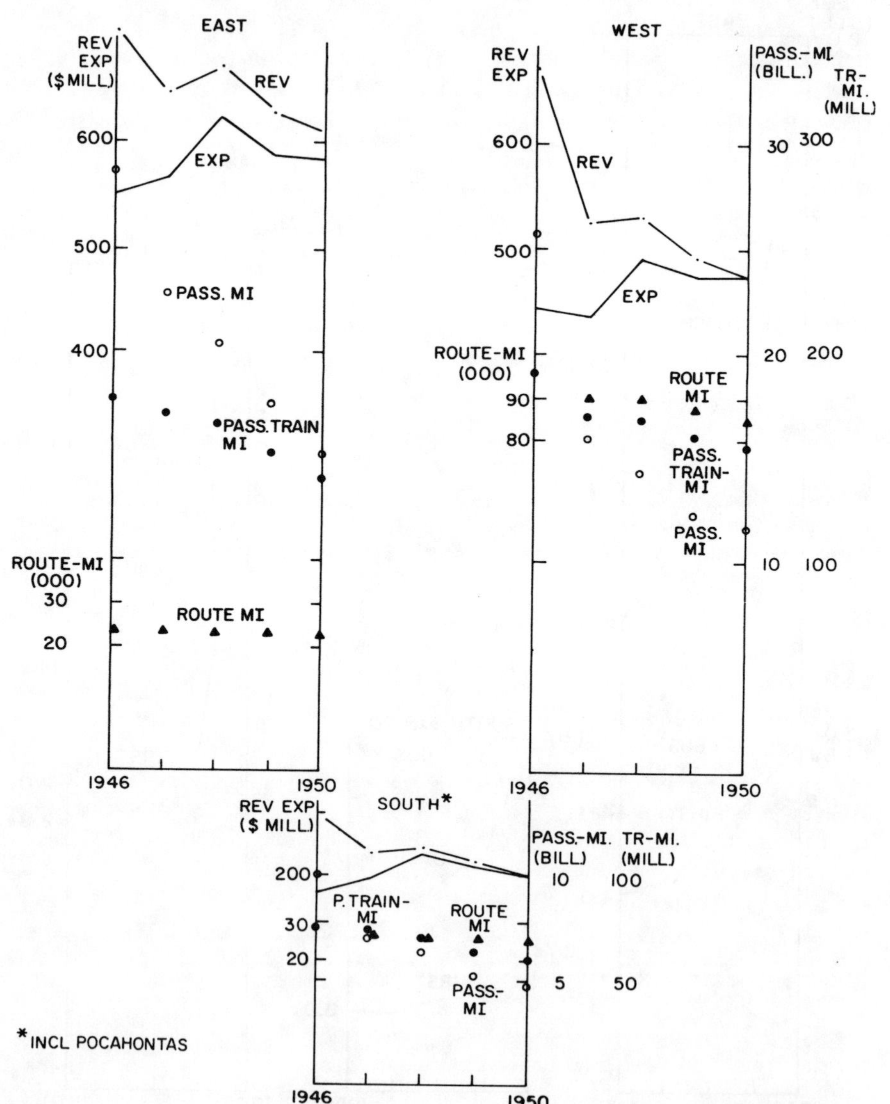

First-class passenger-miles fell some 25 percent—both in the East and West. The equality was despite the much higher eastern fare increase, 35 percent, to a final average 4¢ per mile than the western 29 percent, to only 2.8¢. The western nearly twice the eastern average haul together with the rapid development of air transport, which was most competitive for longest hauls, was a counter to the western lower fares. The southern decline in first-class travel was 17 percent, associated with a 15 percent fare increase to 3¢, somewhat above the western but well below the eastern. Because regional traffic data for air transport were not compiled, regional differences in its competitive role cannot be assessed. But nationwide its gain of 2 billion passenger-miles was of a magnitude to account for a significant proportion of the overall 3 billion rail first-class traffic losses.

Railroad Responses

The railroad response to the 1947 to 1950 declines in intercity traffic and other passenger and allied traffic and to the increasing input prices was to decrease train-miles and miles of route served. However for all regions the rates of train-mile reductions were less than one-half those of the passenger-mile declines. In both the South and West the latter were off 28 percent; the train-mile cuts were respectively 14 percent and 8 percent. The 8 percent was following a relatively much greater cut the previous years. The eastern 38 percent drop in passenger-miles led to a 19 percent cut in locomotive propelled train-miles. Passenger service route miles were curtailed some 5 percent in the East and West, roughly twice that in the South. There was no correspondence of train-mile cuts and declines in passenger (commutation excluded) revenues, which ranged from down 22 percent for the South to 15 percent for the East.

From 1947 to 1950 the relation of changes in outputs and inputs for passenger service must be measured from data that includes both commutation and so-called allied services. The gross revenues fell least for the East, 4 percent, and more than twice as much, 9 percent, for the South (including the Pocahontas region) and for the West. In none of the three could the "solely related" expenses be controlled sufficiently to match the revenue declines. For the western roads with the smallest reduction of train-miles in relation to traffic decline, the sole expenses increased 9 percent and for the southern with the most reduction they increased only 1 percent. Because of the East's initial wider spread of revenues over "solely related" expenses, it still showed some net remainder in 1950, but for the South and West it had been eliminated.

For the country as a whole for intercity coach traffic with hauls in all regions so short as to be critically subject to auto and bus competition the decline was 10 billion in passenger-miles. The tremendous increase in auto passenger-miles, around 70 billion, points up the fact that there was a broad and enormous increase in the demand for personal mobility, and in the course of that growth the automobile and improved highways were the major factor in the decline in rail coach travel. This rail traffic was not at a fare level and mainly not of the trip length for which air transport was then competing. For the higher fare and longer-haul first-class rail service the decline was just under 3 billion passenger-miles. The competitive air carriers posted a gain of 2 billion large enough to account for a large proportion of the rail loss.

The sharp rise after the war in unit rail expense could not be offset by increased fares and other charges, so that the wartime excesses of revenues over "solely related" expenses were eliminated for the South and West and nearly so for the East, a warning of serious problems ahead.

1950–1955

Service Levels

The period 1950 through 1955 was a final testing period for the postwar improved rail passenger services. Passenger equipment had been greatly improved with the heavy capital expenditures of the preceding years. A large number of new coaches and a complete new basic stock of some 1,200 modern sleepers were in operation.

The qualities of rail passenger service during this period may be briefly described. The railroads offered overnight service, with modern equipment, except for that needed to provide extra capacity at peak periods, between most all major cities that had a substantial community of interest and that were within 1,000-plus miles of one another. The spacing of most of the largest cities was such that the overnight services between them could be offered by train. Any gain from higher speeds for the 900- to 1,000-mile hauls would have been marginal and outweighed by operating disadvantages. The schedules of overnight service were predicated essentially on a 5:00 to 6:00 P.M. departure at the close of business and arrival at destination by 9:00 A.M., except where the time zone changes were adverse. In nonmountainous territory for the maximum route distance of the 1,034 miles between Chicago and Denver this meant an overall speed of 63 mph, and between New York and Chicago for the longest route's 970 miles, 62 mph. Day services were offered up to some 450 miles with a 7:00 to 8:00 A.M. departure and arrival for dinner or earlier. Over the longest route between Chicago and Minneapolis, 437 miles, overall speed was 65 mph, between Chicago to Kansas City, 62 mph. For daytime 400- to 500-mile services there was no clear net gain from shorter times at over 65 mph overall speeds. Four routes traversing rugged terrain arrival was on the later side and overall speeds remained below 60 mph.

For transcontinental service across the Rocky Mountains and the coastal ranges from Chicago to the Pacific Coast, the 2,200-plus miles meant two nights on the train. With end-of-the-business-day departure (earlier with adverse time zone differences) and a second morning arrival possible with speeds around 55 mph, there was no opportunity for real gain from possible higher speeds.

The postwar basic fare adjustments were allowed to stand. There was widespread fare experimentation. The wartime coach fares for servicemen in uniform traveling at their own expense was continued at 1¢ to 1½¢ per mile. A variety of reductions for roundtrips on holidays and weekends were tried. In extreme cases the fares were as low as one-way plus 1¢. Trials were made of so-called family-plan reductions, with extra adults carried at half fare. There were many group economy fares. All-expense tours were made available. However, average regional fares revealed only slight impact from these reductions. Aside from fare adjustments, credit cards were issued and travel agents were given commissions on sales.

Competition

During this 1950–1955 period air carriers were experiencing the highest rates of growth in their postwar history, with an increase in passenger-miles of 148 percent in the five years. There had been a slight decline in average fares, 4 percent. This period covered the introduction of the DC-6B's and the Super-Constellations, which brought higher speeds and nonstop flights between even the most widely separated major cities in the United States. Nineteen fifty-one was the year in which hourly "commuter" flights were inaugurated between New York and Chicago, and it became possible for a businessman to leave his home in Chicago in the morning, have a work day in New York, and be back home that night.

In the highway field, by 1955, 100,000 miles of rural highways paved for heavy-duty use had been added to the country's sytem since the war, a 50 percent increase in this cateogry. From 1950 to 1955, 12 million additional automobiles were registered, up 29 percent, and auto passenger-miles were up some 45 percent. Bus traffic declined slightly. The federal tax of 15 percent on fares for all modes of for-hire transport was reduced to 10 percent. Intercity highway passenger-miles increased by 180 billion, air-carrier 12 billion, while the railroads lost 3 billion.

Viewing the changes from 1950 to 1955 by regions, first-class traffic declined sharply: 37 percent in the West, 32 percent in the South, and 22 percent in the East. The longer western average hauls per carrier of 600 miles compared to the 310 to 320 miles of the other two regions made the West more vulnerable to air competition. In contrast, the western coach traffic with some 200-mile hauls increased 12 percent, while that of the South with 170- and the East with 60-mile hauls each declined 8 percent. Looking at changes on a year-to-year basis for the total of all classes of passenger-miles, there had been increases from 1950 to 1951 with the Korean War, particularly in the South and West. Thereafter the war related traffic dropped sharply and further downward pressure came with the 1954 recession.

Railroad (Coach and First-Class) and Bus Passenger Miles, and Annual Average Fares, 1950–1955

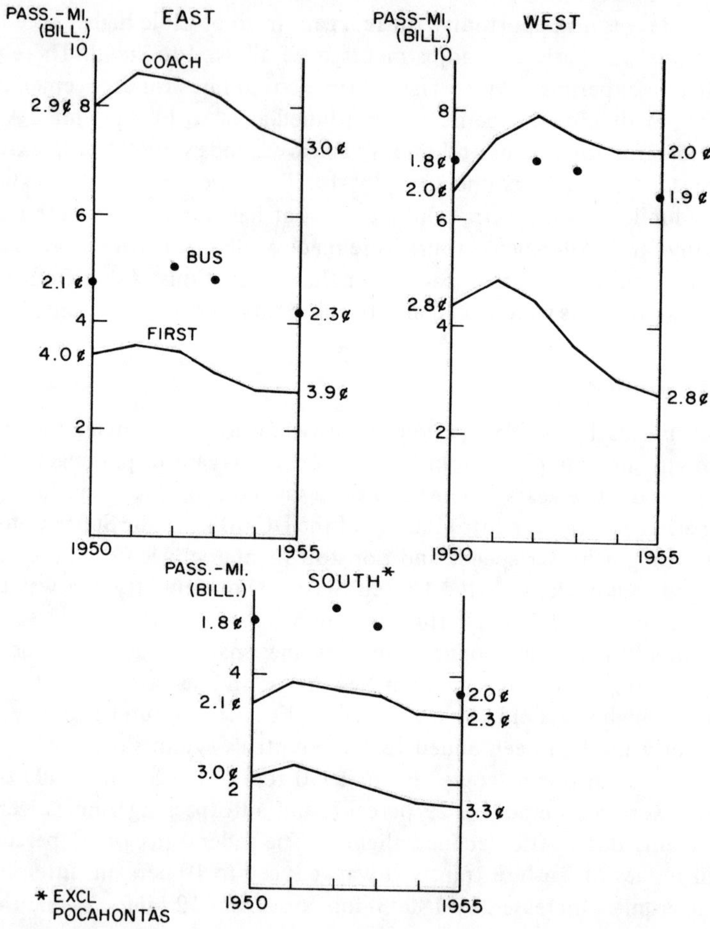

Railroad Responses

With no increases in most types of fares the decline in passenger-miles resulted in serious revenue decreases, sharpest for first class. In addition, mail and express revenue dropped 11 percent. At the same time wage rates rose on the average 31 percent, and material prices rose somewhat less. For this period, in contrast to the immediately preceding years, train-miles and miles of road on which passenger service was offered were reduced more than the passenger-mile declines in the effort to adjust expenses to revenues. Train-miles in the East and South were cut 30 percent more than the passenger-mile decline; in the West, 50 percent, making up for the region's previously slower cutback. The combined result of all factors by 1955 was that for the eastern roads there was still a slight remainder after deducting "solely related" expenses from revenues for all passenger related services combined. For the other parts of the country revenues failed to even meet the "solely related" passenger expenses, short by 5 percent for the South and 12 percent for the West.

* * *

Passenger and Allied Services Revenues, "Solely Related" Expenses, Train-Miles, Route-Miles, and Passenger Miles, 1950–1955

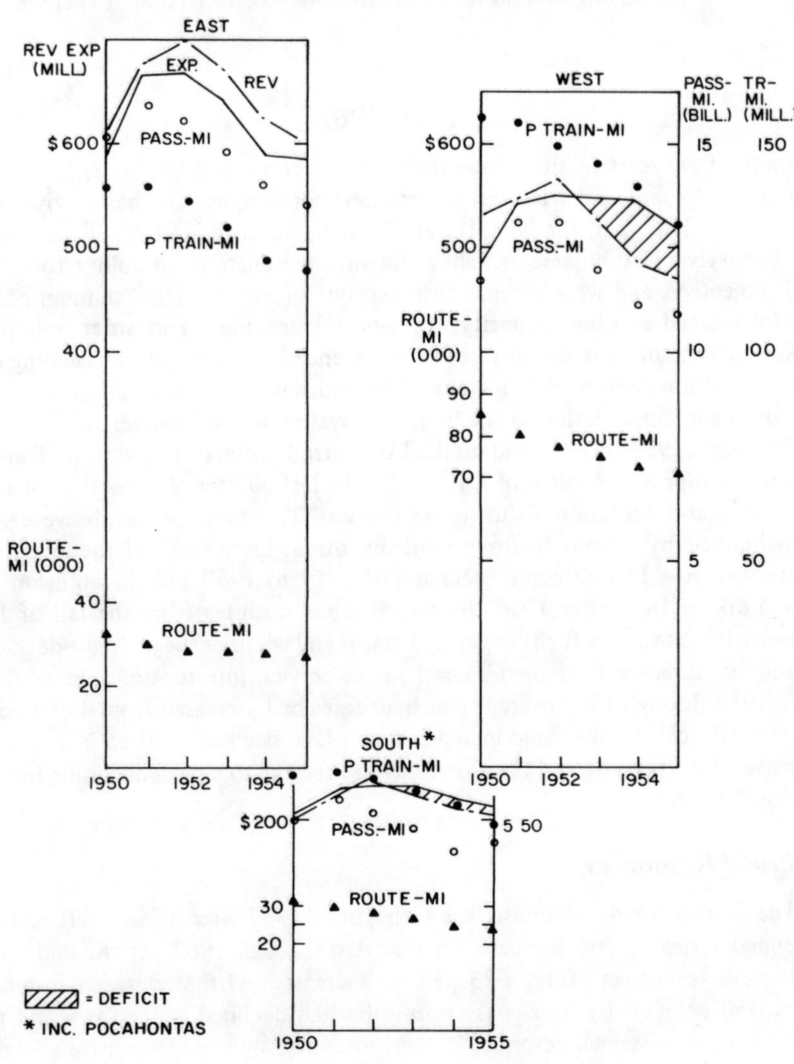

The period 1950 to 1955 confirmed as permanent what had been presaged in the 1947 to 1950 years. That was that passenger and allied service revenues would at best only just cover the "solely related" expenses and in all probability would fall short, as southern and western experiences testified. In fact, in the West the deficit was significant.

These results came from five years of experience without fare increases, with a prior large capital investment in new improved equipment, and with a high level of service. The attractiveness of the automobile and airplane transport was such that all the railroad efforts could neither hold intercity passenger traffic nor make it self-supporting even in terms of only the "solely related" expenses.

1956–1962

In the first years of this phase the railroads continued investment in experimental equipment and tried out several new car designs. The best known were the NYC Talgo train, the New Haven Train-X, the high-level ATSF coach, and the Pennsylvania tubular cars. They did not demonstrate an ability to achieve their objectives and were ultimately taken out of service. The "slumber coach" was introduced as a high-capacity, forty-berth, sleeping car in order to improve productivity and allow coach fares to be extended to passengers in sleeping cars.

Competition continued to increase. The highway system was being continually improved and construction of the interstate system was well underway.

The years 1959 to 1962 had marked the introduction of jets with their contribution to improved quality of service. By the last quarter of 1962 their share of air passenger-miles had built up to 68 percent. This same period, however, had been marked by several features reducing the attractiveness of the air service. There were the Electra plane accidents of 1959 to 1960 and the collision over New York in December 1960. Extended labor disputes from the fall of 1960 through 1962 over the flight engineer's status and whether the jet flight-deck crew should be three or four men caused major service interruptions. In addition, from 1959 through 1962 average coach air fares had increased from 4.6¢ to 5.8¢. From 1959 to 1962 the rapid increase in air plane size had resulted in a seat-mile increase of 32 percent and the above adverse factors to a passenger-mile increase of only 15 percent.

Railroad Responses

The eastern roads' response was to begin in 1956 what turned out to be an extended series of fare increases that carried through 1962. At the end, coach fares were 4¢ instead of 3¢, a 33 percent increase, and first class, 6¢ instead of 4¢, up 50 percent. By 1962 passenger-miles had declined 46 percent, and non-commutation passenger revenue, 23 percent. In response, locomotive propelled

Railroad (Coach and First-Class) and Bus Passenger-Miles, and Annual Average Fares, 1955–1962

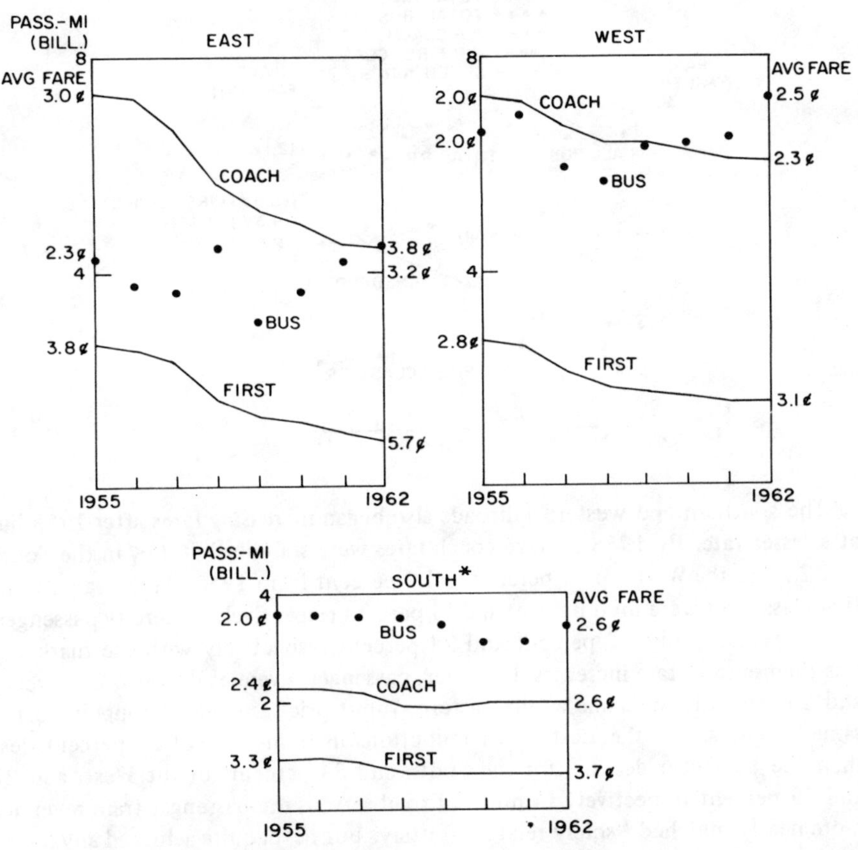

train-miles were reduced by almost a half, about the same as the passenger-mile drop, and miles of line with passenger service, a third. By these means the "solely related" outlays* were controlled to the extent that despite the increases in price of inputs the "outlays" declined 23 percent in seven years. The net result was that the passenger and allied service "solely related" deficit was eliminated in the East. This particularly vigorous response of the eastern roads reflected their severe financial problems, regionally the worst.

*Beginning with this period ICC expense tabulations included also "solely passenger" related taxes and rents, thus enabling the taking into account of the payroll taxes associated with the labor expenses of passenger train crews and station employees together with real estate taxes and rentals for the specialized passenger terminal facilities in larger cities. The sum of these added items and the "solely related" expenses are called "outlays."

Revenue Passenger Miles (Rail, Bus, and Air), 1949–1955

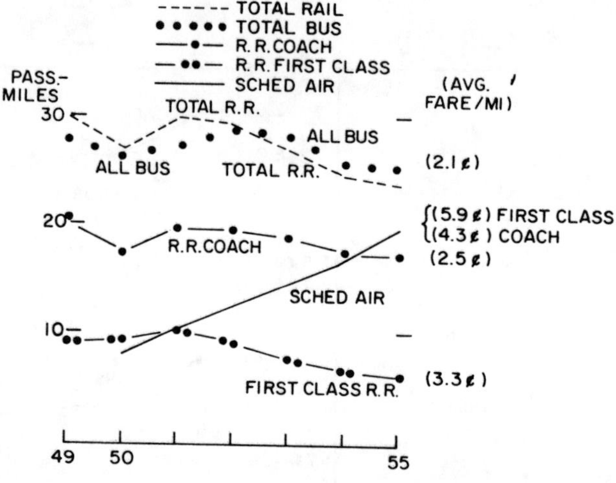

The southern and western railroads also began increasing fares after 1955 but at a lesser rate. By 1958 average coach fares were stabilized at 2.6¢ in the South and 2.2¢ in the West, up 11 percent and 9 percent from 1955. At the same time, first-class fares were up 8 percent and 11 percent respectively. Intercity passenger-miles declined only 21 percent and 24 percent respectively with the markedly less than eastern fare increases. However, passenger revenues declined 23 percent and 24 percent, the same as the eastern. Input prices increased roughly to the same extent as for the East. With reductions in train-miles of 21 percent, less than the passenger decline, for the South and 34 percent for the West, and 21 and 29 percent respectively in miles of road served, the passenger train revenues more nearly matched "solely related" outlays but never quite achieved any more. In the South the shortfall was 9 percent in 1956 and 3 percent by 1962. For the West it had been 18 percent in 1956 and was eliminated by 1962. This last reflected the greater train-mile cut relative to passenger-mile decline in the West than the South.

The 1955 to 1962 period reflected the further downward shift in demand for intercity passenger service. Neither the substantial fare increases in the East nor the lesser ones in the South and West were able to prevent drastic declines in passenger revenue. These were cushioned somewhat by relatively stable mail and express revenue during this period. Reductions in passenger train-miles and miles of road on which passenger train service was offered did succeed in reducing outlays in relation to revenues. In the East the reductions produced an excess over outlays. For the other regions, revenues were brought more nearly in line with, but never full covered, the "solely related" outlays. The eastern railroads were the ones with the greatest overall financial pressure to obtain some passenger

**Passenger and Allied Services Revenues, "Solely Related" Outlays,
Train-Miles, Route-Miles, and Passenger-Miles, 1955-1962**

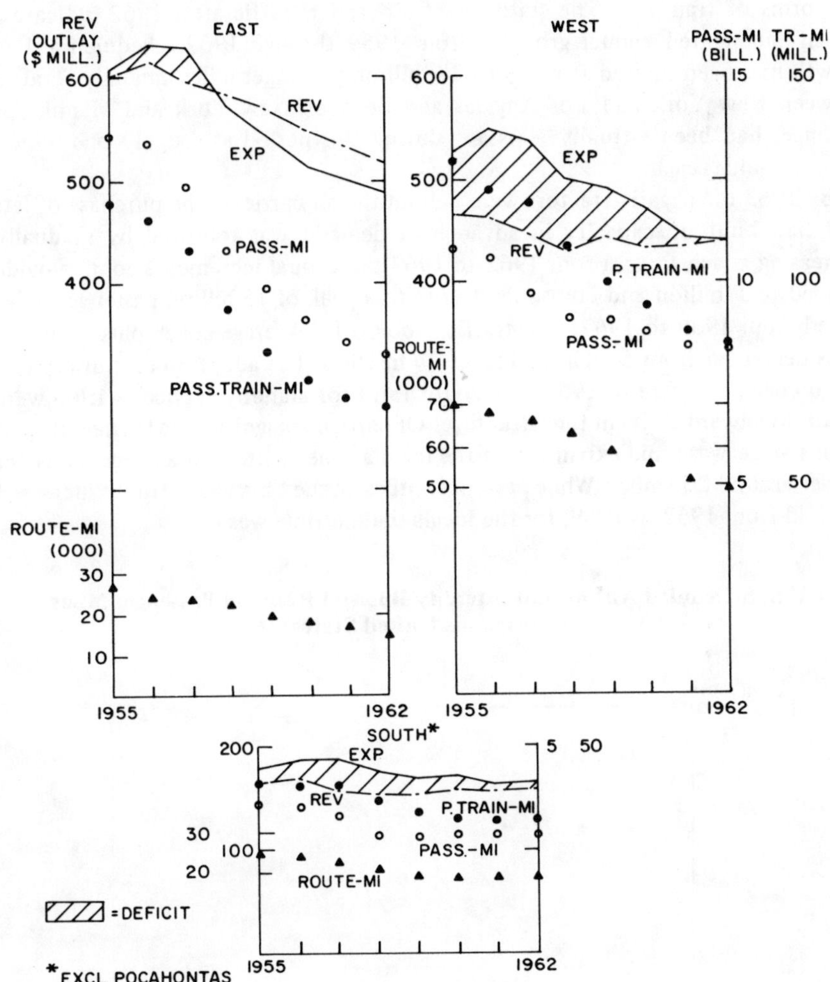

contributions to common expenses. The Pocahontas roads with the least pressure developed the least control and wound up with the proportionately largest shortfall.

1962–1970

The last phase of this passenger service analysis ends with 1970 because in May of the following year the National Railroad Passenger Corporation took over intercity passenger operations from most all of the individual U.S. systems.

Competition

Following 1962, a forward surge in personal mobility dominated the competing forms of transport. The statistics of air-carrier traffic after 1962 indicate a greatly augmented annual growth. From 1959 through 1962 scheduled airline growth had been limited from ½ to 2½ billion passenger-miles annually. Traffic between New York and Los Angeles and between New York and Miami, for instance, had been virtually constant during this period at roughly one billion passenger-miles each.

By 1963 the negative factors were behind the air carriers. The purchase of jets that had built up capacity in advance of demand was followed by gradually decreasing coach fares. From 1962 to 1963 the annual increments country-wide jumped to 5 billion and continued to rise to a peak of 15 billion passenger-miles added from 1966 to 1967. Air traffic "took off." Average coach plus economy fares decreased from 5.8¢ in 1962 to 5.1¢ in 1968. The adoption of military furlough coach half-fare in 1963 and youth fares for standby service in 1965 were major downward shifts in fare structure. Of particular significance to the railroads at this stage was rapid expansion of the local airlines with their average hauls per carrier around 200 miles. While passenger-miles on the "big four" trunks increased 2.7-fold from 1962 to 1969, for the locals the multiple was 4.

**U.S. Scheduled Airline and Intercity Bus and Railroad Passenger Miles
(Contiguous United States)**

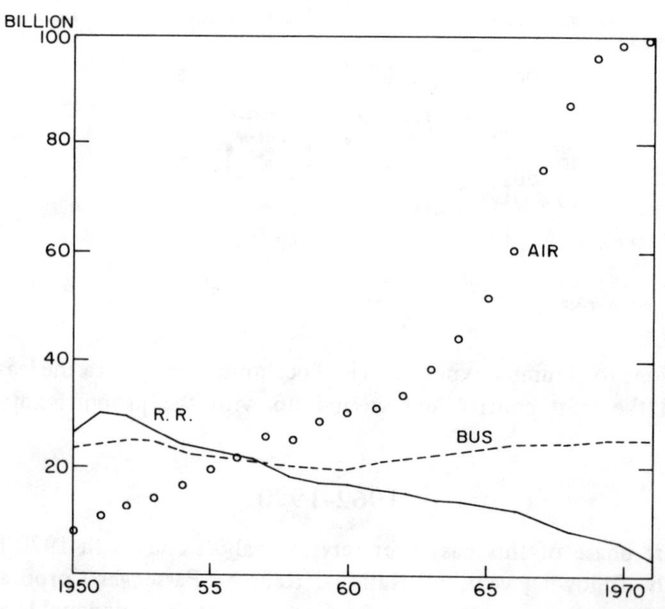

In respect to highway traffic, the further development of toll expressways and the free interstate highway system was of major significance. In 1960 there were some 6,000 miles of four- or more lane divided highways with full access control, in 1962 there were 9,900, and by 1970, 33,000. For the country as a whole intercity bus traffic grew from some 20 billion passenger-miles in 1960 and 1961 to 26 billion by 1970. Automobile passenger-miles, which were of a different order of magnitude, increased by some 80 billion from 1962 to 1970, exceeding all other modes by a wide margin. This reflected the improved highway system and higher per family income levels leading to increased car ownership and use.

Railroad Responses

The intercity railroad services offered on main runs to compete with highway and air were in 1962 and 1963 basically the same as in the middle 1950s. The schedules were much as those described for 1955. The passenger equipment available for the day-in-day-out base load of principal trains was still not much over ten years old. The western roads had made some improvements by way of vista-dome coaches. For the eastern roads from 1962, the southern from 1957, and the western from 1958 intercity average fares remained substantially unchanged until 1967. Then from 1967 on to 1969 the first-class regional average fares increases ranged from 4 percent to 7 percent, and the noncommutation coach were increased 14 percent in the East, 12 percent in the West, and 9 percent in the South. The New York World's Fair in 1964 and 1965 blunted the long-term declining demand for rail service in the East, and the mid-1966 six-week-long airline strike for most of the trunk air carriers temporarily raised the demand for rail transport in all regions.

Viewing the results of all these factors region by region reveals some significant variations. Regional data are available on a more limited base than national. Passenger-miles by regions were compiled only through 1968 for buses. Except for the East, bus passenger-miles throughout the 1960s exceeded rail intercity coach passenger-miles, by the greatest margin in the South. Beginning in 1963 the eastern bus traffic passed the rail coach. The rate of increase in bus traffic in the East, 50 percent in six years, was the greatest for any region in this period.

The least bus traffic increase was in the West, 13 percent. After 1966 bus passenger-miles declined all around, to the greatest extent in the West.

Incomplete regional air traffic data restrict overall explanation of passenger traffic shifts between modes. Local airline data together with that for regional trunk airlines, however, provide an indication of regional air trends. The fourfold growth from 1962 to 1969 of the two local air carriers (Mohawk and Allegheny) in the East, together with the growth of bus traffic, comes near to equaling the decline of rail passenger-miles, coach and first class combined. The fivefold growth of the two southern local airlines (Southern and Piedmont)

Railroad (Coach and First-Class) and Bus Passenger Miles, and Annual Average Fares, 1962–1970

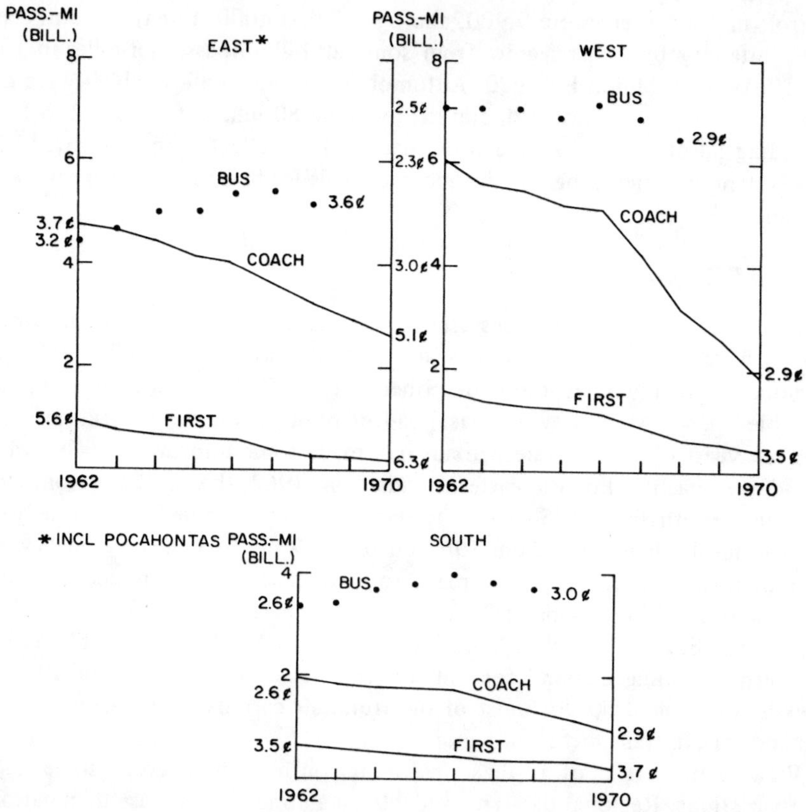

together with the bus increase in the region equaled the southern rail decline. For the West, taking the regional trunk airlines along with the local (the important California intrastate local air carrier is not included in available data), the combined air passenger-mile increase exceeds the combined losses of rail and bus. The long (for railroad) rail trips in the West, something over 300 miles for coach and increasing from 625 miles in 1962 to 825 in 1970 for first class made the air competition a greater factor than in the other regions.

The net result for rail traffic from 1962 to 1970 in the various regions was a 46 percent decline in intercity coach passenger-miles in the East, 50 percent in the South, and 69 percent in the West. First-class traffic in the East with the markedly higher fare level showed the greatest decline of all, 83 percent. The next greatest decline, 75%, was in the West despite the low average fare level of 3.4¢. The length of the western haul probably was the dominant negative factor. In the South first-class traffic with intermediate-length hauls, around 500 miles

**Passenger and Allied Services Revenues, "Solely Related" Outlays, Train-Miles,
Route-Miles, and Passenger-Miles, 1962–1970**

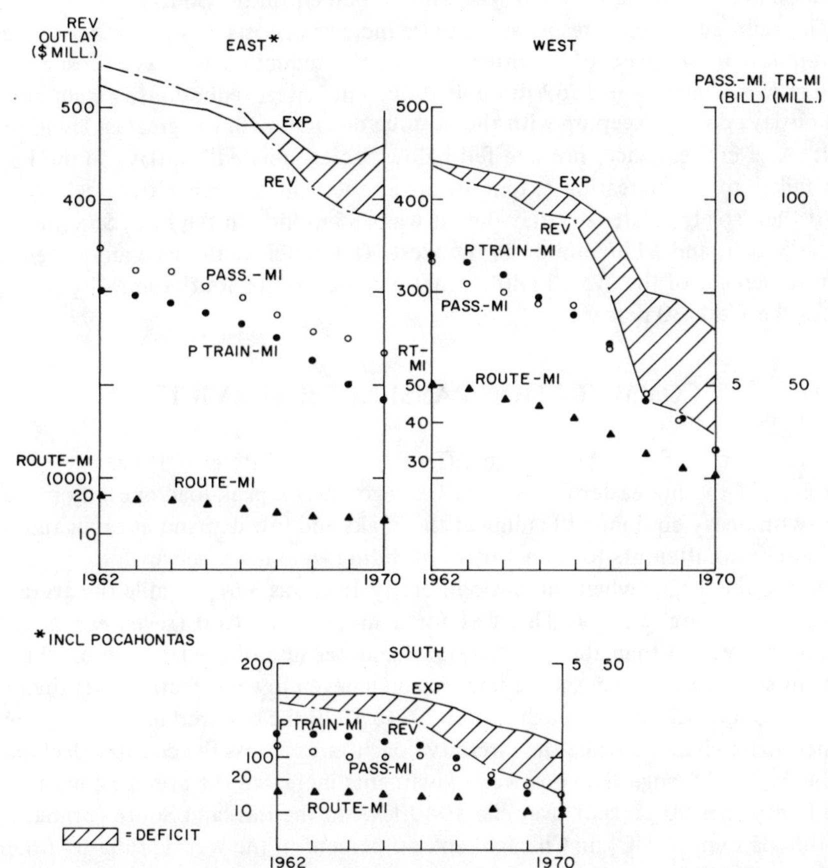

per railroad, and comparatively lower average fares, 3.7¢, declined the least for
that class, 65 percent. In each region the first-class traffic declined significantly
more than the coach.

Compared to earlier periods reviewed, the period 1962–1970 was differentiated
by a precipitate decline in the mail and express revenues earned by passenger
train service. In the West as late as 1966 these together had nearly equaled the
passenger revenue, $169 million compared to $180 million. By 1970 the mail
and express on passenger trains was only $22 million, and the passenger $112
million. Seventy-three million dollars of the mail and express revenue had been
diverted to freight service.

Along with the declines in intercity passenger and allied traffic and revenue
there was an increase in the unit cost of inputs. Average employee hourly com-

pensation increased 37 percent, and material prices, 15 percent. Total "solely related" outlays, this including commuter operations, per train mile rose some 50 to 60 percent in the East and West and 73 percent in the South.

The railroads' overall response to these increasing costs was to further reduce train-miles. In the case of all three regions, the reduction followed closely the decline in revenue from 1962 through 1966. Thereafter reductions in train-miles and outlays did not keep up with the revenue decline, with the greatest lag in the West. As a consequence, revenue fell below "solely related" outlays in the East and failed to an increasing extent to cover them in the other two regions. In 1970 the "solely related" outlay deficit was $85 million in the East, $58 million in the South, and $117 million in the West. The deficit in the East amounted to over 50 percent of the overall railroad net income, in the South some 40 percent, and in the West, 30 percent.

COMMUTATION PASSENGER SERVICE

Commuter traffic has been quite different from the intercity. It has been concentrated in the big eastern cities and Chicago. It is a peak-load one-way movement with heavy equipment loading at the peaks and low demand at other times. The numerous attempts to attract off-peak riding were never successful.

During the 1920s when the basic intercity fare was 3.6¢ per mile the average commutation fare was 1¢. This was for a much short haul (seventeen miles) estimated average) than the intercity fare, and because of the large terminal element in suburban train costs the fare was on an even lower effective level than it appears comparatively. Through the 1930s to 1940 the commutation average remained little changed while the intercity coach fares across the country declined to the 1½ to 2¢ range. The postwar adjustments increased the average commutation fares some 60 percent over the 1940 level in the East and South (primarily the Illinois Central [IC] in Chicago) and 50 percent in the West (primarily other Chicago suburban service). For the East this increase was the same as for intercity coach fares; for the South, slightly more. For the West where intercity fares had been held down, it was markedly more.

After 1950 the commutation fares steadily increased in all regions until by 1970 the eastern and western levels had reached 3.8¢ and 3.7¢ per mile with slightly increasing hauls, 24 and 20 miles respectively. The southern (Chicago) became 3.4¢ by 1970 with a 17-mile haul. In the East the commutation level was still well below the intercity level of 5.1¢ with a 40-mile average per carrier haul. For the other two regions the commuter average fare was much above the intercity coach, which applied for much longer haul per road, 216 miles in the South and 317 miles in the West.

Commutation passenger-miles have in the last decade changed little in the East and South and increased in the West. With the high proportion of terminal costs and the poor load factors in all regions the average fares were in effect much below the intercity fares relative to costs.

PASSENGER TRAIN OPERATIONS

A critical aspect of the passenger and allied services segment of the railroad industry has been the inability to achieve significant gains in either labor or capital productivity in operations, both terminal and line-haul. The latter, in contrast to the case with freight, dominated the overall directly associated expenses by a wide margin. For the line-haul operating the basic producing unit is the train with both capital and labor inputs closely related to it. A discrete amount of both are committed when a train is scheduled. Potential service outputs in turn are related to the capacity of the train determined by the number of cars and the capacities of each. Much of the associated inputs, operating crews in particular, do not vary much with length or car capacity. Further, the call-upon track capacity and its costs are to an important degree determined by the train regardless of its length. Thus, the more cars per train, the greater productivity of its crew and capital productivity of a unit of track capacity.

There are basic constraints imposed by the physical characteristics of passenger equipment. Maximum passenger train lengths have been twenty or so cars, with generally lower limits set by passenger convenience and comfort, loading and unloading delays, and terminal facility constraints. Train lengths have also reflected state-of-the-art motive-power capabilities as they relate to limited grades and curves and tightness of schedules. Productivity is also tied to capacity of the cars that make up the consist of trains. Maximum passenger train car lengths have been 85 feet, a limit based on technical constraints of curvature, vehicular mechanics, couplers, and in-switch territory signal circuit requirements. Car widths and heights have been limited by tracks and roadway clearance dimensions. Within these constraints coach seating has varied from 40 to 50 for transcontinental service, to from 70 to 90 for shorter intercity runs, up to 150 or so where special design has been warranted for commuter operations with peak period capacity problems. Sleeping car and parlor car capacities have depended more upon the amenities offered, ranging from 22 berths per car for first-class accommodations to 40-odd for a bi-level arrangement with restricted quarters. The only significant gains in car capacity have been in the commuter cars.

For intercity operations from 1947 through the mid-1960s, there was only slight gain in regional average train lengths, to ten and eleven cars. Then in the final years, with sharp reduction in passenger-miles and disappearance of mail and express business the average lengths in all regions dropped to eight or eight and a half cars. For the self-propelled car trains in commuter service, train lengths did not vary significantly.

Passenger utilization of intercity trains can only be measured in terms of combined coach and first-class passenger-miles. In 1947 they ranged from 120 per train-mile in the East to 100 in the South, and somewhat less in the West. There was a general decline into the 1950s except for gains during the Korean War. Finally, in the latter 1920s with the sharpest cuts in train-miles, the 1970 average loadings were some 120 in the East and around 100 in the South and West. There were no gains in passenger utilization of trains. Despite the great drop in volume of intercity passenger traffic, there was no significant decline in utilization. Train capacities were kept in line with traffic volume.

The limitations of data permit consideration only of sleeping plus parlor car capacity utilization. In 1947 first-class passenger-miles per car-mile was around thirteen in all regions. By 1950 the figure dropped to eleven all around and to nine by 1960. Thereafter there was significant differentiation between regions so that by 1970 the eastern roads had the lowest utilization, some seven, the western, nine; and the southern, ten. In this class of service the eastern roads had done least well in cutting capacity to meet traffic fall off; the South, the best.

Capital productivity is affected not only by loadings but also by the proportion of equipment life actually spent in service. Meaningful measures of this in terms of annual miles run are difficult because of an inventory of modern cars along with a variety of older cars retained as the economic way of meeting peak requirements. Of some 14,000 non-self-propelled coaches on hand for the U.S. in the mid 1950s, only half, some 7,000, were air-conditioned. Only this part of coach stock was considered likely to see enough service to warrant having the essential amenities. In the case of sleeping cars, the modern vintage were the so-called lightweight ones, all air-conditioned, of which there were 2,000 on hand in 1955, some 1,500 have been added after the war.

Utilization factors may be first reviewed for 1955, that year being the end of the period of a large-scale acquisition of new cars, and sufficiently after World War II and Korea to provide time for adjustment of inventories to normal commercial conditions. In the East average annual per car mileage, considering the whole inventory of non-self-propelled coaches, was around 55,000; in the South, 90,000; and the West, almost 10,000. Taking just the number of air-conditioned stock coaches, on the assumption that these accounted for practically all the coach-miles, annual mileage comes out as some 90,000 in the East, 120,000 in the South, and 140,000 in the West. The eastern roads obtained much poorer utilization.

Labor Productivity

Because there are no intercity versus commuter or regional breakdowns of labor data, productivity in passenger train operations has to be considered overall. The so-called operating members of the crew are the enginemen (motormen of electrically operated trains are considered as enginemen), firemen (helpers), conductors, ticket collectors, brakemen, flagmen, and baggagemen. Basic factors affecting crew size have been several. The introduction of diesel locomotives has done away with double-heading (the use of two locomotives, each requiring a two-man engine crew) for heavy trains. The shift with the rapid intercity traffic decline to a greater share of commutation traffic has increased the proportion of electric "multiple-unit" trains, which do not have firemen or helpers. Decline in baggage and express service has required fewer baggagemen, though there have been minimum requirements in some labor contracts.

The average crew consist has only declined from 5.1 in 1947 to 4.8 in 1970, despite the several favorable factors just enumerated. Passenger-miles per crew hours actually worked only rose from 575 to 593, despite the heavier loads on the commuter trains, and their increased proportion of train-miles. This last factor has led to the average of annual train-miles per crew member declining slightly from 51,000 to 46,000. Despite technological advances in motive power and equipment, the basic physical limitation of passenger train equipment has prevented significant improvements leading to gains in labor or capital productivity.

It may be noted that the standard wage contracts for passenger train service have continued to specify 100 miles as the basic day's run for enginemen and 150 for train crews. The overall average train-miles per crew hours actually worked have varied erratically over the years with some increase recently. Combining these limited productivity gains with the wage increases (without considering added benefits, which are not broken down by type of crew service) has caused average crew costs per passenger train-mile in 1970 to be 4.4 times what they were prewar in 1940, and per train hour, 5 times.

* * *

The postwar quarter century of railroad passenger service began with a vigorous effort with major investment to promote passenger traffic and ended with the gradual withdrawal in the face of greatly expanded automobile use and rapid growth of air transport. The automobile had made major inroads against rail passenger transport before the war. Postwar improvements in automobiles and highways, a greatly expanded network of high-standard roads, and increases in, and wider distribution of, personal ability to provide transport on call, house to house and place to place without transfer; in privacy, single or in groups; and with capacity for accompanying goods was a combination that the railroads could not match at any price. These were the qualities that met human desire for mobility and travel. In turn, air transport so improved its service qualities, comfort, and safety together with speed with jets far beyond the reach of the railroads so that much of the remaining areas of rail demand were syphoned away

61

and their demands replaced with expanding new ones. On the other side, rising unit costs and inability of the railroads to substantially improve productivity greatly increased the burden of passenger costs. Because of the innovations in highway and air transport technology the choice with few exceptions was to move resources away from the older intercity transport mode. The only logical economic response was the private railroad systems' withdrawal.

5

Baggage, Mail, and Express Services

At the end of the war passenger trains were carrying substantial volumes of mail and express. In 1947 out of the $600 million passenger train revenue, $170 million came from mail and $116 million from express. Baggage had declined to a point of producing insignificant revenue, only $3 million, but did continue to require some car space and terminal handling and under labor contracts some extra train personnel. The continuing but declining mail and express services were closely interrelated, using many of the same trains as did passengers for line-haul movement and parts of the same general terminal facilities. Each of the two, however, had its own sorting and pick-up and delivery operations and its own administrative functions.[1]

The only pertinent measure of the relative use these various services made of passenger trains showed that in 1948 for the U.S. as a whole, one-thirtieth of passenger train lineal capacity was for baggage, one-eighth each for mail and express, the remaining almost three-quarters being for passengers. The corresponding revenues were some 18 percent from mail, 9 percent from express, 74 percent from passenger fares, which covered the handling of normal amounts of baggage, and 1/5 percent from excess baggage.[2]

Analysis of the changing transportation demands for the railroad part of the express and parcel post services is difficult because the Railway Express Agency (REA), the post office, and motor carriers and forwarders each provided a complicated array of overlapping services differentiated as to their character and involving different size shipment. The services were competitive within certain ranges but not in others. In competition with the REA some small motor carriers provided a service of the express type. Large motor carriers emphasized shipments of sizes larger than the package class and taking away from the less-than-carload rail service. The REA tended to favor large shipments because of their greater profitability, and actually was involved in carload rail shipments provided with special handling. On the other hand, the postal service had statutory top-size limits placed on parcels it might handle.

The supply of rail service was only one of the inputs for the mail and express operation. Both operations have been labor intensive in connection with terminal handling and pick-up and delivery, so that wages and benefits were more important factors than transport costs. For instance, in 1960 REA payments for transport were 34 percent and for labor 52 percent of revenue. For fourth-class parcel post mail, transport was 33 percent of apportioned expenses; direct labor, 46 percent.

**Surface Parcel Post, Air Parcel Post (including First Class), United Parcel
Service, Rail Express, Bus Shipments
(Est. Aver. Lbs. per Parcel)**

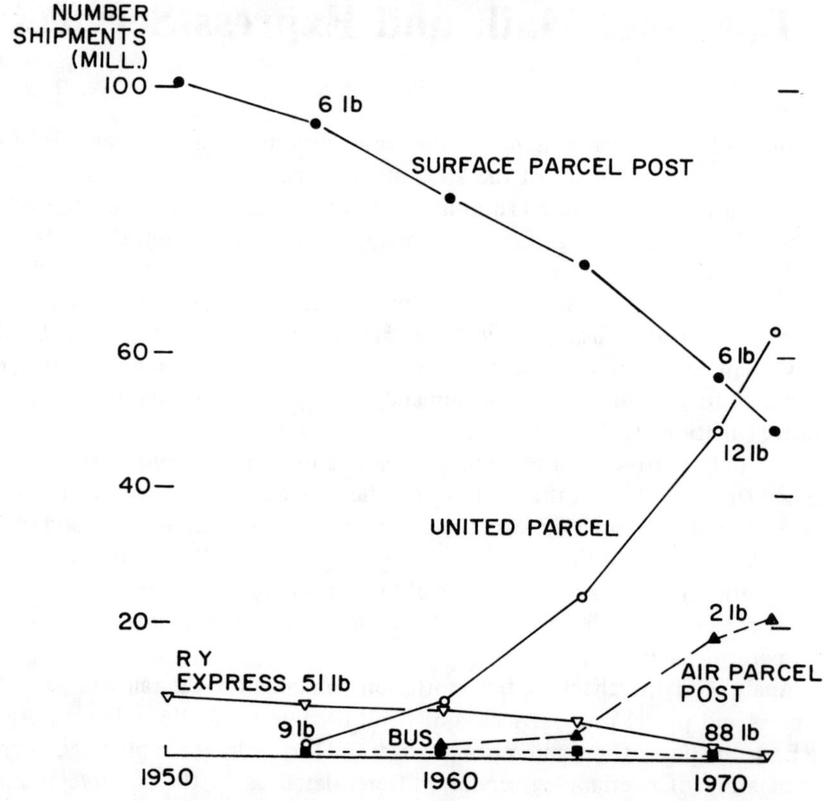

(Source: *TE*, Jan. 1973, p. 5; vol. 1, #3, 1974, p. 11.)

POSTAL SERVICES

The postal services ranged from purely communication by way of letters, first
class and air mail; through an intermediate group, second and third class, news-
papers, periodicals, and other printed matter; on to clearly package transport,
fourth class, which included surface and air parcel post, or "priority mail" as it
was later classified. The railroads traditionally had been involved in the surface
transport of all three general categories. During the period under study, payments
to the railroads for mail transport were established in ICC proceedings. These involved substantial time lags but increases were provided over the postwar years
after having remained at the same level from 1928 to 1947. The first-class and air-
mail letter and the fourth-class mail are the principal categories for analysis.

First Class

The outstanding characteristic of letter mail service is that it has had a generally rising long-run trend in the postwar years from 24 billion surface mail pieces in 1949/50 to 49 billion by 1969/70. Because this class of mail is a matter of communication, speed is of primary concern. Thus quite early, air mail was initiated for long hauls at first with higher than surface charges. A contrasting development was that with reductions in local passenger train service, highway transport took over short-haul and cross-country mail movement. Some railroads provided this service with their subsidiary motor carriers. The railroad share in transport payments for first class letter mail dropped from nearly one-half just before the war to two-fifths in 1950, down to one-sixth in 1968. The air share had become almost two-thirds by then.

Parcel Post—Fourth Class

The principal postal package service was fourth class, mainly the so-called "parcel post." In addition, there was air parcel post. These services competed in the upper weight range of their shipment weights with the lower range of the REA. Parcel post had been established in 1912 as a public service to provide small package service to every household in the country. It aimed to provide such service to isolated rural people and to break up the monopolies of the then regional express companies. The maximum size of package for parcel post has always been a matter of dispute between the post office, express agencies, and various competing types of shippers. In 1950 the REA and other interests pushed Congress into reducing parcel post maximum weights of shipments from the large post offices from seventy to forty pounds within the first three distance zones and from fifty to twenty pounds for the longer hauls. In essence, this was aimed at giving the REA and others the larger, more profitable parcels moving along heavy traffic routes and leaving to the post office the unprofitable parcels of lightweight or over the thin traffic routes. At the same time, Congress ordered that parcel post charges be set so that the service would pay its way. The number of parcel post pieces started a long decline. On the other hand, the book traffic included in fourth class increased steadily throughout the period of the study. The important competitors of surface parcel post were the United Parcel Service for the short- and medium-haul packages (average, 618 miles in 1960) and air parcel post for the longer-haul (average, 1,177 miles in 1960) lightest weight ones. Surface parcel post (per piece average, six pounds) fell from a million pieces annually in 1950 to half a million in 1972 while United Parcel had increased to two-thirds of a million pieces (twelve pounds average). At the same time, air parcel post became a fifth of a million piece (two pounds average) business.

The fourth-class service had always been the biggest user of for-hire transport services, accounting for around 60 percent of total mail payments to the railroads during the years considered. Expedition was not as critical as with first class and economy demanded the use of the optimum combination of alternative transport means and distribution facilities.

The Nationwide Integrated Postal Service Plan initiated in 1960 with its emphasis on a total approach in its move to economize led to the greatest change in the use of transport modes.

There had been a modest increase in the share that railroad payments were of fourth-class transport costs, to 81 percent in 1959/60, but thereafter the combination of greater use of highway carriers and use of the cheaper improved scheduled freight services of the railroads led the passenger revenue share to drop to 42 percent by 1967/68. In that year the post office reported that it had saved $23 million by using freight service for bulk mail. The railroads' improvement in freight schedules was a major factor in this.

EXPRESS

During most of the years of this study, the express services operating over the railroads were by the Railway Express Agency (REA), the stock of which was jointly owned by the major railroads of the country. The directors were railroad officers until the stock was put in a voting trust and shortly thereafter, in 1967, it was decided to sell the agency. In 1969 a group of its officials purchased control. In 1970 the name was changed to REA Express, Inc. The REA was subject to the general pattern of ICC regulations similar to that applying to the railroads themselves. For small packages the REA met competition from parcel post and more recently from various business operators and United Parcel Service. For larger shipments competition was from forwarders, certain motor carriers, and to a limited extent the railroads' own lcl freight service until it was largely abandoned. [3]

Until 1959 the REA's contractual arrangements with the railroads had limited its freedom to use other-than-the-railroad surface transport. In that year a newly negotiated contract specifically provided for use of other modes. Along with a change in management a new course was set. The REA itself applied for and was given by the ICC certificates to operate as a motor carrier over all its routes. By 1970 the REA mileage of motor-carrier routes was twice that of rail. [4]

Up to 1961 railroad revenue from the express operation was not based on unit charges for service provided, but rather on the residual after the agency's direct expenses and taxes had been deducted from its revenues. The individual railroad systems' shares were to be based on proportions of business handled. Under this arrangement the REA never earned any significant net income, a not surprising result of the contract terms. In 1961, the payment agreement was changed to involve a unit cost of railroad service basis. It was set at 7.6 mills per car-foot-mile in the East, 7 in the West, and 6 in the South. These amounts may be compared with the post office estimate of its unit payments in 1961/62 of 15.5 to 17 mills per car-foot-mile for the combined line-haul and terminal rail handling of parcel post.[5]

With the changed policies after 1959 the express operations were gradually revamped, going over to use of TOFC rail freight services, unitizing of shipment handling, and finally a "hub" arrangement of distribution with twenty-four centers covering the country.

In 1964 the Southern Railway discontinued handling of express, and the REA developed its own truck operations by way of replacement in that region. The country-wide reduction of passenger train services led to gradual overall substitution of rail freight and highway transport for REA's surface movement. The result was a sharp drop in railroad use and in corresponding payments for the railroads' services. The final use of the railroads was just along dense traffic routes on the speeded-up freight trains. During the 1950s the railroads' annual express revenues were around $100 million, entirely for service by passenger trains; by 1970 their use was terminated and $22 million worth of freight service purchased.

Major changes in the express rate structure were made in 1962 and 1963. Container all-freight rates for mixed commodities in units of up to 2,500 pounds were published, with initial suspension but final approval by the ICC. The rates were competitive even with ltl truck rates. Similar all-freight rates for smaller shipments were then offered, with competitors voicing strong opposition before the ICC, but with its final approval.[6]

During this period greater emphasis was placed on heavier express shipments, which could be handled more enonomically than the smaller ones. During the 1950s and early 1960s the average weight of lcl surface express shipments varied between forty to sixty-five pounds, by 1970 the average had been raised to eighty-eight pounds. The United Parcel Service was the successful competitor for the smaller packages. After 1965, despite all changes, the express operations resulted in such substantial deficits that they led to ultimate abandonment of what had been REA service.[7]

The railroad express service succumbed to technological change. While it had always been involved with terminal forms of highway transport, the developments in intercity highway and air transport technologies banished the railroads' role in an expedited small shipment service. The labor-intensive handling of small packages as an internal function of the express operation may have been an equally important factor because of declining labor productivity. This aspect seems, however, to have been surmountable with the new independent operation, United Parcel Service.

* * *

While in some respects the railroad mail and express traffic decline can be accounted for by the same sorts of competitive impact as the passenger decline, the ability of a new organization to enter the small-package express business and earn net income calls for added explanation. The new organization was from the start freer to make use of highway transport and did so for short and medium hauls. It did make use of other modes on a selective basis. However, the labor-intensive nature of express operations suggest that the new organization starting fresh was able to significantly increase labor productivity. In addition, some selectivity in respect to items handled enabled the new organization to choose those that could be handled on a large scale most economically.

6

Pricing of Carload Freight Services

The pricing of carload (five tons and more per shipment) freight services has in- volved a vast and incredibly complicated array of rates and divisions, the latter begin the shares of joint rates credited to the individual participating railroads providing a joint service. Among the array there has been a universal set called class rates available for all commodities and between any joints. These are deter- mined by a first-class distance scale of charges and derived scales graded above and below by designated classes or percentages. Then there is formal assignment of some 10,000 specific commodities in the commerce of the country each to a particular percent of the first-class (100 percent) scale. For each commodity there are two principal levels of class assignment, a high one if the commodity is handled in less-than-carload shipment, and a low one if the shipment meets a minimum weight for a carload. To provide some degree of flexibility the basic class rate structure has been supplemented by so-called "exception" classifications and somewhat different scales of rates. In addition, and most important of all, are a vast multitude of individual so-called commodity rate structures established spe- cifically to meet the market situation and railroad circumstances relating to each particular commodity moving in significant volume. For just how many com- modities such rates and structures are provided for has not been counted. The relative importance of the three kinds of rates for carload shipments in the U.S. in 1942 was 4 percent moving under class, 11 percent, "exception," and 85 per- cent, commodity rates. Since the war the proportion under commodity rates has greatly increased to above 95 percent.[1]

After review of the quarter century of rate increases and brief note of the postwar development of the country's class rate pattern, the focus of this analysis is on commodity rate structure changes. First there is a review of the principal innovative types of changes. Illustrations from sample commodity rate patterns are used to portray the factors involved. Then the historical profile of these con- trasting commodity rate structures is taken to show how changes in industries, in rail freight operations, in competition from other modes of transport, and in vari- ous institutional factors have combined to account for the rate changes. This is followed by brief reviews of the adjustments in the rates for the top revenue- producing commodities. Finally, changes in the divisions of revenue from joint through-rates as between the participating railroads are traced.

69

GENERAL RATE INCREASES

During the years covered by this study, thirteen general increases were proposed by the carriers and all came under ICC review. They were all rooted in increasing factor costs, labor the most important, and in declining net income, return on investment, and working capital. It was recognized by the railroads that rate increases would lead to possible traffic diversion to competitors, to decentralization of industry, and to substitution of products requiring less transportation. These possibilities notwithstanding, the railroads argued that their revenues would increase. The proposals sometimes asked for immediate emergency interim increases and sometimes were modified upward in the course of the proceedings before the ICC. After hearings the ICC responded to these proposals with authorization of interim and then final maximum allowable "just and reasonable" increases. By just setting maximums but not absolute amounts, it left open the possibility and practice of individual railroads not to follow allowed increases on particular commodities as their individual appraisal of the market situation might suggest to them. This rejection was known as "flagging out." There is no summary record of the extent of this practice. It can be estimated from the summation of allowed increases and the ICC index of actual rates as indicated in the graph on page 74. Its extent will be sampled in detail in the historical review of the three individual commodity rate structures.

The ICC jurisdiction in respect to the increases directly involved interstate rates, and intrastate rates only indirectly as they might discriminate against interstate ones and create an "undue burden" on interstate commerce. In a number of states there were long delays in getting intrastate rate increases brought in line with interstate ones. For instance, in Montana only after lengthy judicial proceedings did the 1949 U.S. increases become effective on intrastate rates by 1953, and those of 1956 through 1958, by 1959.[2]

The ICC estimated for each of the increase cases the net rise in revenue that would result from the authorized increases, taking into account its approved hold-downs and other exceptions. However, the estimates did not deduct the effects of "flag outs" and the inability immediately to increase intrastate rates. The ICC, and later BLS, indices of carload rate levels derived from waybill sampling take the latter into account and represent what actually happened in respect to rates as a whole.

The fact that soon after the war something well over 90 percent of the freight services of the railroads was priced in the thousands of separate commodity rate structures left little choice with sharply rising factor costs but to ask for some sort of across-the-board increases. To make unique adjustments for every increment in costs in each one of the commodity structures would have been an impossible task. It was, however, possible in general to tailor increases for particular commodity needs by providing differently for particular general types. Such special treatment was quite general for primary commodities, such as fresh fruits and vegetables, grains, livestock, meat, lumber, sugar, basic fertilizer components, coal, coke, and iron ore, and sometimes processed foods.

To provide historical perspective in respect to the general increases, it is necessary to review the happenings at the start of World War II. The rate levels in effect at the beginning of the war had been set in 1938. In 1941 a 12 percent wage increase became effective and prices of materials had risen some 10 percent in the two preceding years. This led the railroads to ask in December for a 10 percent general rate increase. In response, the ICC authorized one of 6 percent, except 3 percent on primary agricultural, mining, and animal items. However, 1942 operations under wartime conditions turned out to produce a railroad net income before taxes of over two and a half times that of 1941. The OPA and others petitioned for a repeal of the rate increase in the interest of price stabilization, and the ICC suspended the increase effective in March 1943. Despite further wage and material price increases during the war, railroad net income before taxes remained at a high level through 1945, primarily because of greatly increased load-factors for both carload and less-than-carload freight and passenger services. No rate increases were requested.[3]

1946–1951

The winter of 1945/46 and spring of 1946 saw abrupt and major changes. Traffic dropped sharply; by April ton-miles were 39 percent below those of a year before. There was a wage increase of roughly 16 percent; material and fuel prices rose rapidly. Most important of all, the high wartime load-factors disappeared. These changes led to the filing in April 1946 of the first of four postwar general rate increase requests, this one for 25 percent. A 6½ percent interim maximum increase was authorized in two months, and in seven months, a final one of 25 percent for the East and 20 percent elsewhere. There were exceptions such as a limit of 15 percent for grain and numerous other agricultural products.

Eleven months after that proposal the railroads asked for a 41 percent further increase for eastern traffic, and 31 percent elsewhere. This time 10 percent was authorized within three months and 20 percent in six. The final authorization came after thirteen months, an eastern 30 percent increase and 20 to 25 percent elsewhere.

In October 1948 the third proposal for 13 percent all around was filed. Roughly half that amount was granted within two months, and 10 percent finally was approved eleven months after it had been requested. In January 1951, a year and a half later, a further 15 percent all around was requested. After two interim increases the whole 15 percent was approved a year after the request.[4]

In each of the four cases, agriculture, mining, and forest product interests in particular pleaded depressed conditions and asked that rate increases for their products be held to a minimum. It was in recognition of such pressuring that the railroads themselves had imposed some restraints on their increases by way of flat rather than percent increases or hold-downs to limit the effect of percent increases for numerous items. The ICC in turn in some cases imposed added restraints of those types.

During these years there were many separate and downward adjustments of individual rate structures by the railroads themselves, which counteracted the general increases. This together with the "flag outs" on the railroads' own initiative of the authorized increases meant that overall actual revenue percent gains were substantially less than the full effect of authorized rates as estimated by the ICC. The ICC carload rate index based on waybill sample data indicated that from 1946 to 1952 the cumulative increase in actual rates was only 52 percent compared to the ICC authorized increases of 79 percent. Apparently, to a significant extent the railroads has asked for, and the ICC authorized as maximum larger, general increases than the market would support.[5]

1952–1960

In 1953 charges for pick-up and delivery of lcl freight were introduced and both parcel post and express rates increased. Wage rate increases were modest from 1952 until latter 1955. There was substantial improvement through 1953 in net railway operating income (nroi) for all regions but the Pocahontas. There were no further requests for general increases until 1956. Nineteen fifty-four had been a year of sharply reduced traffic with 1955 one of recovery. Both years saw reduced maintenance in order to keep up net income and working capital. Then there was a critical increase in wages with new three-year labor contracts. Two requests for percentage rate increases were filed in 1956. For the first it was 7 percent and 6 percent authorized. The southern railroads hesitated in respect to the second because of worries of further diversion to competitors. The allowed maximums, between 9 and 14 percent for different regions, for the second were only some two-thirds of those requested. A third request, which for the most part was not suspended, came early in 1958 asking this time for varied percent increases ranging up to 3 percent for some commodities, instead of across-the-board type of general increases previously requested. This changed pattern was in response to shipper and ICC criticism that the latter type of proposals did not sufficiently take into account the variations from commodity to commodity in elasticity of demand. Then in 1960, at the low point in traffic, there was a really minor two-level, ½¢ and 1¢ per pound, flat-rate increase all around requested. It was granted almost immediately.[6]

These four increases were mostly for lesser percents than the earlier ones and were all authorized in shorter times, none over four months from request. Their cumulative contribution to revenue was estimated to be 21 percent, but the ICC overall rate index increased less than 3 percent. The individual rate structure adjustments independent of general increases were proportionately greater than in the earlier period. The parallel increases in hourly worker earnings were 44 percent, and fuel and material prices, 21 percent.

Up to this point the impact of the general rate increases varied widely among commodity types. For instance, for carload traffic as a whole the ten-year cumulative increases through 1957 amounted to 98 percent. However, they were as little as 59 percent for iron ore, 66 to 70 percent for fresh vegetables and fruits, and 71 percent for coal with a constrasting 111 percent for manufactured and miscellaneous products. Two of the groups in the lower range of increase, iron ore and coal, were least involved in alternate mode competition but rather were ones with changing origins and/or commodity substitution affecting demand.[7]

1961–1972

Over the next five years to 1966 hourly earnings and material prices rose relatively slowly and no rate increases were requested. Downward rate adjustments to keep traffic were continued and the difference between cumulated allowed maximums and actual rates increased. Then 1966 saw a sharp upturn in wage demands and awards. From April 1967 through 1972, six general rate increases with the usual run of exceptions were requested. The first was for flat increases graduated from ½¢ to 3¢ per 100 pounds, according to the levels of the existing rates. The rest were percentage ones, all around 6 percent, except 15 percent in 1971. The 1968 and 1972 ones were commodity-by-commodity group, and the rest, across-the-board. Except for the largest proposed increase in 1917, when the South's proposals were cut back 60 percent, the requested increases were approved by the ICC, all in relatively short order.[8]

The estimated cumulative increase for these six increases was some 35 percent, and the corresponding rate index rise was roughly the same, a reversal of past rate performance. The pressure of the greater than previous factor cost increases were an important element in this. The parallel increase in hourly production railroad worker earnings was 65 percent, and the material and fuel price index, 22 percent.

The graph on page 000 summarizes the postwar quarter century rate increases and the trends in factor costs and average rates. The 1943 cancellation of the 1940 requested rate increases had prevented the railroads from matching the wartime wage and material price increases. Of the four postwar rate increases, the earlier ones came close to meeting the corresponding wage increases but did not make good the earlier deficit. But the parallel railroad cutting of rates substantially offset possible revenue gains from the allowed rate increases. The last of these rate increases, 1949 and 1951, again did not match the wage rate gains because of magnitude of the wage increases and the introduction of the forty-hour week. On the other hand, it was during these years that the rapid introduction of diesel-electric locomotives improved productivity.

BLS, Earnings RR Production Workers (Earnings per Hour); ICC, Index Actual Carload Rates, 1947–1968; BLS, RR Freight Price Index, 1969; AAR, Material and Fuel Price Index; ICC, Estimated Cumulative General Rate Increases

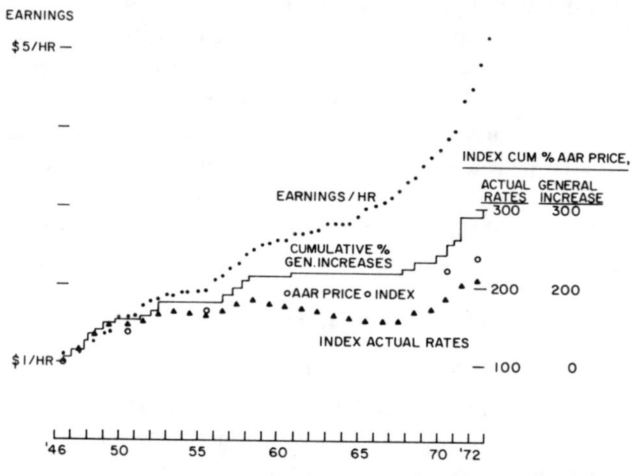

(BLS, *Bull #1312-10,* Employment and Earnings Statistics for the U.S.; AAR, *Yearbook of RR Facts, 1959*; ICC, *TE,* June 1969, p. 9, #1 1976, pp. 11–14; ICC, General Rate Increase Cases just reviewed, by calculation.)

From 1951 to 1956 wage rate and material price increases were modest and there were no requests for freight rate increases. Productivity improvements due to the diesel-electric locomotive and other technical advances were accelerated. In late 1955 new three-year labor contracts started another series of substantial wage increases, which accounted for a series of renewed requests for freight rate increases. Materials prices also rose more rapidly than before. However, the independent downward rate adjustments widened the gap between allowed maximums and actual rates. The improvements in productivity due to dieselization continued, there were increased loads per car, and the low productivity lcl business was on its way out.

The recessions of 1958/59 and 1960/61 led to a stabilizing of material prices and lessened rates of increase for wages. After the 1958 round of freight rate increases, except for a minor request in 1960, there were no further ones until 1967. Actual rates again declined during this period. Incentive carload and multiple-car rates were increasing and gains in load per car and increase in multiple-car and train-load-sized shipments improved productivity further. Nineteen sixty-six was a turning point. The next union contracts inaugurated a sharp accelation in wage increases, and material and supply prices jumped up. A new round of annual general freight rate increases followed with actual average rate increases matching them.

CLASS RATES

The 1940 Transportation Act included a provision calling on the ICC to investigate interterritorial and intraterritorial rate relationships to determine if they were unjust or unreasonable "in and of themselves or in their relation to each other," and then to order appropriate modification. A major factor in the background of this was the feeling in the South, Southwest, and West that their higher than the East's class rate scales were unfair and restrictive of their regions' economic development. In the South in particular there were strong postwar political pressures to equalize the South's rail transport charges with the North's. There had also been prior efforts to achieve national uniformity as a matter of simplifying the country's rate pattern. The ICC after the war actively pushed toward this end. A uniform classification of commodities based on the railroads' existing "Official" (generally eastern) classification was prescribed for nationwide application to replace a number of separate regional classifications, and finally became effective in May 1952. At the same time, as a result of ICC prodding, the railroads developed a uniform scale of class rates, which the ICC agreed to and prescribed for all parts of the country except in and to and from Mountain Pacific territory. Class rates for the latter were subjected in 1955 to an ICC prescription of class rate scales reduced from their traditionally high levels as proposed by the western railroads. With all this, the objective of a country-wide uniformity of class rates was achieved with the mentioned exception. This attainment was ironic since it was in the postwar years that commodity rates were to become the preponderant type of rates. Subsequently, the full amounts of the general rate increases just reviewed were, for the most part, added to the class rate scales. This meant that the class rates increased more than most of the commodity rates. This was a factor in the declining interest in class rates.[9]

COMMODITY RATES

Reform of and Innovation in Commodity Rate Patterns

The postwar quarter century saw major readjustments by the railroads in the patterns of the carload commodity rates. The basic objectives were multifold, to combat motor and water-carrier competition, to develop additional traffic, and to increase railroad productivity. The latter involved improved use of railroad facilities, particularly increased tons per carloading, both for existing older cars and, with the important technical advances, for higher-capacity ones. Along with this were changes by shippers in their facilities and handling practices; for instance, improved packaging, more widely spaced warehouse doors, stronger material-handling equipment, and, in the case of bulk-loading materials, major changes in loading and unloading gear.

The rate structure readjustments thus were bound to be gradual as traditional practices were modified and capital expenditures for the improved equipment and facilities replaced the old. Further, the process of rate change required extended railroad-shipper consultation, interrailroad negotiation of joint rates, and rate association processing of rate proposals. Finally, proposed adjustments brought protests to the ICC, largely from the railroads' competitors, but also from shippers whose vested interests might be hurt. Even competing railroads occasionally protested. The protestants asked for restraints on the degree of modification of rates and the ICC had to rule as to their reasonableness, preference-prejudice, compensatoriness, and competitive need.

As noted earlier, the Commerce Act's 1958 amended National Transportation Policy and its interpretation by the courts liberalized constraints on rate changes aimed at attracting railroads had established a cooperative research group to explore means of reforming rate structures to better compete. The first resultant proposal was a major downward restructuring of paint rates filed after the 1958 amendments. This was approved in an ICC suspension proceeding in the fall of 1959 with the ICC holding that the proposals were lawful since they were reasonably compensatory and, what was critical, that their effect on motor-carrier traffic did not have to be considered.[10]

Incentive Rates

The first postwar rate pattern change came in the form of acceleration in changing of rates so as to be graded according to weight of load per car. This had been initiated prewar and consisted in replacing the traditional rate with a single minimum, which was frequently less than the capacity of the normally available car because traditional commercial practice had aimed to keep shipment sizes down to minimize inventory requirements. Under this arrangement if shipments weighed the minimum the charge per 100 pounds was the published rate; for lighter shipments the effective charge per 100 pounds was proportionally higher as the shipment fell short. For heavier than the minimum shipments the excess weight was charged for at the 100 pound rate; there was no saving for the shipper by increasing the carloading above the minimum. Thus usual shipper's interest was in sending just the minimum.

After the war the railroads moved to emphasize "incentive" rates, the provision of downward adjusted levels of rates graduated according to increased load weights. This provided the shipper the opportunity of obtaining lower average charts per pound by loading a car more fully, and the railroad of gaining lower unit costs. The terms of the tariffs usually insured the shipper of the right to obtain the advantage, even if the railroad did not supply the maximum capacity car. Rate readjustments of this sort increased as the need grew for lower rates to meet the growing truck and other competition. A flat carload rate, independent of quantity or weight of contents, would have been the ultimate form of incentive rate in that it offered zero charge for any added load that could be gotten into a car. The real incentive impact, however, was based upon what minimums went with the previous 100-pound rate and how maximum loadings for different sized cars divided into the per-car rate. The introduction of flat per-car rates was limited to relatively few commodities: fruits and vegetables and automobiles.

Table 6 gives an example of the development of incentive rates as provided by the rate history in respect to green vegetables from Salinas, California, to New York.

Effective December 1962, the western roads put in a flat per-car rate for one particular green vegetable, lettuce. The rate was graduated according to car lengths. The thirty-four-foot-six-inch and under cars were older iced refrigerator ones, the longer ones, new mechanical refrigerator ones. The equivalent per-100-pound charges were graded down from 291¢ to 199¢ for the largest car. The average loading per car as a result of these incentive rates increased from 26.5 tons in 1957 to 51.6 tons in 1963.[11]

The introduction of increased minimums meant that despite the general increases, if shippers loaded lettuce to the highest new minimums their transport rate, 199¢ or 202¢, was little more in 1963 than it had been in 1947. On the other hand, the rate for the 20,000-pound minimum had increased 32 percent. From the shippers' point of view, the heavier loadings tend to increase loading costs because of the difficulty of higher stacking, more bracing, and having to move goods more deeply into a larger car. However, the railroads were providing damage prevention arrangements, which in part countered this. From the railroads' viewpoint there was the great gain in productivity with nearly double the load per car. The transportation expenses in terminal handling were little more for the heavier loaded cars than the light. Where grades were minor and speed high the same was nearly the case for line-haul movement.

There have been other patterns of incentive rates. For instance, a high level of rate might apply for the basic minimum and markedly lower rates applied for in-

TABLE 6

Rate Changes for Green Vegetables, Salinas to New York, 1946–1963

Effective Date of Rates & Associated Minimums	Rates and Applicable Minimums				
	20,000 lbs.	30,000	40,000	43,000	50,000
6/30/46	184¢				
1/1/47	197				
2/15/58	260				
4/14/58	260	250¢	219¢		
6/3/59	260	250	219	213¢	201¢
12/7/62 Lettuce, $790 per 34'6" & under car; $850, 39'; $975, 48' & over.					
7/3/63	261¢	251¢	220¢	214¢	202¢

crements of weight loaded above the basic. For example, in 1969 the southern railroads' lumber rate Hattiesburg, Mississippi, to Chicago was 64¢ for a 60,000-pound minimum, but any pounds over that were priced at 41¢. The latter was only 1¢ over the end-of-the-war rate.[12]

Incentive rates were not without problems. The effort to get maximum loading ran counter to a key competitive selling point of truckers; i.e., their offering lower than rail minimums because of smaller size of highway vehicles compared to rail. Another problem was that the offering of discounts for heaviest loading had to take into account the availability of larger cars. As larger cars were designed and in turn brought into the railroad inventory there were inevitably numerous older lesser-capacity cars still in circulation. During the early years of introducing the larger ones there were bound to be times when shipper orders for them could not be met. Tariff provisions were added so that the shippers would be protected from loss when smaller cars than those ordered by the shipper were placed for loading, assuring him that the lower rate, which applied to the larger load for the car he ordered, would still apply despite his inability to load as much as that. While many shippers might want to take advantage of the maximum loadings and lower rates and order the largest cars, there remained some shippers whose distribution practices were still geared to the smaller quantities and the higher rates.

TOFC-COFC Rates

The mid-fifties' break out of "piggyback," trailer- or container-on-flat-car (TOFC, COFC) service from its experimental stages led to a major restructuring of many commodity rate structures that involved items lending themselves to trailer loading. Over the years, an increasing number of railroads had seen TOFC as a means of making available to rail shippers the motor carrier's service advantages of the direct handling door to door possible for trailer-load quantities and of attracting some of the over-the-road truck trailers to the railroad.

It had been the smaller and often the financially hard-pressed railroads that prewar had initiated TOFC operations and continued them actively after the war. In 1933 the St. Louis Southwestern put in per-trailer-mile rates independent of nature and weight of the contents and based on estimated trucker over-the-road costs. Other railroads in the Southwest opposed this as improving the truckers' competitive position by making available the railroads' line-haul advantages and asked the ICC to order cancellation. It, however, did not suspend the rates because it felt they were an experiment in transport coordination within managements' prerogatives and in the overall public interest. A number of other railroads experimented with TOFC schemes, but only two, the Chicago and Great Western (CGW) and the New York, New Haven, and Hartford (NYNH&H) developed them wholeheartedly. In 1936 the CGW proposed TOFC service west and northwest from Chicago for both trucker and direct shipper use, again with flat rates regardless of trailer contents. Again other railroads in the region protested, opposing railroads proposing the TOFC rates should be in the normal pattern of the truckers' rate structure rather than the uniform flat rates. The ICC permitted the proposed rates to stand. Again the opposition rested on the fear of possible encouragement to truck competition. There was clearly a difference of opinion between railroads, which was taken to the ICC and courts for settlement.

In 1937 the NYNH&H instituted TOFC service between Boston and New York and intermediate points with tariffs and rates open to use directly by shippers and forwarders and with a division of rates arrangement for joint rail-motor-carrier service. The rail charges were flat ones independent of the nature of a trailer's contents. The divisions paid by motor carriers were lower than the open tariff charges. There were no direct rail competitors to the NYNH&H service, and no protests were brought to the ICC. However, after the war in 1953, the NYNH&H itself asked the ICC for clarification and rulings as to the legality of the various possible TOFC rate and service arrangements. In response, among other things the ICC made it clear that the railroads could make use of their TOFC line haulage to offer a service under their own billing and rate structures, something the truckers disliked for fear of the competitive advantage the railroads might thereby gain.[13]

Beginning in 1954 numerous railroads inaugurated large-scale TOFC operations with special expedited trains along heavy traffic routes. Varied types of TOFC rate structures by different railroads reflected the continued difference of opinion as to optimum strategies. Most of the New York-Chicago railroads, the NYC initially excepted, proposed rates to be effective in June 1954 for an all-railroad offering, lowering the line-haul plus railroad provided pick-up and delivery of trailers by local truckers under contract. This was protested by the terminal railroads in the New York area because of their likely loss of traffic to the local truckers handling the trailers. The long-haul motor carriers were worried too, but they were countered by local cartage carriers with an interest in obtaining the business of handling railroad trailers in terminal areas. Local truckers pressured the truckers' association to withdraw its protests. Finally, the major motor-carrier interests did not object so long as the rates for all-rail service were the same as theirs. This had been the railroads' proposal. After a few days of suspension and its lifting by the ICC the proposal went into effect July 10, 1954, with service starting July 12.[14]

TOFC operations spread rapidly. The AAR TOFC revenue carloadings data for the country, first compiled for 1955, showed 168,000 in that year, 208,000 cars in 1956, and 554,000 by 1960. The first regional breakdown, in 1956, revealed the South loading only 1,600 cars; the East, 103,000; and the West, 104,000. By 1960 the eastern loadings had almost doubled, the western increased to 269,000 but the southern were still far behind with only 33,000. In the initial years the railroads' standard flat cars were used, of length sufficient to carry only one trailer. To improve productivity the railroads started to purchase longer, two-trailer-per-car flat cars, and then created the Trailer Train Corporation to build up a commonly available pool of them.

The New York Central (NYC) was a holdout. It initially had restricted clearances on its eastern lines limiting the possibility of handling of trailers. Its position in respect to TOFC also had been shaped by the June 1954 change in its management. Prior to that, the NYC had hoped to develop service in combination with motor carriers. The new president's philosophy was opposed because he feared that it would be an advantage to motor carriers to offer them the use of a rail line haul, which he thought was superior to their over-the-road one. Thus the NYC fostered a proprietary container technique, Flexi-Van, which avoided the clearance problem and would not help ordinary motor carriers with their commitment to the usual type of trailer. Flexi-Van required special fittings on flat cars, unique truck-trailer chaisses for road haulage of the vans, and unique equipment for handling the containers on and off the cars. The NYC inaugurated its Flexi-Van service in April 1958, and was joined by several other railroads in providing it. The Missouri Pacific was the other major advocate of a container-on-flat-car service (COFC), though in contrast to the NYC it handled ordinary trailers as well. While container loadings were as high as 10 percent of piggyback terminations for Class I railways in 1964, the proportion declined after the NYC-P merger to 3 percent by 1970. Traffic joing with water carriers became the principal source of container use.[15]

The sharpest challenge to traditional carload commodity rate structures came from the TOFC offering of flat charges per trailer or per car (two trailers) with only limited regards to the commodities in a shipment (bulk and hazardous items and those of extraordinary value were excluded). The traditional carload all-commodity rate had limited the proportion of one article in a shipment to 60 percent in order to prevent use of the low all-commodity rates by shippers of particular commodities that otherwise would take the higher rates. Forwarders, for whom the all-commodity rates had been brought into use, on the other hand, were consolidating various small shipments and so always had a mixture of articles that would allow unlimited use of the rates.

One type of TOFC service involved handling freight in line-haul movement from loading ramp to unloading ramp with the shipper responsible for providing the trailers and bringing them to and taking them from the ramps. If the shipper owned the trailers this plan could involve shipper payment for returning them empty and thus a cost in addition to the basic charge for loaded movement. In order to avoid this, arrangements were made for "trip-leasing" of trailers to shippers with return of the trailers to the lessor allowed at the destination of the freight movement, thus eliminating empty charges. As of 1959 and 1960 in the East, the charges under this plan, with the by then normal two trailers per flat car, were around 25¢ per trailer-mile, an amount estimated to be competitive with the over-the-road trucking costs. Later the railroads provided this ramp-to-ramp service with railroad provided trailers under a modified plan so that arrangements for the leasing by shippers has not been necessary. Also, shipments of just one item alone were allowed with 7½ percent augmentation of the all-commodity rate in the East, 15 percent in the South, and 66⅔ percent in the West.[16]

Multiple-Car, Train-Load, and Annual Volume Rates

In another direction the combined objective of lowering rates and unit costs were achieved by introducing multiple-car, train-load, and annual volume rates. The ICC had traditionally rejected low multiple-car rates with their greater-than-carload shipment minimums on the grounds that they would impose "a condition which only a few shippers could comply with and consequently was an injustice to those unable to ship the required quantity."[17]

In the late 1930s a southwestern railroad, the St. LSW, had proposed reduced "train-load" rates for petroleum. The proposal had been opposed by competing railroads in the course of rate association proceedings but the rates were published independently only to be suspended by the ICC at the request of the objecting railroads. In the end, the rates were withdrawn by the publishing railroad in response to the threat by petroleum companies of withdrawing all their traffic from it if the rates were published.[18]

In 1941 an association of independent petroleum dealers asked the ICC to require the southwestern railroads to put in lower rates for twenty-five-car shipments, approximately 4,800 barrels, so they could get net transport costs comparable to those of major oil companies with their subsidiary pipeline transport. Though rail and pipeline rates were the same, the pipeline costs were much lower and the difference showed up in pipeline profits, which accrued to the oil company owners of the pipelines. Further the pipelines were common carriers, their use by the independents was limited by the latter's inability to meet the large pipeline minimum shipment requirements, 50,000 barrels. Later, in response to an independent's complaint, the ICC pointed out that it did not have the power to order the railroads to make multiple-car rates, but one commissioner suggested that the railroads study the possibilities.[19]

In 1939, however, formal removal of the ICC's traditional constraint came in response to an Illinois Central proposal for a 14¢-per-pound rate on blackstrap molasses in thirty-eight-car, 1,800-ton shipments, from New Orleans to Peoria, Illinois, to meet barge competition. The existing single-car rate was 17½¢. In addition to the barge protestants of the rate was a major oil company, which opposed the "train-load" rate for fear that the railroads might initiate such rates for petroleum. In changing its traditional stand, the ICC argued that since the shipper was able to get a low 1,800-ton barge rate, any disadvantage to small shippers was present anyway and that, therefore, the railroads should not be excluded from offering the reduced rate to compete for the traffic.[20]

A few multiple-car rates for other commodities were subsequently published without protest and thus without ICC consideration. The St. Louis San Francisco Railroad published one for coal, a $2.00-per-ton one, 2,000 tons minimum, from Arkansas and Oklahoma to St. Louis. The single-car rate was $2.75. The regional rate association protested, but the ICC did not suspend the rate. With the wartime establishment of aluminum electrolytic reduction plants in the Pacific Northwest, a $8.00-per-ton, minimum 1,800 tons, 50 tons per car, rate for alumina to them from Gulf of Mexico points, some 3,000 miles, was published and not protested. The single-car rate was $12.00.[21]

Shortly after the war, multiple-car rates for several other commodities were proposed to meet the competition of barge lines. Upon their protest, the ICC was called upon to pass on the railroad proposals and in a number of cases rejected them as too low relative to the single-car rates. However, where the discount was less 10 percent, they were allowed.[22]

In 1955 the Illinois Central established a rate for western Kentucky bituminos coal traffic to Louisville in competition with barges with a reduction from $1.50 per ton to $1.30 if 4,000 tons per week were shipped. Another innovation was a 1955 rate reduction from metallurgical coal-steel industry from Appalachian mines to Chicago area mills. The Chicago and Eastern Illinois, in order to get a share of the business in competition with all-rail and rail-lake movements, proposed a route by rail to the Ohio River, barge to an Indiana port, and CEI to Chicago. Its single-car reduced rate established in 1953 was rejected by the ICC in January 1955 as noncompensatory, but on rehearing it approved the rate in August, 8 percent under an approved single-car rate, as compensatory with a 2,000-ton minimum. The eastern roads were the protestants in both cases.[23]

Changes after 1955 in the eastern and southern bituminous coal rate patterns provide a picture of the development of innovative rate patterns by way of volume, multiple-car, train-load, and unit-train rates. In 1955 an Eisenhower appointed Advisory Council on Energy Supplies and Resources Policy published a report recommending reduced train-load rates to reflect lower costs of service with train-load shipments. The response to this from the chairman of the rate association of eastern railroads was to the effect that the decline in coal traffic volumes had nothing to do with rates and that such reductions would cripple the railroads.[24]

In June 1957 the CGQ independently established twenty-five–car, 1,250-ton minimum rates, 40¢ per ton under single-car rates, from southern Illinois mines to east St. Louis, after Illinois Freight Association disapproval. Effective August 1958, with the threat of a utility building a mine mouth plant, the Pocahontas roads published volume rates, 1,500,000 tons annually, 35¢ under a single-car rate, for coal from Virginia, West Virginia, and Kentucky. This reduced rate was initially suspended by the suspension board but subsequently allowed to go into effect with an ICC division's approval. The reason for volume rather than multiple-car rates was that they saved the utility from extra expense of multiple-car handling facilities and permitted purchase of coal from small as well as large mines. Also in 1958 Kentucky, Illinois, and Indiana to Chicago multiple-car rates, 50¢ under single-car ones, were established and approved by the ICC. In the same year all-rail, 2,000-ton minimum rates from eastern coal fields to the Chicago steel mill points were established in competition with the earlier CEI rail-barge-rail reduction. These two types of reduced rates were later sometimes combined along with requirements as to minimum car capacity giving a complicated matrix for figuring rates.[25]

The increasing substitution of gas and fuel oil for utility and other users traditionally burning coal was taking potential coal traffic away from the railroads. The installation in 1958 of a coal slurry pipeline and threat of its widespread use together with development of very high voltage transmission to carry energy from mouth-of-mine generating stations to distant load centers was an even greater threat to rail coal traffic. There was further push to publish the various reduced rates, and finally unit-train rates. The latter involved permanently coupled cars especially designed for quick loading and unloading and larger capacities, 90 or 100 tons, than the then standard hopper cars. These unit trains were sometimes shipper owned, which could justify especially low rates. In addition, the new rates called for limited forty-eight-hour loading and twenty-four-hour unloading time and elimination of railroad weighing, and did not allow the holding "no-billed" cars for finding a purchaser. These unit-train rates was essentially negotiated point to point to take into account competing gas, fuel oil, and coal costs, user location factors, and rail transport costs unique to each situation. This was a complete break from the traditional coal rate structure. One railroad raised the objection to the point-to-point reduced rates as representing in effect contract rates providing preferential treatment to one shipper and one consignee. Both being large would get advantages over small shippers. By refusing to suspend the rates the ICC rejected the arguments.[26]

The traditional single-car bituminous coal rate structure had represented a long-term balance between railroad, mine, and user interests, negotiated and preserved by traffic departments and rate associations and the ICC. The rates had produced revenues from coal traffic that were considered a key source of net operating income for the railroads favored with significant coal traffic. The great earning power of coal was demonstrated by the high net income of the few railroads for which a major proportion of revenue was from coal. The tendency to stay with a traditional price structure was strong anyway and one with such proven earning power was even more so. The initial opposition of rate associations reflected this. The ICC's particular interest in preserving revenues against possibly unnecessary rate reductions played its part. But in the face of loss of coal revenue to gas and fuel oil and the increasing signs of possible slurry pipelines and high-voltage-transmission competition the rate associations and the ICC came to accept the various types of rail proposed reductions.

Further insight into multiple-car and train-load pricing innovations is provided by selected aspects of the grain rate structure. Introduction of technical advances in freight car design along with new multiple-car rates was introduced by the Southern (S) in the early 1960s. It had ordered so-called "jumbo" covered hopper grain cars of 100-ton-plus capacity as opposed to the traditional boxcars which were fitted with special grain doors and capable of loading to half or less than the new cars' capacity. To reduce rates as far as possible a "bare bones" multiple-car rate, minimum 450 ton shipment, in five cars, (initially with 900-ton and 1,800-ton minimum were withdrawn) without the usual grain transit privileges and with shortened free loading and unloading time, was published in the fall of 1961. The new rate, was 19.3¢ per 100 pounds compared to 50.5¢ single-car rate for the older cars with the traditional privileges. The S's rail competitors who did not own any of the new design cars countered with the same 19.3¢ reduced rate for 450 tons using older cars with a 50-ton minimum per car, their highest possible per old style car. This would mean nine cars as the shipment unit. Both barge competitors and marketing interests protested the proposals before the ICC, the lower rate undercutting the barging competitive position and the elimination of the transit privileges upsetting the traditional marketing arrangements and the vested interest therein. The ICC suspended the proposals and after controversial hearings allowed the S's rates to go into effect in early 1963 if 16 percent more than proposed and ordered its competitors' canceled as not proven compensatory. There followed long and bitter litigation with the Southern's competitors joining the first two protestant groups. The conclusion was the U.S. Supreme Court's comfirmation in January 1965 of the ICC approval of the S's rates after they had been in use two years.[27]

Another innovation was proposed by the Illinois Central for Gulf export grain from central Illinois points not having access to waterways. It was a "rent-a-train" proposal providing for the annual rental of a whole train with fixed annual-plus-mileage charges. The train tonnage was set at 8,900 and enough shipments for at least forty trips a year had to be guaranteed by the shipper. Minimum speeds were guaranteed by the railroad. With the forty trips per year the effective charges amounted to 19¢ per 100 pounds, with sixty-two trips per year, 15.3¢. The renting proposal introduced strong incentives to maximize utilization of equipment and, with possibility of shipper ownership of cars, relieved the railroad of substantial investment. The provisions of minimum speed and railroad supply of dedicated cars were rejected by the ICC, the latter criticized because in case of a general shortage of grain cars the tying up of a whole train's worth of cars for a particular shipper for a year would interfere with the supply of such cars to other shippers.[28]

A unique proposal relating to volume rates involving another commodity was to tie a reduced rate to the agreement by the shipper to move a minimum proportion, 80 percent, of his total shipments of the commodity involved by the originating railroad. The ICC felt this tying arrangement would amount to destructive competition contrary to the National Transportation Policy.[29]

Overall, these volume and multiple-car rates in various forms were introduced with little ICC constraint for a wide variety of other commodities: newsprint, basic chemicals, iron ore, cement, sand and gravel, and others.[30, 31]

These various pricing innovations led to a major shifting away from the traditional single-car geographically patterned rate relationships between origins destinations, and in-between routes. The newer pricing patterns were developed in light of competition from other transport modes and the basic shifts in the flow and nature of the commerce of the country. The negotiation involved in point-to-point rates in particular represented an emphasis on the part of the railroads in respect to their costs and increasing productivity rather than preservation of intricate balances of competing regional and shipper interests. For the most part, regulator constraints were relaxed to the extent that wide diffusion of the new patterns was possible and the list of commodities involved became extensive.

Speed Premium Rates

Following World War II there was widespread speeding up of scheduled freight trains along main routes in all regions. For the most part, this was not associated with premium rates according to differences in quality of service as measured by speed. The exception was for the long-haul Chicago-Pacific Coast traffic, where the ATSF in 1953 offered a special reduced Chicago-Los Angeles schedule with a minimum of fifteen cars at premium rates. There proved to be little call for this service and nothing was made of it.[32]

A firm move behind a premium rated Chicago and Los Angeles service came fifteen years later with the inauguration of the ATSF "Super-C" with a forty-hour schedule in 1968. The premium was charging $2,800 for two trailers plus 100¢ per cwt for over 70,000 pounds on the specially equipped flat cars of the ATSF as against $1,000 for TOFC plan IV for the sixty-hour plus ordinary elapsed time. This rate pattern was offered for a while by competing carriers.[33] The "Super-C" service handled as many as forty cars per train with U.S. mail and United Parcel Service joining other shippers.

Typical Evolution of Commodity Rate Structures, 1946–1972

Full understanding of the postwar development of commodity rate structures can be obtained only by considering the changes going on in industry as well as in transport. Out of the thousands of commodity rate structures involving the numerous distinct and separate industries of the country, space permits only the smallest sample to be reviewed in these terms. Further, due to complexities of each, only the major elements of the chosen structure can be covered. The choice of samples is based first on the availability of a published record of key rates over the years and second on a rate and industry structure not too complicated. The other objective in choice is that the samples provide variety as to the types of commodities—manufactured versus agricultural, for instance—and as to the different nature of intermodal competition. One commodity group chosen is iron ore and its concentrates, which involves mining and manufacturing industries and water but not highway transport. Another commodity is agricultural, fresh oranges, with both water and highway transport competition. The third is beer, a manufactured item with country-wide distribution and again both water and highway competition. In all three cases the rate adjustments surveyed involved a combination of the general increases reviewed early in the chapter and individual pattern changes. The latter are so definitely involved with developments in each industry that their review is as important as that of the transport developments themselves.

Iron Ore Rates

Industry Location Pattern and Related Transport Needs

Iron ore and its concentrates are bulk commodities of high density, which load to the weight capacity of cars. With the several small railroads in the Lake Superior region with predominantly iron ore traffic, it has been carried in specialized cars confined to that service, with resultant 50 percent empty-car mileage. Elsewhere ordinary open-top cars are used with, in the East, considerable return haul of coal. In general, the ore traffic moves in large blocks of cars, in many cases full trains, and generally with maximum operable tonnage per train. In addition, there have been ancillary services such as sorting and temporary holding of cars so that their contents could be mixed in the course of loading vessels to make shipments of specified mineral composition. With recent pelletizing of ore, this has been largely avoided.

At the beginning of the period under review the main movement was from Lake Superior mines, mostly operated by steel company interests, to lake docks, and thence by vessel to lower lake ports with unloading either directly at lakeside steel mills, to storage, or to freight car loading facilities with further rail haul to so-called interior mills largely in Ohio and Pennsylvania. One large mill was located oceanside at Sparrows Point near Baltimore using primarily foreign ores. Alabama mills originally used Alabama, Tennessee, and Georgia ore but most recently imported ore. There were three major mills west of the Mississippi River: the only prewar one in Colorado; two newer ones near Salt Lake, Utah, and San Bernardino, California, respectively, using ore from Wyoming, Nevada, and Utah; and the latter mill more recently from California. There were small mines in upper New York State and New Jersey supplying small amounts to eastern mills and Texas mines tied primarily to some small mills in that state. There were major shifts over the years in the geographical distribution of ore production. Minnesota sources declined from almost two-thirds to 45 percent. Michigan maintained its 11 percent share. Canada, together with Venezuela, grew from practically nothing to supplying a quarter of the total.[34]

The Minnesota ore movement was handled by western railroads; the small, U.S. Steel controlled, Duluth, Mesabi, and Iron Range (DMIR); and the independent large transcontinental Great Northern (GN). The Lake Superior and Ishpeming (LSI), also controlled by steel interests, shared the upper Michigan peninsula ore with the independent Chicago Northwestern, Chicago Milwaukee St. Paul and Soo systems in a more competitive rail pattern than the Minnesota one. The DMIR and LSI had traditionally been the most profitable Class I roads in the country. The eastern segment of the ore movement, "ex lake" as it was called, was handled by several of the large eastern railroads and the small, U.S. Steel controlled, Bessemer and Lake Erie (BLE). Line haul of ore from the country's other ore fields was by roads operating in general service, obtaining loads from steel company controlled mine access roads.

During World War II there had been major changes in the overall picture with the addition of the two major steel mills in the West—in central Utah and in southern California. This led to the development of new ore sources and movement over western railroads. The second cause of change was the depletion of high-grade ores (around 52 percent Fe) in the Lake Superior district, leading after the war to the discovery and development of mines in Labrador and Quebec, which delivered ore via private railroads to St. Lawrence River ports, and of rich deposits (around 58 percent Fe) in Venezuela. The other development was the innovation of treatment for the remaining low-grade (25 to 30 percent Fe) Lake Superior taconite ores to make pellets (around 62 percent Fe). This led to the erection of large-scale pelletizing facilities in Minnesota and Michigan. Two of the new Minnesota sources were served by private, steel interest owned, railroads for movement to newly established Lake Superior ports. Pelletizing was also introduced at the new mines in Missouri, California, and Wyoming. All this led to the general shifts in origins of ore.

The other change of significance for the ore transportation was the trend in the East of new steel mill capacity to be built at waterside locations. The two completely new locations were on the Delaware River near Philadelphia and on lower Lake Michigan. Most of the additions to old mills were to those at Great Lakes ports and the one on Chesapeake Bay. These decreased the relative need for eastern rail transport of ore.

The Immediate Postwar Rates

During the period covered by this study the railroads faced this sharply changing picture. The older general philosophy about ore rates was that for a basic low-value raw material for manufacturing iron and steel, charges should be relatively low per ton-mile. In turn, the manufactured steel and iron products were high-value items, which could and should be charged relatively higher rates because they would be a lower proportion of the products' value. The lower rates for ore thus would be compensated for by higher rates on the finished products. However, the high rates of return of the railroads primarily relying on ore traffic belied the premise that the ore rates were low in the sense of being unprofitable. Further, the postwar competition of trucking for the manufactured steel products prevented their being charged compensating high rates.[35]

The traditional ore rate structure had as its main elements the mine-to-upper-lake-port rates made by northwestern railroads and so-called ex-lake rates made independently by eastern railroads for the lower lake port to interior mill movement. In-between vessel and port handling charges were separate, with some of the steel companies controlling vessel operations.

The rail rates involved in all this were primarily group rates; that is, most Minnesota mine origins were given common rates regardless of distance to the docks. The hauls were relatively short and terminal services were a large share of the costs of handling the traffic. The ex-lake rates applied to groups of interior mills, with the rate the same from most all ports. This enabled the ore-purchasing mills to reassign vessels to different ports to avoid local congestion without having to consider variation in rail charges. Port and rail competition for the ex-lake ore traffic brought about the equalization. There were also all-rail rates from Superior mines to lakeside and interior mills used in case of lake shipping interruptions. In the East there were all-rail rates from eastern mines to interior mills made to allow their competition with the western ores. Then in 1959 the St. Lawrence waterway brought inland water competition from Canadian mines.

There was a separate southern rate structure involving supply of local ore to Alabama mills and, in recent years, ore imported through Gulf ports. The western pattern was quite separate and more on a point-to-point basis.

Changes in the Eastern, Lake Superior, and Ex-Lake Rates

The development of major foreign ore sources after the war led to major eastern import rate adjustments. The traditional import rate structure had been built around equality of import rates inland from Philadelphia and Baltimore to Buffalo with the ex-lake ones from Erie and Buffalo to the two Atlantic port cities. After the war interior steel interests complained about the high level of the import rates. In response, effective October 1950, the southern tier of eastern railroads, the Pennsylvania (P), Baltimore and Ohio (BO), and Western Maryland (WM), made 28¢ some 10 percent, reductions to points west as far as Pittsburgh. In 1953 the reductions were extended to further west steel centers such as Youngstown and Wheeling so they too could find it economic to use imported ore.

In February 1953, in order to gain a share of the new overseas ore, the northern tier roads—the New York Central (NYC), Erie (E), and others not serving Philadelphia and Baltimore—proposed equalizing New York and Boston import ore rates with those from Philadelphia and Baltimore. In response, the P, BO, etc., reduced their rates by 20¢, to $2.31 for Pittsburgh, for instance. At the request of the latter railroads and the Baltimore port interests, the ICC suspended the New York and Boston rates and the 20¢ reduction by the other roads. Lengthy litigation followed, not ending until over ten years later, in January 1964, with Supreme Court approval of equalization for New York but not Boston. The rejection of the last stage of rate cutting was also confirmed. This case was only one among many over the years where the ICC and the courts were involved in respect to numerous commodities in what was essentially arbitration of railroad conflicts in respect to the North Atlantic port differentials.[36]

Before the St. Lawrence waterway was opened, in order to get a share of new Canadian ore traffic, the NYC joined with the Canadian National (CN) in April 1957 in proposing lowered rates for the imported ore via a port, Contre Coeur, on the St. Lawrence River east of Montreal, thence west by rail. The P proposed to counter this by reducing import rates from Philadelphia. The water transport cost from the St. Lawrence ports around Nova Scotia to Philadelphia was higher than to Contre Coeur, so the NYC-CN rate did not have to be as low as the P's import rates to compete. These proposals were suspended upon other railroad protests but finally allowed to go into effect November 1957. However, the St. Lawrence Seaway as opened in 1959, capturing the import Canadian ore traffic via a Great Lakes route to western Pennsylvania and Ohio mills.[37, 38]

Some of the important interrelationships of upper-lake and ex-lake rates were modified by the regional differences in application of the postwar general rate increases. From 1946 to 1962 three out of the eight general ore rate increases were not applied to the Lake Superior region rates, and for another two general increases the upper-lake ore amounts were only half as much as in the eastern region. The result was that the Superior region rates increased only some 50 percent, while the eastern region rates ex-lake to Youngstown increased 136 percent, and to Pittsburgh, 105 percent. The increased use of imported ores restrained the western railroads in respect to upper-lake rate increases. On the other hand, the eastern roads could count on ore traffic to interior mills whether it was from the Lake Superior region or was imported through eastern ports. Further, the two smaller railroads in the Superior region carrying the highest proportion of ore traffic had such high rates of return, there was pressure not to increase rates in contrast to the eastern railroads, which were faced with serious financial problems to which increases seemed a help. After the latter's move to attract import traffic by lowering rates in 1950, the roads were anxious to take advantage of the ICC allowed maximum with each general increase. Yet it was also the case that the eastern roads faced the possible long-run loss of traffic as steel producers added to their capacity primarily at waterside plants. The net of all this was that the increase in the key Philadelphia to Pittsburgh rate was 8 percent less than that in the ex-lake rates.[39]

By the 1960s the development of ore pelletizing for making Lake Superior lower-grade taconite ores economic was accompanied with the introduction of train-load and annual volume rates and the exclusion of switching and holding traditionally associated with untreated ore movement. These rates were largely negotiated point to point from the new processing plants to the docks. In 1963 such rates were established for upper Michigan peninsula ore to a Lake Michigan port at 92¢ per ton compared to a typical regular single-car 125¢ rate. In the Mesabi field at the end of 1966, the Great Northern quoted a 120¢, 12,000 tons per train, rate. By late 1973 the Michigan peninsula rates, having been "flagged out" in the general increases to maintain the lower Lake Superior ore's competitive position against the Mesabi, had risen only 3¢ to 95¢ while the Mesabi had risen to around 170¢.[40]

In respect to ex-lake traffic, in 1964 the Erie, feeling that because of its poor lake-front access it was losing its share of the traffic, proposed a reduction of 20¢ for shipments of 10,000 tons consigned to not more than two destinations. This was opposed by the other eastern roads and as a result suspended by the ICC. The railroads were already moving the ore largely in train-load or near-train-load lots at the single-car rates and felt that the new rates would only lose them revenue. The ICC, however, found the proposed lower rates compensatory and vacated the suspension. The other eastern roads immediately matched the lower rates. By 1973 the train-load rate with the general increase became 392¢ from the lake ports to Pittsburgh. The comparable Philadelphia to Pittsburgh rate, in connection with which the railroads offered no multiple-car or train-load discounts, was 546¢.[41]

Over the quarter century, the differences between regions in the extent of rate increases was significant. The Minnesota ore to Lake Superior ports typically had increased only 110 percent with the introduction of train-load and annual volume rates. The northern Michigan mines to Escanaba ore rates rose only 22 percent because of the railroads' more competitive position with their not taking general increases and introducing train-load rates. On the other hand, since all general increases were taken advantage of with the ex-lake rates, to Pittsburgh they were up 180 percent, with minimal modification by train-load rate discounts. The import rate from Atlantic Coast ports to Pittsburgh was up 173 percent.

The overall transport cost of Lake Superior ore was a combination of rail and water rates and dock handling charges. In 1950, to Pittsburgh, the import rate had been 64 percent of the sum of the lake rail and ship charges. In 1960, after the forementioned reductions in the import rates, the proportion fell to 55 percent. With the reduction in the rates for the rail segments of the rail-lake-rail charges countering the general increases, the ratio rose to 61 percent. The relationships varied within narrow limits. Western versus eastern rail competitors accounted for a balance between Lake Superior and the new import ore domestic transport costs.[42]

Interior Midwest Structure

Rail rates for midwestern mill destinations developed separately from those for the more eastern ones. While the Lake Superior ores were the principal source used, the important new mines, in Missouri, eighty-five miles south of St. Louis, were developed along with a small one in central Wisconsin and were brought into active production with favorable rates. The introduction of train-load and annual volume rates was a key factor all around. The Chicago and northern Indiana lake-front mills maintained their advantage with the lowest charges of mine to mill, for upper Michigan ore via rail to the port of Escanaba and thence via Lake Michigan vessel. Next lowest were from the Mesabi fields to Lake Superior and vessel beyond. The Wisconsin source was given a low all-rail rate with an annual minimum of 650,000 tons. The Missouri ores moved primarily to Granite City near St. Louis under train-load rates with 100-ton cars. To Granite City, rates for the Mesabi ore were much higher, the same as the all-rail rates to Chicago mills.[43]

Southern Rate Changes

In the South the iron ore rate structure had been developed around an extensive Birmingham destination group. Originally, the ore sources were scattered deposits in Alabama, Georgia, and Tennessee, which led to the adoption of a mileage scale rate structure. In addition, there were also import rates equalized through various Gulf ports such as Mobile and Pensacola to the Birmingham district. This reflected the competition between railroads serving the different ports and mills. With the development of major ore supplies abroad, particularly Venezuelan, the import rates became the most important ones. Domestic sources declined. The Alabama Public Service Commission to help local mining refused to allow all the general rate increases to be applied to the intrastate rates, so they remained at a depressed level. Multiple-car, 1,800-ton minimum, import rates were introduced all around. Typical rates with 360-ton minimums from inland Tennessee mines, however, were kept at a slightly higher level than the import rates.[44]

Western Rate Picture

After World War II far western iron and steel production was dominated by the new Utah (Geneva) and southern California (Fontana) mills. Their competitive impact on the older Colorado Fuel and Iron Minnequa mill near Pueblo, Colorado was a major consideration in ore and finished-product rate adjustments. Heretofore, the latter's far west competition had come from steel shipped via the canal to the Pacific Coast from eastern mills. Under postwar circumstances the Minnequa position was particularly influenced by a 1947 reduction in iron and steel product rates from Geneva to the Pacific Coast. The relative competitive position of the three mills was heavily dependent on their raw material costs for coal and iron ore. Initially, all three mills had as their primary source the southern Utah ore on the Union Pacific (UP). The 1950 rates to Geneva were 194¢, to Fontana, 304¢, and to Minnequa, 415¢, per ton. Minnequa also obtained some ore from Wyoming, roughly 360 miles to the north via the Colorado and Southern (CS). By 1950 the Kaiser interests, owners of the Fontana mill, had developed a southern California source and built their private railroad to bring the ore 52 miles to a connection with the SP, 113 miles to the south of Fontana. The SP in the early 1950s established a 122¢ rate for 1,500-ton shipments. This was one of the early multiple-car rates and was 22 percent below the single-car one. These rates became 245¢ by late 1972 with 5,000-ton-minimum shipments. In the early 1970s the Geneva mill interests developed an alternative central Wyoming ore source with a pellet plant. This was 355 miles from Geneva with a 76-mile private railroad connecting with the UP. The Union Pacific introduced unit-train, annual tonnage, rates, from Utah and Wyoming—from the former with 6,250 tons, minimum, 50 tons per car, and the latter, 7,500 tons, minimum, 90 tons per car, along with annual volume discounts. These rates all limited holding of cars to no more than forty-eight hours for loading and twenty-four hours for unloading.[45]

With the rapid expansion of Japanese steel production in the 1950s and their seeking many sources of ore, both California and Nevada mines exported to Japan, though in irregular fashion. Export rate levels were substantially higher than for the more regular and larger traffic volume to Geneva from Wyoming.[46]

ICC Role in Changes

The major impact of regulation on iron ore rates was in connection with the general rate increases. The aspects of these affecting the upper-lake rates in relationship to the eastern import ones has been mentioned. The general effects are to be noted in per-cent and flat or hold-down rate final requests and approvals. The 1946 12¢-per-ton increase for iron ore request was approved by the ICC. However, in the 1947 proposals for increases of 30 to 40 percent, depending upon region, were limited by the ICC to 20 percent but a 30 to 33¢-per-ton maximum was permitted. Again in 1948 the percent increase was cut from 13 percent to 10 percent with the 35/39¢ maximum agreed to. Then in 1951 a 12 percent instead of a requested 15 percent increase, with no maximum limits, was authorized. With the general rate cases in the latter 1950s and 1961, railroad requests were nearly all approved, as were the 1966 to 1971 ones. In 1972 a 15 percent general increase request was cut to 14 percent with special limitations of 6 percent in the South and 12 percent on imported ore. The negotiated train-load and annual volume rates for pellets introduced in the latter 1960s were not protested and not subject to the general increases but were specially adjusted upward as agreed to along with increased costs.

The role of the ICC in detailed structural changes in the rates has been limited. Only two specific shipper complaints against particular rates were made and both were rejected as not showing discrimination or unreasonableness.[47] There were four railroad protests of reductions proposed by competing roads. The ICC ordered cancellation in 1953 of reduced import rates from Hampton Roads to Toledo and in 1954 of reduced import rates from Philadelphia and Baltimore to interior points generally. The reason given was that of preventing loss of revenue due to excessive competitive cutting. For the 1957 NYC, ex-St. Lawrence, and 1963 Erie ex-lake reductions, the ICC gave its approval. In another matter, after initial denial countered by Court reversal, the ICC finally approved partial equalization of upper Atlantic ports in respect to import rates. In three cases the ICC denied competitive rate cuts. The ICC, at railroad request, was also brought into conflict with state regulatory authority hold-downs of intrastate ore rates.[48]

*   *   *

The competitive elements affecting changes in iron ore rates have been complicated. There has been no trucking competition. The Great Lakes ship movement of ore has from the beginning been an accepted element in the movement of upper-lake ore and, in a way, not thought of as a competitive water movement. In a minor way, the Erie Canal may have affected New York State ore rates, and a threat of river barge from the Gulf to Birmingham, the southern district ones. The important competitive factor has been the independence of the upper-lake railroads from the Official territory ones, with the former's interest in keeping Lake Superior ore competitive with imported ore at eastern interior mills. In addition, there was differentiation in competitive patterns in the upper-lake region. In general, individual Minnesota mines were served by only one railroad, whereas for Michigan mines more than one was the general rule, making for direct rail competition. Further, one of the railroads involved in this was responsible for a low level of rates for an all-rail movement from a central Wisconsin mine to Chicago district mills. The railroad competition was tempered by the ownership of mines by steel interests who controlled several of the railroads. This limited the possibility of shifting traffic to take advantage of competitive alternatives, and led to hauls being determined by mine ownership and mine and pelletizing costs as much as transport costs.

Improvements in railroad productivity has involved increasing loads per car, increasing shipment size with multiple-car rate incentives, and reduction in associated special services. Iron ore traffic after the war had the heaviest loadings per car of any of the commodities important to the railroads, thus limiting the possibility of great gains in that area. The only major ones came in the far west and were tied to train-load and volume rates. This traffic was newly developed and a new fleet of cars could be justified with the incentives. Average far west loads increased from sixty to ninety-eight tons. Finally, productivity gains from multiple-car and train-load shipment incentives depended upon the extent of previous multiple-car and essentially train-load handling of ore movements. Upper-lake handling was traditionally entirely on a train-load basis for the specialized ore-carrying roads. For the other roads multiple-car blocks were general, but not always in train-load lots.

93

Overall, numerous factors have resulted in a decline for the steel industry in the burden of rail transport charges compared to the value of ore. The average price of standard, 51½ percent Fe, ore at the mine rose from roughly $5.00 in 1950 to $8.70 in 1960 to $12.80 in 1973. The total transport charges of ore from the Mesabi mines to Pittsburgh, a typical major flow, dropped from 88 percent of the mine price in 1950 to 76 percent in 1960 to 68 percent in 1973. For Youngstown, it dropped from 79 percent to 63 percent. If the 1973 comparison were made for pellets and their price, the recent cost/price ratios for the two destinations would have been even lower.

The developments in the steel industry illustrate the great influence of industry locational shifts upon the welfare of individual railroad systems. For far western roads the revenue increase was dramatic, from 1950 to 1972 the UP doubling from $7 to $14 million, the SP from $1 million to $6 million (to $14 million if the Japanese imports had been as hauled the year before). In the southwest the MP ore revenues grew from a negligible amount to $7 million. At the same time the Lake Superior carriers only more or less held their own. The DMI received around $36 million in both years, the BN declined from $21 million to $17 million, the CNW held at about $10 million, but the LSI almost doubled to $4 million. In the East, with the addition of the import traffic, there were major gains. The NYC-P jumped from $36 million to $53 million, the BO doubled from $6 million to $12 million, and the Erie increased relatively even more from $3½ million to $8½ million.[49]

Orange Rates

Oranges are the major item among the general agricultural category of citrus. The analysis will be of orange transport except when data are only available in terms of citrus as a whole, and where orange transport is largely at one with citrus. While there had been some transport of oranges before modern refrigeration was available, it was that technical advance that led to large-scale marketing of perishables in general and fresh oranges in particular. The latter are differentiated by having a longer life, up to three to four weeks, than most other perishables.

Production and Use Trends

Climate determines the location of orange production. Central Florida was the earliest area put into cultivation, then California. Later irrigation brought in Arizona and Texas. There has been a regional differentiation in varieties of oranges grown, with Florida emphasizing juice types. The susceptibility of some regions to frost has affected production and in the case of Texas, successive frosts decimated the crop for several years after 1949. The main movement of oranges has been to the large metropolitan markets in the East—New York, Detroit, Chicago, etc.

To begin with, citrus was used as fresh fruit, to be squeezed for juice, or peeled and eaten directly. Then canning of the juice and later its concentration and freezing displaced much of its use as fresh fruit. As a result, the annual per-person consumption óf fresh oranges fell from forty-eight pounds right after the war to a low of twelve pounds in 1963 and became stable at sixteen pounds in the 1970s. In the 1946/47 season, 62 percent of Florida's marketed oranges was shipped fresh; in 1971/72 it was only 7 percent of a threefold increased marketed crop. The California proporation dropped from 81 percent to 63 percent with a 20 percent total increase.

From the point of view of transport, the impact of the processing of oranges at points of origin reduced the demand for transport basically because it eliminated hauling of the weight of water and rind—2,000 pounds of fresh oranges made 1,056 pounds of natural strength juice or 400 pounds of so-called "bottler's concentrated" juice, or, in the extreme case, 288 pounds of frozen concentrate. Sending the latter to market saved 86 percent of the weight transported. Canned juice was the first product to be marketed in competition with fresh oranges; then frozen concentrate was introduced in 1947. In the latter 1950s, chilled straight juice entered the market, transported in tank cars and trucks and, beginning in 1957, in tank ships.

The marketing arrangements for oranges have been a major factor in respect to the negotiations involved in rate adjustments. In Florida, traditionally there were individual producers and packers forwarding oranges to northern markets. In the West, marketing cooperatives have been dominant with Sunkist accounting for over 70 percent of shipments. In general, oranges had been shipped to auction markets in the major metropolitan areas. More recently, the large food chains have played an increasing role with purchasing at origin and direct shipping to their main distribution centers with no intervening auction market. Thus their loading and handling preferences were different from those of the traditional shippers.[50]

The Traditional Orange Rate Structure

There have been two traditional elements in the service provided for transport of oranges, much the same as for other perishables. One element has been the privilege of shipping without specifying the final destination and of diverting en route to the destinations where auction prices were highest, so long as it did not involve significant back-haul. The other was the railroad guarantee of scheduled deliveries to meet auction times and the payment for loss when the sale at a later auction resulted in the shipper receiving a lower price. In 1964, the eastern railroads withdrew their guarantees of this kind on numerous fruits and vegetables shipments, while the western roads continued theirs. There developed a dispute between auction market and chain-market store fixed-delivery interests as to the relation between rates and the special service. The questions were raised again in 1969 when the eastern roads return to the traditional practice.[51]

The orange rates before 1946 had two distinct structures, one from Florida to the North, the other from western origins to the East. The so-called normal rates from Florida to the North had originally been made up of a combination of three parts, a low Florida gathering rate to Jacksonville varying with the location of origins in Florida, another for the through southern railroad haul to Richmond and Ohio River gateways, and the third for the final northern one to destination. During the depression of the thirties with the advent of refrigerated facilities on coastwide ships, the rail rates to northern port cities were reduced drastically to meet competition from the combined truck haul to Florida ports and ships to the North. Relief from the constraint of the long- and short-haul clause was given by the ICC for the railroads to quote the lower rates to meet the water competition at the ports and maintain higher ones at intermediate inland points. The reduced overall rail rates were based on the sum of truck rates to Florida ports, handling charges, plus the water rate from there to Philadelphia, New York, etc. For instance, to Trenton, New Jersey, the rate was 20¢ higher than to New York. Short-haul rates to southern destinations were also reduced to meet direct truck competition.[52]

The western structure was made up of a vast origin group including both California and Arizona so that from all points in those states the same transcontinental rates applied. At the other end, the same rate applied to destinations, Chicago to New York. This reflected the competition from Florida producers who had roughly the same rates to the wide span of northern metropolitan markets because they were not greatly different in distance from Florida. A service aspect of the common transcontinental rate was that it allowed western producers to change the destination of their shipments in the course of reaching the optimum auction market without incurring change in the rate. For Texas producers, rates differentially lower than from the far western origins were established.

In addition to these freight rates, there were so-called "protective," primarily refrigeration, charges in conjunction with all perishable handling. They varied with distance and the amount of icing provided en route. With ice refrigeration, extra switching was necessary to cut cars out of a train to take them to an icing facility and then return them to their train. In 1960 there were 317 icing stations. With mechanical refrigeration, icing was eliminated and ultimately the stations dispensed with. The added inspection and servicing of the car cooling units was done with removing cars from their trains.

Postwar Changes through 1960

GENERAL INCREASES

After the war orange rates and refrigeration charges were raised as part of the general rate increases through 1960. For oranges, the general percent increases were translated into flat cents per 100 pounds calculated from the application of the percentage to the key Lake Wales, Florida, to New York rate. The four immediate postwar increase requests totaled 64¢ per 100 pounds and the ICC approved 54¢ of that as maximums. The actual increases added 66 percent to the Florida-New York and 50 percent to the transcontinental initial postwar rates. The 1956–1958 increase requests were confined to two in 1956, which the ICC cut back roughly 50 percent to 17¢ per 100 pounds. The small 1960 request, 1¢ per 100 pounds, was restricted by the ICC to an effective hold-down of ½¢. During this period seven "protective" charge increase requests were substantial percentage ones, ranging from 7 percent to 41 percent. They were severely cut back by the ICC to just three 15 percent authorized maximums over the whole period. This was justified by the seeming prosperity of the refrigeration car lines and their failure in the last two requests to present evidence in support of the proposed increases. The simple diversion charge was about $3 to begin with, and after 1958, $6.[53]

In the ICC hearings on these increases, the orange producers pleaded their unsatisfactory economic condition and inability of the industry to bear increases. Rising rates were blamed for forcing oranges out of the fresh fruit market to processing plants. Application of the general percentage increases, it was argued, would upset traditional market relationships. The producers, such as California, farthest from the main eastern markets felt that percentage increases would work to their disadvantage as compared to nearer producers in Florida. Conversely, the nearer producers opposed flat increases across-the-board as working against their natural geographic advantage. The flat increase, acting as a "hold-down," was a firmly entrenched rate-making institution particularly in respect to agricultural products, many of whose producers competed in distant markets. Over the years, because of the political strength of agricultural interests, the ICC, as an arm of Congress, has tended to go along with flat increases and hold-downs to limit increases where agricultural products were involved.

REGIONAL ADJUSTMENTS

After the war the Florida to the North rate structure was adjusted in a number of ways. The coastal shipping lines were reestablished. In 1946 they petitioned the ICC to cancel its prewar permission for the railroads to quote lower rates to the northern ports than to intermediate inland points. The lines argued that the depressed port rates were unfair to the water lines. The ICC agreed, and the pre-depression traditional structure with rate increasing consistently with mileage was reinstituted. As a result, for instance, the Florida-New York rail was raised from 69¢ to 84¢.[54]

The more general pressure on rail rates was from the rapid growth of trucking of perishables. This had not been subjected to ICC regulation because of opposition by agricultural interests and their effective political pressure to exempt agricultural truck transport from regulation. Initially, the shorter-haul rail rates for oranges out of Florida were lowered and then in November 1950 rates to more distant points in the Northeast (except the ports) and Midwest were reduced 17 percent and more.[55]

An important local peculiarity of the perishable rate and charges pattern had been the free unloading of refrigerator cars by the railroads for consignees at New York piers and the Philadelphia market. This was handed down from the past and was contrary to the general rule that carload shipments be unloaded by consignees at their own expense. With the great increase in the costs of doing this during and immediately after the war, the eastern roads in 1947 proposed charging for it, in the case of citrus, $1.50 per net ton. Approval by the ICC was forthcoming. However, perishable shippers' and terminal interests' appeal to the Courts led to reversal by the U.S. Supreme Court in 1954. Thereupon, the railroads met the Court's reasons for rejection by providing the opportunity for consignee unloading without the charge if they so desired. With this proviso, the charge for unloading finally became effective in 1958, with the increase by this time making it $2.86.[56]

The increased expense of handling cars of perishables to Manhattan and other boroughs accessible only by floating to piers led the Pennsylvania and Central of New Jersey in 1957 to demand higher rates to such points than to those on the west bank of the Hudson River. The Orlando to New York City piers orange rate was made 120¢; just to Jersey City, 110¢. Opposition was registered by shippers and New York City interests, but in an initial decision in 1964 the ICC through one of its divisions approved establishing the differential. However, on reconsideration, the ICC as a whole (but with three dissents) reversed its division's decision. The railroads were thus required to maintain the traditional uniformity of rates throughout the port area regardless of the difference in costs.[57]

By way of summary, from 1946 through 1960, the combined rates plus protective and handling charges increased from 94¢ per 100 pounds to 152¢ for oranges from Orlando, Florida, to New York, 62 percent. The same combination increased from 155¢ to 248¢ from California to New York, 60 percent.

Rate Structure Changes after 1960

GENERAL INCREASES

There were no changes 1961 through 1966. After that, the more modest general increases, with two exceptions as percentages, as applied to oranges ranged from 3 to 15 percent. The ICC approval all but the 15 percent proposal, which was cut back to 12 percent, 22¢ maximum. However, the TOFC rates out of Florida were increased independently in advance of the general increases. With the percent increases being mostly minor they were not converted to an across-the-board flat increase as earlier.[58]

On the other hand, the railroads' attempts to raise and restructure refrigeration charges were consistently rebuffed. The ICC felt that the railroads' cost data did not support requested increases and that the relationships between ice and mechanical refrigeration charges and between those for frozen and fresh products were not justified.[59]

Over the twelve years after 1960 the basic orange rate California-Arizona to the eastern blanket territory was increased 31 percent, from 202¢ to 265¢, without change in carload minimums. In contrast, the Orlando, Florida, to New York rate was 110 to 120¢ in 1960. The addition of per-trailer TOFC rates, of the special increases and the rejection of some general ones, meant little net change in average charges in the twelve years to 1972. For the average northern destination the increase was only 8 percent, reflecting the importance of truck competition.[60]

REGIONAL ADJUSTMENTS

In Florida, the different railroads serving the orange traffic and the California took contrasting approaches in making rate adjustments to meet the erosion of traffic by truckers. While both introduced innovative adjustments by way of incentive and TOFC rates for deciduous fresh fruits and vegetables, only the southern roads did so for citrus. Within the South, some per-car rates were introduced from Florida origins. These applied with railroad supplied refrigerated highway trailers. Through 1966, considerable enthusiasm was expressed for this arrangement, but the difficulty of getting shippers to load two trailers for the same destination on a flat car and of finding return loads made the service less attractive than was anticipated by the railroads. Rates were increased independently in 1968 by 12 percent to cover increased costs. From the 1966/67 season, the citrus TOFC traffic from Florida declined from 24 percent to only 12 percent of the orange traffic by the 1971/72 season.[61]

The *transcontinental* orange rate structure kept its basic per-100-pound rates with a 39,200-pound minimum, pattern throughout the period under study. The West to Northeast long-haul citrus traffic had minimal truck competition. However, in 1971, it was proposed to change from per-100-pound rates to per-car ones, these to vary with size of car furnished by the railroad. The amount for the smallest car, the old ice-bunker car, was established by multiplying the pounds carried with loading six layers high of boxes, 44,000 pounds by the then 265¢ per 100-pound rate, giving a per-car rate of $1,168. The larger mechanically refrigerated cars were given rates based on their six-layer-load weight multiplied by 248¢. For the shortest of these cars the rate was $1,209 and for the longest fifty-one-foot one, $1,740. If the loading exceeded the six-layer weight, the rate per car was higher. Assuming six-layer loading, there was a substantial gain in unit rate by shifting from ice-bunker to mechanical cars but surprisingly no gain from using a large rather than a small mechanical car, except that the "protective" charge was the same regardless of car size. From the Pacific Coast to New York, for instance, as between the smallest and largest car, this last would provide for a gain of 10¢ per 100 pounds. While most of the suggested adjustments had been worked out in consultation with shippers, some of the chain stores protested because they wanted to be assured of a continuing possibility of using small cars, their load capacity being best suited to the stores' distribution practices.

This proposal of the transcontinental railroads had as its background their desire to increase the per-car loads of citrus, the average load having remained nearly constant, at around twenty tons, over the years. In addition, the railroads hoped to phase out ice-bunker cars, thus eliminating the switching costs of handling cars to and from icing facilities. For the transcontinental citrus plus other perishable traffic, there were still in service some 6,400 ice-bunker cars, a quarter of all the refrigerator cars available. A high percent of citrus was being shipped in the iced cars, 89 percent in 1970/71 for the Southern Pacific, for instance. The railroad problem was to get shippers to give up icing and the smaller cars as they were phased out in the course of building up an inventory of new large mechanical cars.

An added problem was that the car inventory did not have enough of the first and second generation smaller-size mechanical cars to meet probable shipper requests for them. With per-car rates graduated according to size, if a larger-than-ordered car was provided, the shipper unit cost would increase unless it was loaded with more boxes than he planned with the smaller car he had ordered. The shippers' dealing in smaller shipments and preferring smaller cars would be subjected to a penalty, which was not the case with the prior 100-pound basis for rates.

It should be noted that there was a general tariff rule for other commodities providing that if a larger car than ordered was furnished, the rates and minimums associated with the car ordered should apply. The failure to have provided this protection with the proposed citrus structural adjustment was a basis for its rejection by the ICC. All this involved a basic conflict between a carrier's obligation to meet the varied needs of an industry's practices and the carrier interests in increasing productivity by updating its car inventory in accord with technical and capacity advances. The ICC proposed to allow shipper traditional practices to continue at the expense of restraining the railroad attempts at increasing productivity.[62]

Going beyond the period generally covered in this study, the transcontinental roads next proposed, in May 1974, an entirely different structural adjustment for fresh fruits and vegetables in general, this time with citrus being included among them. The citrus rates for the first time would be graduated downward with increasing loads over a range of minimums from 50,000 pounds to 90,000 pounds. From lowest to highest, the reduction amounted to about one-third. From California and Arizona to Chicago, for instance, the rates were graded from 373¢ to 233¢. The rate to be superseded was the then 334¢, minimum 39,200 pounds. The other charge was a major break with tradition, namely to do away with the equality for rates from the far west to all destinations between Chicago and New York. The proposed New York rates were, for instance, made 140 percent to 150 percent of the Chicago ones, roughly in proportion to the added haul involved. The ICC rejected the overall proposal, including the citrus rate adjustment, for several stated reasons: that the proposed rates would mostly exceed conventionally calculated variable costs, that the carriers were not suffering such massive losses with present rates as to justify such radical divergence from traditional marketing patterns, and that the diversion to trucks that the proposed rates would bring about would largely eliminate rail transport for many of the items, thus working an extreme hardship on producers and consumers. This was an extreme illustration of the ICC's emphasizing protection of vested interests.[63]

* * *

The quarter century of changes in rail transport of fresh oranges for reasons of data limitations must be considered in terms of citrus as a whole of which oranges are the greatest part. The changes reflect a combination of the regional differences in production characteristics, the shift from fresh to the processed forms, and the impacts of the highway and water competition.

Substitution of processed for fresh citrus led to a 55 percent drop in fresh orange consumption for the Northeast. This is close to the 58 percent drop in California and Arizona. Official citrus traffic where the great length of haul, 2,850-mile average, has ruled out significant truck competition. The rates for this traffic also show the greatest increase, 83 percent. In contrast, the volume of western traffic to the South decreased by 83 percent despite nearly as long a haul and similar rate increases. The fact that the South grew its own citrus in Florida could account for a more elastic demand and thus rejection of the high increase in costs of oranges delivered from California.

At the other extreme, from Florida to the other southern states, the shortness of the haul has meant maximum truck competition so that rail traffic essentially ceased despite the relatively minor rate increases, at most 20 percent, over the years. The Texas-Midwest traffic, with intermediate-length hauls, 1,300-mile average, was also taken over by truckers after the initial decimation by frost kill of the crop. This loss of production due to frost also played a part in Texas dropping out of the eastern market, where it had initially been in strong competition with southern producers. This last eliminated a potential source of long-haul traffic suitable for the railroads.

Florida to the North fresh citrus traffic was subject to both the general decline in consumption and the fact that Florida's dominant type of oranges was the most suitable one for processing. By 1971/72 only 8 percent of that state's marketed oranges went as fresh fruit. With the great improvements in highways and decreasing scale of markets, truckers became a dominating competitive factor. By 1966 the rail traffic volume had dropped by over two-thirds. The loss continued after 1966 despite the introduction of TOFC service, and the modest average rate increase from 1947 to 1972 of 26 percent. Nineteen seventy-two volume was only 16 percent of 1947.

In respect to rail productivity, the average load for Florida to the North cars actually decreased from 1947 to 1972, twenty-three and a half tons to twenty tons, and for the West to East cars, twenty-three to twenty-two tons. Only from the West to the Western Trunk-Line Territory was there an increase, twenty-three to twenty-eight tons. Thus for most flows of citrus traffic little improvement in productivity was achieved. The restructuring of the rate patterns so as to provide incentives to heavier loading was resisted by shippers and the ICC protection of their position. In addition, the ICC imposed serious restraints on proposals to increase rates, though the severe competition from trucks, except for the longest hauls, probably would have countered the possible raising of revenue by greater rate increases.

In all this the railroads' problems with the citrus traffic had been compounded by the entrance of chain stores in the fresh citrus trade, and the resultant conflicting shipper viewpoints in respect to optimum loading and special services like reconsignment and diversion.

Malt Liquor

During the depression before World War II the malt liquor, beer, ale, etc., traffic again became available to the railroads, upon the repeal of Prohibition. By 1940 there were more than 600 breweries in the country producing 55 million barrels. After the war, production gradually increased from 87 million in 1947 to 95 million in 1960 to 140 million by 1972, 61 percent overall. The brewing industry was characterized by important economies of scale and company ambitions to control increasing shares of the market. The number of breweries decreased to 404 by 1947 and 108 by 1972. The major companies increased capacity at their own original breweries and built or acquired others at new locations. The eight largest companies accounted for 30 percent of the shipments in 1947, 70 percent in 1972. Most local breweries either dropped out or were taken over by regional or national companies. A few successful and aggressive locals continued and expanded. Added capacity was built primarily in parts of the country with growing demand, like Florida, Texas, and California.[64]

In the early years most of the national company production was at a single location from which they distributed nationwide. The three largest, Schlitz, Pabst, and Anhauser-Busch, were located in the Midwest—St. Louis and Milwaukee. Toward the end of and after the war the big national companies decided to serve markets remote from the Midwest with their own local breweries. Anhauser-Busch acquired land for a plant in Newark, New Jersey; Pabst purchased the Hoffman plant in Newark. Further construction and acquisition provided the major brewing companies with production in Florida and Texas and on the West Coast in the Los Angeles area. This displaced their long-haul traffic. On the other hand, some of the smaller breweries—Olympia in Washington, Coors in Colorado, and Heilman in Lacrosse—sought wider markets leading to longer hauls for their traffic.

Malt liquor had always been transported in draft form in kegs and barrels and in bottles and, since the war, increasingly in cans. Protection was required against extreme cold and in summer some cooling was used. Refrigerator cars because of their insulation were used for a substantial proportion of shipments. Traditionally, the kegs and bottles were sent back to the breweries as return movements for the cars handling beer outbound. With the coming of no-return containers an important part of the return loading disappeared.

Malt liquor rail transport costs had unique elements by way of special car supply requirements associated with the use of refrigerator cars. Along certain routes it was said that the return hauls of such cars as were used for West to East fruit and vegetable traffic made them available to fill empty return movements westward at lower than usual cost.[65]

Prewar Rate Structure

The pre-Prohibition beer rate structure had been based on 35 to 40 percent of first-class rates, minimum around 30,000 pounds, with complimentary 12 to 15 percent rates for the returned containers. With the revival of beer traffic in the depression and at the same time the beginning of truck competition, there was a reduction in the classification to 25 percent to 20 percent of first class. Commodity rates played an increasing role with introduction of incentive rates graduated downwards as applicable carload minimums went from 30,000 to 40,000 to 50,000 pounds. Empty container return rates were also reduced, for instance, to around 9 percent of first class.[66]

In the late 1930s barge lines became active in hauling beer from the Midwest to the Gulf Coast markets and in connection with shipping lines through the Panama Canal to West Coast ones. The Midwest companies were pushing for low rates to keep themselves in distant regional markets against growing local production. The 1937 rail rates from St. Louis to the Pacific points ranged from 118¢ per 100 pounds for 30,000 pounds minimum to 89¢ for 50,000 pounds. Publishing of barge-ship rates of 70½¢ with the latter minimum led to an 80¢ rail rate based on beer weight alone, with a 60,000-pound minimum. Similarly, to help St. Louis production keep in the Florida market the rail rate to Miami, minimum 40,000 pounds, was cut from 69¢ to 57¢.[67]

Postwar Rate Structure

With decentralization of brewing and widening of markets, there developed a more complex structure of rates best considered in terms of rate averages rather than specific point-to-point or group rates as were best considered in respect to iron ore and oranges. The ICC published waybill statistics provide the basis for such analysis. Also there were so few challenges of rate changes brought before the ICC that only occasional historical data by way of specific rates are available in the published rate cases.[68]

GENERAL RATE INCREASE ADJUSTMENTS

From 1946 through 1961 malt liquor rate increases were requested by the railroads and authorized as maximums by the ICC in connection with seven of the eight general rate increases discussed earlier in this chapter. None was requested in 1958. The sum of authorized maximums came to 121 percent in the East, around 94 percent in the South, and 84 percent in the West. In actual practice the railroads did not take advantage of a large share of the increases, rather there were special adjustments meeting changing marketing patterns and trucking and water competition. Despite the continuing series of authorized increases, in general, rates having peaked in the mid-1950s receded thereafter to lows in the mid-1960s.

As noted earlier, general annual increases began again in 1967 following the general ICC granting of requests for them. The cumulative total of the 1967 through 1972 ones applied to malt liquors was in the neighborhood of 30 percent— somewhat less in the South, more in the East.[69]

RATE STRUCTURE CHANGES

At the end of the war malt liquor movements within Official (O) and Southern (S) territories and between them were largely at class and exceptions, rates with only some 10 percent at commodity rates. For the rest of the country there were largely commodity rates particularly tailored to the circumstances of the industry. However, by the latter 1950s the traffic had been provided with commodity rates all around. In parallel with this the incentive rates to induce heavier loading of cars were expanded as to the range of weights and the discounts for added tons per car. In general, from 1947 to 1966 this, along with provision of cars with greater capacities, led to average loading rising from around twenty-eight to thirty-seven tons, with some few special traffic flows reaching forty-three tons. In the following six years the general level increased to forty-four tons with two flows reaching the extremes of fifty-six tons within the Mountain Pacific territory (MTP) and sixty-one and a half tons from the West to the Southwest respectively.

The other major change in rate patterns came with the introduction of TOFC service in the mid-1950s. The railroads in the MTP territory were early promoters of this for malt liquor traffic. Initially, in 1956, 40 percent of their beer tonnage was TOFC, with average tons carried per car only twenty compared to thirty-two for regular carloads. However, by 1966 the TOFC tons had declined to 24 percent with its average load increasing to twenty-six tons to be compared to fifty-four tons for the then railroad carloadings. Other regions were slower to initiate TOFC service, by 1966 with 13 percent in O territory, 23 percent in WTL, and only 10 percent in SW.*

ADJUSTMENTS FOR PARTICULAR MOVEMENTS, 1947–1966

For major long hauls, while there was a general rise in long-haul rates with the last of the postwar annual increase, the Midwest to Atlantic seaboard ones were reduced some 20 percent to forestall possible loss of that traffic because of major Midwest brewers increasing their East Coast production capacity.

---

*Proportions calculated by proportions of traffic handled on flat cars.

Thereafter to the mid-1950s average charges increased all around, up 15 to 20 percent, to reach the peak ones of this phase. An exception was for barge competitive movements such as that from Louisiana to Texas. There was no general increase in loadings.

Subsequently, to 1960, with increasing average tons per car, there were decreases in long-haul rates to Florida and Texas again to forestall added destination territory brewing capacity. The previously stable subnormal barge competitive charges did decline further. The averages for the long hauls from the Midwest, Washington, and Colorado to California did not change significantly.

From 1960 to the last year for which detailed waybill statistics were published, 1966, there were little changes in charges from the Midwest to the East but a further 17 percent decline to Florida from Missouri and New Jersey. To Texas from the Midwest there was a 9 to 10 percent decrease. These reflected the interest in maintaining the long-haul traffic from the breweries in the Midwest. For the barge competitive traffic from Louisiana there was again no change. For the so-called transcontinental traffic from the Midwest to California, there was no change in spite of major loading gains. The most drastic change was for the state of Washington to California movement with the greatest of any increase in loading, thirty-six to sixty-four tons, and a 21 percent decrease in average charge, this involving Washington expansion into the California market.

For local hauls, as mentioned earlier, short-haul traffic declined greatly due to truck competition. However, in some regions with new breweries and increased brewing capacity there was the opportunity for medium-haul rail traffic to grow. Between 1949 and 1966, with average hauls of around 250 miles, the rail tons handled intrastate increased 180 percent in Texas, 390 percent in Washington, and from nothing to over 100,000 tons in Florida. For this traffic, average charges from 1950 to 1966 showed little change.

ADJUSTMENTS FOR PARTICULAR MOVEMENTS, 1966–1972

For the six years after 1966 the lack of published state-to-state data makes necessary the use of the grosser intra- and interterritory rate figures. For the shorter hauls the average increase in average charges per 100 pounds for those years was around 25 percent, for the middle-length nearly 30 percent, and, adjusting for changes in haul, the longest movements showed considerably greater increase. Increase in tons per car were for the most part modest, 20 to 25 percent. However, for the WTL to SW territory traffic there was a major gain, 40 percent to fifty-two tons, and within the MTP, 30 percent to fifty-six tons. In terms of volume of traffic there was a 17 percent loss within Official territory and 40 percent from it to the Southern, the latter a reflection of the growth of production in S territory. The major gains were in the traffic within the S and MTP territories, the former almost fivefold.

Beginning with 1966 the compilation of motor-carrier commodity statistics makes it possible to compare over the six years to 1972 railroad with motor-carrier traffic (private truck haulage not included) for each of the gross regions, East, South and West. In the East motor-carrier revenues initially were a fifth of the rail and they were slightly less in 1972. On the other hand, in the South the motor-carrier revenues rose from an eighth of rail to a little over a fifth. This was despite a substantial growth in southern rail tonnage. The growth of local production provided the opportunity for increasing local distribution and reduced the importation from other regions. In the West, distances involved were greater, resulting in motor-carrier revenue being only one-seventeenth of rail with no increase in the proportion.[70]

Comparison of Malt Liquor Average Charges, Intra- and Interterritory, 1966 and 1977

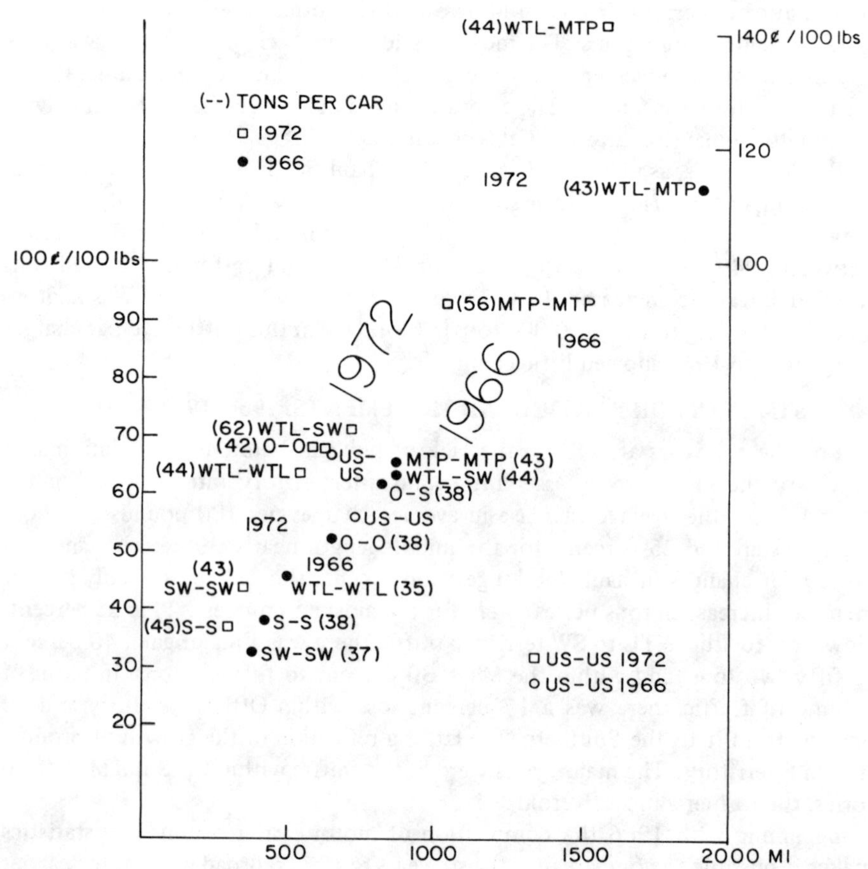

REGULATORY CONSTRAINTS

Regulatory constraints on proposed rate changes were asked for in connection with only three railroad proposed rate adjustments in these years. In early 1949 slight reductions in Midwest to Pacific Coast malt liquor rates were published by the railroads, 110¢ per 100 pounds from a range of from 115¢ to 123¢. Local California, Oregon, and Washington brewing interests protested, being fearful of strengthening of the Midwest breweries in the western market. The railroad motives were to forestall further decentralization of the latter's production and loss of long-haul traffic. The ICC did not suspend the changed rates and in December decided they were not unlawful. In September 1950 the railroads filed rates of 23¢ instead of 26¢ from New Orleans to Texas cities on the Gulf to meet barge and motor-carrier competition. At the barge lines request, the rates were suspended, to April 1951. In an August decision they were found to be compensatory and reasonable and the suspension vacated.[71]

In February 1956 the railroads filed for reduced long-haul rates without lowering intermediate ones from the Midwest brewing points to Texas ports to meet barge competition as well as to forestall decentralization. For instance, from St. Louis to Texas 57¢ per 100 pounds for 70,000 pounds minimum loading was proposed in place of 70¢ for 60,000 pounds. A barge line protested and the rates were supended. In a decision rejecting the rates the ICC said that they were not shown to be compensatory because no cost data were presented.[72]

This review of malt liquor rates shows the impact of several competitive factors. In the background has been the influence of railroad system network patterns that have provided interrail competition. For instance, in respect to both eastward and westward traffic, different rail systems provided service for the Wisconsin brewers from systems providing it for the St. Louis ones. The impact of motor-carrier and of water competition for particular lines of traffic flow was important. A third factor was the big Midwest producers' move to decentralize production and contrariwise some others' to expand their markets from local to regional and even broader ones. But the associated long-haul "transcontinental" rates, which felt the least truck competition, showed the least decline in the long run. Overall these competitive pressures resulted in 1966 rate levels being generally lower than in 1950. With two exceptions there was not a major breakthrough in loading practices to provide increasing productivity to match the rise in rail input prices over these years. TOFC was introduced in the far west in the latter 1950s but was not attractice enough to maintain its initial proportion of shipments.

After 1966 the greater pressures of sharply accelerating input unit costs led to all-around rate increases of some 30 percent in six years. As with the previously examined commodities there were not sufficient productivity gains to counter the pressures of rising input prices.

The overall picture of malt liquor traffic was one of successful adjustment to changing location patterns of the brewing industry, recognized loss of short-haul traffic to truck competition, and active development of wider markets for aggressive regional brewers. Only under special circumstances was it possible to increase per-car loading in any spectacular way, otherwise the increase was below the average for other classes of commodities except products of mines.

Development of Rate Structures for Major Revenue-Producing Commodities, 1950–1972

Further understanding of postwar rate developments is provided by review of five of the six principal rail revenue-producing commodities. In contrast to the cases of iron ore, oranges, and beer, the detailed examination of changes in these industry patterns are omitted and the focus is on the major traffic flows, carloading, and rates, and the factors accounting for the changes. The initial year chosen is 1950 because it was the first year of complete waybill data and after the rate increases to compensate for the wartime and immediate postwar inflation. Intermediate measuring points, 1963 and 1964, are necessary because between those years there was a change in commodity classifications to insure homogenity of each commodity. The trends are reviewed in two segments, 1950 to 1963 and 1964 to 1972, the latter being the first year after 1966 for which reliable waybill data are available, as well as the final year covered in this study. In general, 1966 charges are slightly less than 1964. Average ton-mile charges are calculated based on short-line mileage between origin and termination points, real mileage ranging 15 to 20 percent more.[73]

The five commodities are bituminous coal, lumber, fiber- and paperboard, assembled autos, and motor vehicle parts. These items accounted for a quarter of rail freight revenue in both 1950 and 1972. (See Table 7.) Wheat, the other major commodity, is not considered because the interruption of the complete hauls of wheat by transit stop offs for milling storage, etc., prevent the statistics of average regional charges, hauls and loadings region by region, from being meaningful.

TABLE 7

Class I U.S. Line-Haul Railways

	Tons Orig. Revenue 1950		Tons Orig. Revenue 1972	
Bituminous Coal	362 tons	$1,119	371 tons	$1,361
Lumber & Plywood	29.5	440	26.6	749
Motor Vehicle Parts	9.7	202	16.4	494
Assembled Autos	2.8	103	8.7	430
Paper-, Fiberboard, Pulpwood	4.8	66	16.8	266

(Source: ICC, *SRUS,* 1950, Table 51;
———, *Frt. Commod. Stat, Class I Rys.* 1972.)

Bituminous Coal

Bituminous coal was the biggest revenue-generating commodity for the railroads. Truck competition was involved only for the shortest hauls and motor carriers received negligible revenue from coal. On the other hand, water transport was significant on the Great Lakes and the Ohio River and its tributaries, and segments of a few other rivers, but traffic data have not been collected. A 104-mile coal slurry pipeline placed in operation in 1958 across Ohio was a competitive threat, though it did not continue in operation following rate reductions. Increasingly, high-voltage transmission lines were also competitors. Important overall was the increasing substitution of gas and fuel oil for coal, particularly in Official territory (O) where coal had traditionally been the dominant source of heat energy.

From 1950 to 1963 within O territory the average charge per ton-mile for an average short-line 285-mile haul there was a decline of around 8 percent, taking into account for the slight lengthening of haul. There was only an 8 percent increase in load per car in Official territory compared to 20 percent in the South, the roads in the South starting off with somewhat smaller cars and loads. Beginning in 1955 multiple-car, and then annual volume and train-load, reduced rates were introduced and by 1963 were widely promoted to counter substitution of the cheaper competitive fuels and stave off possible future coal pipelines.[74]

In the next phase, 1964 to 1972, the full impact of substitutes for coal was felt within Official territory with a 33 percent decline in rail coal tonnage. Average ton-mile charges, adjusting for a shortened 235-mile haul in 1972, were up around 30 percent despite both a 23 percent better load per car and further use of the train-load and annual volume rates. On the other hand, within the South with its counteracting general economic growth and fewer waterside coal-using power plants there was a 90 percent increase in coal traffic. there was a somewhat less increase in average charge, 26 percent, adjusted for the lengthening haul, with only 18 percent better load, but as in the North with increased proportion of train-load rated shipments. No regional data are available in respect to the proportion of train-load shipments. Despite continued competition from gas and oil and the railroads' greater productivity gains than in the earlier phase, the more rapid rise in factor costs after 1966 forced substantial increases in charges after the 1966 lows. Despite the pressure from substitutes, the rate increases were only slightly less than for commodities as a whole. For most regions the increases were around 30 percent to 40 percent; the exception was within the South, only some 20 percent.

A sharply contrasting picture in this last phase was the beginning of the growth of eastern Mountain Pacific territory to Midwest (WTL) coal traffic, up from practically nothing to 8 million tons. The haul averaged 959 miles, and with new cars dedicated to the service average loads of 98 tons were attained, far above averages for coal originating in the East and South. For this traffic the 1972 average charge per ton-mile was 0.64¢ with what were essentially negotiated train-load incentive rates reflecting the increased productivity of combined maximum tons per car and maximum-length unit-train operation and reductions in terminal handling costs.

Coal has been a heavy loading commodity with minimum of claims for loss and damage. Many of the shippers as large-scale producers or users of coal have tendered and received cars in multiple or even train-load lots quite regularly even before the introduction of rate incentives to do so. Shipments from mines to Great Lakes and Atlantic ports had traditionally been in solid coal trains. These circumstances make it difficult to estimate the extent of savings for the railroads arising from the multiple-car and volume rates.

Traditionally, coal shippers had the privilege of forwarding cars without having sold the coal and therefore without destination, thus necessitating repeated switching in yards until a consignee was found. Further, export coal shippers could request holding and sorting of cars so they could be delivered in special order and finally spotted at docks so as to provide cargoes of particular chemical specifications, much as had been traditional with upper-lake iron ore. Weighing of coal was another service that was provided. These all involved extra expenses above those for just simple transport. One of the gains associated with the new train-load rates was elimination of these extras and requirement of shorter free loading and unloading time.

There were roads in the early years of the period under review whose traffic was largely just coal, before their merger with roads with general run of traffic. These roads were the Pocahontas group. They provide a look at coal revenue in relation to associated costs. Their net railway operating income was a higher proportion of revenue than other roads with the general run of commodity mix. Net income percents traditionally highlighted coal traffic as one of the railroads' highest earning commodities despite the extra services and the generally 50 percent empty car-miles associated with coal handling. The so-called "low" level of rates necessary to attract coal traffic because of its low value per unit of weight were in fact not low in the sense of producing revenue only slightly over associated costs.

The postwar rate developments resulted from the powerful forces of produce substitution and improve technology for energy transport breaking down a traditional rate structure. The railroads initiated a rate pattern, and brought in new equipment and simplified service so that productivity could be increased.

Lumber

The next largest revenue source was dimension stock lumber and its complement plywood. Together they accounted for 30 million tons originated by the railroads in 1950 and 27 million in 1972. Truck competition was strong for the short and medium hauls and negligible for the transcontinental long hauls from the Pacific producing region to the Atlantic Coast. In 1963 regulated motor-carrier revenues from lumber and plywood amounted to only 3 percent of the rail revenues, and in 1972, 5 percent. There are no corresponding data for private trucking. Only a minor proportion of lumber tonnage was transported by water, 3 to 3½ percent of the tonnage shipped. With rates for plain plywood being related to those for basic lumber, the charges for the latter are the basis for analysis.[75]

Traditionally, there was competition between southern, southwestern, and northern Pacific Coast producers so that the rate structure reflected in part their respective pressures on the southern and western roads. It also carried over the earlier impact on Panama Canal competition, which had led to uniformity of rates from the Pacific Coast to all points east of Chicago, a blanket rate much the same as with orange rates but for different reasons.

In the initial year 1950 there was substantial local traffic within both the Official (O) and southern (S) territories, with average short-line hauls of 346 and 286 miles respectively. By 1963 the average intraterritory charges per ton-mile were up from 1950 by about 5 percent in the O territory and down 10 percent in the S, taking changes in haul into account. These differences in part reflected active use of incentive rates in the South with that territory's per carloading rising from twenty-nine to forty-one and a half tons while the Official was up only twenty-nine to thirty-four tons. By 1963, due largely to truck competition, the volumes of these intraterritory traffics had both declined by roughly 75 percent, and the length of haul increased by 23 percent and 12 percent respectively. From 1964 to 1972 the intra-O charges rose some 26 percent and the southern only 16 percent, the southern loads increasing fifty-seven tons, the Official only to forty-seven. The tonnage carried in the South increased 23 percent with average hauls remaining the same, while the Official decreased 25 percent with hauls 30 percent longer. In general, western lumber was taking over from local eastern sources.

From 1950 to 1963 the important S to O flow decreased, 90 percent, even more than the intraregional despite having double the haul and a lesser, only 6 percent, increase in ton-mile charge. Loads per car increased from twenty-six to thirty-four tons. In the 1964 to 1972 phase the load for this traffic jumped to forty-eight tons, average charges were up only 15 percent, and there was a 13 percent growth in the tonnage handled. This traffic was particularly sensitive to the competitive standing of southern versus western lumber.

The long hauls from the Pacific producers to the East were not subject to truck competition and the once active Pacific to Atlantic Coast, Panama Canal, shipping had declined. From 1950 to 1963 there was around a 25 percent increase in the transcontinental ton-mile charges with loadings increasing 10 percent, and from 1964 to 1972 from 30 to 36 percent with average loading reaching forty tons. This range of increases was well above those just reviewed for the shorter hauls where there was active truck competition. The decline of Panama Canal water competition was also a factor. The increases from 1950 to 1963 were significantly greater than for the other commodities reviewed.

Lumber rates were associated with a traditional service feature of starting a car off without consignees and routing it over circuitous routes to lengthen the journey to market so as to get the maximum time to find the highest bidder for the contents. This was the basis for a well-established country-wide brokerage system with railroads providing daily a count of the moving inventory upon which brokers based their solicitation of orders from lumber dealers. In 1958 the railroads proposed to allow fifteen days for holding lumber cars at key points together with one free diversion to eliminate excessively long hauls. The Canadian roads had initiated this arrangement and it applied on shipments in competition with U.S. ones. While the ICC and courts restrained the various attempts at limitation of the service arrangements, in the end the privileges were curtailed.[76]

Fiber-, and Paperboard

Fiber- and paperboard, manufactured wood products, have been top growth items for the railroads with tons originated in the U.S. in 1972 over threefold those of 1950. With improvements in stowage and protective techniques, larger cars, and incentive rates, average loading per car increased steadily from a U.S. average of 25.3 tons in 1950 to 39.0 in 1963 to 49.3 in 1972, nearly doubling overall. Neither intra- nor interterritorial length of hauls have for the most part changed significantly. From 1950 to 1963 charges for the major flows were reduced from 10 to 20 percent except within MTP territory where loadings to begin with had been higher and charges lower than elsewhere. From 1964 to 1972 with the continued rise in per-car loading, increases in charges ranged from 20 to 30 percent (except near 40 percent, within Official territory), significantly less than commodities in general. Motor carriers accounted for a small percentage of the traffic. In 1966 and 1972 their revenue was only 12 percent of that for rail. Fiberboard was a commodity for which methods for heavier per-car loading could be devised with resultant competitive advantages over trucking with the latter's limited loads. It was also a commodity much of which was produced and used at large-scale plants. This favored rail handling because of the processing in large-quantity lots and of universal presence of railroad sidings. The nature of the commodity and of its industry pattern where physical aspects that the railroads were able to take advantage of to build strong intermodal competitive position.

Assembled Autos

The most radical rate structure changes among the five commodities were for assembled passenger autos. For several years after the war loading of autos continued in loading-device-fitted assigned boxcars with loadings averaging six to seven tons per car. Motor carriers had devised a rack trailer, the advantages of which had cut down the rail handling of assembled autos from a 40 percent share in 1946 to 6½ percent by 1959. The rail innovation of the open-rack cars, bi-level and tri-level, was introduced in 1959 and 1960 by southwestern railroads. By 1960 they had been adopted sufficiently in the Southern. WTL, and southwestern territories to raise loading per car significantly. Rack highway semitrailer-on-flatcar service was also instituted. By 1962 rail rack handling was widespread enough to raise the national carload average to twenty tons, three times what it had been in 1950. This moved autos from being one of the lightest loading commodities handled by the railroads to one of the better loading ones among finished manufactured products and led to rate reductions that increased originated tonnage almost fourfold from 1950 to 1972. To compete with what had been decimating highway competition the productivity gains of increased loading were passed on in the form of drastic cuts in rates. By 1963 in terms of cents per ton-mile below the 1950 levels, the reductions were between 30 and 50 percent, depending upon region. However, from 1964 on there was little further increase in loading per car, and rates increased by the same general range of percents as for most other commodities.

The rack car innovation resulted in recovery of a large share of the traffic that had been lost to motor carriers. By 1972 the railroads were carrying over four times the ton-miles of autos they were in 1950 and average per-car-mile revenue was up almost three times. The railroads regained the longer-haul traffic. In 1972 they originated 8.7 million tons, which provided $430 million revenue. The motor carriers retained the shorter haul, originating 16.8 million tons with $367 million revenue. The service advantage of making direct store delivery to retail dealers without transfer from a railroad siding at a distance from the dealer's premises was sufficient to keep the shorter-haul traffic with the motor carriers.

However, the specialized rack cars committed the railroads to more expensive cars, to ones assigned to particular flows of traffic with little chance of return loadings or use for other commodities. In addition, because the autos were critically in the open they were exposed to damage, which made for significant increase in claims against the railroads.

Motor Vehicle Parts

Motor vehicle parts were not a homogeneous category, but ranged from relatively light loading items like body parts to the heavy loading engines with rates for the different categories varying with differences in loading, possibility of damage, etc. From 1950 to 1972 the tonnage originated had increased 69 percent. The traffic originated predominantly in Official territory and from 60 to 70 percent was destined to that territory. For the 1950 to 1963 phase, average parts-loading per car was low and did not increase greatly, for the U.S. as a whole, only from 17.0 tons average to 18.1 tons. From O to other territories the gains were greater than within O territory. Average charge increases per ton-mile was 38 percent within O territory, and to other territories ranged from none to Southern to 21 percent to the southwest.

From 1964 to 1972 substantial improvements were made in stowage and protective features and per-carloads gained 34 percent to twenty-four tons average. The average ton-mile charges for traffic local to Official territory increased 35 percent, to other territories, around 26 percent with only slightly higher loading.

In respect to motor carriers, they played a lesser role in parts shipment than in shipment of assembled cars. Parts involved shipment from a large-scale manufacturer to an assembly plant. This meant they were going to plants with railroad sidings in contrast to the assembled auto going to off-track premises of automobile dealers. Shipments were largely multiple car due to the large scale of the assembly plant operations. In 1972 the railroads originated 17 million tons of motor vehicle parts and accessories with $498 million revenue, while the motor carriers originated 6.6 million tons with $158 million revenue. Because of the importance of this traffic to the railroads and the critical demands of closely timed assembly lines at destinations, the associated services of the railroads were given more attention than most other commodities. This traffic involved special service features by way of scheduled car movements and supervision of car and train movements closely and continuously. This meant staff dedicated to this end and, when necessary, special handling of errant car movements all at added cost.

Overview

1950–1963

Comparison of the changes (see Table 8) in rates as reflected in average charges for movements within and between different regions for the five commodities shows a dominant influence of the productivity factor of tons per car. The threefold gain in loadings per car of assembled autos from 1950 to 1963 produced the maximum reductions in charges for any of the five commodities for all length hauls and in all regions. Autos were the only one of the three commodities with transcontinental hauls that showed a rate reduction. The strong competition from motor carriers with early losses for all but the longest hauls of this traffic made the railroads pass on to the shippers the savings from improved productivity to the extent necessary to regain a substantial share of traffic. The pass through for the longest hauls as well can be seen as an attempt to combat the decentralization of auto assembly plants and resultant losses of traffic.

The next greatest loading increase in the 1950–1963 phase was for fiber- and paperboard with most flows showing a gain of over 50 percent. There were charge reductions averaging from 10 to 20 percent. The motor-carrier competition in this case was very much less than for assembled autos. An aberration with the one fiberboard flow with only a small increase in loading showed the average charges were increased. Lumber within and from the South had the next greatest load increase, 30 to 40 percent, but was accompanied by lowered charges only within the South. Overall for the commodities with less than 20 percent loading increase, there were increases all around, except for coal intra-South.

TABLE 8

Changes in Average Ton-Mile Charges and Carloadings for Five Major Revenue-Producing Commodities—Principal Intra- Interregional Movements, 1950–1963

	Local Hauls			Longer Hauls		
	O-O	**S-S**	**S-O**			
Bituminous Coal	+3%	−8%[e]	+11%			
	60-65t.	55-65t.	54-60t.			
				MTP-WTL		**MTP-O**
Lumber	+1%	+25%	+8%[e]	+27%		+22%
	29-34	29-42	26-34	33-35t.		33-35t.
				SW-O	**MTP-MTP**	
Fiber-Paperboard	−14%	−7%	−18%	−13%	+12%	
	23-35	25-39	26-42	26-37	33-40t.	
			O-S	**O-WTL**		**O-MTP**
Autos	−32%[e]	−25%[e]	−40%[e]	−38%[e]		−39%
	6½-21	6½-20½	6½-21½	6½-21		7-22½
Motor Vehicle Parts	+38%		0%[e]	+14%		+9%
	17-18		17-20	17-20		16-19

(e = estimate taking in account significant increase or decrease in haul)

There were significant regional differences in the changes. Intra-South charges all decreased, even with minimal loading gains. Intra-Official charges all increased, except for autos and fiberboard with their maximum loading gains. For inter-continental-length hauls with minimal truck competition as well as limited Panama Canal competition, there were, again excepting autos, only increases.

1964–1972

In the 1964 to 1972 phase there were substantial increases in average charges per ton-mile all around. (See Table 9.) For the shorter hauls they were greater for the intra-Official than the intra-South movements. The latter region, except for coal, had greater gains in load per car. There were not the earlier phase's marked differences in magnitude of average ton-mile changes as between the shorter and longer hauls. Loads per car were increased less than earlier except for motor vehicle parts. The commodity with minimal gains in loading, assembled autos, had the highest percent increases. In general, all this suggests that adjustments to meet truck competition had been built into the rate structures in the earlier period and that differentiation between commodities as a result of relative gains in loading per car was largely eliminated. Overall, the rapid increase in factor costs, particularly the large labor cost increases after 1966, dominated the extent of cents per ton-mile increases.

TABLE 9

Changes in Average Ton-Mile Charges and Car Loadings for Five Major Revenue-Producing Commodities—Principal Intra- Interregional Movements,

1964–1972

	Local Hauls				Longer Hauls	
Bituminous Coal	**O-O** +31%[e] 66-81½t.	**S-S** +26%[e] 67-78t.	**S-O** +42% 63-71t.			
Lumber		**S-S** +19% 42½-54	**S-O** +14% 36½-48	**MTP-WTL** +32% 36-40t		**MTP-O** +30% 36-39½t.
Fiber-Paperboard	**O-O** +37%[e] 36-51½	**S-S** +22%[e] 41-51	**S-O** +26%[e] 45-51½		**MTP-MTP** +17% 42½-53½t.	**SW-O** +18% 38½-52
Passenger Cars, Assembled	**O-O** +37%[e] 22-23	**S-S** +21% 21-23½	**O-S** +38%[e] 23-22	**O-WTL** +31%[e] 23-23½		**O-MTP** +37% 23-24
Motor Vehicle Parts	+35% 21-24		+26% 21-24	+37% 24-25		+25% 23-25

(e = estimate taking in account significant increase or decrease in haul)

Overall, the diverse trends of these five commodities and the three previously reviewed ones indicate the railroads had significant flexibility in matching rates to the varying demand and supply factors, and relative competitive pressures. The ability to produce large rail productivity gains was especially influential. This flexibility involved the railroads' passing up of general rate increases and making, from time to time, of separate rate adjustments for particular commodities. Also, there was a regional difference in flexibility with southern roads resisting increases compared to other regions.

DIVISIONS

When more than one railroad was involved in hauling a shipment, freight revenue was allocated to each railroad according to what were called "divisions." The unit value of these was the part of a rate going to each railroad system for its part of the haul. Divisions have not been published as rates have been. Traditionally, they have been determined privately except that since 1920 when railroads could not agree on divisions the ICC has been asked to arbitrate their terms. Divisions have been, for one, set in terms of percentages applying to each railroad's segments of a joint haul, usually applying between so-called gateways or key points. Alternatively, they have been based on the application of distance prorating scales against which to measure each railroad's share. The scales could be uniform as between different segments or at quite different levels. Other bases have occasionally been applied. Sometimes before these bases have been applied, "arbitraries" involving bridge, special handling, or other factors involving individual railroads which have been subtracted from the revenue to be divided. Overall, the division patterns are more complicated than the rate structures themselves.

Before passage of the Transportation Act of 1920, divisions were entirely a matter of hard private bargaining. For instance, originating railroads tended to get more than their length of haul proportion, particularly if there were competitive possibilities of playing off one system against another for the share demanded by a following segment or segments of movement. When unable to agree, the last resort was for the road collecting the freight charges, usually the destination road, to pay the preceding carriers according to its contentions. Changes in 1920 put regulatory constraints on divisions mandating that they be "just and reasonable" and not unduly prefer or prejudice any participating carrier. When considering divisions the ICC had to consider "among other things" efficiency of carrier operations, revenue needs to cover costs, importance of services provided by the carriers involved, "whether any particular participating carrier is an originating, intermediate, or delivery line" and whether there was any other fact that "would ordinarily, without regard to the mileage haul," enter into determination of relative proportions.[77]

The first major consideration of divisions by the ICC came in response to a complaint of the New England railroads in 1921 to the effect that they were not getting a large enough share of joint rates in conjunction with hauls to and from the rest of the country and that this was the cause of their financial problems. From then on several regional groupings of railroads took their complaints about divisions to the ICC. In these cases, the role of the ICC was that of an arbitrator working out a compromise between contenders who could not agree among themselves, but the basis for compromise was different from that of purely private bargaining. Emphasized among points enumerated in the statutes were relative costs of service.

After the war, the deteriorating position of the eastern railroad systems relative to the prewar and predepression times led them to press for a greater share of the revenue on traffic carried jointly by them and southern or western systems. The earlier view had been that the southern roads' position had warranted the proportionately higher originating road share. The western roads too had received higher shares in proportion to length of haul than the eastern, reflecting the western roads' greater origination of traffic and their mountainous profiles with higher costs. More generally, the main eastern systems had been considered the wealthier with high-density traffic and heavy profitable coal traffic and without as great revenue "needs" as the others.

The adjustments of divisions in the 1950s and 1960s have been by way of both changing percentages allowed on either side of key gateways and restructuring the patterns of prorating by use of changed scales.

The history of several division patterns illustrates the developments during the period of this study. Before 1939, North-South interterritorial joint-rate divisions were in terms of specific amounts derived from the factors that had been used to calculate the rates themselves. In 1939, upon complaint by the northern roads that they were not receiving large enough shares, the ICC instituted an investigation and ordered that divisions for general traffic should be based on mileage prorating scales, with the southern one to be 25 percent higher than the northern. This was based on the ICC's conclusion that the southern costs were roughly that much higher than the northern. An exception was when the interterritorial rates, which were to be divided, were at the same level distance for distance as those in Official territory, then the prorating scales should be the same. It should be noted that there were special other privately settled bases for divisions applying to revenues from certain particular and important commodities such as lumber, citrus, and coal.[78]

At the end of World War II northern carriers again complained. After five-and-a-half years of proceedings, the ICC concluded that there were no longer regional differences in revenue needs and costs. In 1953 it prescribed that equal scales apply for northern and southern segments. It was estimated by a dissenting commissioner that this would increase the northern revenues by 22 to $25 million. They had wanted a still larger share and at their request the case was reopened in 1959. Six years later, after hearing further evidence and arguments, the ICC concluded that costs were then greater in the North and that a higher scale should apply for the northern divisions, 27 percent more for a 100-mile segment, 20 percent at 200 miles, gradually reaching equality at 500 miles. On appeal, the courts questioned the costs data analysis in the case and remained it back to the ICC in 1968. After minor adjustments in favor of the South, the final basis for divisions was prescribed in 1970.[79]

Western railroads had a similar history starting from the privately established divisions based on the level of first-class rates for the segments in the respective territories. After complaints by midwestern railroads the ICC in 1948 prescribed prorating scales, a common one for eastern and the eastern part of the Western Trunk-Line territory (roughly between Chicago and St. Louis to the Missouri River), and for the further western part a scale on average 20 percent higher. Upon further eastern complaint and upon recognition of continued decline in the fortunes of the eastern roads in 1962, the ICC prescribed the use of a common scale for all segments of traffic between the East and Western Trunk-Line territories.[80]

The most complicated and bitterly contested divisions were the so-called "transcontinental." These involved percentage allocations for segments either side of key

TABLE 10

Divisions of Numerous Transcontinental Rates

	New York- Chicago	Chicago- Pacific Coast	Chicago- Missouri River	Missouri River- Pacific Coast
Proportion of				
Average Mileage	30%	70%	15%	55%
1925 Divisions	27½	72½	12½	60½
1963 Divisions,				
ICC prescribed	34	66	13	53

(Source: 203 ICC 299 [1934]; 321 ICC 17 [1963]; 323 ICC 491 [1963]; 238 Fed. Supp. 528 [1965]; 381 U.S. 326 [1967].)

Midwest gateways with prorating scales for intermediate segments. Table 10 shows the generally applicable proportions between New York and the Pacific Coast, one of the many transcontinental routes that had to be provided for (lumber, citrus, and other items again were dealt with separately and individually).

The 1925 divisions were reviewed and in 1934 not found unlawful despite "most unsatisfactory evidence." Twenty years later the Official territory roads complained again to the ICC and after lengthy consideration the ICC in 1963 prescribed changes that would transfer $50 million from "transcontinental" lines to the others. The decision was rejected by a U.S. district court in 1965. Rather than start all over again, the "transcontinental" and eastern carriers reached agreement privately in 1966. Adjustment of intermediate midwestern roads' shares was settled later after ICC reconsideration and Supreme Court approval of the findings in 1967.[81]

The ICC role in divisions was as arbitrator between regional railroad groups, one or more of which were unwilling to accept the privately established allocation of revenues. This arbitration process was time consuming and costly, with long delay before final decision. In one critical case, the decision in the end was rejected in favor of a private settlement.

* * *

The postwar pricing of carload freight service evolved along two distinct lines. One was broad upward adjustment initially rapid in response to continually rising input prices. The other was the adoption of innovations in rate structures to meet increasing competition, shifts in raw materials and their sources, and new location of processing and distribution facilities, as well as to promote better carloading and larger shipment sizes to improve productivity. This involved greater use of commodity rates and a variety of downward adjustments until the mid-1960s.

As to the first, after government denial in the interest of price stability of requested rate increases during the war, the railroads got approval of a series of general major increases, scaled down by the ICC from the railroad proposals, in response to the inflation of input prices from the beginning of the war to 1950. Cumulatively, the rate increases were estimated to add some 60 percent to freight revenues if all were to be applied. In practice, however, the approved rates for many of the commodities were not increased by the full amount in response to competition and changing basic demands for transport service.

For some sixteen years following 1950, although input prices continued to rise, general increases were less frequent and of smaller amounts and there were independent downward adjustments. This was despite continued increased factor prices. Over the whole sixteen years, despite the initial upward trend, downward adjustments were enough so that the index of overall rates adjusted for change in commodity mix for 1966 was only 4 percent above its 1950 level.

With the sharp upturn in wage rates and benefits following organized labor's 1966 initiation of demands for substantially greater annual increases, the railroads turned to annual rate increases, which for the most part were put into effect in amounts they proposed. These general increases cumulative to 1972 were estimated to produce 35 percent more revenue and the index of average actual rates rose about the same amount.

Early postwar years saw the final crystallization of a country-wide structure of commodity classification and class rates. It was a monument to years of negotiation and pressure for uniformity that was to fall into disuse for commodities moving in significant volume. Commodity rates were to take over.

Thus the other line of change was by way of innovations in the pattern and terms of commodity rates. Most of these had been introduced before the war by a few pioneering roads. The most extensive changes were the replacement of single or double carload minimums traditionally associated with the rates for most commodities by pricing that provided a wider range of discounts graded in line with shipment size. For many commodities this resulted in increase loadings per car. This change was aimed at increasing productivity and creating rates the better to meet competitive mode rates. These changes were paralleled by acquisition of increased-capacity cars. This was of necessity a gradual process so that conflicts developed as to the application of the new incentive rates and the acceptable extent of the discounting process. Overall, from 1946 to 1972 the average loading for all commodities, except for products of mines, rose from thirty to forty-five and a half tons, 51 percent.

The second innovation was the trailer- (container) -on-flat car (TOFC) rate structure. After prewar experiments it became generally accepted and accompanied by new train services on key routes, in the East in 1954, and spreading throughout the country thereafter. One element of this structure was based on rates of the motor carriers. Another was an extention of the all-commodity rates designed for freight forwarders to use by shippers generally, thus by-passing the segments of the traditional structure of rates based on value, density, etc. Ultimately, a large number of TOFC plans with different rates and charges and service conditions were established with some based on estimated over-the-road truck costs. The vast volume of these new rates, which were filed with all this, resulted in less-than-usual critical review by rate associations and protests under regulatory procedures and provided a significant relief from prior restraints. By 1972 TOFC traffic had reached some 2 million trailers and containers terminated annually by the railroads of the country.

A third area of innovation was the introduction of multiple-car and train-load discount rates with "no frills" service providing important productivity gains. The rate reductions was initially aimed at water competition but extended to combat competing new raw commodity sources and to develop and hold flows of numerous commodities that moved between large-scale shippers and consignees. These innovations were frequently accompanied by restriction or elimination of ancillary service features such as blending, weighing, and free holding time of cars. There also were incentives for use of maximum available capacity cars. These changes to significant extent were initially made by smaller roads, which were in weak competitive positions or under financial pressure. When there were competitive other roads they often initially opposed the changes in the rate associations and before the ICC.

Overall, the changes in rates varied widely between commodities, length of hauls, and regions. A major differentiating factor between commodities was the extent to which carloading could be increased, the extreme case being from 1956 to 1963 for assembled automobiles with the use of multiple-level cars as opposed to the traditional equipped boxcars, improving loads from eight tons to twenty-five tons, over 200 percent and under competitive pressure, rates dropping more than any other commodity. From 1950 to 1963 among the major revenue-producing commodities, except assembled autos, unit revenue decreases occurred for the shorter-hauls with maximum truck competition and loading increases. For the longest hauls with less competition and least loading gains, there were significant unit charge increases.

For the period of universal rate increases, 1964 to 1972, the lack of the previous period's accomplishments by way of increased loading limited further productivity gains. The ton-mile revenue increases followed no overall pattern that could be related to loading changes or other-mode competition, but involved basic demand changes unique to each commodity's industry and market.

7

Less-than-Carload Freight—
Service and Pricing

Even more drastic changes than in the passenger services have occurred in respect to the less-than-carload (lcl) railroad freight operations. These involved the freight traffic of shipment sizes not big enough to qualify for carload loading with the rates and minimum that go with them. Less-than-carload traffic contrasts with the bulk commodity type, like coal, wheat, and sugar beets, or large configuration items like automobiles or steel ingots. For collection of data lcl is defined as shipments of under 10,000 pounds in weight. The rates under which lcl moves have largely been those based on the Official classification and the class rate scale but at levels on a higher percent of the first-class rates than that would be charged for the same commodity qualifying as a carload shipment. However, there have been especially tailored commodity rates provided for items moving in substantial and regular quantities.[1]

During the early 1920s more than 40 million tons of lcl freight were shipped and a half billion dollars of revenue collected annually. The volume as late as 1947 produced that magnitude of revenue.

Less-than-carload operations were markedly different and more complicated and labor intensive than the carload. For the latter, with very few exceptions, the railroad did not load and unload cars at terminals nor did it rehandle the freight en route from on car to another except in case of car failure. But with lcl traffic the railroad loaded most of the individual shipments into cars at the originating freight houses, rehandled them on the average of twice at intermediate ones, and finally unloaded them at destination stations. For manufacturers with sidings and lcl shipments in quantity, so-called "pool" cars were spotted at their plants to collect such shipments rather than have delivery by the shipper to the railroad freight house. After the early thirties "store-door" pick-up and delivery by truck of lcl shipments was also undertaken to compete with trucker comparable service. The expenses of all this were a substantial addition above the costs incurred for carload traffic.

Further, a carload of lcl shipments weighed much less than the average carload load so that line-haul costs of the former were substantially higher than the latter. The coming of the motor truck and improved highway and the resultant motor carrier provided a new means of handling the small shipment traffic. The possibility of direct movement from shipper's door to consignee's regardless of whether they had rail sidings or not was a natural advantage of operating over the highway and street networks. These carriers were built up rapidly by small entrepreneurs whose initiative was devoted to improved speed, cheaper handling, and quoting rail competitive rates with a view to garnering as much of the railroad lcl freight as possible.

FORWARDERS

The 1920s also saw the expansion of the domestic forwarding companies, which consolidated small shipments into carload ones and provided local truck door-to-door pick-up and delivery service. These companies paid for their expenses out of the differences between the carload freight rates they paid the railroads and the higher less-than-carload ones, which set the level of forwarder rates. Because they saw forwarders as keeping lcl on the rails, the railroads provided this new type of rate, the "all-commodity" or "all-freight" rates, these were in contrast to the usual classification of commodities into different rate groups and to the special commodity rate structures for most carload traffic. A main selling point of the forwarders was provision of more reliable and faster service than the railroad lcl service. As rather larger shippers on the railroads, forwarders had enough bargaining power along main routes to play one railroad against another to obtain good service, favorable terminal handling, and most advantageous "all-commodity" rates.

By 1929 the railroad lcl traffic of 36 million tons originated was one-third less than it had been at the beginning of the decade, despite a substantial increase in the amount of goods produced in the country during that interval. In 1932, trucks, motor-carrier and privately owned, probably were originating twice the amount of that type of traffic as the railroads. The forwarders were handling some 2 million tons.

LESS-THAN-CARLOAD FREIGHT TRAFFIC

The truck competition led the railroads in the early 1930s to add collection and delivery door-to-door in connection with their handling of lcl traffic, limited generally to shipments over 260 to 300 miles but occasionally regardless of length of haul. There were accelerated freight train schedules established to handle this traffic. The costs per car-mile were higher for this type of service than for the usual carload car handling because of the lighter train loads necessary for higher speeds.

Some railroad management had during the 1930s decided to take advantage themselves of the possibilities of forwarders as means of combating truck lcl competition and set up their own or bought into independent forwarding companies. Other managements viewed the use of intermediate organizations of this sort as syphoning off part of revenues and attempted to improve their lcl service costs by using containers as a means of consolidating small shipments into more economical and secure units for handling. This did not prove effective after years of use. In addition, railroads started to use trucks as a substitute for way-freight handling of lcl. There was some feeling that the railroad that provided its own lcl service would have a strengthened competitive position in respect to soliciting carload business. In sum, the thirties witnessed some serious railroad experimentation with various means to reduce its lcl costs and to keep the lcl business and even regain it from the truckers. There were gains from the low of 14 million lcl tons originated in 1935 to 17 million in 1937, but probably due to the general increase in economic activity. There was a downturn in the subsequent years and by 1940 the tonnage was back to its 1935 level, in contrast to the 28 percent gain shown in the five years for carload traffic.

The only overall measurement of the unit costs involved in lcl service was made for 1932 by the Federal Coordinator of Transportation. It was found that, taking just operating expenses and taxes, lcl revenue did not quite meet even the narrowest possible definition of association variable costs. These included estimates of lcl line-haul cost elements based on overall average car-mile costs. The comparative lcl to carload traffic utilization of cars was indicated by the revenue ton-miles per loaded car-mile, which for the lcl was 3.6 tons compared to that for the average carload, 27 tons. On a fully distributed basis (but not including capital costs), expenses plus taxes were shown to exceed revenue by 92 percent. For the year 1932, one-third of all freight cars loaded and 18 percent of the loaded car-miles were just for lcl services. Yet lcl revenue ton-miles amounted to only 3 percent of all ton-miles of freight. For 1939 another less thorough cost calculation indicated that lcl bare "out-of-pocket" costs exceeded revenues by something between 17 percent and 25 percent. In this year such provisions as were made for pick-up and delivery or allowance for its nonuse was shown to equal 19 percent of lcl revenues.[2]

A post-World War II, May 1947, sample analysis of country-wide lcl traffic and operations broken down between rate territories concluded that for shipments of under 300 pounds, revenues failed to cover "out-of-pocket" costs for all but the longer-haul movements between western and Official territories and between western and Southern. For shipments between 300 and 10,000 pounds, the average longer-haul movements within western and again between western and Official and Southern were the only ones to meet "out-of-pocket" costs. Overall, only for distances of over 1,000 miles did lcl shipments of any weight bracket have "out-of-pocket" costs significantly less than freight charges.[3]

By 1947, an early year of the period under consideration in this study, the railroads were originating 22 million tons of lcl compared to 36 million in 1929, down some 40 percent, a span of years over which carload tonnage increased 18 percent. By this time the motor-carrier less-than-truckload originated tonnage was of the order of 50 million. There was no estimate of privately carried small shipment tonnage. The forwarders were originating some 4 million tons, most of which then moved as carload freight on the railroads.

In the initial postwar years the railroads made further efforts to improve lcl service, in particular several named trains with fast schedules were added and widely advertised. However, it appeared by now to most managements that there were substantial and increasing losses being incurred with the lcl business. So far as rates for lcl service were concerned, the general run of rate-level increases was applied with some special increases for shipments under certain levels, for instance, under 2,000 pounds. An attempt to add a lump sum regardless of distance was suspended because the class rate increases were considered sufficient to cover increased costs and no analysis of terminal costs was presented that would justify such an increase. The pick-up and delivery costs mounted rapidly, taking as much as 20 percent of the increased rates, so that by 1950 there was a general move under all conditions to change for that service.[4]

With the increasing deficits incurred by lcl operations, despite rate increases the railroads undertook a variety of control measures. Where there were alternate routes for the traffic, movement over those of low density were canceled. Competing railroads pooled their services. Pick-up and delivery service was withdrawn at smaller stations. The lcl business was not actively solicited and finally the service was suspended by one railroad after the other. By the fall of 1967, only seven of the major carriers of the country were in the business and only two of them seriously trying to attract the traffic.[5] The possibility of this withdrawal rested in a large part in the ability and desire of the motor carriers to take over the lcl business as less-than-truckload (ltl) traffic. From 1950 to 1964 the railroad lcl traffic dropped from 11 to 2 million tons carried, the truck ltl increased from 53 to 73 million tons. Forwarder tonnage remained practically unchanged. By 1972 rail lcl traffic in the East and South had disappeared and the western volume amounted to only some ½ million tons. The forwarder traffic was still at the 4 million-ton level, and the Class I motor-carrier ltl, 85 million. Cooperative arrangements among shippers for consolidating small shipments into carloads accounted for 5 million tons. This was lcl traffic consolidated into carload traffic. Another category of so-called mixed shipments moving by rail at all-freight rates, which included items that earlier would have been lcl traffic, amounted to 15 million rail tons originated.

The shift out of the lcl business has meant a major redeployment of resources used by the railroad system of the United States. The analyses of the Federal Coordinator of Transportation for the early 1930s, after there had been substantial erosion of the lcl business, estimated that 24 percent of the overall railroad variable expenses, rents, and taxes could be related to lcl services.

This estimate of the lcl share cannot be interpreted as the magnitude of the expenses that might have been avoided if lcl had been completely given up at the time. The parallel estimate of 18 percent of total costs suggests that the avoidable proportion could not be less than a sixth and might be well over a fifth.

* * *

Because lcl operations tend to be labor intensive even with modern technology and because it is the labor component of railroad inputs that has risen most in unit price, the resources that might have had to be devoted to lcl'in 1972 had the service been restored probably would have been even higher in relation to those involved for the other services. Motor carriers, by competitively taking away the railroads' lcl business, have played an important part in improving railroad productivity in respect to both manpower and capital equipment. As a consequence, the ability of the railroads to maintain a viable balance of revenues and costs was significantly enhanced.

Railroad, LcL; Motor Carrier, LtL; Freight Forwarder; Air Freight and Forwarder

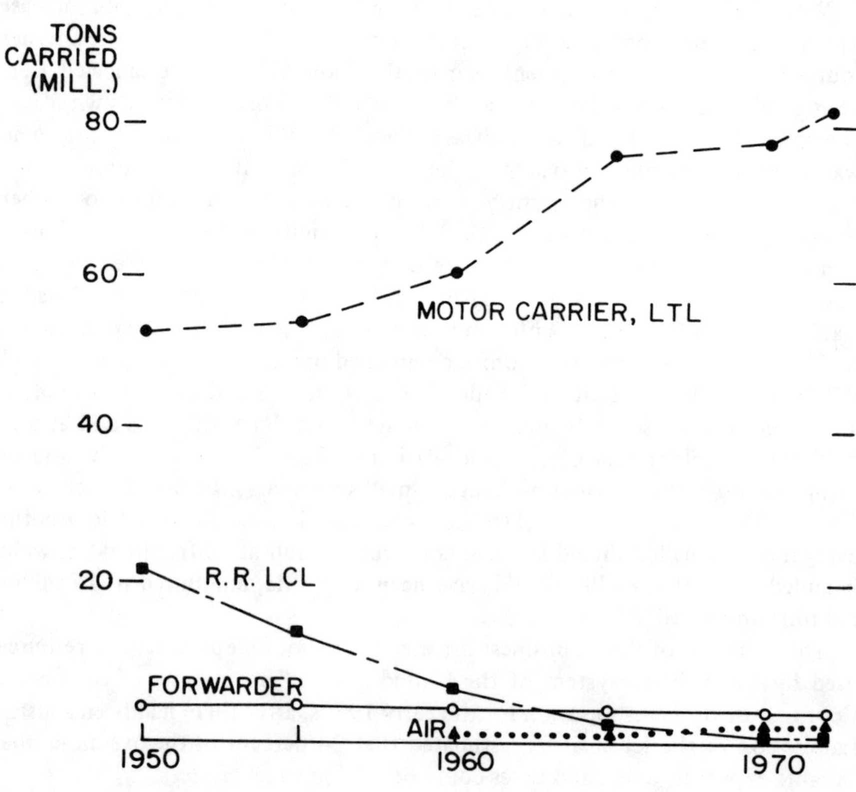

(Source: *TE*, Jan. 1973, p. 5; Vol. 1, #3, 1974, p. 11.)

8

Freight Operations

TRAIN AND SWITCHING OPERATIONS

The greatest opportunities for exploitation of technical innovation have been with respect to freight operations. The biggest single advance has been the development of diesel-electric motive power with its replacement of steam. Like innovations of all kinds, this was introduced experimentally by several pioneering railroads, initially as far back as the 1920s. After prewar refinement and proving its worth, followed by war interruption, the acquisition of diesels gradually filled the country's inventory of locomotives. By 1960 the diesel had totally taken the place of steam. The second major area of advance was for improved freight cars with increased capacity and critically valuable new designs, for instance, rack cars for motor vehicles and large covered hoppers for grains and other dry bulk items. These first appeared in the late 1950s after the diesel revolution was pretty well over. These were the basis for major items of capital expenditure for the U.S. by 1972, three times that for locomotives. Advances of lesser magnitude in yard facilities, in signaling, and in communication were developed and installed, resulting in improved operating productivity and quality. The theme then is of innovations and their contribution to the increase of productivity.

The production of railroad freight services involves two broad operating functions, the line-haul movement in trains and the switching of cars in the course of being assembled into or distributed out of trains and being placed for loading or unloading. The only complete U.S. railroad cost analysis undertaken showed that for the country as a whole costs of these two functions were of equal order in the mid 1930s.[1]

Line Haul[2]

The task of moving freight in line haul is, in practice, divided between two types of trains. One is the through freight, which moves maximum loads between major train assembly points; the other, the local or way-freight, which does the delivery and pick-up of cars where there are no switch crews and performs some line haul in the course of going between those points. Overall, during the period of this study, some 80 to 90 percent of gross ton-miles have been produced by the through trains.

Normally, through freight trains are operated in the direction of prevailing freight traffic at the maximum tonnage or car length possible reflecting locomotive capacity, type of cars and loads, siding lengths, grades, other track characteristics, as well as type of service. Occasionally, working-condition rules established in local union contracts have imposed added limits. In the reverse direction, when significant proportions of empty cars were likely to be carried, it was not usually possible to utilize full potential tonnage-hauling capacity. To some extent, railroad alignments have been laid out to minimize grades in the originally expected direction of prevailing traffic; grades in the reverse direction might then be such that the lighter trains with predominantly empty cars operate to full locomotive capacity too. The available data have not been separated by direction for recent years and thus only allow analysis in terms of the averages of heavy tonnages in one direction and lighter ones in the other.

The basis for through freight crew payments has been normally "miles run," the rates per mile varying with weight of locomotives or number of cars, both reflecting train-load.[3]

Local freight trains usually have runs of less than the 100-mile standard day basis so that their crew wages have been either the full, or 100-mile eight-hour, standard day's pay, or that plus overtime when runs took over eight hours. The unit rates of pay are somewhat higher than for through crews. The latter are defined as not making three or more stops en route to set out or pick up cars.

The output of line-haul freight train operations is measured in terms of hauled gross ton-miles (gtm), which include the weight of the cars and their contents. The application of more and more tractive effort and horsepower per train with diesels increased per train gtm. The gains from diesel were not only with the basic dieselization but also the subsequent introduction of increasingly powerful units. The mid-1940s ones were 1,350 H.P., and by 1950, 1,500 H.P. By 1960, 1,750-1,800 H.P. had come into general use and 2,000 and 2,400 H.P. were appearing. Finally, 3,000–3,600 H.P. units dominated new acquisitions. Diesels also provided gains resulting from greatly increased reliability of output enabling reduced elapsed scheduling times.

For heavy-grade territory these locomotives were equipped with regenerative braking over and above air brakes to allow greatly improved downgrade control of trains. More recently, crewless operation of diesel units in the middle of the train further increased possible train-loading without extra crew members. These motive-power advances were paralleled by improved car brakes, strengthened car couplers, draft gear and under-frames, and lengthened sidings, all of which were necessary to utilize the greater locomotive capabilities. In addition, there were improved operating practices taking advantage of all these advances.

For the span of years, 1948 to 1962 (the last year for separate Pocahontas data), during which full dieselization was accomplished, the southern roads showed the greatest increase rate of through freight train tonnage, 80 percent; the Pocahontas next, 63 percent; the western, 33 percent; and the eastern least, 16 percent.

Regional Averages of Combined Through and Local Freight Train Gross Loads by Type of Motive Power during Period of Dieselization

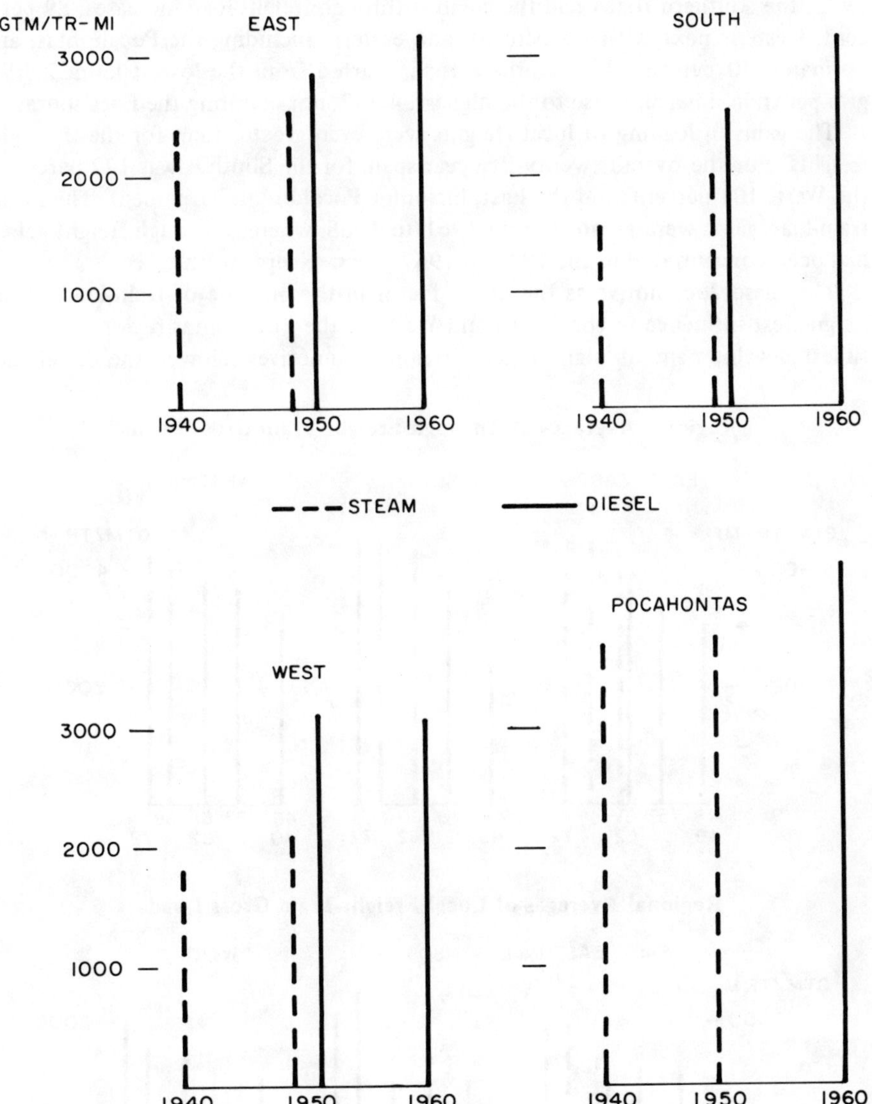

(Source: ICC, *SRUS,* 1940, Table 17; 1950, Table 18)

The Pocahontas roads with their heavy-loading predominantly coal movement at all times had the heaviest train-loading, with 4,354 gtm per through freight train-mile in 1947/48 and with 7,083 in 1961. For the overall twenty-five years to 1972, the southern roads had the greatest through freight load increases, 89 percent; western next with 47 percent, and eastern, including the Pocahontas, an estimated 30 percent. The southern roads started from the lowest level, 2,408 gtm per train-mile, and rose to the highest, 4,597, not counting the Pocahontas.

The gains in loading of local freights were even greater than for the through freights. For the overall twenty-five year span, for the South it was 122 percent; the West, 101 percent; and the East, including Pocahontas, 71 percent. The local train-load gains were greatest from 1961 to 1968, whereas through freight gains had been concentrated in the 1948 to 1957 years, except for the East.

The diesel locomotive as the major factor in the increase of train-loads, had its greatest influence in the South and West. In the Pocahontas region the prior fullest development of high-capacity steam locomotives allowed the diesel the

Regional Averages of Through Freight-Train Gross Loads

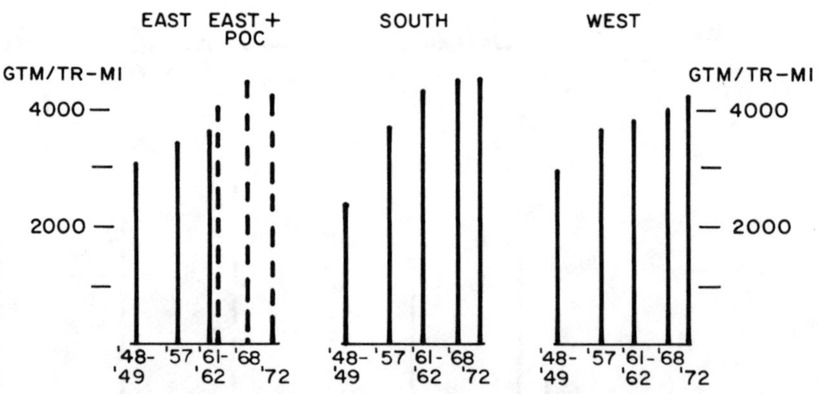

Regional Averages of Local Freight-Train Gross Loads

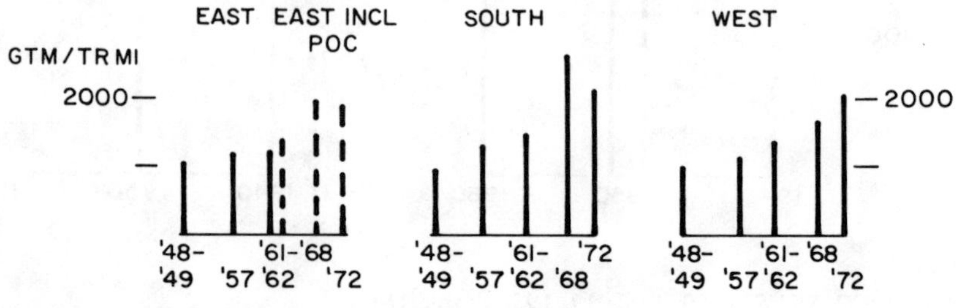

(Source: ICC, Bur. of Accts. #'s 1–50, 6–57, 3–62, 6–69; ISC-72.)

least possible gain, and the high carrier interest in coal traffic led to a substantial delay in going after the gain. For the East the diesel influence was intermediate between that in the first two regions and the Pocahontas. In the South other influences played a major role in the rate of increase. The South had started with the lowest steam train-loads, had the greatest proportionate possible gains, and by 1960 reached the highest diesel loads, the special Pocahontas ones excepted. The western roads had been the earliest to utilize the diesel and to develop its potential. They had widely used petroleum for fuel in steam locomotives, had petroleum resources in their region from Louisiana to California and to some extent in Montana, and with a few exceptions had least interest in coal as a source of energy.

Variability of Train Productivity with Traffic Changes

The control of freight train inputs with changes in traffic volume is an important aspect of performance. Gross ton miles (gtm) measure the volume of traffic

Changes in Gross Ton-Miles versus Changes in Adjusted Train-Miles
(Annual Changes of over 3 percent, 1950–1962)

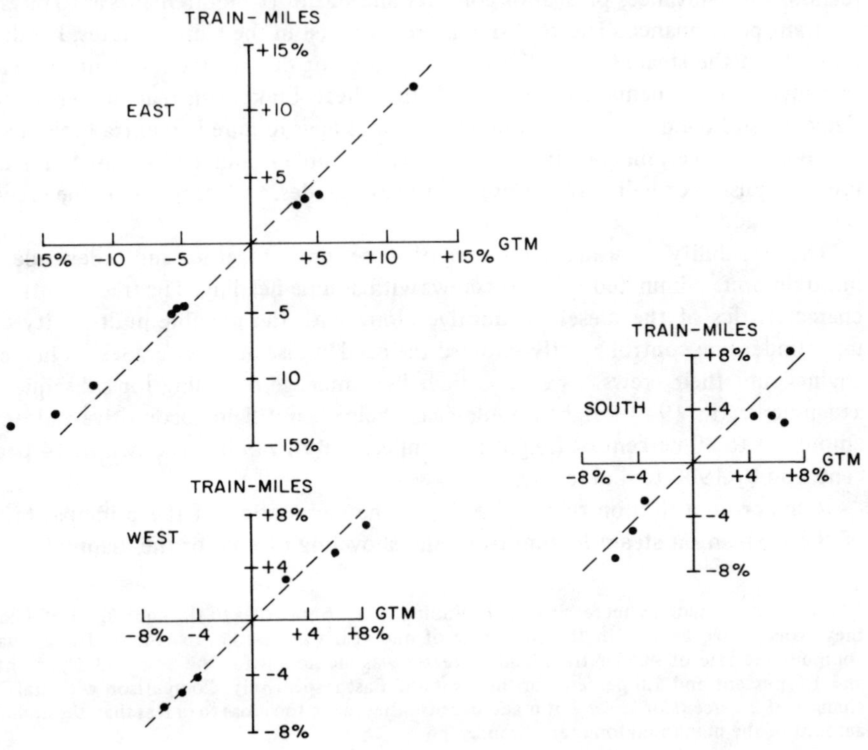

as it is presented to those responsible for its line haul, and train-miles are a basic measure of inputs. The train-miles were in part determined by the long-term trend of improvements in train-loading just discussed. Therefore, for this analysis, adjustment is made for long-run, secular increase in train-loading for each region.*

Only during the period 1950 to 1962 were increases intermixed with declines so that meaningful analysis of variability is limited to that period. The graphs on p. 216 show the degree of control in the major regions. On the downward side, the western roads uniformly cut train-miles closely in line with traffic declines. The southern on occasion went slightly further. The eastern, on the other hand, did not quite control train-miles sufficiently to match the more severe declines. In the case of upward movements, there was less consistency in response to changes in traffic. Half the time the southern roads kept train-mile increases well under those of traffic. The close correspondence of train-miles with traffic changes most of the time for the eastern and western roads indicated for the twelve years covered a near 100 percent variability in the short run of their line-haul direct costs.

Train Service Labor Productivity

Labor productivity in the operation of freight trains was dependent upon the technological advances plus labor contract and statutory requirements as to physical train performance. The traditional crew consist in the United States, handed down from the steam locomotive and hand braking days of the last century, was five men: an engineman, fireman or helper, head brakeman, rear brakeman or flagman, and conductor. In a number of states laws required an extra brakeman on trains over certain specified lengths. With double-heading of steam trains or use of a pusher or helper locomotive for heavy grades, two or more engine crews were also added.

The possibility of using a number of diesel units together and independent midtrain units eliminated the extra crews with double-heading. The tractive-effort characteristics of the diesel locomotive along with the possible multiplicity of units under one control greatly reduced the need in case of heavy grades for helper engines and their crews, as well as their light mileage returning for subsequent assignments. In 1940 freight double-head, helper, and light locomotive mileage amounted to 30 percent of freight train mileage. By 1949 it was down to 14 percent, and by 1960 to 4 percent.

A major contribution of the diesel was the elimination of the principal task of the fireman on steam locomotives, the shoveling of coal or the manipulating

---

*Adjustment is made by increasing the beginning year's train-miles to the equivalent of what they would have been with the advantage of one year's secular improvement. The annual compounded rate of secular train-load increases was maximum for the South, 3.2 percent, and 1.8 percent and 1.6 percent for the West and East respectively. Comparison with traffic changes of 2 percent or less is not made because they were too close to or less than the annual amount of the maximum long-term trend.

of mechanical stokers and otherwise tending to steam generation. In freight service there was a head brakeman on the locomotive available for lookout and other duties. After years of futile attempts to change the relevant labor contracts the railroads in the middle sixties effected arrangements to gradually reduce the firemen in freight service, firemen with over 5 years of service being retained until promoted to enginemen. Nineteen sixty-four was the first year for freight fireman hours and miles run to differ significantly from those of enginemen. By 1972 on trains whose crews were paid on the local train basis firemen were 42 percent of enginemen, and those on a through train, 51 percent.

The technological advances that have affected the work of train crews as distinct from engine crews have been the train radio and "walkie-talkie" sets for individual crew members, the improvement in car-bearing performance with reduction in setting out of cars for hotboxes, and the increasing signal instead of train order control of train movement. Changed operating practices have resulted in eliminating trainmen walking on the tops of cars. Longer trains, on the other hand, have made for longer walking distances on the ground. Attempts were made with some success in the middle sixties to eliminate one brakeman from crew consists, but labor negotiations in 1968 resulted in the reinstatement of a major proportion of those eliminated. The statutory constraints of state "full-crew" laws were a factor in maintenance of crew sizes despite these changed labor agreements. Total crew requirements per train unit in the end were reduced by about a sixth for local and a fifth for through trains.

Locomotive Utilization

Gains in utilization of road locomotives must be analyzed in terms of combined through and local train use, since the available data does not keep locomotive use separate as between the two services. From a utilization point of view, the possibility of extended locomotive runs on through trains offered the maximum possibilities while the short hauls of local trains with local switching work limited improvement.

The use of steam locomotives in freight service had involved the need for servicing and refueling after trips of 100 to 175 miles, generally between division points. Though improved designs of steam locomotives had lifted some of these limitations, their impact remained substantial. The diesel, on the other hand, only needed running inspection at division points and refueling after many hundreds of miles. In 1947 with steam locomotives still dominant in road freight service, locomotive average annual mileage ranged from 27,000 miles in the East to 34,000 in the West. Diesel mileage with its advantages attained averages ranging from 48,000 in the South, 77,000 in the East, to 100,000 in the West. The high mileages represented use predominantly in through freight service. By 1956 the diesel mileage had dropped to around 50,000 with their use extending to local freight trains.

In the postwar twenty-five years the average miles per unit owned and assigned to road freight service increased just over 100 percent in the South and at most to 220 percent in the West. In the East without the Pocahontas region the annual locomotive mileage increased somewhat over 100 percent from 1947 to 1965, and in combination with the Pocahontas the overall increase from 1947 to 1972 was around 90 percent.

An important complementary gain with dieselization was the elimination of the substantial water and coal facilities for steam-powered locomotives. The corresponding diesel fuel facilities were far simpler and less expensive to operate and maintain. Likewise, facilities for running inspection and servicing of diesel were substantially reduced.

Reduction of Freight Train Schedules[4]

From a starting point just after the war the railroads made a series of moves to speed up freight train schedules largely to compete with trucks. Merchandise trains and then their new TOFC trains were speeded up sharply. In parallel, the guaranteed service for perishables from the West and South to eastern markets was cut drastically, and service improvement for general freight movement followed. This progress covered all major routes but will be traced for a sample of key ones—Chicago-New York; the so-called "transcontinental" routes between the Pacific Coast and Chicago; and Florida-New York.

Less-than-carload merchandise and later TOFC movements were heaviest between Chicago and New York. They were offered by three single-line carriers, the NYC, P, and E, and several end-to-end joint combinations, they were highly competitive and tried to match the best times, though route-operating characteristics were different. The first phase in speedup was to provide overnight schedule for intermediate distances, New York-Buffalo, for instance. Train departures were established late enough to allow cars to be assembled from various parts of the originating metropolitan districts and morning deliveries to be made at destination. Route segments like the New York-Buffalo were where even with the immediate postwar state of the highways trucks were making overnight runs.

The next step was to provide second-morning merchandise service between New York and Chicago, with thirty-two-hour more or less elapsed time. For this route the general freight schedules were reduced by twenty-four hours by the mid-1950s to provide second-morning delivery. Newly introduced TOFC trains, with cars of special design standards, cut the time to twenty-nine hours. By the mid-sixties these shortest times were further reduced to twenty-four hours or slightly less, but only the most favorable routes could offer the fastest schedules. In the East, with hauls of 1,000 miles and less and consignor wanting end-of-day pick-up of loaded cars and consignee desiring to have morning delivery, schedule shortening basically had to be in twenty-four-hour units, which limited the amount of schedule cuts possible for the 1,000-mile-and-less hauls for traffic within the East.

Two southern systems and their northern connecting roads from Florida to New York had traditionally provided fourth-morning Florida perishable service. In 1947 and 1948 a day shorter schedules were offered for perishable shipments, which waived the usual diversion or reconsignment privileges, but the demand was not sufficient to warrant continuation of this expedited service. However, in 1952 the normal guaranteed perishable services were cut to third-morning. The southern roads were later than the eastern in starting general TOFC service and special TOFC trains. In the early 1960s second-morning TOFC service was initiated from Atlanta to New York and one-day-a-week TOFC perishable service from Florida fruit origins. The TOFC service between New York and Tampa was put on a thirty-two-hour service. By 1970, following the ACL-SAL, merger the time was slightly lengthened.

The so-called "transcontinental" service between the Pacific Coast and Chicago had taken around 130 elapsed hours for eastward perishables guaranteed schedules. By 1950 emphasis was given as well to merchandise service. During the 1950s several 24-hour cuts were made in schedules. In 1953 the ATSF experimentally offered a premium-rate service, minimum fifteen cars, with a 62-hour schedule between Los Angeles and Chicago. This was matched by a competitor. There was little demand and very few trains were run. Regular schedules were finally cut to a little over 60 hours to provide so-called fourth-morning service in both directions. Fifteen years after the initial trial, in early 1968, the ATSF and again competitors offered another premium-rate service, this time approximating the fastest of passenger train times, 40 elapsed hours. This was used by United Parcel Service, the U.S. Post Office, and by a variety of shippers who needed specially prompt service for parts used in a mass assembly line or needed for replacement of equipment breakdowns. In the twenty-five years Pacific Coast-Chicago perishable and TOFC merchandise service along all main routes was cut to a half, and a premium service to a third of immediate post-war elapsed times.

These service improvements were in part in response to truck competition and in part reflected rail system competition. They were possible because diesel locomotives provided more reliable performance and greater power with a single engine crew than steam locomotives. Freight car improvements by way of roller bearings, better draft gear, and mechanical refrigeration eliminated a large part of intermediate stops and servicing. Improved signaling allowed high speeds and less interference with continuous movement.

Switching[5]

The other transportation function performed in connection with freight service output is the switching of cars to and from the places where they are loaded or unloaded, between yards and interchange points, and in and out of trains that produce the line-haul service. Switching is performed by yard crews and local freight train crews, and to a minor extent as a secondary operation by through freight trains. A significant amount of switching is done by separate switching and terminal companies distinct from the line-haul railroads.

The only portrayal of different basic types of switching functions again was a 1932 sample study. For the U.S. as a whole it showed that 40 percent of switching hours was for the classification of cars, that is, assembling cars into trains and distributing them from trains. Twenty-eight percent was for handling of cars to and from team and freight house tracks and private sidings where they were placed for loading or unloading. Twenty-six percent was for transfer from one yard to another and only 6 percent for interchange between railroads.[6]

The continuously available data for analysis are in terms of the overall switching function for which the measure of output is the number of cars, revenue and nonrevenue (company supplies), loaded in the country as a whole. The simple per-car unit is a valid measure because the time and effort involved is only slightly affected by the weight of a car and its contents within the range of weights and capacities general during the period of this study. The available physical measure of inputs is yard-engine plus train switching hours. The recording of the latter excludes switching stints involving less than thirty minutes. The yard inputs include those of switching and terminal companies as well as the line-haul roads.

Factors Affecting Switching Productivity

The gross measure used for switching productivity for the country as a whole is U.S. revenue and nonrevenue carloadings per switching hour. The movement of cars from and to Canada and Mexico was sufficiently minor and stable a proportion so as not to affect trends significantly. Consideration of switching productivity is complicated by the need to take into account the effects of the gross changes in mix of traffic. Nonrevenue traffic, largely the hauling of company material, particularly coal for steam locomotives in the earlier years, dropped by a half. Nonrevenue traffic accounted for 3.5 million carloads in 1947, and only 1.8 in 1972. Even more important was the essential disappearance of lcl service, which declined from 6 million revenue carloadings, 14 percent of total in 1947, to a negligible amount by 1969.

Other factors that might affect switching are the lengthening of car trips, reduction due to unifications in number of systems handling each car in interchange between them, and the increasing proportion of empty miles associated with loaded movements. The average "short-line" haul (measured by minimum direct-route distance between origin and destination points) increased from 432 miles in 1950 to 460 miles in 1966 to 512 miles in 1972. Longer hauls might be expected to require more switching. However, there is no evidence that there is a greater amount of car sorting to fit cars into their origin-destination routines with the longer hauls than shorter. There have been changes in operating practices over the years by way of pooling of cabooses, through blocking of cars and running

TABLE 11

Cars Loaded vs. Train and Yard Switch Engine Hours

	Revenue plus Nonrevenue Carloadings (Million)	Revenue lcl car Carloadings (Million)	Revenue cl car Carloadings (Million)	Switch Engine Hours per a Composite Carloading
1947	48.0	6.1	38.4	1.6
1953	41.0	3.5	34.8	1.6
1957	37.5	2.8	32.8	1.6
1966	31.8	0.4	29.3	1.5
1971	27.2	neg.	25.2	1.6

(1972 not shown because switch hours for swt. and terminal cos. were not published; composite carloadings-revenue cl cars + $\frac{1}{2}$ [lcl and nonrevenue cars]; yard swt. hours = swt. loco-miles $\div$ 6.)

of trains without switching at intermediate terminals, all of which would have reduced requirements. Mergers might be expected to decrease intercarrier interchanges, but the average number of roads involved in handling a carload revenue car has only decreased from 2.0 in 1950 to 1.9 in 1972.

The declines in lcl and nonrevenue carloadings can be taken into consideration. The switching required for lcl cars was less than for cl revenue cars. The concentration of lcl cars at centrally located freight houses and sorting facilities required less than the handling of cl cars to widely scattered and decentralized industrial sidings. Further, lcl cars when unloaded generally would be used immediately for outbound shipments with a minimum of problems as to car condition and needs for relocation. An estimate of one-half the switching required for lcl cars compared to carload revenue cars offers a basis for adjustment in calculations. Nonrevenue cars have some of these latter characteristics that would suggest less switching. Table 11 shows surprisingly stable inputs for the adjusted carloadings figure. The statistics point to a lack of improvement over the years in the switching performance of the U.S. railroads as a whole.

U.S. Switching Productivity

Regional comparisons in switching productivity are difficult to deal with because the proportions of movements local as opposed to just originating or terminating vary between regions. However, in the three major regions in recent years, originated carloads handled locally have been a substantial proportion of all carload loadings and not too different as between the regions. In 1972 local carloads were 76 percent for the southern region; for Official (approximately

East plus Pocahontas), 82 percent; and for the western, 85 percent. Data for ascertaining these proportions are only available in the waybill samples broken down by rate association territories, which can be grouped so as to approximate the major geographic regions. These data cover just revenue carload loadings, not lcl or nonrevenue ones. For recent years the lack of lcl data is not of consequence because those loadings are negligible, and the lack of nonrevenue loadings is minor with their decline to only 7 percent of the total.

In 1971, the last year for which complete switching hours including switching and terminal companies were compiled, the originated plus terminated cars per switching hour were 1.0 for the Official territory, 1.1 for the overall western, and 1.7 for the southern. In these terms, the southern productivity appears sig-

Changes in Carloadings versus Changes in Switching Hours (Annual Changes of over 2 percent, 1950–1969)

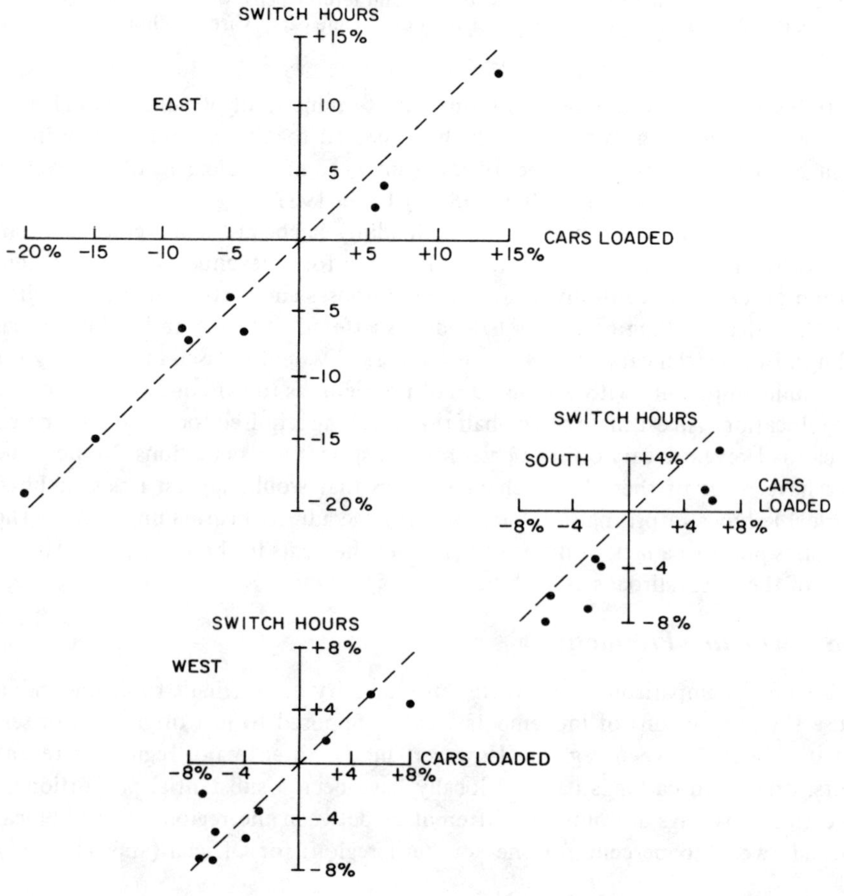

nificantly higher than that of the other two regions. The southern superiority is so great as to suggest that it reflects more than just possible favorable traffic and network characteristics.

The control of switching inputs with changes in carloadings was not as consistent as that of train inputs relative to gtm changes. Nevertheless, the basic performance as shown in the graphs on page 226 indicates the ability to vary inputs at least generally in line with output changes. There was no country-wide secular trend for which to adjust as with train inputs. For the South increases in cars handled tended to be followed by less than proportionate switching input increases, and decreases in cars by more than proportionate input decreases. This points to a downward trend for that region.

Modernization in Switching Facilities

The lack of improvement in switching productivity was not for want of technological advances and investment in improvements. There were both the visually spectacular large-scale projects of new automated classification yards and the incremental small-scale improvements in communication, car-checking and testing devices, automatic weighing, and the like. The diesel switch engine was an innovation important from the point of view of fuel and maintenance savings and improved utilization of investment but not in respect to switching productivity itself. The innovations in connection with large hump yards back in the 1920s had started with mechanized braking of cars by retarders and power operated switches and the consequent replacement of brakemen and switch tenders. This was accompanied by the early communication improvements such as teletypewriters and pneumatic tube handling of waybills, and later radios on engines, walkie-talkies for personnel, and by 1972 automatic identification of cars. These improved yards represented capital-intensive investments economically justified where traffic was dense, so their application was confined initially to eastern railroads and the eastern border terminals with western and southern railroads. In the immediate postwar years for the first time retarder yards were built west of the Mississippi River.

Nineteen fifty-two saw the installation of the first of another generation of yard innovations by way of automated functions, involving improved retarders, switches, scales, journal-box oiling, and so on. These labor-saving innovations together with rapidly rising wage rates led to widespread construction of new yards and upgrading of the strategically placed older ones. In the six years from 1953 through 1958 from $80 million to $100 million was spent in each of the three main regions on the new yards, the southern railroads spending the most. Setting this off against the cars originated plus terminated in each region in 1954— 22 million in the East, 10 million in the South, and 22 million in the West— emphasizes a much higher investment per car in the South. After the 1950s this surge of investment in large yards continuing to be built was at a much slower pace in all three regions.[7]

Labor Productivity

The available data for man-hours is for Class I line-haul and terminal railroads, freight and passenger switching combined. Since freight was the major element, 93 percent in 1940 and 1950, increasing to 97½ percent by 1969, the data are representative of freight-switching manpower. A measure of labor input in yard service is man-hours of crews associated with switch engine hours.

Not all men are directly tied to a switch engine as, for instance, some of the brakemen who, in the earlier years, rode and braked cars as they rolled off a hump in a classification yard and did not accompany engines. These brakemen are nevertheless an element in the total switching process.

Beginning with the prewar period an average of 5.1 crew man-hours per engine hour increased to 5.4 by 1950. There was essentially no change in the next thirteen years. There was a one-to-one ratio, firemen to enginemen. This was not reduced until after 1964 with the final agreement for reduction in firemen on diesels. It had become 0.3 to 1.0 by 1972, a decline of some 67 percent. The ratio of brakemen to conductors had been some 2.4 and declined to 1.9 by 1972. The greatest impact of investment in advanced facilities was in respect to switchmen, a group somewhat independent of engine hours and a relatively small category. There was a greater decline in their ranks relative to the rest from 1940 to 1969, with a near 80 percent decline in hours. The hours for enginemen and conductors remained level to as late as 1969. The diesel locomotive and other improvements resulted in no more than a 16 percent gain in the postwar years.

The hours of supervisory staff, yard masters and assistants, relative to switch crew hours, have remained relatively constant throughout. There were fourteen crew man-hours per supervisory hour in 1950, the first of the years in which the pertinent data are available. It was fourteen in the 1960s and fourteen and a half in 1972. Automation and improved communication and information systems offered no gain in supervisory productivity.

Switching Locomotive Utilization

Utilization of yard engines for switching service can be measured by locomotive hours per day per locomotives available. Statistics available with respect to assignment do not distinguish between use in passenger and freight operations, so the indices of hours per day reflect performance in both categories. The low passenger proportion makes the utilization reflect primarily freight. Dieselization was the principal factor in improving engine utilization because the diesel units required less servicing than steam locomotives and could work nearly continuously. In 1947, when steam locomotives were still dominant, their hours per day for the major districts ranged from eight and a half to eleven and a half compared to the diesel's eighteen to nineteen hours. At this stage in the introduction of the diesels, because of their substantially higher capital cost than the steam, they were assigned to those jobs giving maximum hours per day. Later, as the last of the steam locomotives were being displaced by diesels, the latter's assignments were taking on the less intensive jobs and the average diesel utilization declined.

Optimum utilization of units owned came with the highest levels of traffic since the size of the yard engine fleet could not be adjusted in the short run to changes in traffic levels. Utilization trends for years with highest volumes of traffic showed the greatest gains for the South, from ten-and-a-half hours per day in 1947 to nineteen in 1970. The East showed scarcely any change from a near thirteen-hour level, and the West increased from thirteen to fifteen hours.

FREIGHT CAR PROVISION AND USE[8]

In the postwar years the provision and use of freight cars has become a vastly more important part of the railroad business than ever before. From 1946 through 1972 for the U.S. as a whole the investment in freight cars has more than trebled, almost twice the increase in that for locomotives and more than that for all the rest of the facilities. Thus, from the point of view of capital investment productivity, the trends in provision and utilization of the freight cars have taken on greatly increased significance in the overall performance of the railroads.

Carloadings and Car Productivity

Increases in loads per car both directly affect car productivity and compound the train and switching productivity just reviewed. The latter is based on the fact that inputs for train and particularly switching operations do not rise proportionately with increases in load per car. The loads depend on both basic car capacity and on the actual use made of it.

Car Capacities

The postwar period witnessed substantially increased capacities with newly added cars both in respect to weight and cubic dimensions. Ton capacity has been significant for dense loading commodities, on the one hand bulk loading ones like coal, cement, and grain, and on the other, particularly concentrated items like metal ingots and coils of strip metal. Cubic capacity has been significant for the less dense mostly finished products like automobiles, furniture, and some basic materials like wood chips, foam rubber, and insulation. The first year of large-scale orders after World War II when specifications were free of wartime limitations was 1950. In that plus the following year 241,000 freight cars were ordered, more than one-eighth of the total inventory of cars. The designs were essentially those of the immediate prewar period. For instance, boxcars were fifty-ton nominal capacity; forty-foot long, open hoppers, fifty-five- and seventy-ton; and most refrigerator cars were forty-ton, thirty-three to thirty-six feet long. The largest tank cars were of 11,000 gallons' capacity. There were a few slightly larger ones in all classes. A few automobile boxcars of fifty-ton capacity, fifty-one feet long, were evidence of pushing toward new capacity levels.

Within the next five years there was a limited increase in sizes. There were more fifty-foot boxcars, but the hopper car capacity remained seventy tons. This was also the period of introducing mechanical as opposed to iced refrigerator cars. Again there were a few larger models ordered.

In the years just before and after 1960 there were some major design break-throughs and the beginning of a new generation of freight cars, eighty-five-foot flat cars for TOFC service to carry two highway trailers rather than one, open rack cars for automobiles and covered hopper cars of high capacity for dry bulk cargos like grain were all introduced. Improved types of shock-absorbing draft gear were applied to better protect fragile items. Roller bearings had become standard. Boxcars of eighty-five-foot length were tested. Increased capacities for all types of cars were the order of the day, 70-ton refrigerator cars, 100-ton hopper cars, covered and open. Removal of the requirement for side running boards on tank cars enable the increase to 30,000-gallon capacity.[9]

All aspects of the structure of freight cars were being reexamined, in particular the need for larger diameter wheels for the heavier loads. In 1961, reflecting improved strength and quality of car components, a 5 percent increase in the allowable loads for existing cars was authorized. Both car manufacturers and railroads were increasingly involved in standardized designs to be ordered by more than one railroad in order to temper rising costs. Further incentives to private car owners to increase capacities were provided by changing from a flat mileage hire rate paid by the railroads regardless of car size to rates based on car size, so 100-ton capacity cars ultimately became economically attractive. In turn, refrigerator capacities were increased with adoption of mechanical refrigeration and the build-up of frozen foods traffic. Seventy-ton capacity cars came into use first in 1956 and by the 1960s became standard. By the 1970s, 92 tons was reached. Underlying all this had been the general strengthening of track structures and bridges and enlarged clearances that had been gradually made by the railroads since the war. In addition, the loading and unloading facilities of shippers had been modified with wider spacing of loading dock doors, larger loading shutes and receiving hoppers, and the like.

The overall results for railroad cars of the acquisition of the large-capacity new ones, the rebuilding and upgrading of some of those in the inventory, and the retirement of large numbers of older low-capacity cars is shown in Table 12.

TABLE 12

*Average Capacity of the Major Types
of Cars in Service, Year End*

	Boxcar	Gondola and Hopper	Gondola	Open Hopper	Covered Hopper	Flat
1947	47t.	57t.	na.	na.	na.	49½t.
1960 vs. 1947	+5½%	+ 8½%				+12%
1960	49t.	62	62t.	60½t.	69t.	55½t.
1972 vs. 1960	+22%		+19%	+25%	+25%	23%
1972	60t.		74t.	76t.	89t.	68t.

(Source: ICC, *SRUS,* Table 26;
      ———, *TSUS,* Table 26.)

Capacity Utilization

Given the increased capacities of cars, the loadings actually practiced involve still other variables. Maximizing utilization of capacity (except for bulk commodities, which are loaded to visible cubic capacity or load limit tons) increases the expense to the shipper of loading and unloading of cars and the chance of damage to the contents. Also, other things being equal, there may be significant gains to consignees with small-scale operations from shipping minimum quantities so as to even the flow of goods and minimize inventories. The "floor" under loading is the tariff minimum weight of commodity for application of carload rates; with loadings below that the effective charge per pound of shipment rises. The traditional minimums had often been more related to commercial practices than to maximums that capacities would actually permit. The emphasis after the war on a broad range of "incentive" rates provided an important force for better utilization. Increases in loading that have come about are thus a result of both increased car capacities and incentives for shippers to better use those capacities.[10]

Some examples of loading improvement showing the wide range in the better utilization are given in Table 13.

The gains for passenger automobiles, fresh vegetables, and corn have come with new types of cars, auto rack, mechanical refrigerator, and covered grain hopper. The maximum increase in capacities and utilization of traditional car types is reflected in the coal, rock, and sand figures. The limitations on increase because of the physical nature of commodities, which limit load densities and dimensions, and practices entrenched in the commercial patterns of an industry are evident in the case of tires, citrus, and furniture.

TABLE 13

*Average Tons per Car, Carload Cars
Originating, for Selected Commodities*

Class I RR-US

Commodity	1947	1972		Commodity	1947	1972	
Passenger Autos	6.8t.	22.6t.	+232%	Sand & Gravel	58t.	75t.	+30%
Fresh Vegetables	13	23½	+80	Iron, Steel scrap	41	55½	+30
Paper-, Fiber-							
board, Pulp	26	49½	+88	Vehicle Parts	19	24	+28
Corn	50	81½	+62	Citrus	22½	23½	+4
Bituminous							
Coal, Lignite	57	80½	+40	Tires	17	19	+11
Phosphate Rock	53	80	+51	Furniture	9	8½	–7

(Source: ICC, *Freight Commodity Statistics,* 1947, 1972, [by calculation].)

For the country as a whole from 1947 to 1972, taking all the changes into account including the shifts in commodity mix, the average revenue tons per carload car originated has increased from forty-one to fifty-six tons, 38 percent. Because of regional variations in commodity mixes there have been significant regional differences as shown in Table 14.

TABLE 14

Average Tons per Carload Car Originated and Carried by Region

Class I RR

	East, incl. NW, CO & RFP	East, excl. NW, CO, RFP & merged rds.*	Pocahontas, NW, CO, RFP plus merged rds.*	South	West
		Originated			
1947	43½t.	na.	na.	39t.	38½t.
	+25%			+52%	+45%
1972	54½t.	na.	na.	59t.	56t.
		Carried			
1947	41t.	40t.	44½t.	36t.	36t.
	+29%	+29%	+29%	+51%	+43%
1972	53t.	52t.	57½t.	55t.	51½t.

(Source: ICC, *Freight Commodity Statistics,* 1947, 1972;
Moody's *Transp. Man.,* 1948, 1973; [by calculation].)

*The NYCStL, W, PM, WLE, & PWV, which were included in the eastern district in 1947 and within the CO & NW in 1972.

Both with respect to cars originated and carried, the southern region roads showed the maximum gains, as well as the highest final level, the Pocahontas roads excepted, in 1972. The western roads' levels were somewhat lower in both respects. Finally, the eastern and Pocahontas were substantially below in percent improvement. The Pocahontas roads had the highest average loadings because of their preponderance of coal traffic.

Table 15 shows that for the eastern systems the decline in their coal traffic was a key major negative factor against improved overall loading per car. In contrast, the southern roads had a large increase in coal traffic. For the western there was some increase, and the tons per car reached the highest level for any major commodity.

The eastern roads also lost around half of their originating tonnage for each of four other of their heavy loading commodities—cement (73 tons per car), crushed rock (70 tons), fluxing stone (82 tons), and wheat (85½ tons). The southern and western systems, on the other hand, showed gains for all four.

The numerous increases in tons loaded per car have provided important gains in net switching productivity despite the little or no gains in productivity per se as measured in terms of cars handled. Since the larger cars and loads have been

TABLE 15

Coal Originating Tons by Regions

(Millions)

	East, excl. NW, CO, RFP & merged roads*	Pocahontas, plus merged roads		South	West
	Anthracite	**Bituminous & Lignite**			
1947	49t.	175t.	148t.	72t.	51t.
	−95%	−47%	−17%	+43%	+10%
1972	2½t.	92t.	120t.	103t.	56t.

Aver. Tons/Car Orig.

	East + Poc.	South	West
1972	79	81	85

(Source: ICC, *Freight Commodity Statistics*, 1947, 1972; *Moody's Transp. Man.* 1948, 1973; by calculation.)

*The NYCStL, W, PM, WLE, & PWV.

handled with little extra input per car the gains have been as much as 25 to 30 percent for the eastern and Pocohontas roads, and close to 50 percent for the southern and over 40 percent for the western.

The load-per-car increases have also added to the direct gains in line-haul freight car productivity. The effects of heavier carload loading, the elimination of lcl traffic, and changes in nonrevenue loading is measured by the increases in net ton-miles per loaded car-mile. Table 16 shows the gains are slightly greater than those just reviewed for loadings per carload car.

The effect of near elimination of lcl movement and of heavier carload carloadings on line-haul productivity involves possible changes in empty to loaded car-mile ratios and decreases in tare weight of cars relative to weight of loads. The elimination of lcl loaded cars removes the movement of boxcars that were very lightly loaded and therefore with a high proportion of tare weight to tons loaded. But those boxcars were ones with which the minimum of empty hauling is associated. For carload traffic, increase in tonnage capacity of cars tends to decrease tare weight per ton of load. However, much of the use of such cars is for movements with higher than usual empty return mileages.

As far as measuring these factors the only data are net ton-miles (ntm) of loads and the gross ton-miles (gtm) of freight cars, which are the sum of tare and load weights. These reflect the combination of all the factors just reviewed as they may affect line-haul productivity. The ratio of the ntm to gtm indicates the net productivity of the gtm since it reflects the proportion going to hauling freight and as opposed to that hauling tare weight along with the load or just in empty movement. Table 17 shows that in 1947 the Pocahontas roads had the most favorable ratio, the eastern next, and the western substantially worse than the others. Over the period reviewed the eastern roads lost most ground, the Pocahontas nearly as much, while the southern and western held their own. The twenty-five

TABLE 16

Net Ton-Miles, Revenue and Nonrevenue per Loaded Car-Mile by Regions

	East, excl. NW, CO RFP & merged roads*	Pocahontas, plus merged roads*	South	West
1947	34t.	41t.	31½t.	30t.
	+30%	+32%	+55%	+48%
1972	44½t.	54t.	49t.	44½t.

(Source: ICC, *SRUS*, Tables 158, A-1;
     ———, *TSUS*, Tables [by calculation] 159, A-1 [by calculation].)

*The NYCStL, W, PM, WLE & PWV.

TABLE 17

Net Ton-Miles Percent of Gross Ton-Miles by Regions
Class I RR

	East, excl. NW, CO, RFP & merged roads*	Pocahontas, plus merged roads*	South	West
1947	49%	53%	47½%	44½%
1972	45%	50%	47½%	44½%

(Source: ICC, *SRUS*, Tables 158, A-1;
      ———, *TSUS*, Tables 162, A-1 [by calculation].)

year effect of the factors just enumerated reduced line-haul train productivity in the East and Pocahontas regions, while there was no change for the South or West.

Freight Car Utilization

With freight cars always being a major item of investment for the railroads and becoming the critical one in the late 1960s, car utilization has always been a highly controversial matter with very combative positions taken by most all of the many interests involved. With the responsibility for provision of the cars divided among the numerous railroad systems, their car-line subsidiaries, and certain shippers, there are numerous opportunities for differences as to the control of the common use of cars. With the failure from time to time to meet shipper needs for cars, there are strong and numerous incentives for controversy as to responsibilities and remedies. Overall these have provided continuous and prime grist for politicians. The lengthy congressional hearings on car shortages go back to the turn of the century.[11]

Basic Problems Inherent in Demands for Cars

The most critical problem of car supply and utilization grows out of peak demands, and extreme example of which is created by crop harvesting concentration in a few weeks of the year. Another type grows out of what might be called cyclical variations in demands, for example in automobile manufacture, from peak months to depressed ones. Recently, the peaks created by large orders for export grain from inland storage have created even more serious problems because of their unpredictable random nature.

*NYCStL, W, PM, WLE & PWV.

Unbalanced Commerce

Another fundamental underlying factor in car utilization is the geographically oriented flow of the commerce of the United States. Perishables are produced in the warmer southern and southwestern parts of the country, and refrigerated rail transport carries them to the populous northern and eastern parts. There are few or no balancing flows of commodities suitable to fill returning refrigerator cars. Coal comes from the middle Appalachian region and moves to industry and utilities located to the East, West, and South with nothing going back to the mines in hopper cars. Increasing use of specialized cars for more and more items leads to still further movements with empty return hauls. Bi-level and tri-level automobile rack cars seldom find loads to carry back to assembly plants. Wheat, which used to move in boxcars, which were usable by a wide variety of commodities, now moves in covered hopper cars from grain-producing plains states to Gulf and eastern ports with limited return traffic. Overall directional imbalance has been least for commodities making up boxcar traffic. On the other hand, it has been the greatest in the East with east and northward loaded refrigerator car movement four times that in the reverse directions, and with loaded open hopper cars five times.

A quite different problem for car utilization comes with the addition of improved new cars to the country's inventory. For instance, new boxcars have been provided with wider doors to meet the needs of mechanical loading and unitized packaging of shipments and with new devices developed to protect against switching and train shocks. Incentive rates based on heavier loading leads to preference for the new increased-capacity cars. All this makes the new cars preferred and ordered by many shippers as opposed to older design ones. Yet the whole inventory cannot be brought up to the new standards every year, so the older equipment must continue to serve and be placed in response to shipper requests even though it is not what might be wanted. However, in this case tariff provisions provide some protection to shippers and thus insure use of older cars if the highest-capacity ones cannot be supplied.

Suitability of Car Condition

Still another factor in utilization is the conditioning of cars to be acceptable for certain types of use. In connection with the hauling of bulk agricultural commodities and food stuffs, grains, for instance, the highest standards of waterproofing and interior surface cleanliness are necessary so as not to damage or contaminate the loads. The previous load may have left odors or damage so that car time and labor effort must be spent in inspection and if necessary in cleaning and repairing. One of the most troublesome related details is the failure of consignees to clear cars of all debris and dunnage in the course of unloading. This requires the switching of an empty car of the type ordered is on hand does not necessarily mean it can be used immediately to fulfill the order.

Responsibility for Supply of Cars

The supply of the vast majority of freight cars has been dependent upon individual railroad system acquisitions by purchase or by long-term leasing. These cars make up the main pool of cars available for common use throughout the country. When rail systems use cars not of their own inventory, called "foreign" cars, they have paid rent on a "per diem" basis. Certain types of cars have been provided in other ways. Refrigerator cars have largely been supplied by railroad controlled car-line companies, and the rental has been in the form of mileage payments. Tank cars and other special types that have been supplied by privately owned car lines have also been reimbursed on a mileage basis. To a more limited extent, shippers have supplied their own specialized cars, again with mileage charges.

The supply of cars by an individual system has traditionally been based primarily on its need to provide cars for shippers located on its own lines. An originating system has the incentive to do this because otherwise when cars are in short supply there could be a direct and immediate loss of revenue to a transport competitor or indirectly due to the shipper's loss of a sale. Thus systems serving coal-mining regions have provided hopper cars; those in grain-growing regions, grain-carrying cars; and those serving automobile assembly plants, special auto-parts- and auto-carrying cars. Sometimes it is possible for a railroad to use cars made empty from traffic destined to it if the type of car is compatible with its own originating traffic. Arguments have arisen as to the extent of the obligation to acquire cars if the use of others' cars is possible. Guidelines as to the kind and number of cars the various systems should own have been promulgated, but compliance has been voluntary.

The Car Supply

The total supply of cars at the beginning of 1947 was made up of 1¾ million freight-carrying cars in the fleets of the United States railroads, together with around 110,000 owned by refrigerator car lines and some 150,000 otherwise privately owned and used. By the end of 1972 the numbers were 1.4 million, 35,000 and 270,000. While the number of cars in the railroad fleets decreased 17 percent in number, their total nominal load capacity increased roughly 7½ percent due to the addition of increased capacity cars. Data as to total capacity of nonrailroad cars are not available, but the increase was substantial. In somewhat different terms, a measure of the cars available to the U.S. railroads is the average cars "on line," which includes Canadian and Mexican cars in addition to most but not all the aforementioned U.S. cars. This excludes cars in use for long-term storage or held for retirement. This in 1946 was an average 1.95 million, and in 1972, 1.56 million, a decline of 20 percent.

Demurrage

Demurrage has been the basic charge assessed shippers for the time they have held cars longer than the forty-eight hours free time (Saturdays, Sundays, and holidays also were generally counted as free) allowed after time of placement for shipper or consignee. Longer free periods were allowed at ports, up to twenty days for grain at Boston and Norfolk, for instance, because of difficulties in assembly of shipments and uncertainties of shipping. For the first four days after the free time a first-level daily demurrage rate was charged and thereafter still higher rates. Beginning with 1964 the second-level rate was made to apply for four days, and thereafter a still higher charge applied. Demurrage charges were viewed as a combination of payment for the daily costs of cars and a penalty for keeping them out of use and thus reducing the supply of cars available to other shippers. Traditionally, the charges were uniform regardless of capacity, cost, or age of cars. The basic one up to 1953 was $2.20 per day for the first four days, and $5.50 per day thereafter. By 1964 the charges had reached $5.00 and $10.00, and a higher $15.00 after eight days. In 1971 they were doubled.[12]

Viewed in terms of opportunity costs, the lack of adjustment of demurrage charges in response to car surpluses or shortages was irrational. However, the ICC by emergency service orders did temporarily increase charges in 1952 and include Saturdays in counting. Again in 1966/67 and 1969 temporary increases were ordered. These orders were in response to severe car shortages. At various times the free time at ports has been curtailed as well. In addition, to prevent accumulation of cars that might be delayed in unloading at ports, embargoes were ordered or shipping permits required. Beginning in the 1960s tying limited terminal car holding times to reduced multiple-car and train-load rates was initiated.

Rental Arrangements between Railroads and with Shippers

The use of freight cars not part of the fleet of a using rail system, so-called "foreign cars," traditionally involved a daily rental charge called "per diem." This has purported to return the costs of providing the cars and to act as an incentive to return cars promptly to the providing system. Along with this there were rules as what to do with foreign cars made empty in order to guide them back to the roads owning or leasing them. For refrigerator-line and shipper owned cars charges were generally on a mileage basis with the interest of the owners in policing their traffic being presumed sufficient to expedite movement. The importance of these arrangements for foreign car use is indicated by the fact that in 1947 an average of 66 percent of on-line cars were foreign, and in 1972, 52 percent.

The per diem charge had traditionally been a flat amount regardless of size, age, or type of car. It was based on railroad estimated average costs associated with provision of cars. From 1920 to World War II per diem had been $1.00. During the war it was raised to $1.15 and by 1947 to $1.50.

Some of the short-line railroads complained to the ICC that the increased $1.50 per diem was too high. The New England roads joined them. On the other hand, some of the western systems objected to per diem as being so low as not to cover costs and thus to discourage investment in much-needed equipment. In 1949 the ICC found the $1.50 rate lawful. With a subsequent increase in per diem, the New England roads refused to pay it, arguing that because they were more of the nature of a destination terminal operation with the extent of shipper holding cars proportionately greater than elsewhere and thus the railroads were liable for more per diem charges than the long-haul roads to the South and West. To counter this, the western and other roads asked the ICC to consider prescribing a charge based on mileage and time. But nineteen major roads asked that the ICC find the objected to per diem rates lawful and should be observed. In 1955 it found the by then $2.40 per diem level reasonable. But this was rejected by the courts with their requiring that the ICC consider both the possibility of the combined mileage and time charges and a more acceptable basis for determining what would be compensatory.[13]

The railroads increased the per diem to $2.88 in December 1959, and in 1964 changed to a multilevel rate graduated over several depreciated investment value brackets, the minimum, $2.16, and for instance for cars valued from $5,000.00 to $10,000.00, $3.58. In the meantime the ICC had proceeded with its investigation in line with court suggestions and January 1, 1968, and prescribed a mileage-plus-time basis, the mileage part varying with the original cost, and the time part, with age and original cost.

The western roads felt under this formula that they would be overcharged for eastern cars on their lines because of their long hauls and would lose still more than ever on their own cars held by the eastern roads with short mileage use and greatly lowered daily rental for their proportionately longer holding time in terminals. At western road request, the proposed pattern of charges was enjoined, but a 1970 Supreme Court decision finally upheld it. This was a case of conflict between regional railroad groups with the ICC called upon to arbitrate and the courts to approve. Over fifteen years elapsed before suggested changes of a traditional pattern of pricing became effective.[14]

Car Utilization

Changes in freight car utilization over the postwar quarter of a century has varied significantly by car type. (See Table 18.) The most important change has been in the case of boxcars with the near disappearance of lcl traffic. In 1949 the latter had accounted for somewhat over a third of all boxcar loadings, but by

TABLE 18

Year End Freight Car Inventory—U.S. Railroads and Switching
and Terminal Companies, Car Lines, and Shippers—Approximate

Type of Car	1948	1957	1968	1972	1972 vs. 1948
Boxcar	746	745	600	535	−28%
Gondola		285	210	190	−33
Hopper	875				
Open Top H.		535	420	400	−25
Covered H.		55	122	179	+23
Refrigerator	130	120	75	56	−37
Tank	150	120	160	150	0
Flat (incl. rack)	67	90	95	100	+50
TOFC	Under 1	Under 1	55	65	+00
Total (incl. other)	2025	2070	1790	1720	−15
Average On-Line, Total	1949	1950	1630	1600	−18

(Source: ICC, *SRUS* & *TSUS,* Tables #21, 24, & Pt. 9 [Cars leased to RR's not included];
———, Statement #Q240, 1969;
———, Statement #100, 1972 [including estimates for switching and terminal companies] [by calculation].)

1966, only 3 percent. The other major shift has concerned covered hopper cars. In the early years they handled principally short haul cement, traffic, but in recent years grain and bulk dry chemical items have become dominant.

The review of performance is restricted because of limited by-car-type car-mile data. They have been collected for only five sample periods, 1948/49, 1956/57, 1961/62, 1968, and 1972.

There are three measures of car utilization that can be calculated from the regularly published data—annual loadings per car, proportion of empty to total car-miles, and annual miles run per car. Comparisons to show trends must be in respect to periods having near normal traffic, since low levels of traffic affect these measures adversely independently of the basic factors accounting for long-run trends. Annual loadings for each type of car for years of near normal traffic volumes is indicated in Table 19. The inventory data were most reliable in the case of box-, gondola, and open hopper cars.

The decline in lcl loadings from 6 million in 1947 to 300,000 in 1966, all in boxcars, was the major factor in the early decline of annual boxcar loadings. The shift of typical boxcar commodities to TOFC with loading on flat cars with higher utilization was another adverse factor. For these reasons the overall decline in boxcar annual loadings exceeded those of any other car type. All types but the

TABLE 19

Approximate Annual Loadings per Car

Type of Car	1949	1957	1966	1968	1972
Boxcar	22	19	17	15	14
Gondola	18	18½	16½	15½	15
Open Hopper	19	23½	24	23	22
Covered Hopper	25	20	14½	15	16
Refrigerator	13½	11½	14	15	19
Tank	15	13	10	9½	9

(Source: ICC, *TE,* Feb., 1968, p. 7; Apr., 1973, p. 9;
AAR, CS54-1B, CS 8A;
Ibid., previous table, by calculation.)

covered hopper and refrigerator cars failed after the first few years to show an increase in annual loadings, and for the three major categories there was a significant deterioration despite the changes in pattern of charging for car rental aimed at improving use. The practice of assigning cars to particular shippers was a factor; in 1964 their turnaround time was twenty-six days as opposed to eighteen for all cars.[15]

Another aspect of car utilization has been the empty proportion of total car-miles. (See Table 20.) The basic factor determining this, as has been noted, has not been a railroad generated one but has the flow patterns of the different commodities in the commerce of the country. However, added to this has been the extent to which particular commodities have been provided with special car types that are not useful for hauling any commodities which might be hauled in the reverse direction along the route taken by the initial commodity. Coal, for instance, is principally hauled in open-top hoppers, and there is little possibility of finding bulk, weatherproof materials to move back in open cars to the coal fields. Movement of imported iron ore from Atlantic ports to Ohio and western Pennsylvania in the Appalachian coal-mining region from which metallurgical coal was exported was a rare exception. Movement of petroleum company supplied tank cars with refined petroleum products from refineries to distribution points is not likely to be matched by any reverse flow.

The trends in empty mileage reflect these two elements. Open hopper cars have had somewhat under 50 percent empty movement, and there has been little change in the ratios from 1948 to 1972. In the case of tank cars, with a near 50 percent empty share, there has been a slight improvement since 1968 despite the recent elimination of payment for empty miles hauled. The gondola and flat

TABLE 20

Proportion Empty to Total Car-Miles

	1948/49		1956/57	1968	1972
Boxcar	24%		26½%	35½%	42%
Gondola	} 43		40	44	47
Hopper		Open	46	47½	47½
		Covered	53	51	50½
Refrigerator	38½		42	41	43½
Tank	50		51	52	49
Flat	35½		40	44½	49
		TOFC		24½	32

(Source: ICC, Bur. of Accts., Statements 1-50; 6-57, 6-69; 152-72, by calculation.)

(other than TOFC) car empty-mile proportions have all increased significantly. In the case of refrigerator cars, these have had to some extent a return movement of containers, paper, and miscellaneous manufactured items to keep their empty miles below that of types so far considered, but the empty porportion has increased 5 percent points from the initial years. Boxcar use for lcl service originally kept empty miles low, but its discontinuance has led to their increase by probably around 10 percent points. The introduction of boxcars of special design or equipped with load-protecting and stowing devices for certain commodities has contributed to their empty-mile proportion increase. An added factor was the increasing dedication of these cars to particular shippers or routes. In 1964, 70 percent of equipped boxcars and 60 percent of covered hoppers were in assigned service. In 1961/62 general service boxcars had a 30 percent empty ratio and the special ones 42 percent; in 1968 the corresponding ratios were 35 and 47 percent, and in 1972, 40½ and 49½ percent. Despite modifications and high charges for per diem, empty-mileage ratios increased.[16]

An overall measure of car utilization, which combines the annual loadings and the proportions of empty mileage and the character of traffic, is the loaded miles per car per year as shown in Table 21.

The overall loaded-mile utilization of boxcars has not shown significant change. The decline in annual per-car loadings noted earlier has been offset by longer trip lengths. There has been a slight net decline in gondola and open hopper car performance. The increase in covered hopper usage reflects the shift in nature of traffic using them. The early heavy share of short-haul cement loadings has given way to long-haul grain and dry bulk chemical ones. Flat car figures are not shown because of the uncertainties in classification of subtypes, such as rack cars, in the inventory count.

TABLE 21

*Estimated Loaded Car-Miles (Revenue and Nonrevenue) per Year
per Car for Years of High Traffic Volume*

(000)

Type of Car	1948/49	1956/57	1968	1972
Boxcar	13½ mi.	14 mi.	14 mi.	14 mi.
Gondola		5½	5	5
Open Hopper	6	6	5½	5
Covered Hopper		6½	8	9
Refrigerator	20	18	15½	15
Tank	8	7	5½	5½

(Source: Previous two tables, by calculation.)

Car Shortages

Severe car shortages in 1963, worse than the last serious ones, in 1955, led Congress in 1966 to hold another of its many hearings on the subject. In conclusion, it required that the ICC to study the problem and mandated that it insure the adequacy of the national car supply. As a result, the ICC entered into a far more active role than ever before. Most radical of all, it ordered a scheme for financing additions to the general service boxcar inventory out of increased per diem charges collected during peak periods, September through February, each year. The ICC also issued a series of orders that among other things penalized consignees who did not clean out cars as they unloaded them, required railroads to handle cars in terminals within twenty-four hours, greatly increased demurrage charges, limited the time cars loaded with lumber could be held for reconsignment to five days, and established a permit system to control movement of coal cars to ports for export. It also tightened the railroad agreed-upon rules for handling of empty foreign cars and made them government rules to ensure improved compliance. A sample had shown 50 percent of these cars were not handled according to the rules. Shipper pressure on their congressional representatives and inadequate control by the railroads led to this increased direction by the ICC of car handling by both shippers and railroads.[17]

All through the years these institutionalized arrangements for dealing with car utilization were paralleled by undocumented activity of railroad staff in making the actual decisions as to the use and handling of cars. This staff kept track of cars, received the shipper requests for cars, notices of release and readiness for forwarding, as well as dealt with interrailroad interchange. During the period under review the improvements in these activities have been primarily in improved communication and recording. Speeded up information and more available facts have improved the decision-making process. However, it was not until after 1972 that the railroads through the AAR undertook an analysis of the car service institutional arrangement and possible improvements with a view to upgrading utilization.[18]

* * *

The underlying contribution to increased productivity in both line-haul and terminal freight operations was the increased capacities of all types of cars. Line-haul train operations in their own right had shown substantial productivity gains, due primarily to dieselization and then the increasing power of locomotives. Not for eighteen years after adoption of diesels were savings from smaller crews attained. Heavier train loads and higher and more reliably sustained speeds increased track capacity. Together with discontinuance of passenger trains this enabled abandonment of multiple-track mileage. These improvements in line-haul productivity were only possible with numerous other innovations and upgrading of less spectacular character. Terminal operations showed no gains in engine productivity and little in labor aside from reduction in firemen. There were no improvements in respect to freight car utilization, no decline in proportion of empty miles, or reduction of turnaround time. Shortages persisted. There were significant reductions in train schedule times, but shipper to consignee elapsed times still were burdened with time-consuming terminal handling and, except for specially monitored traffic, with a degree of variability that was generally not acceptable to users.

9

Labor

The labor for the U.S. railroads has been by far the most important among the broad categories of the industry's inputs. It has amounted to some two-thirds of operating expenses and taken around one-half of railroad revenues. Thus the continuous rise of wage rate and benefit levels has been critical in the performance of the railroad industry. The step-by-step upward adjustments in both have been as complicated and hotly contested as any aspect of postwar railroad developments and have involved a long series of union-management-government encounters. The review of a quarter of a century of this must consider a vast array of fundamental labor market factors, union institutional elements and government participatory roles. All together they were the determinants of the bargaining results. Only a somewhat detailed consideration of the long series of encounters from 1946 through 1972 can provide a feel for the part the various elements in the array have played and the extent of their influence. It is the details of the numerous negotiations that add up to the overall impact on the twenty-five years' performance.

THE INSTITUTIONAL BACKGROUND

The Unions

Bargaining has been done by a number of national craft unions, each of which has had an effective monopoly over the labor input of its craft for nearly the entire industry. There was a gross differentiation among unions, five being called the "ops," whose members ran trains and switched cars, and the seventeen "non-ops," representing the rest of the employees, clerks, maintenance workers, etc.

In 1970 there was a merger of the "ops," except for the Brotherhood of Locomotive Engineers (BLE), into the United Transport Union (UTU). The "non-ops" were divided among the large Brotherhood of Railway (Airline) and Steamship Clerks, Freight Handlers, Express and Station Employees (BR[A]C), eight shop-craft unions, and ones for maintenance of way workers, carmen, signalmen, telegraphers, etc. The "ops" considered that they represented the elite crafts of the industry. They tended to be independent both among themselves and in respect to the "non-ops," though they did have common interests. Overall there has been a National Union Executive Conference of all the unions, which provided consideration of common objectives and strategies. However, there has been occasional breaking away of an individual union or group of them to negotiate settlements on its own, noticeably so after 1968.

157

The power of any one of the individual unions was projected beyond its own craft because of the control of the work input of others by way of the key tenet of unionism, the respecting of each other's picket lines. One union's vote to strike and the posting of pickets upon striking have denied, with only a few exceptions, the railroads' labor input of all crafts.

The railroad companies as employers joined in regional and then the national groupings to establish bargaining units to match the scope of those of the unions. Since 1963 there has been the National Railway Labor Conference, whose chairman has been the rare exceptions the chief negotiator for the railroads in respect to national contracts. Throughout, there has been individual handling of a variety of details with the union general chairmen of the local lodges of individual railroads. The conference procedure for the most part has provided a unified front, but individual railroads have on several occasions made concessions as to basic terms that have forced the rest to follow. The unions sometimes attempt to deal with the individual railroads separately by limited or selective strikes in order not to create the bad image of crippling the country's transport. In this way it is possible to exert concentrated pressure on a particular struck company to capitulate. To counter this, the railroads have created mutual assistance agreements whereby the diverted revenue received by those continuing in operation is shared with those out of service. A lockout by all nonstruck railroads in support of a struck one has been theoretically possible but very rarely even threatened because of public resentment against the crippling of the country's commerce. The monopoly powers of the unions over the labor inputs have not been matched by any corresponding power of the collective railroads.

The Government Role

The other institutional element has been the government participation in the negotiating process. The foundation for this in recent years has been the Railway Labor Act of 1926 and its amendments. After private negotiating fails, federal mediation efforts are mandated. These failing and a strike having been authorized, the president can appoint an Emergency Board to review the situation and report out recommendations. This staves off the strike until thirty days after the recommendations are made. These are to contribute to a consolidated public opinion, which hopefully will prevail and provide a basis for a settlement. The general union attitude toward such recommendations was epitomized by the 1950 statement of one of the union leaders that "not a single report has ever approached acceptability."[1]

Over the postwar years the unions frequently rejected board recommendations while the railroads generally accepted them. Following rejection there have been varied ad hoc procedures adopted by the executive branch of the government, and more recently, upon their failure, by Congress. In turn, these have been backed up by the injunctive powers of the courts. The final steps have ranged from federal government takover of the railroads to congressional mandate of arbitration or even setting final contract terms. These steps have all been premised on the assumption that a prolonged stoppage of a major railroad and certainly of several or all railroads was not compatible with the general welfare of the country. In fact, since World War II there never has been a shutdown of major railroads for more than a few days. Longer strikes have occurred on switching and terminal railroads, industrially owned railroads, and the smaller local Rutland and Florida East Coast railroads.

The key effects of all this have been twofold. One, for the major roads the certainty that there will not be an all-out testing of the strengths of the opposing parties by a lengthy strike makes for bargaining strategies different from those in the usual industrial situation where that possibility exists. Two, many negotiations have been so long drawn out as to incur large sums for retroactive wage payments, which cannot be recovered from past shippers and riders.

Finally, another unique institutional government related aspect of the railroad industry has been its pension, unemployment, and disability benefits have been handled by a special government agency, the Railroad Retirement Board (RRB). The financing has been by special railroad industry payroll taxes and under deficit conditions by borrowing and transfer of funds from nonrail related government sources. Both employers and employees have paid taxes for retirement benefits, only employers for the remainder and unemployment. The terms of a large share of the benefits are settled by congressional action mainly at the behest of the unions but to some extent in response to carrier suggestions. As a result of the particular strength of railroad unions, the annuities paid have been substantially higher than those for general industry social security benefits, and the unemployment benefits have accrued to employees on strike.[2]

The Operating Pay Structure[3]

A critical institutional heritage has been the unique terms of wages for freight and passenger train and engine crews known as the "dual basis of pay," the foundation of which has been the "basic" day, eight hours for freight crews, five for passenger engine, and seven and a half for passenger train crews.

A particular aspect of the railroad pattern was that there were also mileage rates of pay related to the basic day pay by its division by a speed factor, $12\frac{1}{2}$ miles per hour for freight and 20 for passenger service. The speed factors originated back in the late 1880s and have carried into modern times the limitations of old-type steam locomotives and long since obsolete operating practices. The only modification of this was in 1968 when the speed factor in the case of freight trains was slightly increased to some 14 mph for any miles run over 100. At $12\frac{1}{2}$ mph, the eight hour day was equivalent to 100 miles, so that a 100-mile trip was the alternative basic measure of a day's work in freight service. At 20 mph the five-hour passenger day also came to 100 miles for engine crews, but the seven-and-a-half-hour one came to 150 miles for train crews. No trip was compensated for at less than the base day's amount. If a 100-mile or under trip took over eight hours the base pay was augmented by an amount equal to the excess time at the punitive one and a half times the regular hourly rate. Trips over 100 miles were paid for at the mileage rate even when time on duty was not over eight hours or was even much less.

The incidence of all this on a crew member's compensation varied widely between types of trains. For example, 51 percent of enginemen in freight service local or way trains whose principal function was to set off and pick up cars along their route got punitive overtime whereas only 3 percent of through freight enginemen did.

Another structural wage element has been the gradation of these mileage and hourly rates for enginemen and firemen according to the size of locomotives, providing a productivity and responsibility factor. Also, since 1955 freight conductors' and trainmens' rates have varied with the number of cars in a train.

There have been monthly mileage limitations, the minimums being another form of monthly guarantee, and the maximums, a means of spreading earnings among those on the roster of employees. For instance, in 1960 maximums for freight engine crews were generally 3,800 miles per month; for passenger, 4,800.

Along with the basic 100-mile day has been the continuation of many "crew change-point" locations from the days of early steam locomotive operation with the close spacing of those points, 80 to 150 miles. Change in these locations or running through one of them without crew change has been resisted because of employee objections to resultant reduction in number of jobs and to moving their residences. The consequences of this and the mileage piece-rate are illustrated by the eighteen crews required for a regular some sixty-hour Chicago-Los Angeles through freight. The average crew trip over the 2,225 miles is three and a third hours running time and 124 miles, until recently paid for at one and a quarter times the basic day rate. For the fastest freight run on this route the average time per trip was two and a fifth hours.

In addition to these elements of the wage structure, there are numerous items of payment by way of arbitraries, special allowances, and guarantees, some of which are in the national contracts and many are local to individual railroads. During the period under consideration the only data measuring these are for the country as a whole in 1962. For the "ops," compensation from arbitraries, etc., ranged from 11 percent in through freight service to 3 percent in straightaway passenger. These special features of the wage structure are not only a generally significant addition to the regularly negotiated basic wage rates, but they also have come to vary regionally in their impact. If the compensation for "allowances," vacations, arbitraries, etc., are added so that for the basic straight time and overtime, the gross hourly earnings level in the East has been 6 percent higher than in the South, and in the West, 1½ higher.

This has reflected local bargaining, some managements having allowed the accumulation of special work rules and others having aggressively restricted them. The difference between individual systems has been more pronounced than between regions.

GENERAL DEMAND AND SUPPLY ELEMENTS[4]

In broad terms the basic demands for labor input are derived from the demands for the great variety of railroad services; the lcl and passenger categories of service declining precipitately during the period under consideration. The continuous introduction of labor-saving technological advances with increased productivity is the other important factor in declining demand. This, of course, has not been unique to the railroad industry.

Overall, the railroad demand for labor inputs has been continuously downward in the postwar years, except for a minor bulge during the Korean War period. There was a decline from 1947, the first year after the immediate large postwar adjustment, to 1971 of 62 percent in production employees on Class I railroads. These have been the employees involved in major labor contract bargaining.

A sensitive measure of the change in demand for labor is the changes in annual number of persons employed who had never before worked for the railroad industry. In 1947 there were 400,000 such new employees, while during the 1960s they were down to from 45,000 to 75,000 per year. The annual number drawn from the country's labor force had declined some 80 percent, substantially more than the 62 percent decline in average employment. The effective draft on the country's labor force was substantially less than these amounts because out of a year's accessions, a half worked for the railroads less than a year and were thus back in the general labor force.

On the supply side, the relevant labor force has been that of the country's white males in the lower age brackets. Only 5½ percent of the Class I railroad employees have been women, and a very minor share, nonwhite. The percent unemployment for twenty- to twenty-four-year-old white males provides an available rough measure of changes in supply conditions over the years. Substantial tightness for this category, that is, unemployed less 3 percent unemployed, existed in 1951 through 1953, 1955 through 1957, and again 1965 through 1966. Slackness, measured by 7½ percent or over unemployment, occurred in 1949, 1950, 1954, 1955, 1958 through 1962, and 1970 on. Possible influence of these conditions of supply is noted in the following history of railroad wage adjustments.

HISTORY OF LABOR INPUTS COSTS[5]

The trend of labor inputs is reviewed in terms of the changes over time in basic wage rates, major incillary elements of compensation, basic working conditions, and overall levels of benefits. The vast number and complexity of working conditions and benefits forecloses the possibility of considering all their details. For comparison with developments in other industries, two, namely steel and auto, are recognized as "key" ones with the changes for a principal firm in each considered. As the wage contracts of the trucking industry become standardized in the 1960s, their terms are also brought in for comparison, as those of the principal competitor of the railroads. Finally, in later years, as indices of overall industry changes become available, they too are reviewed for comparison. Because the "ops" and "non-ops" on a number of occasions have negotiated settlements for different amounts and at different times, the two groups are dealt with separately. Because many of the "non-ops" crafts are comparable to those of general industry, the cross-industry comparisons are largely with "non-ops."

Pre-1946

An important factor relative to the postwar developments is the wartime negotiation for wage increases. At the beginning of the war, effective December 1, 1941, the "non-ops" obtained a wage increase of 10¢ an hour (=15.6 percent average overall), and the "ops", a 9½¢ (=10.6 percent) wage increase. Because of the institutional factors in negotiations it is noted that the settlement came after the unions had rejected Emergency Board recommendations and had forced negotiations to the White House level. President Roosevelt pushed the board into a mediation role, which led to a 1¢ increase over the board's original recommendation for the "non-ops," giving roughly the same as parallel increases for the steel and motor vehicle industries, and the 3 percent added for the "ops." Next, in the middle of the war, 1943, the rail unions made further demands. There were Emergency Board reviews, a final strike call following rejection of the recommendations, a takeover of the railroads by the government, and final presidential arbitration. It led again to more than the board's awards, 9¢ to 11¢ for the "non-ops" and 9¢ for the "ops." The Economic Stabilization director refused approval for the 11¢, but this was overridden by a Senate resolution introduced by Senator Truman and approved by Congress. The final 1943 railroad settlement amounts were considerably more than the comparable increases of 5½¢ for U.S. Steel and 8¢ for General Motors. The 1941 increases were a case of a common industrial wage pattern; the 1943, a case of union militancy with a threat, even in the middle of war, of shutting down a critical industry together with the use of political friends, all against the background of a short labor supply.

1946–1949

1946

Nineteen forty-six was a year with industrial production 16 percent below 1945. For the railroads, traffic declined sharply and net railway operating income (nroi), excluding a large carry-back tax credit, dropped below the level of the worst depression year. The consumer price index (CPI) after relative stability with wartime controls jumped 18 percent during 1946.

In early 1946 the Wage Stabilization Board was still functioning for nonrail industries and under its influence settlements for U.S. Steel and General Motors were in an 18½¢ to 19½¢ per-hour range, and meat packers who were thought not able to absorb as much of a rise, only 16¢. The average increase for all manufacturing was 14½ percent. The railroad negotiations carried through to later in the year. All the unions but two "ops" agreed to arbitration. Awards of 16¢ were announced in April. Despite the agreement to accept arbitration, the awards were rejected as being too little. In the meantime, the two "op" demands went to an Emergency Board whose affirmation of the 16¢ was also rejected. A strike was called but prevented by President Truman ordering a government takeover of the railroads. He entered the negotiations and suggested settlement with an added 2½¢. The two "ops" rejected this, and finally went on strike, only to be brought around two days later by a fighting speech of President Truman and his threat of drastic legislation to curtail railroad union bargaining power. Militancy and strategy on the political front were successful in gaining for the railroad unions more than had been granted by government appointed boards for industries in deteriorating financial circumstances and roughly the same as the key steel and automobile companies.

1947

For the second round, 1947, railroad settlements were preceded by other "key" industry agreements. In February, U.S. Steel had agreed to increases equivalent to 15¢, and in April, General Motors, to 11½¢. A September arbitration award gave the "non-ops" +15½¢, and two of the "ops" settled for that amount. The other three "ops" carried negotiations through to government seizure, and again with White House intervention finally were to settle for the 15½¢ pattern to which were added extras for particular classes of their membership. This increase came against a background of improved financial performance of the railroads.

1948/49

Industrial production peaked in mid-1948 and turned down from November to a low a year later. There was a rise in country-wide unemployment from 1.6 to 4.1 million. The CPI turned down in late 1948 to reach a slightly lower level a year and a half later. All this removed the pressures for large wage increases in 1949. Nineteen forty-eight had been a good year for the railroads with net railway operating income (nroi) more than double that of the low year 1946 and 28 percent above 1947. However, this was followed by a sharp reversal in 1949 due to the general decline in the economy, coal mine stoppages, and October and November steel strikes. The nroi in the last half of 1949 was below the previous postwar low.

In 1948 both U.S. Steel and General Motors had agreed to two-year contracts, the former with reopening provisions, the latter with cost-of-living escalation based on the CPI. The steel contract signed in July gave a base increase with increased job-spread differentials, averaging in all 13¢. Upon reopening during the downturn in May 1949, existing wages were continued without increase but with largely a noncontributory pension plan costing the equivalent of 25¢ per hour being agreed to. The contract termination date was extended to the end of 1950. The General Motors contract signed in May introduced an innovation by way of an annual improvement factor of 3¢, plus 3¢ more in the first year to make up for the previous rise in the CPI. These adjustments gave an 11¢ gross increase for 1948 but what turned out to be none in 1949 because the CPI decline totally offset the improvement factor.

For the railroads the 1949 "non-op" negotiations resolved a long-standing demand, based on the forty-hour week established prewar for other industry, for conversion to a five-day week without loss of pay. The bargaining was carried out in a turbulent atmosphere because of strikes by some of the "ops" and again government takeovers. The pattern was set by the December 1948 decision of an Emergency Board reached while economic conditions were still generally favorable and increase in unemployment was not yet under way. The recommendations were accepted without appeal by the unions and were for a two-year contract. The increase was 30½¢ an hour, the effect of conversion to a five-day week.

The "ops" in the latter part of 1948 settled on a 10¢ an hour increase with extras for certain crafts and classes of service. In addition, paid vacations for the "ops" were increased from one to two weeks for employees with over five years of service. In 1949 the engineers' and firemen's requests for additional crew members on multiple-unit diesel locomotives were rejected by an Emergency Board. The "ops" had presented demands for conversion to a shortened week for yard crews but no decision was forthcoming. No wage increases accrued to the "ops" in 1949.

Overall 1946–1949

The wage rate adjustments during this four-year phase were plus 46½¢ per hour for steel and 60¢, including cost-of-living adjustments, for General Motors. For the railroads the total, including conversion to the short week, was 64½¢ per hour for the "non-ops" and 44¢-plus difficult to average wage structure changes for the "ops." In all years the "non-op" rates increased substantially more than the CPI. With initial inflationary, double-digit CPI rises and improving railroad net income, the unions aggressively pushed for large increases. The demands continued but were more temperate but with no question as to the "non-op" conversion to a forty-hour week.

Percent Changes in Year for Railroad "Non-Ops" and for All Industry Wage Rates; January to January Percent Changes, Consumer Price Index; Annual Class I Railroad Net Income; Percent Unemployment among Whites Twenty to Twenty-four Years of Age, 1946–1949

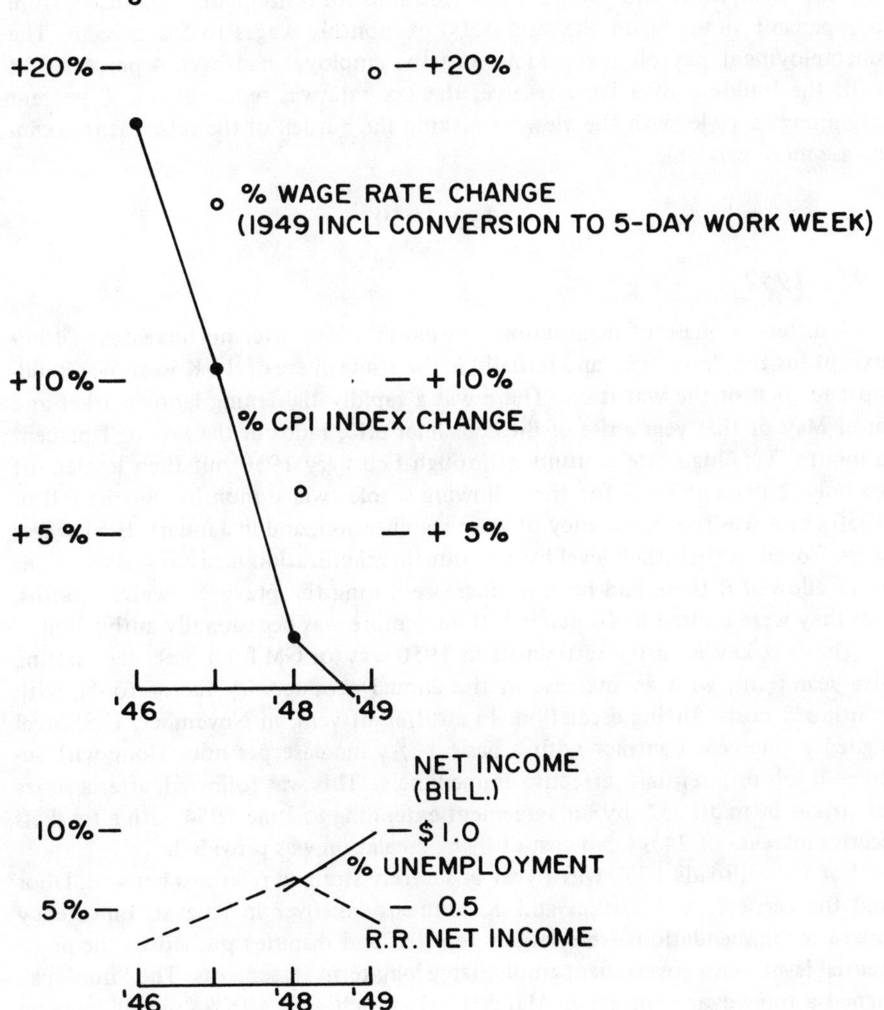

1946–1949 Retirement, Unemployment, and Other Benefits[6]

In this phase for nonrailroad industries private fringe benefits (social security was in effect) had been minor. The major change was the agreement to noncontributory pension plans in the key industries, steel and auto. For the railroads the equal employee and company contributions for retirement were raised, from 3½ percent annually on the first $300 of monthly wages to 5¾ percent. The unemployment payroll tax paid by just the employer had been 4 percent, but with the build-up of a large reserve, the tax rate was reduced to a ½ percent beginning in 1948 with the view to making the burden of the retirement tax increase more palatable.

1950–1959

1950–1952

A different phase of negotiations started in 1950, after no increases in 1949 except for the "non-ops" and initially in the atmosphere of the Korean War build-up and then of the war itself. There was a rapidly tightening labor market and after May of that year a rise of the consumer price index at the rate of 1 percent a month. This high rate continued through February 1950 but then leveled off to only 2 percent total for the following whole twelve months. By the fall of 1950 there was the expectancy of wage stabilization, and in January 1951 wages were frozen at their then level by government stabilization measures. Exceptions were allowed if there had been no increase during the previous twelve months, but they were limited to 10 percent, though more was occasionally authorized.

The first key industry settlement in 1950 was for GM for a precedent-setting five-year term, with an increase in the annual productivity factor to 4¢, with continued cost-of-living escalation. In a different vein, in November, U.S. Steel signed a one-year contract with a basic 12½¢ increase per hour along with increased job differentials, effective immediately. This was followed, after a series of strikes in mid-1952, by an agreement extending to June 1954 with a total effective increase of 24½¢. No cost-of-living escalation was provided.

For the railroads 1950 was a year of severely strained relations between labor and the carriers, with strikes and government takeover in August. Emergency Board recommendations were largely rejected and disputes pushed to the presidential level, with government emphasizing long-term agreements. The "non-ops" signed a three-eyar contract in March 1951, which gave a 16½¢ overall increase plus a 14¢ for cost-of-living add-on, considerably more than the steel increases.

Negotiations with the "ops," which had begun in 1949, were long drawn out and complicated primarily because of the conversion to a forty-hour week for terminal crews. The various "op" settlements spanned twenty-one months, with terms running to October 1953. For road crews the total increase was 16½¢ per hour, and for terminal ones, 31¢. The cost-of-living escalation turned out to add 7¢ in both 1951 and 1952 and to subtract 1¢ in 1953.

1953/54

Nineteen fifty-three started with a rising trend in production but ended with a downturn beginning with September. The trough extended through to October 1954. Railroad traffic fell sharply through the fall of 1953 into early 1954 and did not recover fully until mid-1955. Unemployment was sharply up in 1954. The CPI leveled off in mid-1952 and did not push upward until April 1956.

In May 1953, under reopening provisions of the five-year auto industry contract, its annual improvement factor was increased from 4 to 5¢. In June reopening of the steel contract provided a basic increase of 8½¢ per hour. Both settlements came before the downturn. In 1954 the continuing auto contracts netted only a 3¢ increase because of the decline in the CPI. The next steel contract provided only a 5¢ increase in June 1954.

The railroad agreements had expired in the midst of the downturn. After exhausting the early steps in negotiation the "non-ops" accepted an Emergency Board recommendation of May 1954 that gave no wage increase but provided for the establishment of a company nealth and welfare plan with contributions by the carriers equivalent to 2¢ per hour. In the meantime, the various "ops" reached agreements giving 5¢ more per hour, effective in December 1953. Being in a recession, the unions were not prepared to sign long-term contracts and rejected cost-of-living escalation following experience with negative adjustments. Negotiations with respect to 1954 demands carried over into 1955 and "op" increases for 1954 were passed over.

1955

General economic conditions turned up at the end of 1954, and industrial production rose to new high levels through 1955. There was no rise in the CPI in 1955. Railroad freight traffic moved sharply upward through the year. Quarterly nroi for the middle quarters of 1955 were near or at postwar highs, though net income before taxes remained below the highest quarters of 1953.

The steel contract was reopened in August 1955 and a 15¢ gross increase was obtained. A new three-year auto contract was agreed to in August, again with an increase in improvement factor of 2½ percent, minimum 6¢, plus 5¢ in the first year for further correction of inequities and increased differentials for skilled workers.

For the railroads the "non-ops" signed a one-year contract with a 14½¢ per-hour increase effective December 1955 plus carrier assumption of the full cost of the welfare plan, equivalent to 2¢ more. One-year contracts for the "ops," except the engineers, provided basic increases in October ranging from 8 to 10½¢, of which 4¢ was in lieu of the contributions obtained by the "non-ops" for their welfare plan. The conductors in addition got an extra 2 percent for an increased differential over brakemen. Yardmen obtained a still further increase for the shortened week conversion, ranging from 12½ to 16¢ more. The engineers settled separately for a 5 percent basic increase plus 2 percent corresponding to that which the conductors had won.

In the meantime, in the summer of 1953 an old aim of the road conductors and trainmen was brought up, to have their pay graduated with the size of trains, much as engine crews long have had their pay graded according to weight on the drivers (wheels) of locomotives. Effective June 1955, both road conductors and trainmen were given a flat 2½¢ per-hour increase plus additives graduated according to the train length. For 126- to 145-car trains, for instance, it was equivalent to a 12½¢ increase per hour. All this meant a basic restructuring of the road train crew pay terms accompanied by a substantial increase. With the resumption of an upward business trend the unions pushed forward for major additions to compensation.

1956–1958

Industrial production continued to increase until a downturn began after September 1957, reaching a low in April of 1958. This was followed by a sharp reversal upward, terminated, however, in the second half of 1959 by the long steel strike. Railroad freight traffic followed these trends but did not return to the prior 1956 high levels in the upturn of 1958/59. The CPI continued stable in the first part of 1956, but by December was 3 percent above that of the year before. The increase in 1957 was 3½ percent, and in 1958, 1 percent. While non-financial corporate net income fell off in the 1957/58 recession, it came back quickly to higher levels. On the other hand, railroad net income before income taxes fell more sharply and did not recover, 1958 being 20 percent below 1957, and 1959 being no better. After 1954 the unemployment rate first fell to a low in 1956 but then doubled by 1958.

Contracts for this phase were all three-year ones with cost-of-living escalation. The first to be negotiated was for steel in August 1956, following a five-week strike. There was a 7½¢ basic increase for the first year and 7¢ in each of the two following, and again greater job differentials adding 2 to 3¢ more. The 1958 auto contracts continued the previous improvement factor and only added a 1½¢ extra for the first year.

For the railroads a three-year "non-op" contract was signed during the rising traffic in November 1956, with a 10¢ per-hour increase for the first year and 7¢ each year thereafter, along with added contributions to the welfare fund, equivalent to 2½¢. Aside from the engineers, the "op" contracts were basically the same as the "non-op," except that the first year increase was 12½¢, the extra being specified as in lieu of the "non-op" welfare contribution. The engineers continued use of percent increases to maintain their proportionate differential over other

Percent Changes in Year for Railroad "Non-Ops" and for All Industry Wage Rates; January to January Percent Changes, Consumer Price Index; Percent Changes in Annual Class I Railroad Net Income; Percent Unemployment of Whites Twenty to Twenty-four Years of Age, 1950–1959

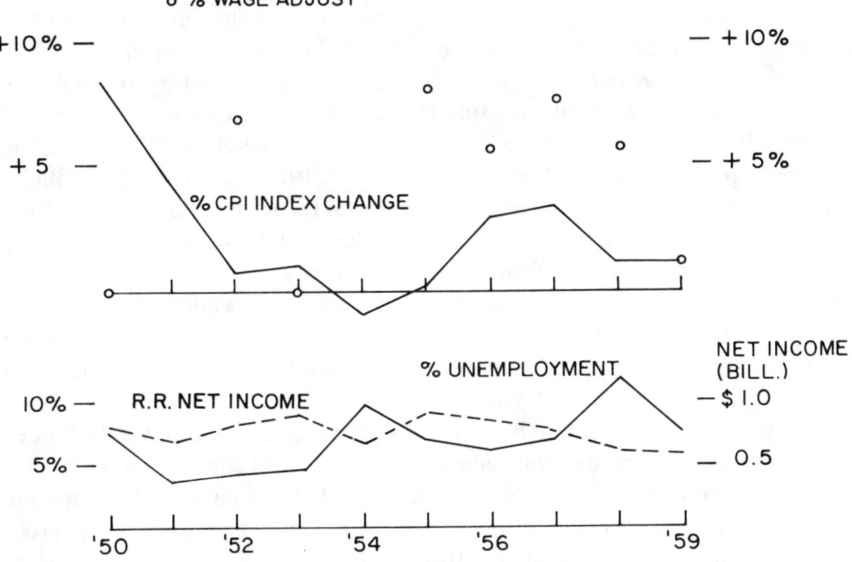

classes with the first year's increase 6 percent and 3½ percent for each of the next two. With the sharp downturn in freight traffic in the fall of 1959, the 1958 rise in unemployment, and a two-year decline in rail net, when these contracts expired there was no immediate new settlement.

Overall 1950–1959

For this phase key steel and auto gains were not too different. The "non-op" ones, including the forty-hour-week conversion increases were roughly the same. While the basic "op" increases were less than the key industry ones, the numerous increased differentials for particular classes brought the "ops" total to roughly the same as the others. Relative to the CPI increases in five of the ten years, the "non-op" increases were twice or more than the CPI increase. For the rest of the years, price and wage changes were close to the same, if 1950 and 1951 be considered in combination.

During this phase railroad employees obtained an additional week's paid vacation (bringing the total to three weeks after fifteen years) and seven days of paid holidays. The key nonrail industries had obtained comparable arrangements somewhat earlier. For the full-time hourly paid railroad employee the pay for holidays and vacations in effect added 8⅓ percent to hourly compensation.

1949–1959 Retirement, Unemployment, and Other Benefits

In the years 1949 through 1959 contributions of industry for retirement, unemployment, and other benefits became a substantial and very complex element in labor costs. Among nonrailroad industry only U.S. Steel has provided usable data as to annual total company contributions. In 1949 they amounted to $39 million; in 1959, $221 million, about 16 percent of employee payroll.

In the case of the railroad industry, benefits were handled by the Railroad Retirement Board (RRB), but its funding has not been comparable to nonrail industries. In 1949 railroad payroll taxes going to the RRB were $253 million, just under 6 percent of employee compensation; in 1959 they were $374 million, 7½ percent. But in that year there were transfers to the RRB of $337 million from government general social security funds. The RRB benefits were increased greatly between these years. In 1951 retirement allowances were given to a broader list of beneficiaries and increased 15 percent to retirees. There were further increases of 10 percent in both 1956 and 1959. Unemployment benefits were doubled and in the case of employees wtih over fifteen years of service, their payment extended from twenty-six to fifty-two weeks.

In addition to all this, the railroads had become involved in privately funded company health and welfare arrangements. The amount of contributions for these were not shown in published accounts until after 1959. They were $120 million in 1961. The proportion railroad contributions for all benefits were to payrolls rose from 6 percent to an estimated 10 percent in 1959, the last not including the transfers from outside government funds. This latter represented a funding source that the unions had garnered, and which relieved the railroads from a substantial additional burden accruing from the growing benefits.

1960–1964

The next phase of labor negotiations, 1960 through 1964, was in a period of relative price stability. In no year did the consumer price index rise more than 1⅔ percent January to January. The annual average increases in nonagricultural hourly straight-time earnings did not exceed 3 percent, or some 7½¢ per hour. In the mid years of this phase the Council of Economic Advisors urged wage guidelines tied to the extent of increase in productivity from the whole economy, stated to be 3.2 percent annually in 1964. Total nonfinancial company corporate profits had peaked in the third quarter of 1959 and did not reach that level again until the final quarter of 1963. Unemployment rates remained above 7 percent.[7]

Key Nonrailroad Industries

In response to the first year's declines during this phase, pensions rather than wages, health, vacation, and other benefits were the important items in new contracts. Steel negotiations were delayed by the 119-day strike in the fall of 1959 so that a new contract was not reached until January 1960. It extended over 30 months with two basic 7¢ per-hour increases along with greater job spreads, annual increments being the same as in the 1956 contract. The normally expected annual increase for 1959 had been skipped, but beginning with 1960 U.S. Steel agreed to insurance payments equivalent to 6½¢ an hour on average partially funded by the cost-of-living wage adjustments. The next contract in June 1962 came after the 1960/61 "growth-recession." The emphasis was on benefits. They were equivalent to an annual 7½¢ per hour, and a year and a half later, 9½¢ more.

The General Motors previous three-year contract had carried on to the fall of 1961. The following settlement was for another three years, the improvement factor remaining at the same level, with 2¢ of it in the first year being diverted to pension funds. The next negotiations came at the end of 1964 when stabilization was being emphasized. The resultant contract was again a three-year one, with no uniform improvement factor but 2½¢ for inequity adjustments in the first year, 1964. The second year had a 2½ percent, minimum 6¢, improvement factor. These modest increases were, however, added to by increased benefits.

Since the over-the-road trucking industry and the teamsters were coming near to a national agreement in this phase, their key Central States contract can be considered at this point. The trucking industry had been growing rapidly and had steadily increasing net income, except for 1960. Net income before taxes for motor carriers of general freight had doubled from 1959 to 1964.

In January 1961 a three-year agreement was reached providing for terminal employees 10, 8, and 10¢ annual hourly increases, and for over the road, three ¼¢ per-mile ones, both with cost-of-living escalation. The previous three-year contract had provided 10, 7, and 7¢ increases per hour and ¼¢ per mile annually.

The Railroads

For the railroads this next phase was a period of uncertainty as to both the direction in which the railroad competitive position would develop and how their financial problems, particularly in the East, would work out. The downturn of 1960/61 had hit the railroads more severely than industry in general. Average annual employment had declined for the mid-1950s level of around a million, to 815,000 in 1959, down to 700,000 in 1962. But because of wage rate increases, total employee compensation had declined only 7 percent.

The unions proposed substantial increases, but the carriers for the first time in some years countered with demands for wage reductions and for relief from work rules restrictive of improvements in labor productivity. Study of union demands became the task of a Presidential Railroad Commission appointed by President Eisenhower on December 22, 1960 and reporting in early 1962. From the labor side a growing dissatisfaction by the skilled workers both "op" and "non-op" with the narrowing relative differences between skilled and unskilled worker pay as a result of the numerous flat per-hour wage increases led to demands for a change to percentage increases.

The "Non-Ops"

The first two rounds with the "non-ops" were expedited with their acceptance of Emergency Board recommendations in 1960 and then 1962. The 1960 one gave a flat 5¢ per-hour increase and improved health and welfare benefits equivalent to 8½¢ an hour specifically in lieu of a further wage increase in 1961. The 1962 one provided two increases totaling 10.3¢ with no further change allowed until May 1963. The third negotiations carried on through November 1964 and ended with acceptance of Emergency Board recommendations for three annual flat 9¢ per-hour increases by seven "non-ops" but met rejection by the machinists, sheet-metal, and electrical workers reflecting their demands for better "pay differentials" for skilled workers. These three crafts settled belatedly in February 1965 for the flat 9¢ (=3.4 percent for skilled crafts) for 1964 but 4 percent and 3½ percent increases for the following years.

The "Ops"

The first round for the "ops" in this phase was settled June 1960 by arbitration for the engineers. Mediation for the other "ops" except the switchmen and Emergency Board recommendation for them led to a 2 percent increase in July 1960 and another 2 percent in March 1961.

The next two years involved bitter dispute over the basic work-rule changes that had been recommended by the Presidential Railroad Commission's report issued in February 1962. The issues were principally in respect to elimination of firemen on freight and yard diesel engines and of a brakeman under limited conditions on freight trains. It is of interest to note that a presidential commission for the airlines in May 1962 had endorsed the reduction of jet plane flight-deck crews from four to three, and another commission for marine workers in December 1960, the elimination of the third deck hand on tugs. The proposed railroads' rule changes were further reviewed by an Emergency Board and a special review panel appointed by President Kennedy. The unions took the matter to the courts and finally to the Congress, which responded by creating an arbitration board, this time with the unusual power of issuing a binding award. Forthcoming in November 1963, it approved the crew member eliminations, but effective only for two years, so the whole controversy was to be reopened again. The board's key awards were one, the phasing out by attrition of 90 percent of freight and yard service firemen's jobs on diesel locomotives, and two, the reduction in size of a limited number of freight train crews from a conductor and two brakemen to a conductor and single brakeman, the exact trains involved to be decided by individual carriers reaching binding local settlements. Third was that any pay rate increases for road crews during the following four years would be added just to the daily basic rates and not to the mileage rates. This last broke with the long-standing relationship of 100 miles being equivalent to eight hours and the basic day, and excess mileage paid for on the basis of the 12½ or 20 miles per hour divided into the basic day's pay. The unions challenged the award in the courts and not until Supreme Court affirmation in May 1964 did its terms become effective.

In the meantime, two "op" wage increases had been negotiated. First in the winter of 1963/64 the carriers, in lieu of a wage increase, assumed the costs of a health and welfare plan in an amount equivalent to 10.3¢ per hour of wages, in effect a matching of the 1962 "non-op" increases. Then in mid-1964 general increases were agreed to ranging from the equivalent 18¢ to 22¢ per hour, depending upon job class. In addition, enginemen without firemen were given an additional 19¢ per hour. There were also special increases for yardmen equivalent to from 8¢ to 13¢ to pay for the liberalized rules allowing road train crews to switch in lieu of yard crews in a wider range of situations.

Stabilization of employment was another area of change. From 1958 to 1961 with receding traffic there had been widespread layoffs. Then the merger proposals became active and their heralded savings forecast still further loss in jobs. All this led to intensification of demands for restricting the elimination of jobs. At the end of 1961 the Southern Pacific settled for a rule prohibiting abolishment of telegrapher positions in excess of attrition, except in case of abandonments and centralized traffic control installations. Other local job stabilization agreements were achieved. Union opposition to the NYC-P merger in May 1964 forced those two roads to agree that attrition alone be the basis for eliminating redundant employees and that there be no layoffs unless there was 5 percent or greater decline in revenue in any thirty-day period. These concessions led to negotiation in 1964 and 1965 of a radical new restrictive work rule, for the "non-op's," namely that employees with two years' or more service as of October 1964 be guaranteed permanent employment except for retirement, disability, and discharge for cause. In addition, jobs, as distinct from employees, were forbidden to be abolished in excess of 6 percent per year, and employment might be temporarily reduced only if revenue and net income over any three-month period declined more than 5 percent, and then only to the extent of 1 percent for each percent point over the 5 percent decline in revenue. In return, the carriers obtained formal recognition of freedom to make organizational changes and adopt technological advances and to transfer employees in connection therewith. Nineteen sixty-four and 1965 were years in which labor obtained work rules that placed the first basic constraints on managements' ability to control major categories of labor costs in line with traffic fluctuations.[8]

Overall 1960–1964

For the first time industry-by-industry wage adjustment averages were compiled by the BLS, thus making possible broad-based comparisons between key

Percent Changes in Year for Railroad "Non-Ops" and for All Industry Wage Rates; January to January Percent Changes, Consumer Price Index; Percent Changes in Annual Class I Railroad Net Income; Percent Unemployment of Whites Twenty to Twenty-four Years of Age, 1960–1964

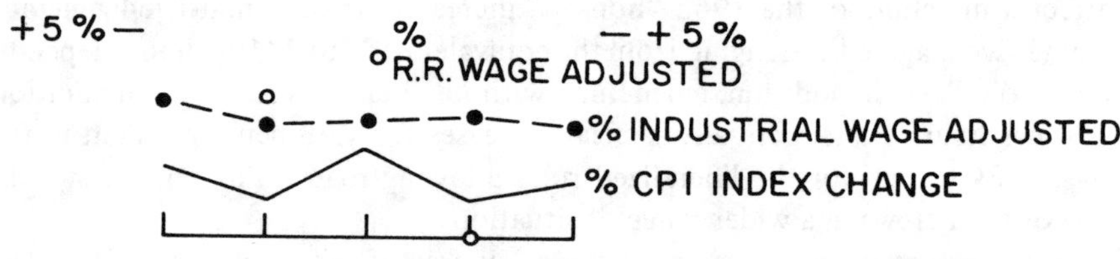

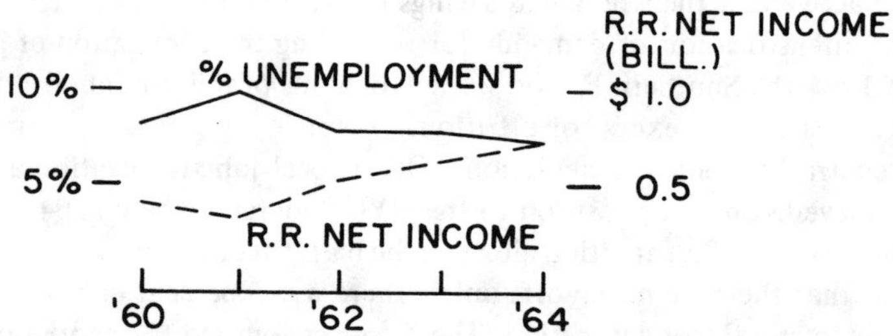

industries and railroads. Comparison of basic wage-rate increases, including cost-of-living escalation and benefit contributions specifically in lieu of wages, indicates that the "non-ops" gained the same amount as the steel industry and that the "ops" somewhat more than the higher amount for the auto workers. The increases for the trucking industry were substantially higher than the others. It was the industry of greatest growth during this period and the most aggressive union leadership. The railroads, on the other hand, had the least growth and in contrast to the past negotiations were never carried beyond the Emergency Board stage, and the boards' recommendations were accepted by the unions as well as the carriers. The strength of the "op" unions was reflected in the greater "op" gains and great resistance to the management pressure for the rules' modification.

Gains in addition to those in wage rates came from an increase to four weeks of vacation with pay after twenty-five years and a reduction in years of service required for shorter vacations. The railroads gave an eighth holiday; the auto industry, an eighth and ninth; and U.S. Steel, an every-five-year "sabbatical" for the senior half of its employees.

1960–1964 Retirement, Unemployment, and Other Benefits

For this period comparison between industries with respect to the level of benefit contributions can be made in terms of proportions that contributions by employers were of payroll. (See Table 22.) In the case of the railroads, this again does not include the transfers to the RRB from government sources.

TABLE 22

*Annual Company Contributions for Retirement, Unemployment,
Health, and Welfare, etc., as Proportion of Wages and Salaries*

	Class I RR	Class I Motor Carrier General Freight	U.S. Steel
1959	Est. 10%	6.7%	12½%
1964	13½	10.4	14½

It can be seen that by 1964 the interindustry differences in benefits had become less marked. Except for the catching up of the motor carriers, the percent increase in level of contributions was modest as compared to previous phases.

1965–1972

The final phase in the review of labor costs started with an upward trend in the country's economic activity. Industrial production rose rapidly through 1966, tapered off, and then continued up until the end of 1969. A decline started then and continued through the first quarter of 1971. The CPI rate of increase was modest to begin with, accelerated and peaked in 1969 at three and one-half times that of 1965, then receded to twice that in 1972.

From 1961 on, there was increasing pressure on the labor supply as economic activity increased and, the military cut into the twenty- to twenty-four-year-old male category, taking 20 percent of it in 1966. Overall, blue collar unemployment moved sharply downward from a high of 9 percent average in 1961 to 6 percent in 1964, to around 4 percent from 1966 on through 1969. There was a sharp upturn in 1970 to 8 percent and 9 percent in 1971. The trend 1966 through 1969 weakened employer bargaining strength and increased that of employees and their unions. In 1966, for instance, workers voted down more tentative agreements than in many years. In addition, there was generally expressed dissatisfaction in union circles with the modest 2½ to 3 percent annual wage increases of the first half of the 1960s. Beginning with 1965 there was first a gradual acceleration in the increases and then an explosive rise in many of the contracts covering 1970 and beyond. This phase is therefore reviewed in two periods.

1965–1968

Key Nonrail Industries

The steel and auto industry negotiations reflected these changing influences. The first contract was a two-year one for steel, agreed to in August 1965. The first year increase was 12¢ per hour all around plus 2¢ additional for skilled crafts, and the second year, 7¢. There were no cost-of-living additives. The just previous year's basic wage increase had been some 9¢. Initially, the auto industry carried on with its 1964 contract annual improvement factors of 2½ percent, minimum 6¢ per hour for 1965, and 3 percent, 7¢, for 1966, to which cost-of-living escalation was to add 11¢ and 2¢, respectively. In the last months of 1967 the big "three" auto companies signed new three-year contracts providing an immediate basic 20¢ per-hour all-around increase plus 30¢ additional for skilled crafts. For each of the following two years the improvement factor was increased to 3 percent, minimum 9¢. Over the three years, cost-of-living escalation was to add successively 5, 8, and 8¢.

Over-the-road truckers also continued with an earlier contract providing for terminal drivers an 8¢ per-hour increase in 1965 and 10¢ in 1966, and for line-haul, ¼¢ per mile in both years plus cost-of-living adjustments. A February 1967 three-year contract jumped the annual hourly increases to 14¢ for the first year and 15¢ each for the next two years. The mileage rate increases were doubled to ½¢.

During these years industry-wide average annual wage increases rose from the earlier level of about 7¢ each year for 1962 through 1964, to 9¢ in 1965, 10¢ in 1966, and then 13¢ in 1967. In percents these increases were from around 2.8 percent in the earlier period, rising to 3.3 percent for 1965, to 4.4 percent in 1967.

The Railroads

From 1963 on through 1966 there was a continued increase in railroad revenue and a substantial gain in pre-income tax net income, from $816 million to $1,089 million (well below the 1953 peak of $1,436 million). Nineteen sixty-seven brought a temporary downturn in revenue and sharp drop in the pretax net to $620 million. Nineteen sixty-eight provided slight improvement with net at $650 million. The East minus the Pocahontas pretax net was hardest hit in all this, becoming a deficit. In respect to railroad demand for labor it may be noted that by the mid-1960s the previous major reductions in jobs had leveled off to between 2 and 3½ percent annually. Average weekly insured unemployed railroad workers declined from 47,000 in 1963 to some 20,000 in 1966 through 1968.

The general attitudes of railroad labor at the beginning of this phase was indicated by the complaint of the president of the Railway Labor Executives Association in a statement of the Joint Economic Committee of Congress in 1966 complaining of the "great inequity in wage treatment of railway employees over the past eight years." A year later the editor of one railroad union magazine lauded the 1967 contracts as a "breaking of the old patterns."[9]

The "Non-Ops"

The first new contract of this phase was the clerk's December 28, 1967, settlement for one year for a 5 percent increase retroactive nearly a year. There followed a two-year agreement that gave a 2½ percent and then a 3½ percent rise plus 5¢ per hour for reclassification of jobs for 1968. The other "non-ops," shop crafts excepted, settled for the same pattern.

The parallel shop-craft negotiations turned into a long bitter dispute carried through more procedural steps than ever before. The initial demands were made in May 1966. By January 1967 the National Mediation Board's mediation attempts had failed. An Emergency Board was appointed and on March 12 published its recommendations of a 5 percent (equivalent to 15¢ per-hour average) increase for 1967, pointing out that this was in line with the general railroad pattern and better than many other industry increases that year. It also recommended a job revaluation study to determine satisfactory job pay differentials for skilled crafts and the collection of funds to be held in escrow to provide for such adjustments as would be found desirable. The shop crafts rejected all this and voted to strike. To prevent a stoppage of the railroads during the Vietnam War, Congress stepped in twice to pass legislation postponing any strike action, each time hoping that a settlement could be reached. By April, President Johnson appointed a special mediation panel in an attempt to reach an agreement. Its proposal was in excess of the Emergency Board suggestions, with a 6 percent increase over eighteen months plus three consecutive 5¢ per-hour supplements for skilled workers to meet their demands for elimination of skilled craft inequities. This too was rejected and finally the shop crafts actually went out on strike July 16. On the following day Congress passed, and the president signed, the final resolution of the dispute. Striking was postponed for another ninety days until still another special board was to mediate but this time with authority to make a binding determination. The board was of unusually prestigious make-up partly reflecting its congressional creation. There were two senators, Morse and Saltonstall; the head of the AFL-CIO, Mr. Meany; the professional labor-relations negotiator, Mr. Kheel; and a former AT&T president, Mr. Kappel. As might have been anticipated, mediation proved futile and the board itself set the final terms. They were the increases recommended by the previous board plus an additional basic 5¢ per hour effective July 1 and an added skilled crafts supplement of 5¢, October 1, 1968. Mr. Kappel challenged the board's additions as "inflationary." Senator Morse characterized the package as a "just and equitable middle ground."[10]

The "Ops"

During this 1965 to 1968 period the affected operating crafts continued their attempts to reverse the 1964 elimination of firemen and of a brakeman on some freight trains. The 1964 two-year limit with respect to firemen had expired in March 1966 leading to another special board to review again the merits of the elimination. It reported January 1966 that there were no adverse effects and elimination should be continued. This led the firemen to selectively strike eight major railroads beginning March 31, 1966. A federal court enjoined the strike action because the unions had failed to follow Railway Labor Act required procedures, and the strike ended after four days. The final "official" step in the "fireman manning" issue came much later in July 1970, following strikes against the BO, SP, and LN, and talk of a lockout threat by all the country's Class I railroads. An Emergency Board appointed this time again concluded that the evidence relating to safety and work burdens did not support the union asserted need for the restoration of firemen. The board proposed to soften the impact of the elimination by creation of a combination fireman-brakeman craft, which would lead to greater promotion opportunities for firemen through provision for their advancement to either conductor or engineer.

The issue of brakeman elimination followed a different course. In January 1965, Mr. Saunders, chairman of the Pennsylvania, and Mr. Luna, the president of the BRT, entered into a local agreement for the NYC, P, and EL railroads to retain a minimum of a conductor and two brakemen in train and yard service with the agreement by BRT to withdraw its opposition to the repeal of state full-crew laws. In February, Mr. Tuohy, president of the BO, and Mr. Luna agreed to similar terms for the BO. How much this may also have been tied to union withdrawal of opposition to ongoing merger proposals is not clear. Subsequently, other eastern roads followed suit.

The southern and western railroads continued for a while without such minimum crew agreements. Finally for some roads there was individual bargaining leading to 190 individual crew reduction agreements eliminating 8,000-plus brakemen jobs. However, on February 5, 1968, following BM, S, SCL, MP, TP, and UP promulgation of rule changes allowing management freedom to reduce crews, the BRT called strikes on three of these railroads. Settlement was reached between the presidents of the struck roads and the BRT on February 8 providing for immediate restoration of 50 percent of the eliminated brakemen jobs and individual negotiation with respect to the other 50 percent. In the following months most other roads settled on these terms. However, the IC and LN did not do so, and the latter was struck on November 6 and another Emergency Board was appointed. It recommended in December that since most other railroads had been able to reach agreements these last roads too should do so. Little was done during these years in respect to the other work-rule modifications that the Presidential Railroad Commission had suggested.

In the meantime, "op" wage adjustments came up for negotiation in 1966. The first settlements came in November with the BRT and BLE-F agreeing to a sixteen-and-a-half month contract with a 5 percent increase effective August 12. The BLE delayed settlement until the following June and obtained a 6 percent increase plus a 6 percent additive for engineers without firemen. The ORC-B, representing primarily the conductors, threatened a strike and following Emergency Board proceeding and mediation settled for the same 6 percent effective August 1966 but with added increases effective a year later in the car-length additives amounting to 5.6¢ per hour for each additional twenty cars above eighty.

1969–1972

Key Nonrail Industries

In this phase a more comprehensive review of nonrail industry awards is necessary to bring out some of the background for the rail negotiations. The August 1968 three-year steel contract established the initial pattern for this period with an immediate basic 20¢ per-hour increase along with ½¢ more for each spread between job classes, estimated to give a 32½¢ overall increase. For each of the following two years the basic increases were 12¢ with further job-spread factors of declining magnitude. This estimated overall average increase in 1969 was 21.2¢, and in 1970, 18.2¢.

Other industry negotiations produced the largest increases at this point and, in relation to rail negotiations, possibly the key ones. The last-minute New York Metropolitan Transit Authority, January 1, 1970, settlement under threat of a shutdown of New York City transit services provided an 8 percent increase immediately and 10 percent on July 1, 1971, along with large added supplemental benefits. Next came the widely heralded General Electric settlement. After a three-month strike, agreement was reached on January 26, 1970, for a first-year hourly increase of 20¢ per hour and 3¢ for back cost-of-living plus from 5 to 25¢ more for skilled crafts, followed by 15¢ basic increases in February 1971 and 1972.

The master truck negotiations came next. There was an initial national agreement reached in May giving drivers a three-year total increase of $1.10 per hour and 2¼¢ per mile through 1972. The Chicago area teamsters, however, held out for more and after three weeks of striking won three-year increases of $1.65 and 2¾¢. These became the master contract terms under a national clause that had provided for modification if any other settlements were higher. The teamsters union magazine had pointed out that the initial terms even without allowance for cost-of-living escalation would add $5,070 a year to hourly paid drivers' basic pay and $5,720 to over-the-road drivers'. In addition, there was the possibility of as much as 16¢ an hour more in 1971 and again in 1972 by way of cost-of-living escalation.[11]

A later key other-industry agreement was that of General Motors, November 4, 1970. The immediate increase was for 23 to 35¢ per hour, depending on job class, plus 26¢ for back cost-of-living adjustment not taken care of in the previous escalation provisions. Averaged over all employees, these totaled 51¢. Then for November 1971 and 1972 there were to be increases of 3 percent, amounting to from 11 to 22¢ per hour, this time along with unlimited cost-of-living escalation.

The terms of these contracts provided the setting against which the terms for new railroad ones were to be negotiated.

The Railroads

In this last period differentiation between the financial performance of the East and other regions became particularly noticeable. For the country as a whole, revenues continued upward from 1968 to 1972, in the East up only 10 percent compared to 20 percent in the West and 26 percent in the South. In the East pretax net (ordinary) income declined to a deficit of $225 million in 1970 and with continued deficits through 1972. In the South pretax net increased continuously from $131 million in 1968 to $204 million in 1972, and in the West net ended up at $506 million in 1972 after starting from $424 million in 1968 with a low of $381 million in 1970.

The various railroad crafts entered the 1969–1972 negotiating period at different points in time in respect to expiration of their previous contracts. The 1969 increases for most of the "non-ops" and "ops" were the earlier awards of 2 percent on January 1 and 3 percent on July 1. The shop-craft negotiations had come a year later and carried over into 1970. In this case the issues were (1) increased wages and (2) carrier desire to ease restrictions on the range of work allowable for particular craftsmen. These restrictions went back to World War I federal control when the kinds of work performed by each craft had been narrowed by elaborate classification rules that led to the splitting up of particular maintenance tasks among several employees.[12] An Emergency Board recommended in November 1969 a settlement with a 2 percent and 3 percent increase in 1969 plus 20¢ more per hour for Class I mechanics above regular mechanic's rates along with special increases for improved productivity resulting from modification of the working rules. This was rejected by the metal workers because of the concomitant modifications that would allow workers of one craft to do incidental work in other crafts at outlying points where there was so little work that members of each craft could not be fully employed. This dispute was finally carried to the congressional level with legislation passed once again, imposing roughly the board's terms. The final outcome provided the 2 percent and 3 percent plus 10¢ for 1969, a basic 5 percent increase January 1, 1970, plus 4¢ per hour on April 1 and on August 1 that year, and an additional 7¢ for skilled crafts on February 10, 1970. This might have been expected to set the 1970 pattern for other crafts, but the greater gains established during 1970 in other industries beginning with the General Electric January settlement and culminating in the truckers' final settlement for a 50¢ 1970 raise made such a possibility fade further into the background as months went by.

Negotiations for 1970 increases in other than the shop-craft wages started early in that year. A new grouping of crafts, the "non-ops" other than shopmen and the "ops" cooperated in bargaining. The dominant bargaining unions being the BRAC and new UTU. After selective strikes in September by the clerks on the S, BO, and CO railroads, still another Emergency Board was convened. It recommended on November 9 the largest increase in any one contract in railroad history: 5 percent retroactive to January 1, 1970, plus 32¢ (equivalent to some 9 percent) November 1, 1970, 9 percent in 1971 and 10 percent in 1972. Compounded over the three years, these totaled 34 percent. Rule changes were recommended to reduce labor costs, largely in respect to the "ops." Principal were the lifting of requirements that interchange crews had to return empty following delivery of cars to a connecting railroad and that road crews could not make delivery of blocks of cars in interchange directly to other road crews but rather had to turn them over to intermediate yard crews. Another was the easing of limitations on road crew handling of cars, locomotives, and cabooses of their trains in terminals. Still another was providing the right to institute interdivisional runs. The board also recommended that compensating benefits be provided for employees who would be adversely affected by these changes. The recommendations were rejected in early December and a vote approved striking. Again negotiations carried to the congressional level and on December 11 a law was passed and signed putting into effect the wage increases recommended for 1970 but omitting any requirement as to easing work rules. Union members were ordered back to work for two months while further negotiations were carried on. In February 1971 the maintenance of way workers and then the clerks accepted the Emergency Board's recommendations with the addition of an extension of the contract life by six months with an added 25¢ per-hour increase for January 1, and 10¢. April 1, 1973, making an overall 46 percent increase through 1970 to mid-1973.

In the meantime, the signalmen rejected this pattern because they felt it did not provide pay raises commensurate with the greater skills involved in working with the increasingly complicated signal technology. They went out on strike in May 1971. This again led to congressional involvement in order to keep the railroads operating, with legislation enforcing settlement on the general pattern terms. On May 13 the engineers agreed to them with some modifications advantageous to their craft. Finally, the UTU group of the remaining "ops," after breaking off discussions with the official bargaining agent of the railroads, met with the presidents of the S, PC, and SP in August and settled for the general pattern with certain modification. Ther had never been such combined congressional and individual system presidential involvement and such massive wage increases.

Percent Changes in Year for Railroad "Non-Ops" and for All Industry Wage Rates; January to January Percent Changes, Consumer Price Index; Percent Changes in Annual Class I Railroad Net Income; Percent Unemployment of Whites Twenty to Twenty-four Years of Age, 1965–1972

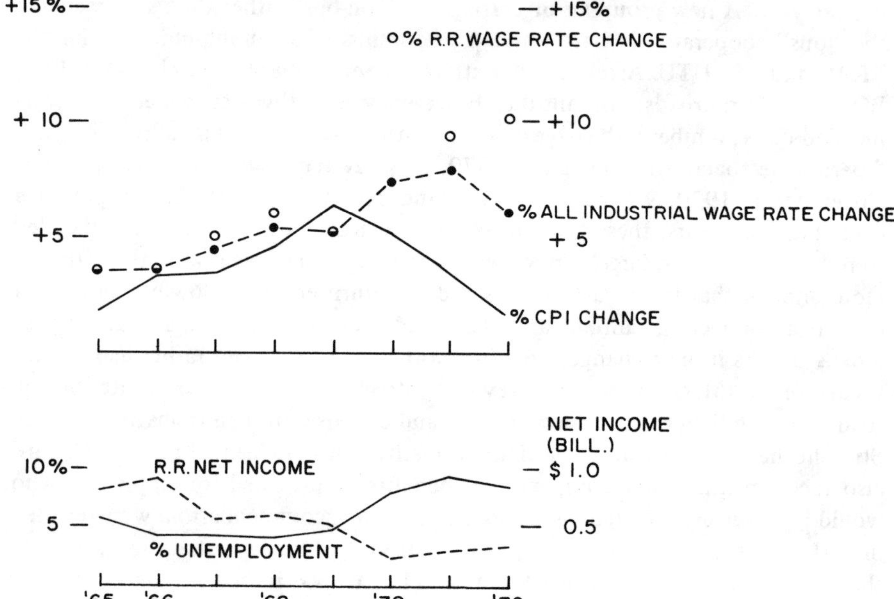

Overall 1965–1972

A cross-industry summary comparison for this phase of wage adjustments is made difficult because of the varying use of percent and absolute amounts for annual increases. Numerous extra increases for skilled workers make necessary for the comparison calculation of the sum of the two types of increases averaged over all workers. Comparable increases can be calculated for the "non-ops." For the first two years of this 1965–1972 phase, average overall wage rate increases were in low key for the individual industries surveyed and for industry as a whole. The 1965 increases were greater than the CPI rise; the 1966 increases were close to it. With 1967 both the automobile and trucking wage contracts had major breakthroughs with heavy front loading of their new three-year contracts and substantially raised levels for the following two years. The railroad "non-ops" contracts showed similar trend jumping from the early years' 3 percent plus increases to 5 and 6 percent. The auto and "non-op" increases were somewhat over the all-industry averages, in 1968 greater than the CPI increase and in 1969 under. With 1970 (1971 for steel) the increases going into effect for the individual industries listed far exceeded the industry-wide increase and the 5 percent CPI rise.

In particular, the railroad increase was some 13½ percent compared to 7 percent for all industry. Thereafter for the railroads the increases were 9 and 10 percent compared to 8 and 6 percent for the all-industry average. The large gains in the key industry contracts beginning in early 1970 and the unusually large teamsters' gains set an example that the railroad unions insisted on at least matching. The high level of their militancy with numerous rejections of Emergency Board recommendations, an unusual number of strikes, and carrying of negotiations to the point of congressional involvement led in the latter years to the highest level of wage increases far above the CPI rise.

1965–1972 Retirement, Unemployment, and Other Benefits

The changes in railroad employee benefits during the 1965–1972 phase were largely made by Congress. Basic retirement benefits were increased 7 percent in 1966 and 15, 10, and 20 percent in the three years 1970 through 1972, these latter without any provision for their funding. Additional supplemental benefits were agreed to be paid for by a 2¢ (increased later to 7½¢) per-hour-worked contribution by the railroads. Just following this phase the employee-employer retirement contributions were revised by reducing the employee share by a half and increasing the railroads' by 50 percent to make up the loss. In total, from 1965 through 1972 the railroad taxes for retirement and expenses for private health and welfare both almost doubled while taxes for unemployment compensation remained the same. By 1972 overall benefits paid out were over $2,700 million with the railroads' contributions just over $1,000 million, equal to a sixth of total employee compensation, and transfer from other government funds to railroad retirement accounts had reached $800 million. Precise benefit comparison with other industries is no longer possible with this increasing governmetnt subsidy for the railroad ones. However, it may be noted that the Presidential Railroad Commission in 1972 observed that "as a group, railroad retirement beneficiaries receive higher benefits and total income than most people dependent on social security and/or other pension plans."

In five years the widening of eligibility and increasing of levels resulted in a cumulative increase of 68½ percent in average monthly benefits. The funding of most of this increase was left to transfer from other government funds, toward which neither employees nor the railroads paid anything. Further, at the end the unions pressured the Congress into cutting employee contributions in half and requiring the railroads to increase theirs correspondingly.

Supplementary Aspects of Wage Structure[13]

A supplementary component of compensation during the period under review has been the adding to hourly compensation the pay for holiday and vacation days, etc. For all hourly paid classes, train and engine employees excepted, payments for these days amounted to some 4.4 percent of straight-time compensation in 1946 with a continuing rise over the years, to 7.6 percent by 1959 and 10.5 percent by 1972.

Another component is the overtime element in compensation arising from labor contract rules requiring that anyone called for work must as a minimum be paid for eight hours and that for hours over eight, at a punitive rate most generally one and a half times the straight-time rate. During World War II there had been unusually heavy use of overtime as a result of overloading of facilities and scarcity of labor. Data for 1945 reflects this with overtime hours amounting to 12 percent of straight-time for "non-ops" employees other than executives and their staff. The average for the "non-ops" declined to 7 percent in 1946, 2½ percent in 1954, and 2¾ percent in 1958, depressed traffic years. A peak of 6 percent occurred in the heavy traffic year 1969, and there was a decline to 4¾ percent in 1972.

There have been significant regional differences in proportion of overtime hours of work. For the period for which regional data were available, 1951 to 1962, in the East the proportion of overtime compensation to that of straight-time was 6 to 6½ percent, half again as much as the South, with the West beginning the same and ending somewhat less.

Changes in Job and Wage Structure with Service Shifts and Technological Change

An overall view of the labor input of the railroad industry over the postwar quarter century points to the changes in the operating functions performed resulting from the shifts in kinds of services provided and the technological and organizational advances introduced. Table 23 shows the effects on employment for such crafts as can be identified as being involved in the principal areas of change.

The near elimination of lcl operations phased out a large number of relatively unskilled "platform" employees—loaders, truckers, etc. The reduction in passenger service was not as complete but dropped some 60,000. The changes in maintenance technologies and related organizational changes had wide-reaching effects in respect to reduction of the less-skilled types of jobs and introduction of the specialized higher-skilled types. For track work the traditional section men were reduced by 84 percent while portable track equipment operators increased 22 percent. For rolling stock maintenance it was helpers and apprentices that were cut back 91 percent while the journeymen declined only 61 percent. The absolute numbers involved were large, around 100,000 less section men, and as many less skilled equipment repair workers. Through freight train and engine crews were reduced by nearly a half, 40,000, while ton-miles of line-haul service increased almost by a third, as a result of dieselization, larger freight cars, along with elimination of lcl service and reduction in transport of light loading commodities. All told, there was a decrease of 61 percent, over 800,000 employees.

In the early part of the postwar period the predominance of cents-per-hour increases in wage rates narrowed the proportionate differences between rates for

TABLE 23

Reduction in Jobs of Particular Crafts by Cause, 1946–1972

(Average mid-month employment)

Crafts	1946	1972	Reduction
Phasing out of lcl service			
Loaders, callers, truckers, station laborers, etc.	60,000	3,000	95%
Primarily reduction in passenger train services			
Coach cleaners	13,000	2,000	84%
Baggage agents, assistants, station attendants	10,000	1,400	86
Passenger train & engine crews	46,000	8,000	83
Changes in technology and organization-maintenance of track (Also reflects elimination of maintenance to passenger service standards)			
Section men	126,000	21,000	84%
Crossing elimination and automatic crossing protection			
Crossing watchmen, etc.	13,000	1,100	92%
Changes in technology and organization-maintenance of equipment (Also reflects phasing out of lcl boxcars and passenger equipment)			
Machinists, boilermakers, electrical workers, etc.	92,000	35,600	61%
Helpers & apprentices,	96,000	8,700	91
General laborers (shops, engine houses, etc.)	22,500	5,400	76
Changes in technology and operating methods for road freight service			
Crewmen	87,300	45,800	48%

**Typical Craft Average Hourly Earnings per Hour Worked Including Holiday
Pay and Allowances, Excluding Overtime; Through Freight Conductors per Mile**

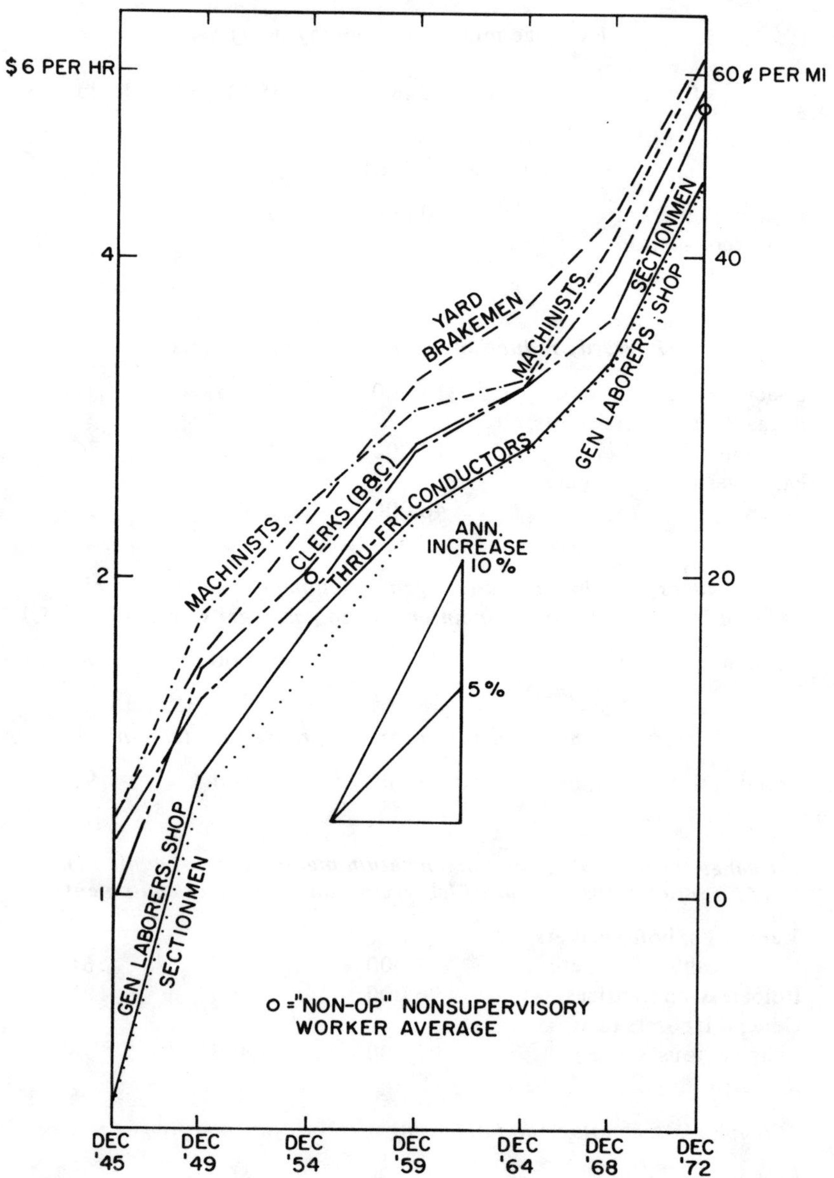

**Four- and Five-Year Phase Annual Rates of Increase: BLS—Production Workers
—Average Hourly Gross Earnings Class I Railroads, Motor Vehicle, Blast Furnace
and Steel Mills, Intercity Trucking, and All Manufacturing Industry,
Cost-of-Living Index**

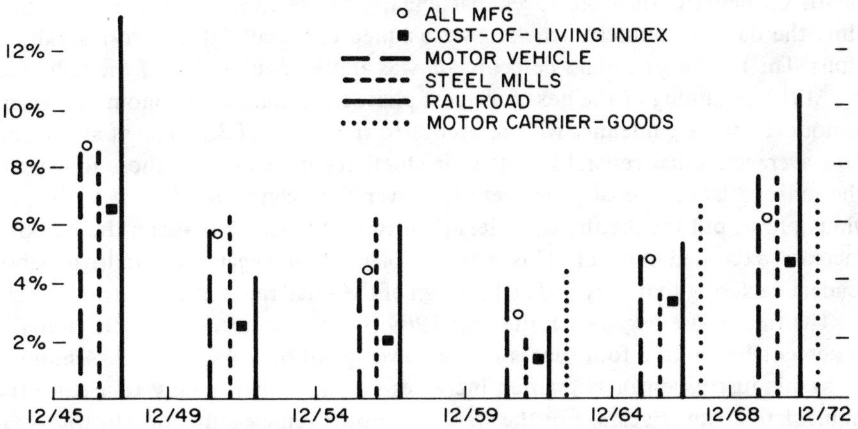

skilled and less-skilled jobs. It was not until after 1966 the increases, with few exceptions percentage ones, that the skilled crafts' rates moved up toward restoring their traditional advantage. Over the whole twenty-seven years section-men rates increased 643 percent and the lowest increase for the skilled crafts charted, for the conductors, was 381 percent.

* * *

By way of summary, the trends of railroad employee average overall compensation or so-called earnings rates in comparison with those of key industries and with the consumer price index (CPI) provide an overview of the quarter-century developments free of the details of cost-of-living adjustments, overtime, arbitraries, vacations, etc., but still taking them into account. While indices showing these trends are not in every detail exactly comparable, each is consistent over time so that comparison of the rates of increase of each is meaningful.

During the four years of postwar adjustment, 1946 to 1949, the average annual rate of increase of railroad employee earnings per hour was more than half again as much as that of the key steel and motor vehicle industries and over double the CPI increase. During the next five years to the recession year 1954, the railroad increase was still twice the CPI, but that of the two industries exceeded the railroads by a substantial margin. Over the following five years through another recession to the low railroad traffic year, 1959, the railroad labor earnings gain was almost three times the CPI rise and considerably more than for manufacturing as a whole, though less than for steel.

From December 1959, following the long steel industry strikes, to 1964 through the 1960/61 depression was the period of lowest CPI rise and earnings gains. The railroad increase was again twice that of the CPI but close to that for manufacturing indusry in general. It was in these years that there was more emphasis on benefits than on wages, particularly in the steel industry. For the first time the data for intercity trucking were added to the available historical tabulations. The trucking earnings percent gain was almost double that of the railroads.

At the beginning of the next four-year phase the Council of Economic Advisors announced wage guidelines with reference to the figure of 3.2 percent as the current average annual general industry productivity increase. For those four years the railroad labor annual gains were just over 5 percent, double that of the previous phase, but for the first time less than twice the CPI rise. Again the trucking increase exceeded the rail. This was the phase that began with railroad labor leaders declaring that they had had enough of the small raises of the previous years.

The final phase began with the year 1969, the CPI annual rise jumping initially 6 percent but with a four successive year average of only 4½ percent. A number of key industry contracts granted increases far more than at any time since the immediate postwar years. For the steel and motor vehicle industries the four-year annual gains averaged just over 7½ percent. For the railroad industry the average was 10½ percent and well over twice that of the CPI.

Yearly "Non-Op" Basic Hourly Wage Rate Increases and Consumer Price Index Changes, January to January

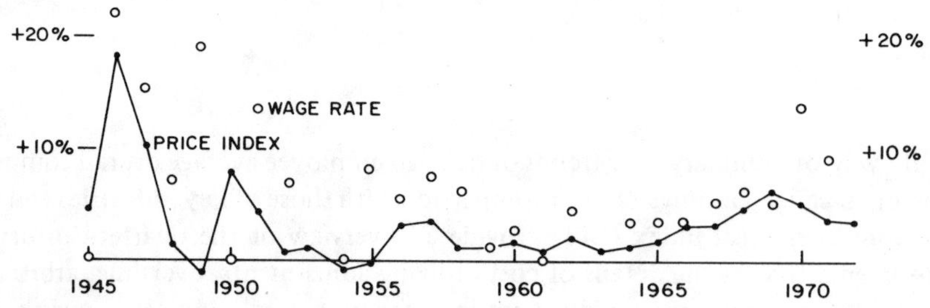

Annual Average Mid-Month "Non-Op" Employment and Percent Unemployment of U.S. White Males Twenty to Twenty-four Years of Age

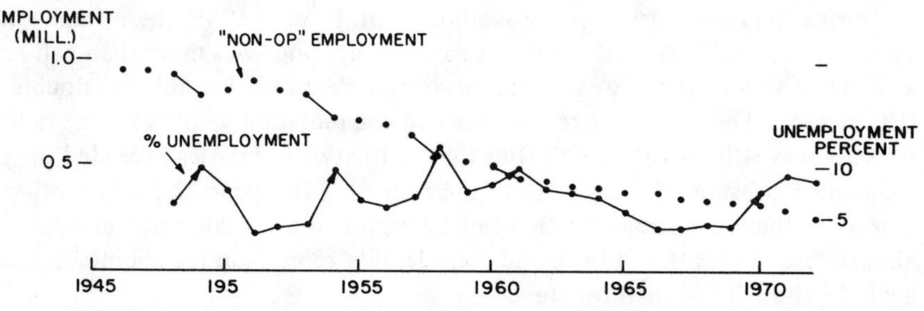

Over the whole twenty-seven years the railroad hourly gross earnings increase was some 450 percent; all manufacturing, some 300 percent; and the key steel and motor vehicle, 360 percent. The CPI rise was 133 percent. The railroad unions' strong bargaining had pushed their members' earnings up more than three times the rate of the CPI rise and half again the rate of the manufacturing industry.

It was this phase that also saw the highest rate of increase in level of benefits, over 60 percent, with little funding provided for, so that the costs were left to the government to cover. Further, the sequel was the reduction of the employee payroll tax contributions by half and forcing that loss to be made up by a 50 percent increase in the railroad payroll tax contribution, to 15½ percent.

The terms of labor input supplied to the railroad were controlled by a conglomeration of craft unions. Their bargaining strength was maximized by the critical public interest in avoidance of service interruption by strikes, the highly organized political power of the several unions, and the presence most of the time of at least one aggressive, competitive personality among the union heads.

Share of Operating Revenues for Labor Costs by Major Regions, 1940–1941 and 1945–1970

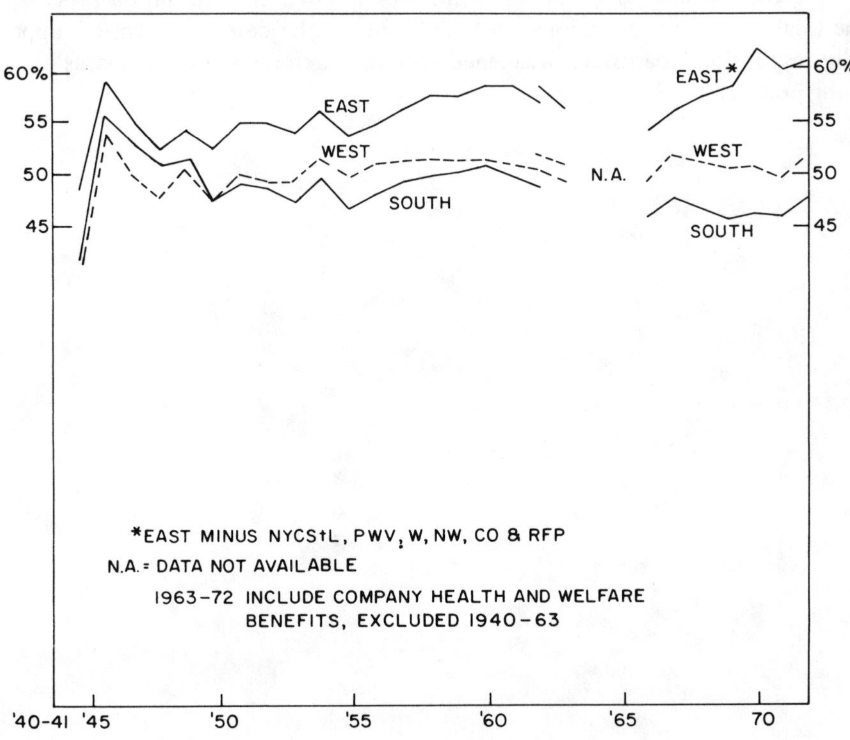

The comparatively greater railroad than other industry compensation rate gains reflect this. The pattern of the wage structure for a major group of railroad employees, the train and enginemen, was extremely complicated with key structural elements based on operating conditions of the distant past. The unions consistently opposed and largely prevented the modernizing of these elements. The industry was a mature one with little or no growth possibilities by expansion of its facilities and minimal opportunity for increased labor productivity in two important segments of its operations, lcl and passenger. This was countered by withdrawal from those two services. Investment in the technological developments in respect to maintenance tools and machines and heavier track components did increase productivity in respect to fixed facilities. Advances in motive power and freight cars markedly increased productivity in carload freight service. The higher than for most industry rate of increase in unit labor costs garnered for employees a large share of returns from these increases in productivity. The railroads' withdrawal from major segments of their operations reduced employment substantially. This along with the southern roads' labor share of revenue declining and the eastern rising consistently, the western remaining almost constant. The regional cultural differences as they affect labor relations and management attitudes remain to explain these regional contrasts.

Overall, the willingness of top politicians to enter the arbitration process at the final stages in negotiations, with additions to the determinations of supposedly responsible boards, has weakened both management's and the boards' stabilizing powers.

10

Management

Management is possibly the most critical input in respect to the performance of railroad systems. A definition of what comprises management and review of how it is chosen and functions are necessary in assessing its performance. Management is responsible for a system's organization with its structured array of positions, the personnel occupying them, and the lines of communication, which will energize the cooperative efforts of all. Management also has the responsiblity to formulate the organization's objectives with an eye toward, among other things, the changing environment in which it operates. Who effectively comprises management depends on the assignments of authority and responsibility to formal positions and even more on the forcefulness of particular personalities involved.[1] In general, the chief executive officer (ceo), be he chairman, president, or ceo, in association with some of his immediate subordinates, constitute top management, and he, its responsible leader.

The role of directors or, in the case of bankruptcy, of trustees, may vary widely. Their role has been, most generally in the period under consideration as passive advisors and routine approvers of the top officer's decisions.

Since for the most part stock ownership is widely dispersed, seldom as much as 1 percent in a single ownership, the board members are not beholden to any particular stockholder and become in effect a self-perpetuating body principally chosen by, or at least with the approval of, the top executive. Trustees, on the other hand, are court appointed with different loyalties, but often one of them is the former system top leader. There are important exceptions to this when a significant share of stock is in particular hands, in which case directors represent that share.

From the point of view of assessing performance, the crucial role of directors or trustees is in their choice of successors to retiring executives or, in the extreme case, to a top executive who is being replaced ahead of retirement. In their generally passive role directors have tended to be approving of existing management. Succession has been from existing officers as recommended by the top officer. This sequence reflects loyalty to him originating with his approval of the director appointments and his bemutterings of rising personnel in his organization. However, if performance has been exceptionally poor the directors on occasion have overridden loyalties and on their own replaced top executives with someone from outside. In the unusual case with an outsider's acquiring working stock control, replacement has generally been because of changed objectives, quite aside from any assessment as to strength or weakness of management.

191

Appraisal of the performance of the country's railroad managements is difficult because of the difficulty in finding ways of evaluating it objectively. In carrying out the directors' responsibility just indicated, their unusual action of bringing in outsiders as top executives provides an objective sign of critical inadequacy in management. This action indicates that the existing leadership has not acquired, trained, and brought along personnel capable of meeting top officer standards. Obversely, an indication of good management is when the personnel brought along appear to other companies to be particularly capable and, therefore, are sought after as replacements on foreign systems. Another objective sign of poor performance is frequent and extensive replacements throughout upper management. All these drastic personnel changes are a matter of public record.[2]

In another vein, objective measures such as statistics of operating and financial results and rates of growth are tempting, but they are greatly affected by other variables, particularly the underlying strategic strengths or weaknesses of systems and the impact of external changes. Thus they are not a sure basis of judgment of pure management ability. The appraisals of such rating agencies as Duns and Moody specifically related to efficiency, rather than to financial success, do effectively discount these other variables and will be reviewed. This analysis of management over the postwar quarter century rests on these few objective bases of appraisal, as applied to the larger railroad systems, those with over $25 million revenues in 1960.

REPLACEMENT UPON RETIREMENT

Immediate Postwar

The postwar replacement of wartime leaders was a critical phase in the management of the country's railroads. It was significant that with so many eastern systems, the NYC, NYCStL, DH, WM, CEI, and CIL, directors decided it was necessary to go outside their own organizations. The choices were all for persons with operating backgrounds except on the WM and CIL, who had financial experience. For the largest eastern system, the P, the directors indicated uncertainty about succession by choosing a sixty-five-year-old traffic vice-president, who, however, had not had the usual engineering training. The appointment was only for a short five-year term before going back to the traditional choice of their own operating vice-president. In the southern region one road, the ACL, did not choose from within, taking a president of a jointly owned subsidiary. In the West five systems the CNW, CRI, StLSF, WP, CGW chose presidents from other systems, all choices with operating training. Of the total of these twelve choices, all but five served to their normal retirement. The NYC and CNW appointees were displaced after only a few years because of a change in stock control of their systems. Two others of the outsiders moved on to more attractive presidencies, being replaced by choices within their organizations, and one was replaced early by a traffic officer of his system.

Next Generation

The subsequent successions of top officers involved fewer instances of outside choices. Excluding the abnormal situation on the NYNH&H, the only eastern region outside ones were for the P in 1963, to bring in a NW lawyer president as its leader, and the E, to relieve its president seven years before normal retirement. On the southern systems there was a higher proportion of outsiders appointed than previously, with legally trained choices on the IC and the S, both in 1967. The former choice was from the Railway Express Agency and the latter from a private law practice in Washington, D.C. Five western roads imported outsiders—the CMStP in 1958, the KCS in 1961, the MP in 1961, influenced by a new controlling interest stockholder, and the CBQ and NP in 1965/66. All but the first, a lawyer, were with operating backgrounds. In this second phase, for the country as a whole, half of the choices had had legal careers and three of the western five had had chief executive experience. The change toward lawyers may be attributed to emphasis on merger problems and interest in the possibility of diversification. Of particular note was the fact that two cases, the E and CRI, in 1965, involved early replacement of executives, reflecting an unusually strong negative assessment of existing management performance.

Overall, this history of bringing in outsiders reveals a substantial degree of mobility of executives in the railroad industry. The high proportion of operating-trained choices emphasizes stress on the physical technology of the industry and the control of expenses rather than the marketing of its output. Strangely, with the interest in the marketing rather than the simple sales approach developing around the 1960s, none of the later replacements were from market departments.

Executive Replacement upon Change in Stock Control

Changes that came with the acquisition of working control of a system's stock or a shift in such control from one group to another involved other factors. In such cases, the new executives have several times been the financial operators who acquired the control. Twice in the case of NYNH&H, in 1948 and 1956, and once in the case of the BM, in 1956, these choices led to traumatic results. On the other hand, the unusual choice could be considered successful for the CNW. Most of the time, however, the new groups chose operating-oriented new chief executives.

Systems Supplying Replacements

The obverse of these negative assessments is the evidence of organizations bringing up their personnel to upper management levels whose qualities excelled sufficiently to make them attractive to other systems as top management candidates. Because any organization can just by chance have single individuals who develop top qualities on their own, the criteria for successful management must be that several individuals have been exported and that this was not the result of a top officer who himself was exported and wanted to take along with him some of his old associates. More of the S system upper-level officers than any other road have been chosen by other systems. An S general manager was chosen to head the StLSF in 1947, and an operating vice-president to head the PC in 1970. Another S operating vice-president had been chosen in 1966 for a similar post on the P and still another in 1970 for one on the WP. The StLSF is the only other system that qualifies as to numbers of exports. In 1965 its president went as president to the CBQ, and then to the NP. A StLSF vice-president became TPW president in 1966 and CNW operating vice-president in 1968. Another StLSF officer was taken on as marketing vice-president by the IC and then the PC vice-president in 1968 and 1970 respectively. The two systems identified as producing good executives were also ones whose performances were among the most successful in the country.

EVIDENCE OF INADEQUATE PERFORMANCE

By way of contrast there was strong negative evidence as to management performance in the case of three systems, all eastern, the NYNH&H, the P, and the EL.

The NYNH&H

The former case arose with change of stock control and needs to be examined in some detail to appreciate the traumatic effects. After the NYNH&H had come out of bankruptcy in 1946 it had a new operating vice-president and two well-trained young vice-presidents, one as assistant to the president and another in charge of traffic. A year later, an eighty-four-year-old New England industrialist, Frederick C. Dumaine, Sr., and his associates purchased stock control and installed as president a former legislative representative and presidential assistant on the Boston and Maine. The latter and Dumaine, Sr., were only able to work together for fifteen months, whereupon Dumaine himself took over the presidency. Within eighteen months he died and his son, who had had no railroad or managerial experience was voted to take his place. In the two months short of three years of Dumaine control the road's storekeeper and purchasing agent was second in command. There were major departures from the upper management in particular the operating vice-president and the two young vice-presidents.

Then Patrick McGuiness, a Wall Street financial advisor who had been a Dumaine aid in his purchase of control and who earlier had been criticized by the ICC about his performance as chairman of the Norfolk and Southern together with associates acquired control of the NYNH&H. McGuiness became the fourth president in six years. He immediately announced that he was looking for outside personnel for five departmental vice-presidents. Outsiders were brought in for three posts. Then suddenly after nineteen months McGuiness himself resigned. The directors replaced him with one of their own members, George Alpert, a Boston lawyer with neither railroad nor executive experience.[3]

Alpert started off with the former storekeeper and purchasing agent again as chief of operations, but soon brought in several western railroad officers to take over operations, a CIL officer as traffic vice-president and an outside accountant as comptroller. However by early 1960 Alpert found it necessary to reappraise his operating team. He publicly acknowledged the inadequacy of management in announcing the need to put "responsibility for management and operations back in the hands of long-time employees" in order "to restore the faith and morale of New Haven employees and patrons."[4] The western operating outsiders were dropped. By July 1961 the NYNH&H was in bankruptcy following which there was yet another policy-making group, the trustees. They appointed still another outsider as chief administrative officer. In turn he too did not work out and in less than two years the trustees brought in still another outsider as operating head, but in effect kept the overall presidential function to themselves.

In the meantime, the U.S. secretary of commerce had appointed a group of railroad specialists from various railroads in the U.S. to appraise the NYNH&H problems. Among their conclusions were that it was necessary "to intensify [efforts] to revitalize the management..., this to include educating the managerial force in both modern railroad and managerial techniques." The group also observed "that for at least fifteen years top management has not only not made its policies and wishes clear, but in addition has not set the example of making wise decisions or following sound managerial principles."[5]

Later, the ICC in 1966 was to comment that the company "was plagued with the failure of its management to develop any long-range plan of operation. Additionally,...suffering such problems as the speculative practices of a particular management..., a locomotive policy marked by poor judgment, drift and indecision..."[6]

The survey of these organizational changes makes clear the impossibility with the unsatisfactory and frequently changing leadership of attaining the effective cooperative relationships and formulation of and stability in objectives emphasized by Chester Barnard.

The Pennsylvania

Another case of negative assessments of management was that of the largest of the eastern systems, the Pennsylvania (P). In the fall of 1955 the newly installed president of the P announced a major restructuring of its operating department in order to gain the "close supervision of service typical of a smaller railroad" and at the same time to "capitalize on the advantages of size." A review of the P's management structure by outside consultants had been authorized, and the 1955 changes followed. They were drastic. The older pattern of three gross regions each in the charge of a vice-president and an average of six operating divisions under each was replaced by nine regions characterized as largely autonomous small railroads headed by regional managers without subregional divisions. This eliminated a whole layer of supervision at the operating division level, each division having previously had a superintendent and numerous trainmasters.[7]

That the results were unsatisfactory was evidenced by the announcement some nine years later by the P's next chief executive officer that there was to be a reversion back to the previous three gross regions, this time with an average of four divisions for each. This was "to regain leadership in excellence as well as size,... better managerial control of costs and operating efficiency" and "closer direction of day-to-day operations." It was to make the P "again the standard railroad of the world."[8]

Just before this, with the retirement of the system's chief executive officer, the directors did not promote one of its own but chose the Norfolk and Western's president instead, contrary to the long-established traditions of the P. All this was indicative of serious deterioration of management performance, an important part of which was its failure to provide for future leaders. The further and penultimate problems of the P's management, which developed in connection with its merger, are discussed in another chapter.

The EL

The other publicly stated criticism of a management involved the EL. In mid-1963 its directors formally revealed that a change was "highly desirable." This came four years after the E-DLW merger.[9] Management during those four years was almost exclusively of prior Erie officers. Four of five EL vice-presidents were from the E, so were all regional general managers and assistants, and six of the seven division superintendents. With the announcement the directors brought in as a new chairman and top executive the president of the DH, who many years earlier had been the president of the DLW. In addition, the president of the Terminal Railroads Association of St. Louis was brought in as executive vice-president, shortly to become president. This replaced both the existing president and operating vice-president several years before normal retirement. This is one of the rare instances of disavowal of key top system officers.

FINANCIAL RATING ORGANIZATION APPRAISALS

In contrast to these indications of a negative nature, there is the identification of top managements in terms of efficiency and growth independent of financial standing by the editors of *Moody's Bond Survey* and *Dun's Review*. These appraisals discount the effects of external changes and inherent characteristics not subject to management control.

Over the years *Moody's* was sparing of optimum ratings and kept them separate and distinct from their ratings as to credit standing.

In the 1950s only three systems, the New York Chicago and St. Louis, NYCStL Gulf Mobile, and Ohio GMO and Denver and Rio Grande Western DRG, were characterized by *Moody's* as being "among the most efficient" or "highly efficient." They were also credited with "favorable traffic prospects" or "superior revenue trends." One of the three was from each of the three major regions, and all were medium-sized roads. In the early 1960s the Missouri Pacific was added as "more efficient than railroads as a whole."[10]

A 1960 *Dun's Review* first polled executives of major businesses of all types as to what were the twenty "best-managed" companies in the country, and no railroads were chosen. But in the subsequent poll of 1974, a railroad, the Southern, was among the five best.[11]

*   *   *

Considering both these positive and negative judgments, the eastern region was heavily burdened with inadequate managements and organization weaknesses. It lost its only "highly efficient" management, the NYCStL, through merger in 1964. The southern region was favored with two well-managed systems, one, the GMO, to be lost in 1972 by merger. The western region was credited with two of the higher-rated managements.

The East's lack of highly rated managements and the burden of several clearly demonstrated inadequate ones must have played a significant role in the poor performance of that region's systems.

11

Growth of Railroad Systems—Internal

A key aspect of the performance of railroad systems is their growth or decline. On the one hand, it is basically related to factors external to a railroad system, to changes in the use of the resources adjacent to it, in the level of transport-generating economic activity of the area served, and in the competitive strength of other-than-rail modes of transport. On the other hand, growth or decline is dependent on the internal factors of a system's own strengths or weaknesses, in its route network, the attractiveness of its pricing policies and service, and its entrance into other-than-rail transport activity.

REGIONAL ECONOMIC ACTIVITY VS. SYSTEM GROWTH

The analysis first deals with the effects of the external factors—changes in general economic activity and competitive strength of nonrail transport. Growth by way of system entrance into development of other-than-rail modes is then considered. In the next chapter the review and analysis covers system growth from acquisitions of other rail systems by merger and unification.[1]

Satisfactory measures of rail growth must be chosen carefully. Historical trends in dollars of revenue and of investment in road and equipment assets are distorted upward by inflation, and in number of employees, downward by improving productivity. Physical volume of traffic avoids these biases. Because of the phasing out of lcl service and the decline in passenger traffic, growth has been a matter of changes in level of carload traffic. The overall physical unit of this, revenue ton-miles, which avoids the mentioned distortions, is taken as the best choice as to measure of growth, recognizing that it provides only a rough estimate due to the possible distorting effects of shifts in the mix of commodities involved. When nonrail activities are considered it is necessary to fall back on revenue or sales dollars because dollars are the only common denominator available.

GROWTH BY WAY OF INTERNAL INCREASE
OF RAIL TRAFFIC

Growth of Larger Systems

The measurement of rail growth has been described in chapter 3 along with the choice of a proxy for economic activity relevant to overall demand for freight transport. Only the larger rail systems can be expected to fully reflect regional

198

differences in rates of growth. Small systems tend to rely too much on a limited number of shippers and their products for originating or terminating business and/ or on high proportions of overhead traffic that depend upon activity levels outside the system's area. Therefore only the twenty systems with over 5 billion annual ton-miles of traffic are considered in this analysis of the relation of transport-oriented economic activity growth and rail system growth. The Pocahontas roads are excluded because of their substantial dependence, some 30 percent, on export coal traffic, the volume of which has reflected changes in foreign rather than domestic regional activity.

The graph below shows the twenty considered systems with the 1950 to 1969 percent changes in revenue ton-miles and in the proxy for activity calculated for the states served by each system. The year 1969 is chosen for the last year to be considered because it is the last one in which the three important western systems—the CBQ, GN, and NP—still separately reported ton-mile data and is a year for which deflated data is available. The year 1950 is chosen at the beginning

Changes in Independent System Revenue Ton-Miles versus Index of System Area Industrial Activity, 1950–1969
(Systems with over 5 billion ton-mi. in 1960, excluding those with over 33 percent overhead traffic)

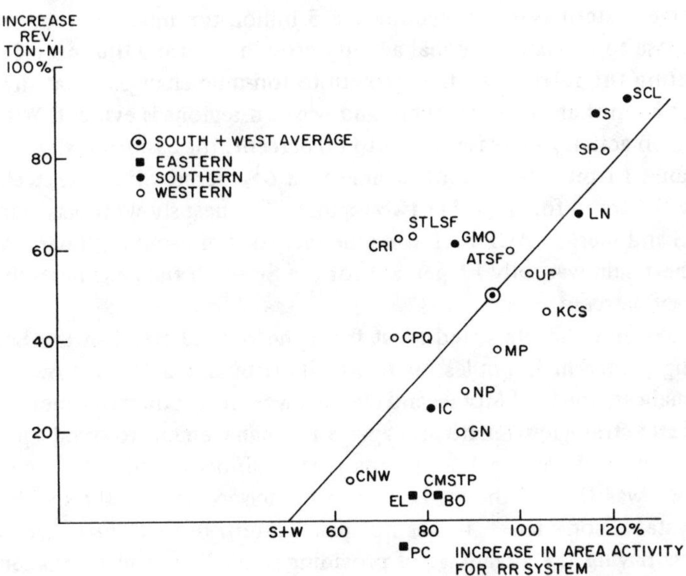

East: BO, EL, NYC-P-NH; South: ACL-SAL, GMO, IC, LN, S-CG, West: ATSF, CBQ, CMStP, CNW, CRI, GN, KCS-LA, MP-TP, NP, StLSF, SP-StSW, UP.

(Source: ICC, *SRUS* and *TSUS*, Sections A-1; U.S. D. Comm. *Sur. Curr. Bus.*, v54, #4, April 1974, pp. 34–45 [by calculation].)

because, as noted in chapter 3, it is the earliest postwar year for which constant-dollar state-by-state data are available. The 1950 data for what were initially the originally independent systems are combined in accord with their mergers to match the final make-up of the systems.

The correlation of revenue ton-mile changes and tributary region activity increases for the seventeen southern and western systems indicates that 52 percent of the ton-mile changes was associated with increases in the proxy measure of area activity growth. This leaves 48 percent associated with the other variables—management, pricing, service, strategic aspects of location, etc. For the country-wide average system there was a 93 percent increase in activity and a 49 percent increase in its ton-miles. Estimates of country-wide rail shares of all-mode (rail, motor vehicle, inland waterway, and pipeline) transport revenue ton-miles were 56 percent in 1950 and 41 percent in 1969. (There were no regional estimates.) With the 56 percent rail share of all-mode ton-miles initially in 1950, there would have to have been a decline to a 43 percent rail share to produce the result of only a 49 percent rail ton-mile increase. The 41 percent estimated 1969 share would have resulted in a somewhat lower rail increase than the 49 percent, which actually occurred.

Growth of Roads—Over 5 Billion-Ton-Mile Scale

The three eastern systems meeting the 5 billion-ton-mile size requirement all had very close to the same regional activity growth rates and thus provide no basis for estimating the relation of that growth to ton-mile changes. That the relation is different from that of the southern and western regions is evident. With overall eastern region activity increases of 75 to 80 percent, the eastern system's ton-mile changes ranged from 5½ percent decline to a 6½ percent increase, well outside and below the trend for the other two regions. The best showing was in the South with the S and merged ACL-SAL ton-mile increases of around 90 percent. In the West the best gain was only 81 percent for the SP, with the next best, the ATSF, just under 60 percent.

Of the systems that departed most from the general trend in the South, the outstanding gainer in ton-miles relative to its tributary activity growth was the region's smallest, the Gulf Mobile and Ohio. It was the product of a merger in 1947 and had basic strategic strength and aggressive management to build up traffic in competition with its regional counterpart, the Illinois Central. An even superior performance was that of the St. Louis San Francisco, next to the smallest of the western systems considered. It was not just western but extended well into the South, thus having the advantage of providing single-line service between part of the South and the Midwest. Still better was the gain for the Rock Island, which was a middle-size western system with slightly higher than usual overhead traffic for a road of its size. It had a traditional role in transcontinental traffic through its western connection with the Southern Pacific via El Paso. The other better-than-average system was the Chicago Burlington and Quincy, again a road with important western connections for participation in long-haul traffic between the Northwest and both the Southwest and the East. The poorest performer was the Chicago, Milwaukee, St. Paul, and Pacific. It had long been strategically weak, with a transcontinental extension in the early part of the century attempting to invade the territory of two already well-established systems.

The only relation of scale of systems to growth was that the largest systems, those over 20 billion ton-miles in 1960, deviated little from the overall trend of traffic increase relative to regional activity growth. The medium- and small-size systems among the seventeen provided both the extremes of the best and the worst performance.

Growth of Smaller Roads—Under 5 Billion-Ton-Mile Scale

East

In the East between Buffalo and Pittsburgh and the Atlantic seaboard there were eight systems of 1 to 5 million-ton-mile scale. With one exception they were roughly parallel to the three larger eastern systems. Of the eight, annual ton-miles declined between 30 and 33 percent from 1950 to 1969 for the LV, CNJ, and R, and for the DH and NYNH&H, between 23 and 24 percent. The former were particularly hard hit because anthracite coal had made up a major part of their traffic, accounting for 20 percent of freight revenue, and was to be lost to fuel oil. These three were also highly dependent upon traffic with western and southern connections for which they had to compete both among themselves and with the bigger systems. But the key factor was that all were involved in traffic demands that were dampened by the general slow development of goods-producing industries in the overall eastern territory.

On the other hand, in the slowest growing part of the territory, northern New England, two roads, the BM and MC, did significantly better than the other because of the important share of their traffic being related to the local potato and wood and paper production. The BM's loss was only 9 percent and the Maine Central had a gain of 20 percent.

The WM, the southernmost of the eight roads, with the advantage of a role in a through east-west general merchandise traffic route and a significant amount of coal and blast furnace fluxing stone traffic, showed a 10 percent growth.

There were several still smaller Class I roads in the East. Their fortunes varied but the Bangor and Aroostook remained as a viable independent road because it originated agricultural and paper products that provided a 44 percent ton-mile growth from 1950 to 1969. On the other hand, another northern New England road, the Rutland, primarily in Vermont, could not find enough traffic there to survive as a private operation. The state took it over and parceled parts of its operation out under contract. A third road, the New York, Ontario, and Western, running west from the lower Hudson River, controlled by the NYNH&H, was poorly located as a part of a through east-west route and after loss of its anthracite coal had no local traffic to help. It was liquidated and parts of its line were taken on by the larger adjacent lines. Still another small road dependent on cement traffic, which was lost to trucks, was liquidated to gain tax advantages.

South

In the South the Class I roads with below 5 billion annual ton-miles were mostly affiliated with larger systems with which their operations became consolidated. The exception was the Florida East Coast (FEC), extending 366 miles from Jacksonville to Miami, which, with 1 billion ton-miles in 1960, remained independent. Originally a heavy passenger carrier, it had financial problems that led to its receivership in 1931 and long years of reorganization problems until its return to private operation in 1960. With Florida the fastest-growing state in respect to the proxy index of goods-generating growth, the FEC increase of 77 percent in ton-miles from 1950 to 1969 and 19 percent more to 1972 is not surprising. After several years of labor difficulties the new management obtained a uniquely simple and labor-efficient set of union contracts, built up the physical property, and maintained a successful independent operation. Takeover by a larger system would lose the gains of the labor contracts, so the system remained independent.

The other independent southern road was the Norfolk Southern (NS), running south from Norfolk diagonally across North Carolina to Charlotte, 398 miles. The NS did not possess strategic strengths or particularly profitable special traffic that would make it an especially attractive candidate for acquisition by one of the adjacent larger systems. While it had managed to pay dividends through 1957, it had only just been able to earn its interest through the 1960s. In 1973, the NS stockholders agreed to an exchange of S securities for their stock.

There were six other smaller (less than a quarter of a billion ton-miles) independent Class I southern roads that had shown traffic declines by 1964 or before. These roads had some earnings in the 1950s, but the 1960s proved difficult financially and two went into bankruptcy. Between 1962 and 1970 five of these were acquired by major connecting lines for cash amounts varying from $1\frac{1}{2}$ to $16 million. A sixth was formally abandoned in 1969, but subsequently some half of its route miles were taken on by adjacent larger roads.

These smaller southern roads fared better than their eastern counterparts. One continued as an independent with substantial growth, and all but one of the others were taken on by the larger southern systems. The greater increase in general economic activity of the South differentiated the fate of the eight from their counterparts in the East.

Midwest

In the Midwest there were eight independent Class I roads below the 5 billion-ton-mile size. Two of them, the Chicago and Great Western (CGW) and the MStL, were in the highly competitive Chicago to Missouri River region. Their network route structure was weak both in respect to on-line traffic sources and bargaining strength for joint through hauls. Both had failed during the 1930s and came out of bankruptcy in the early 1940s. Both lost around 11 percent in ton-miles between 1950 and 1960, somewhat more than the 4 to 9 percent loss of the larger roads in the same slow-growth midwest area. Both were finally taken over by the CNW.

Two more, the Monon (M) and the Chicago and Eastern Illinois (CEI) were roads with access to the Chicago area from the south. The M had ealier been controlled jointly by the LN and S, providing entry for these southern roads into the Chicago gateway. The CEI had been an important line between Chicago and St. Louis with branches to the Ohio River at Evansville and to southern Illinois and Missouri where it connected with southwestern roads. Both these two roads had also been through reorganization. Between 1950 and 1960, the M had lost 21 percent in ton-miles; the CEI had gained 33 percent. Their strategic value to southern or western connections was considerable, leading to the ultimate takeover by larger systems.

There were three much smaller midwestern Class I roads all with less than one-third billion ton-miles, the Toledo Peoria and Western (TPW), the Akron, Canton, and Youngstown (ACY), and the Green Bay and Western (BGW). They all connected with larger systems, which wanted to use the three for participation in long-haul through routes. By mid-1955 the TPW was taken over jointly by two of the country's largest systems, the P and ATSF, and its ton-miles by 1969 were 61 percent above 1950's. The ACY became an adjunct to the NW merged system and its ton-miles rose 40 percent. The GBW remained independent and its traffic increased 20 percent.

There were also two still smaller Class I roads, which grew out of electric railways. One remained as a very small independent with no growth. The other was taken over jointly in 1954 by eight larger Class I roads running through Illinois. Only minor growth followed.

These smaller midwestern roads with modest growth of traffic had fared better than their eastern counterparts. Their growth did not make for continued independent existence, but it did insure their value as candidates for acquisition by their larger neighbors.

West

In the Southwest the Missouri, Kansas, and Texas (MKT), with 4 billion ton-miles in 1960, was just under the size limits considered in the initial analysis of internal growth of twenty systems. The MKT had a long history of financial difficulty and had deteriorated from a freight traffic and fixed physical plant point of view through most of the years of this study.[2] Its ton-miles increased only 6 percent from 1950 to 1969 while the increase in the activity of its areas was 85 percent. In relation to trends for the larger western and southern systems, these figures place the MKT in lowest rank. Because of its lack of relative traffic strength and its inheritance of excessive financial burdens, the MKT did not have suitors for merger. Over the years it was a tempting challenge to a series of changing independent groups who acquired control of its stock. It was placed under a holding company, Katy Industries, for speculative possibilities and possible tax benefits.

A smaller system, the Kansas, Oklahoma, and Gulf, operating north-south across Oklahoma between Kansas and Texas, with a half billion ton-miles in 1960, had shown little growth and was acquired by the MP system for $8½ million, with one segment in turn sold to the ATSF.

Further west there were two independent systems of a size to have been considered along with the twenty first considered but with such a high proportion of overhead traffic to exclude them from that analysis. One carrying 5.5 billion ton-miles in 1960, the Denver and Rio Grande Western (DRG), crossed the Rocky Mountains from Denver and Pueblo to Salt Lake, some 570 miles. It was an important segment of a transcontinental route, which was competitive with the SP-UP route from Ogden across Wyoming. The DRG's bargaining strength was improved during the years as a result of an ICC order effective in 1968 restricting longstanding UP, SP preferential traffic solicitation in their own favor.[3] There was a substantial growth of industry in the two states the DRG served. It became an important originator of coal, which accounted for about a third of its carried tonnage both in 1950 and 1969. Revenue ton-miles increased 59 percent from 1950 to 1969.

The second western independent system was the Western Pacific (WP) with its subsidiaries. Its main line was the western segment of a transcontinental route with the DRG. It had a branch north to Oregon, part of a north-south inland route connecting with the GN on the north and the ATSF on the south. Both routes met strong competition from the SP. Some two-thirds of the WP traffic was to and from connecting carriers and only 14 percent local. Its 1969 traffic had grown by 32 percent above the 1950 level. There had been a 125 percent gain in the proxy measure of northern California, Nevada, and Utah activity growth. Since the WP traffic was so much related to activity levels in other parts of the country because of its high proportion of overhead traffic the system's growth did not match this local growth.

The possible value of the WP network as an addition to the systems connecting or in competition with it was substantial so that it was actively sought after as a merger partner. However, its takeover would unbalance the western half of the transcontinental railroad pattern and it had seemed to have been able to perform satisfactorily, so the ICC quashed the attempts at takeover.

*   *   *

Internal growth of carload freight traffic for the larger rail systems came only with substantial increase of rail transport-generating economic activity in the regions they served. The increase had to be sufficient to counter the decreased rail demand due to the decentralization of industry, the introduction of processing and distribution methods requiring less transport, the tendency of industry to produce lighter and smaller products, and the increasing competition from other modes of transport. In the South and West a 50 percent increase (inflation compensated for) in region activity kept a rail system's traffic (ton-miles) just level, while a 100 percent increase resulted in 50 percent traffic growth. Under the less favorable conditions in the East north of the Potomac River it took 80 percent activity growth to provide just a 6 percent increase in traffic.

For larger systems of over 5 billion ton-miles of traffic the possibility of gaining by merely increasing their share of their region relative to other rail systems was limited. In an industry as mature as the railroads with empires already staked out and new entry possibilities very limited there was little opportunity through just better marketing to overcome a system's strategic weakness. The only single clearcut case of such gain was the GMO. A possible second case was the StLSF. On the other hand, impossibility of improving a basically weak position was clearly demonstrated by the CMStP and, among smaller systems, the MKT, both of whose traffic increases were much below the normal expectancy associated with their region's growth.

Overall, the twenty large systems, with the exception of the PC constituents, were all able to post some gain from 1950 to 1969, with the proxy for countrywide transport-oriented activity increasing 86 percent.

For the smaller systems of 5 to 1 billion-ton-mile scale the traffic growth possibilities were rare and decline likelihood great. Of the thirteen of this scale only four showed a ton-mile increase from 1950 to the latter 1960s. These four were all sought after by the larger systems. Nine did not have networks with sufficient traffic-attracting power as independents to grow in line with regional growth. However, three of the latter, in the Midwest, were still attractive enough to be sought as acquisitions.

Of the nineteen still smaller Class I roads, with under 1 billion ton-miles, six registered increases. These were attributable either to particular on-line growth industries or an unusually strategic position of their routes relative to their connections. The four with the latter characteristics were all candidates for takeover by connecting roads, two begin consummated during the years covered by this study. Of the thirteen whose traffic declined, four were formally abandoned with segments of their lines remaining in service under new auspices. Two remained in operation as independents. The rest were acquired by larger connecting roads at such low prices as to make it worthwhile.

GROWTH BY TRANSPORT MODES OTHER THAN RAIL

Forwarders

Of the forty more or less Class I railroad systems a substantial proportion had subsidiaries involving transport operations other than rail. After World War II, two, the Erie and New York Central, controlled forwarder companies that had been started twenty years or so earlier as a means of retaining some of the lcl-type traffic. The gross revenues of these forwarders, in 1954 $52 million for the E's and $64 million for the NYC's, were far larger than any derived by rail trucking operations at that time. However, by 1962 both railroads had disposed of their interests in these forwarders, the NYC to its stockholders in 1956 and the E to a major trucking company, Pacific Intermountain Express, in 1962. It may be noted that the forwarder industry was a static one having received 4.7 million tons from shippers in 1947 and only 4.2 million in 1972.[4]

With the fast growth of air freight in the 1960s a new type of air forwarder operation was inaugurated. Several railroads saw intermodal possibilities. To most it was unrewarding but the Burlington Northern starting in 1972 was highly successful, producing $4½ million net income before taxes by its fifth year.

Air Transport

Railroad direct moves into air transport operations were limited to that of New England road involvement in Boston and Maine Air and New England Airways during the 1930s. Under grandfather provisions these operations obtained regulatory approval but with their increasing financial demands the railroads voluntarily relinquished control in 1940.[5] There had also been railroad involvement in independent airline development. For instance, the P had directors on Transcontinental Air Transport, and the P and ATSF in the early years of air transport provided joint rail-air service.[6] Of more general significance, in 1947 the CAB expressed the opinion that it was essential to air services' ultimate success that they be conducted independently of railroad and bus operations.[7] Earlier, in rejecting shipping line control of American Export Airlines, the CAB had referred to the earlier ICC investigation of the NYNH&H attempt to establish a monopoly of the then three modes of transport—rail, electric trolley, and water—and the conclusion that the failures of that monopoly indicated that different modes should be kept distinct so that each might operate most effectively in its own sphere.[8]

Highway Goods Transport

A number of railroads entered into trucking operations from the latter 1920s on. For the most part, the objective was substitution for line-haul train service on branch lines and for way-freight service in respect largely to lcl traffic. In addition, railroad trucks provided various terminal services such as pick-up and delivery services and handling of TOFC trailers. Practically none of the subsidiaries undertook to compete directly with trucks for over-the-road service. The exceptions were the Boston and Maine; the New York, New Haven, and Hartford; the St. Louis and Southwestern; and the Chicago, St. Paul, and Omaha (part of the CNW system) trucking subsidiaries. These had gained permanent rights for the operations because they were established before federal regulation of motor carriers was effective.[9]

Of the railroad system trucking subsidiaries in the years just after the war, only two had intercity common-carrier freight-traffic revenues of more than $5 million, the ATSF's with $8 million in 1947 and the SP's with approximately $11 million. In general, trucking revenues were 2 percent or somewhat less of the parent railroad system's rail-operating revenues. From that point on, trends for these subsidiaries varied widely. The one with nearly complete freedom to enter into competition with independent truckers was the NYNH&H. However, the latter's managements made no serious effort to take advantage of its subsidiary's unique opportunities and promote its operations. Its operating revenue, almost entirely from freight, was only around $3 million just after the war and still only around $3½ million in its final year, 1967. The other New England roads that had grandfather rights to varying degrees likewise did not take advantage of them and in fact the BM leased what rights it had to a major independent trucker.

In general, with the exceptions mentioned, railroads have not been able to compete for over-the-road traffic because of regulatory constraints that limit railroad related trucking to operations auxiliary or supplemental to train service. Despite this, several western railroad systems, the ATSF, CBQ, DRG, CRI, MP, and SP have continued to pursue the development of their trucking subsidiaries.[10] Estimated growth of their intercity traffic from the latter 1940s to 1969 can only be measured in terms of revenue, individual company ton-mile data not being available. Growth has been nearly fivefold for the SP and CBQ systems, almost fourfold for the ATSF, and around threefold for the others. In proportion to parent rail-operating revenues, the trucking revenues in 1969 were highest for the DRG, 8 percent; for the SP and CBQ, 5 percent; and between 3 and 4 percent for the others. The railroads that had no or partial regulatory constraint had not attempted to develop their trucking business. On the other hand, the named western roads have pushed their trucking operations as far as the constraints have permitted.[11]

Waterway Transport

Rigid regulatory restraints on rail involvement in domestic water transport kept railroad systems from entering this form of transport. Two railroads that had grandfather rights, the Southern Pacific, from Texas to New York, and the Central of Georgia, from Savannah to New York, did not attempt to reinstitute these services after the war. The CG turned this over to Sea Train Lines. In 1962 the Illinois Central and Southern Pacific joint request to take over the J. I. Hay inland water operations in the Southwest, with $4 million revenues, was denied by the ICC. On the other hand, in 1972 the Southern system was allowed to acquire a coal-carrying barge line on the Tennessee River, and Katy Industries, the Missouri, Kansas, and Texas Railroad holding company, to control the Cena Towing.[12]

Pipelines

In respect to petroleum pipelines, there was no constraint on railroad entrance. However, there was very little attempt to obtain growth by pipeline construction. This was the fastest developing transport field—ton-miles increased over three times 1950 to 1969—and was the most profitable mode. The only major railroad construction of general service pipelines was by the Southern Pacific system starting in 1957. It handled refined products from the Los Angeles area and El Paso, serving intermediate points such as Tucson and the Imperial Valley. Later lines were built east from the San Francisco Bay area to Reno, from Portland to Eugene, Oregon, and jointly with the ATSF from near Los Angeles to San Diego. Southern Pacific Pipeline Company revenue grew from $14 million in 1960 to $39 million in 1972, and net operating income before taxes from $8½ million to $17 million.[13]

In connection with oil found on NP and adjacent lands, the NP took a 10 percent interest in the Butte Pipeline Company, beginning operations in the mid-1950s with revenues of $4½ million in 1960 and $4 million by 1972. Further developments led to a 50 percent interest in the Portal Pipeline Company east to Minneapolis, which had $3 million revenue in 1972. Neither of these proved to be growth situations because the supplying oil fields' output did not increase. The Union Pacific was involved in a products line from southern California to the Reno area starting in 1961. Its revenues leveled off at 4 to $5 million.

A $72 million petroleum products pipeline from the Southwest to the Midwest was built under the auspices of Missouri, Kansas, and Texas system officers and directors. Kay Industries, a MKT subsidiary, held 19 percent of the pipeline company's stock. This stock, however, was sold in 1966.

The ATSF system on its own entered the pipeline field with a 117-mile line for jet fuel from Amarillo, Texas, to a military post at Clovis, New Mexico. The ATSF's major later moves were by way of a 739-mile line completed in 1971 from western Texas and New Mexico to near Houston to carry natural gas liquids. Its revenues were $7 million in 1972. In the fall of 1970 the ATSF put into operation an anhydrous ammonia pipeline extending from Louisiana producing plants to Midwest corn-growing states. This involved an investment of over $100 million, the largest single commitment of any rail system toward building its own pipeline operation.

The most radical entrance into pipeline activities was the SP system's construction of the Black Mesa pipeline, carrying a coal slurry 273 miles to a large power plant near Mojave on the Colorado River. The SP won in the bidding for the cheapest way to get coal to the plant and made an investment of some $40 million with initial operation in 1970. In 1972 the gross annual revenue was $10 million, and net income after taxes, $3.7 million.

*   *   *

While the railroads had been free to enter the pipeline field, their ability to find shippers ready to use rail-owned lines was limited. The major oil companies had long seen the transport of crude oil as having many aspects of value to them and thus built their own pipelines. With the advent of refined product pipelines, most of these too were oil company developed, but independent operations were more possible. However, only the SP and ATSF systems among railroads took the opportunity to build their own facilities as a means of participating in a significant way in a new area of transport growth.

In the postwar period a few of the western roads reached out to develop other-than-rail modes of transport as a means of maintaining their share of the transport market and providing a base for growth. It was the western roads that pioneered in viable coal slurry and anhydrous ammonia pipeline transport. It was western roads that pushed hardest to get the maximum opportunity to use trucks that the regulatory constraints on their use could be interpreted to allow. The revenues from the nonrail operations did not become a significant percentage of that from freight rail services or a significant element in growth.

Overall, the growth of the mainstay of the railroads, their freight traffic, from 1950 to 1969 in raw physical terms was around 40 percent for the two most successful large systems, the S and SCL, and 80 percent for the third-ranking, the SP. In dollars of revenue, because of changing traffic mixes and price changes, the increases were somewhat less, 62 and 13 percent for the top two. Three western systems also achieved that range of revenue gain. At the other extreme of major system performance, the lowest growth was for two principal eastern ones, the PC and EL, whose revenue gains were just under 2 percent.

With such important regional differences, the variance in growth rates could not be attributed to basic factors, which were uniform country-wide. Wage terms were basically the same for all systems; capital markets were pretty much homogeneous. Regulation was largely in federal hands with the rulings applying equally all around. As we have seen, management can vary markedly, system to system, and be a potentially strong factor in relative growth. Concentration of problem managements in the East have been a significant factor. The high proportion of mergers in the East may be a cause of traffic loss and they may be prompted by lack of traffic growth. Clearly, the lack of gains in and loss of economic activities productive of transport demands have been the dominant factor.

209

12

Growth by Acquisition of Other Railroads and Results of Unification

In the twenty-five years following World War II there have been a number of systems achieving growth by means of acquisition of other railroads. Almost all Class I systems in existence at the end of the war had reached their then size as a result of a past history of acquisition and unification. With fewer independent systems left, the significant opportunities for this type of growth had sharply declined. In the period under study the large share of unifications has involved tidying up subsidiary or minor company control. These have not been of significance in the broad picture so will not be considered. The field of interest then comprises the formally proposed acquisitions submitted to the ICC for approval by one of the independent Class I systems. It is this that has preoccupied top management to an increasing degree as the years have gone by after World War II.[1]

It is important to recognize that the acquisition process can involve much more than simply an attempt at growth per se. Other possible objectives included the reduction of the number of competitive routes, and of firms involved in the rate-making process, the diversification of traffic mix, and the broadening of the characteristics of region served. Still other possible goals have been improving use of management skills, getting better use of car supply, reducing facilities to match diminishing levels of traffic, making optimum use of alternative facilities and hoped for economics of scale. These considerations along with growth will be covered in the case-by-case review.

From 1947 through 1972, twenty-four of the acquisitions were consumated by merger or unification. Of these, eight involved acquired systems large enough when compared to the acquiring system (former's freight revenue at least 25 percent of that of the latter) to make comparison of before and after performance data reveal the result of merger or unification. The proposals advocating combination state that five years must elapse to allow all readjustments to be made. Thus comparisons are of the precombination averages with post-five-year averages. Since the last year generally under review is 1972, unifications consummated after 1968 are not analyzed in this way. Parallel or otherwise comparable systems that were not involved in unification, when available, are presented as control cases.

210

HISTORICAL BACKGROUND

By way of general background the prewar build-up of the major systems is reviewed. In the East and Pocahontas regions, the major systems had in the early years of this century expanded their control to involve wide-ranging empires. These had been subjected to cutbacks with the enforcement of antitrust constraints. For instance, the New York Central (NYC) had to give up control of the parallel New York, Chicago, and St. Louis (NYCStL). So did the Pennsylvania (P) of the Baltimore and Ohio (BO).

Subsequently, in the 1920s important realignments were effected through acquisitions by holding companies, which avoided regulatory constraints. Largely through this means, the Van Sweringens had built up a family of eastern roads including the Chesapeake and Ohio (CO), Pere Marquette (PM), NYCStL, Wheeling and Lake Erie (WLE), Chicago and Eastern Illinois (CEI), and to the West, the Missouri Pacific (MP). The Pennsylvania system had purchased a controlling block of Norfolk and Western (NW) stock early in the century and in the 1920s acquired either directly or through subsidiaries a large share of Wabash (W), Lehigh Valley (LV), and Detroit, Toledo, and Ironton (DTI) stock. It also obtained shares in the two main New England carriers. The BO had acquired an interest in the Reading (R) and Central of New Jersey (CNJ) to protect its access to New York, although it shared this with the NYC. Then the BO purchased 43 percent of the preferred and common shares of the Western Maryland (WM) to control a parallel route over the Allegheny Mountains and prevent its acquisition by competitors. It had joined in with other eastern roads to establish an east-west through route that was competitive with the BO. The BO also took on two smaller carriers, in northwestern Pennsylvania, to provide access to Buffalo, and in the Midwest, the Alton, to get more extensive coverage of that area and access to western traffic at the Missouri River. The NYC was the least expansive during the 1920s and '30s, its principal efforts involving the stock ownership in the R and CNJ just referred to. Following the promulgation of the ICC 1929 consolidation plan proposing the Delaware and Lackawana Western's (DLW) inclusion in the NYC system, the latter purchased 8 percent of DLW common stock. In a series of ICC decisions after 1930, based on antitrust and public interest policy objectives, some of these acquisitions were restrained by orders to place stockholdings in the hands of independent trustees. Thus operating control of the E, WM, and LV was separated from the railroads that had purchased their stock.

In the South, the broad pattern had been established before World War I. The 1920s were years of unification of smaller carriers within the ACL and the S families. In the West, the super empires planned by the Harriman and the Hill interests in the early 1900s were cut back by antitrust constraints, and a more fragmented basic pattern remained. The Gould empire financial failures led to its disintegration, leaving an MP family and a number of independent systems. In the 1920s there were some unsuccessful attempts to reassemble these and other independents into new family alignments. In 1930 the proposed three-way merger of the GN and NP along with their common controlled CBQ was in effect denied by the ICC with its conditioning approval of the merger of principals upon divorce of the CBQ.

Thus coming into the post-World War II period, there were for the most part generally well positioned systems or families of affiliated roads, a few of which had been strengthened and enlarged in the interwar years. In addition, there were a number of medium- or small-sized Class I properties that had been independent since pre-World War I days or had become so because bankruptcy and consummated plans of reorganization had liquidated the position of the old stockholders. In a few cases there had been voluntary severance of affiliation or changes in systems that were tantamount to independence as in the case of the WLE. Finally, there had been the three systems, E, LV, and WM, that became independent but not available because of the trusteeing of their stock.

In the post–World War II period, as noted earlier, the effective constraints on acquisition of control and merger are those in the Transportation Act of 1940. Its main thrust is "to foster and encourage," even "to facilitate," control and merger so long as it was "consistent with public interest."[2] Certain guidelines of a specific nature had to be followed: Weight had to be given to the effect upon service and the public interest of inclusion or failure to include other railroads. Consideration had to be given to the resulting fixed charges. Finally, the interest of affected employees had to be protected by fair and equitable arrangements.

POSTWAR ACQUISITION PROPOSALS

End of the War Merger Proposals

As World War II came to a close, active moves toward merger appeared in three parts of the country. In Florida the ACL tried to acquire the Florida East Coast (FEC). In the middle of the country the reorganization of the Alton (A) was the focus of the GMO merger. Along the routes of east-west commerce, Chicago-Detroit-Cleveland-Buffalo, the CO proposed merger of some parts of the old Van Sweringen empire.

Atlantic Coast Line-Florida East Coast

The FEC had long been an independent road serving the eastern coast of Florida from the Jacksonville gateway where it connected with the Southern (S), Atlantic

Coast Line (ACL), and Seaboard Airline (SAL) systems south to Miami and the tip of Florida, 396 miles. Despite an apparently strong bargaining position as a generator of traffic, with a heavy passenger business and a double track line, it had not proved to be a viable operation and had gone into receivership in 1931. In the prolonged course of working out a plan of reorganization for the FEC, the ACL in 1945 entered the picture with a takeover proposal. The ACL's final maximum proposed payment for the FEC was $46½ million in par value of securities, and cash to the extent of $4 million. FEC revenue ton-miles added to the ACL systems would have provided an immediate 10 percent increase in the latter's freight traffic. Further additions were anticipated from increased routing via the ACL of the FEC traffic moving north of Jacksonville. The two principal competitors of the ACL, the S and SAL, naturally opposed the proposal.

So did the local Florida interests, which through ownership of a large part of the bankrupt road's mortgage bond issue held the key residual interest in the FEC. They were a large paper company, local banks, and the estate of Alfred I. Dupont. The driving force behind them was Edward Ball, a Dupont relative. The ACL versus these Florida interests battle was fought over thirteen years, with several successive ICC approvals of the ACL acquisition and court rejections of them. In 1958 the ACL finally withdrew, and after further extended proceedings the FEC was launched free of court jurisdiction as an independent road on January 1, 1961. The early subsequent years of its operation were highlighted by intense labor conflict as the new management pioneered a unique, simplified, cost-reducing wage structure. This would not have been possible if the merger with the ACL had taken place because the ACL was fully unionized and its unions would have demanded their representing of the FEC employees and adopting the ACL contract. The FEC's operation remaining independent was accompanied with ton-mile growth of 111 percent from 1950 to 1972.[3]

Gulf Mobile and Ohio-Alton

The GMO-A merger in the Mississippi Valley involved as the principal actor a recently formed southern system assembled in 1940 from the Gulf Mobile and Northern (GMN) and the bankrupt Mobile and Ohio (MO). The latter had been part of the S system but the MO's performance was such that it was allowed to go into bankruptcy in 1932, and in 1940 its mortgage bonds held by the S were sold to the GNW for $7 million, giving it control of the MO. As for the A, it had been in receivership during most of the 1920s and was, as just noted, taken over by the BO in 1931. The BO had not been able during the depression to successfully develop the A and had allowed it to fall again into bankruptcy in 1942. The A was without effective leadership while the GMO had an aggressive management team looking for possibilities of growth.

The GMO entered the reorganization proceedings via the protective committee for holders of the A's refunding mortgage bonds. The other participants in the reorganization proceedings proposed plans for continued operation of the A as an independent. The GMO argued for merging with the A as offering reduction of capitalization and fixed charges and greater assurance of future return.

The merger extended the GMO's 673-mile New Orleans-St. Louis line by 284 miles north to Chicago and 323 miles west to Kansas City and added the 483-mile A route from Chicago to Kansas City. The plan was consummated in May 1947 and the GMO system ton-miles were immediately increased 54 percent. The subsequent growth of the system in the Mississippi River Valley region, with its only middling growth rate of economic activity, was 61 percent in ton-miles from 1950 to 1969.[4]

In respect to one of the A's constituent companies, the Kansas City, St. Louis, and Chicago, there was an attempt in 1948 by the Atchison, Topeka, and Sante Fe (ATSF) and the Chicago, Burlington, and Quincy (CBQ) to acquire it to improve their strategic positions. The GMO use of the tracks would be allowed to continue, and it would be relieved of the mortgage debt on the line. The ATSF wanted to gain access to the St. Louis gateway and the CBQ to shorten its Chicago-St. Louis route by acquiring the Kansas City to Mexico segment. This was opposed by major roads in the Southwest as strengthening two already strong systems in the region at the expense of the protestants, which were clearly weak, four of them, the MP, StLSF, StLSW, and CRI, being in bankruptcy. In August 1948 the ICC found that the protestants could not stand the probable diversion of traffic and denied the proposal. Three dissenters to the decision argued that "competition unless it was clearly shown to be destructive still has merit as spur to progress." This decision opened the way for the GMO takeover.[5]

The GMO-A merger qualifies for expense and financial analysis. It produced major decreases in transport and repair expenses. In the repair category much of the gain rested on the premerger upgrading of fixed facilities and introduction of diesel-electric locomotives. Complete dieselization was achieved a year after the merger. The decreases in repair expenses thus were major in comparison to the trends in similar items on the parallel Illinois Central system. In respect to overhead-type expenses, the merged system did not show improvement compared to the IC. Trafficwise, the merged system made significant gains in other-than-coal compared to the IC. Overall, the pre-income tax net railway operations income (nroi) of the CMO increased sharply as a proportion of revenue, from around 6 percent before the merger to 18 percent average 1951 to 1953. The GMO credit ratings were significantly upgraded and in the latter 1950s were not reduced as were the IC's. The GMO started paying dividends immediately after the merger and increased them to a level that was comparable to the IC's and then did not reduce them as sharply as did the IC in the 1958–1961 depressed period.

Chesapeake and Ohio-Pere Marquette-New York, Chicago, and St. Louis-Wheeling and Lake Erie

In the eastern region in 1945 Robert R. Young, who had gained control of the Van Sweringens' holdings, the Allegheny Corporation and Chesapeake and Ohio (CO) proposed to combine the CO with the Pere Marquette (PM), New York, Chicago, and St. Louis (NYCStL), and Wheeling and Lake Erie (WLE). These were three of the five eastern roads that comprised the family of eastern properties assembled during the 1920s by the Van Sweringens. A measure of the CO's possible growth with these additions was that the combined ton-miles of the three were 62 percent of the CO's in 1946. The proposal was approved by the ICC upon finding that the previous years of common control of the properties had shown that Young's managements had brought about substantial improvement in the operation of their railroads and that unification would be "in the public interest."

However, NYStL preferred stockholders' dissatisfaction with the CO proposed terms of exchange for their stock led to their opposition, so the NYCStL and with it the WLE withdrew from the proposal. The CO distributed to its own stockholders its NYSStL stock and proceeded to merge with the PM alone, effective August 1947. The PM ton-miles were around 16 percent of the CO's. The addition diversified the CO's traffic mix from one of primarily coal by adding substantial amounts of manufactured products and broadened the markets to which the CO coal could be shipped on single-line routing.[6]

1947–1959 Merger Proposals

New York, Chicago, and St. Louis-Wheeling and Lake Erie

Following the NYCStL withdrawal from the previous merger proposal, the CO and its affiliates decided to sell their WLE securities to the NYCStL, enabling it to acquire the WLE by lease in December 1949. This would add to the NYCStL two lines across Ohio, from Toledo southeast and from Cleveland south, totaling 355 miles. The former as part of the "alphabet route," an actively competitive joint east-west route made up of the NYCStL, WLE, Pittsburgh and West Virginia, Western Maryland (WM), and others to the East would consolidate the NYCStL's competitive position relative to the P and BO in the flow of traffic between the eastern seaboard and the Midwest. As far as growth of the NYCStL was concerned, the WLE ton-miles would add some 30 percent.

In January 1950 the NYCStL queried the Pennroad Corporation as to the possibility of leasing its Pittsburgh and West Virginia (PMV) to provide a 111-mile eastward extension of the WLE from Ohio to Connellsville, Pennsylvania, and thus a connection with the WM. The PWV ton-miles were only 4 percent of the

NYCStL's. The PWV had access to Pittsburgh industry. However, no acceptable terms for agreement could be reached and the matter was dropped in June.[7]

The postunification trends for the WLE-NYCStL of transport, traffic, and general expense ratios showed no significant gains. The combined companies' share of traffic in the Great Lakes region did improve.

This unification is the second one to qualify for analysis. In comparison with other primarily freight competing roads in the region, the Wabash and Erie, pretax nroi proportion of revenue of the unified NYCStL did not decline as much as the others' did. Premerger to five years after merger, during the general weakness of the eastern railroads, the NYCStL ratio declined only 9 percent while its two competitors in the same period declined 22 percent. After solution of security structure and preferred dividend problems the unification was followed by initiation of common dividends, which were maintained at a constant level even through the 1958–1961 downturn. Compared to the E and W in the same region, this was a decidedly superior performance. However, these accomplishments could also be credited to the change in management initiated with the premerger bringing in of a new executive vice-president in 1948 who became president a year later.[8]

Chesapeake and Ohio-New York Central

When the NYCStL opposition to merger with the CO became evident, Young and his associates turned their attention to possible affiliation with the New York Central (NYC), ton-miles-wise 120 percent larger than the CO. In late 1946 and early 1947 the Allegheny Corporation acquired a total of 6 percent of NYC common stock, placing it in trusteeship as required by a 1945 ICC decision. Young publicly stated that the two companies could do a lot for each other. The CO could improve the NYC management and help in rehabilitating the property. The two could contribute to each other's traffic and provide a more diversified commodity mix. The attitude of the Young interests toward affiliation, however, was one of caution, characterizing it as a "trial marriage," because of the NYC's precarious financial situation. There were suggestions of ultimate merger. A plan to include in addition the Virginian (V) to take care of its opposition was announced in May 1948. The NYC was the V's connection to northern and western markets and its loyalty to the V would be lost with CO affiliation. But by December 1948 the CO president announced that there would be no actual merger proposal until the NYC looked better financially.

In March 1947 the president of the NYC had recommended on the basis of the 6 percent CO holding that two directorships should go to the Young interests, one to Young himself, the other to Mr. Bowman, chairman and president respectively of the CO. However, the ICC would have to make exceptions to the statutory antitrust constraints to permit the two to hold dual railroad directorships. It decided in May 1948 that there was extensive competition between the NYC and

NYCStL that would be substantially lessened with either a community of interest or a unification, and therefore the proposal should be denied. Instead of achieving maximum growth for his key railroad enterprise, the CO, Young had twice so maneuvered as to run afoul of private interests or government constraints, which denied him his objectives.[9]

Delaware Lackawana and Western-New York, Chicago, and St. Louis

Soon after the CO system had cut its ties with the NYCStL the president of the DLW, William White, announced in January 1948 his system's purchase of 15 percent of the NYCStL stock with merger in mind. This was to give the DLW control of its principal western connection and thus direct access to Midwest markets. Mr. Davin, president of the NYCStL, rejected the idea and took legal action to oppose the acquisition. In 1952 the DLW requested formal approval from the ICC for two directors. The merger would have been an end-to-end one, 396 miles of DLW, Hoboken to Buffalo, and 524 miles of NYCStL, Buffalo to Chicago, with no elimination of direct competition. However, there was also the question of how the NYCStL interchange at Buffalo with other eastern connections that were competitors of the DLW would fare. NYCStL representatives argued that neutrality would get the NYCStL the maximum share of traffic. It is obvious the DLW felt one way about this and the NYCStL the opposite. The DLW hoped for substantial savings in a single management, and thus help in meeting its New York region commuter burdens. There would be an over 200 percent increase in its ton-miles. Personalities were a critical factor. White, in his first formal meeting with the NYCStL representatives in January 1948, had suggested that upon takeover their directors resign except for its president, Davin, who would become chairman of the merger company. The NYCStL rejected all this. Davin died soon afterward, but his successor, Lynn White (who had been brought in from the CNW in August 1948), and the directors continued a vigorous opposition. In 1955 the ICC rejected the DLW proposal, pointing out that the NYC owned 8 percent of DLW stock and that until just previously one of the NYC vice-presidents had been a director of the DLW. Since the NYC was a direct competitor of the NYCStL for its full length from Buffalo to Chicago these links to the NYC would "tend to lessen substantially competition." Effective December 1955, the DLW trusteed its then 15 percent NYCStL stockholding, then withdrew the request for representation on the NYCStL's board, and finally disposed of its holdings in 1959.[10]

New York Central-Pennsylvania

Still pursuing an interest in eastern mergers, Young dissociated himself from the CO and Allegheny Corporation in January 1954. Control of the CO was transferred to friendly Cleveland bankers. Young, together with associates, bought substantial blocks of NYC stock on the open market and acquired from the CO the 800,000 shares that it had trusteed earlier. Freed of antitrust constraints, Young started toward control of the NYC. This led to a spectacular proxy fight, which Young won. He then reconstituted the NYC management by bringing in an outside president, Alfred Perlman, executive vice-president of the Denver and Rio Grande, and changing many of the NYC policies. Young and Perlman had early agreed on merger as a key means of improving the eastern railroad situation. It was stated by Perlman that the president of the P initiated talks about a NYC-P merger. Studies of NYC and P consolidation were started in January 1957. However, Young's suicide in January 1958 took the country's most aggressive empire builder out of the picture. A year later Perlman announced the NYC withdrawal from further negotiation with the P and no application was made for merger.[11]

St. Louis San Francisco-Central of Georgia

In the South the Central of Georgia (CG) came out of reorganization in 1948, free of its earlier control by the Illinois Central. CG stock was initially held by a voting trust, but became available on the market with the trust's dissolution in 1954. In the early 1950s the St. Louis San Francisco (StLSF) had acquired a Class II railroad in order to gain entrance to Mobile. The StLSF then considered purchase of CG control to give it direct access to a greater volume of traffic to and from the southeastern states via the Birmingham gateway. Acquisition came under fire as a violation of requirements for ICC authorization of control. From 1954 through 1956, 64 percent of the CG voting stock was acquired but necessarily placed in the hands of a trustee. CG ton-miles were some 35 percent of those of the StLSF.

The StLSF purchase was opposed by the IC, SAL, and GMO. In an initial decision, the ICC approved the idea of StLSF control but called for investigation as to legality of the purchase. The continued purchase after initiation of the investigation and the StLSF failure to agree to terms of trusteeship that completely separated StLSF control from its ownership together led to the ICC's in effect denying the StLSF project in 1958 and to finally rejecting it upon review in 1960.[12]

Atchison, Topeka, and Santa Fe-Pennsylvania-Toledo, Peoria, and Western

In the early 1920s the P and CBQ had jointly controlled the Toledo, Peoria, and Western (TPW). It extended 224 miles from the Indiana-Illinois line to Keokuk, Iowa, on the Mississippi River. It went into receivership and in 1927 was sold at auction to independent interests, who in subsequent years built up the road as a neutral connecting link between eastern and western systems. In 1927, it made a connection with the ATSF near the latter's Mississippi River crossing.

In the mid-1950s the estate of the principal stockholder decided to sell. At this time, 71 percent of the interline cars handled by the TPW were with the ATSF and/or P. In June 1955 the Minneapolis and St. Louis (MStL), which connected with the TPW at Peoria, with a view to growth by TPW acquisition offered first $69.50 and then $80.00 per share for its stock. In competition, the ATSF, with an agreement to sell the P half of the shares purchased, made a $100.00 offer. The MStL raised its bid to $133.00. In mid-1955 the ATSF countered with a winning $135.00. Thus, the largest eastern system and the ATSF jointly obtained control for $12 million of a connection that enabled them to save fifty miles and avoid the congested Chicago gateway for transcontinental traffic, as well as to gain direct access to Peoria industry. The control protested the P and ATSF against other systems gaining any strategic advantage by obtaining an interest in an interconnecting road with access to important traffic. The TPW was continued as a separate operation and ICC approval included orders to maintain traditional traffic interchange with other roads. Its ton-miles increased 54 percent, 1950 to 1972.[13]

Union Pacific-Spokane International

The Spokane International had long been a Canadian Pacific controlled road extending from the Canadian border to Spokane 139 miles. It had gone into bankruptcy in 1933. The reorganization plan consummated in 1941 resulted in

Principal Lines: Chesapeake and Ohio—Pere Marquette—New York, Chicago, and St. Louis—Wheeling and Lake Erie, 1947–1949; New York, Chicago, and St. Louis—Wheeling Lake Erie, 1949

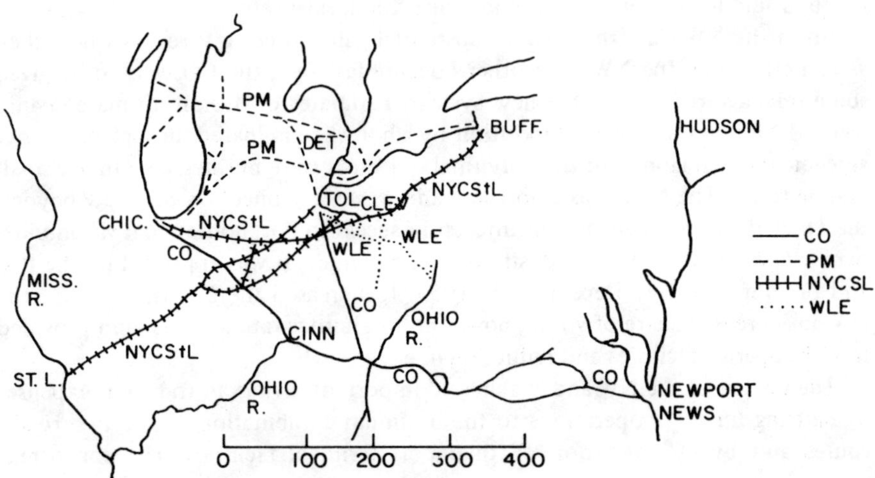

an independent road. In October 1958 the UP obtained control by a 1.04 for 1 exchange of UP stock for SI, amounting to some $6 million at average UP stock prices for the year. It was operated separately from the UP. Its ton-miles, minor compared to the UP's, increased some 54 percent from 1950 to 1969.[14]

Norfolk and Western-Virginian

In early 1959 the directors of the Virginian (V) and the Norfolk and Western (NW) approved merger of the former into the latter. The Virginian extended some 440 miles the last built of the trans Appalachian coal roads, from the Hampton Roads to a point 88 miles south of the Ohio River. It had been one of the most prosperous systems in the country. Coal-mining and utilization interests had acquired a major stock interest in the V in 1937. It paralleled the NW and in some sections had superior line characteristics. Of the fifty-six active mines served by the V in 1953, twenty were also served by the CO and one by the NW. The V ton-miles in the latter fifties were around 25 percent of those of the NW. During World War I, under government control, the NW had jointly used V trackage to improve operations. In 1925 the NW had asked ICC authority to lease the V, but this had been denied because of resultant reduction in competition among the Pocahontas roads. The ICC consolidation plan tied the V to the New York Central.

In 1959, again seeking control of the V, the NW argued that as part of the NW the Virginian would lose its heavy dependence on coal traffic and thus insure against losses through depletion of local coal reserves and mine stoppages. Also merchandise service would be improved with the joining of its traffic and operations with the larger, more extensive NW. It was also alleged that a small road could not meet the challenge of a dynamic and changing transport market. It was pointed out that the consolidation of engineering, traffic, and other departments would lower unit costs for administration, sales, etc.

From the NW side, there were substantial gains in using V routes where they were better than the NW. The other Pocahontas road, the CO, was to be given some trackage rights over the new system. Estimates of overall ultimate savings were $12 million per year. Opposition by labor was eliminated through protective agreements with labor and the only final objectors were businessmen in one small on-line town. The NYC was a northern and western connection for the V beyond the Ohio River and had had an interest in access to Pocahontas coal via an independent V but voiced no opposition to the merger. It was approved by the ICC and became effective December 1, 1959. It increased the NW traffic, gave the NW an increased share of voting power in Pocahontas rate matters, and provided it with superior facilities and reduction in expenses.[15]

The merger of the NW and V achieved important savings in transport expenses by shifting line-haul operations to the optimum combination of the two roads' routes and by consolidation of their port terminal facilities. The concurrent dieselization of the NW starting just before the merger and continuing afterward accounted for additional transport expense savings along with locomotive repair economies. The gains were augmented by the consolidation of repair facilities. NW repair expenses both for equipment and way and structures had started to decline prior to merger with the change in president in 1958 and continued downward after merger, suggesting that a change in executive policy to tighter control of those expenses was a factor independent of merger. The general expense proportion of revenues for the NW plus V also declined slightly after the merger. These reductions in expense ratios contrasted sharply with an upward trend in transport and general expenses and no decline in repair ones for the parallel CO. Trafficwise, the merged NW-V continued a premerger upward trend in their combined share of the region's coal traffic but lost slightly in share of other-than-coal traffic.

Overall, the ratio of pre-income tax nroi to revenue for the NW-V improved from premerger 35 percent in 1957/58 to postmerger 40½ percent in 1962/63. Correspondingly, the CO ratio worsened from 23½ percent to 15½ percent. NW dividends rose from $4.70 in 1959, eleven months of which year were before the merger, to $5.50 in 1962 and $6.00 in 1963. The CO dividends remained at $4.00 over those years and were throughout a higher than the NW proportion of net income.

Principal Lines: Erie—Delaware Lackawana and Western, 1960

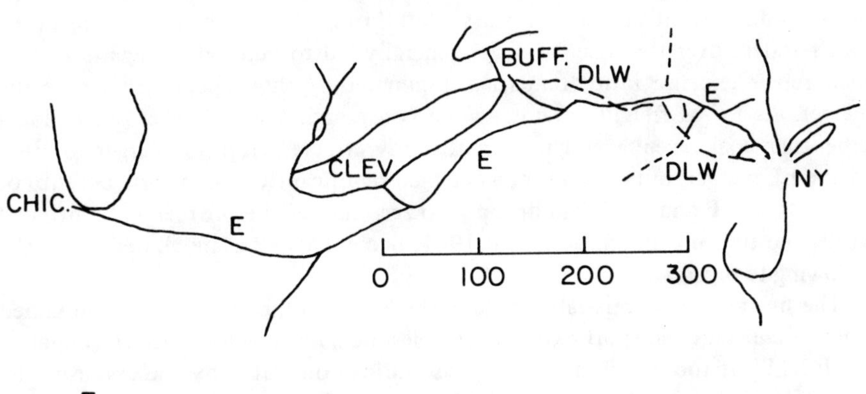

Erie-Delaware Lackawana and Western

Both the Erie (E) and the Delaware Lackawana and Western (DLW) in common with other eastern roads had experienced generally declining financial fortunes after 1955. In 1956, in an effort to find a solution, they joined with the financially stronger Delaware and Hudson in a study of possible merger gains. By March 1959 the conclusion was that there was no basis for a three-way merger equitable to all stockholders because of the roads' widely disparate characteristics. Further analysis indicated that an E-DLW combination was a desirable alternative. Joint director approval followed on June 24, 1959, and application to the ICC was made on July 6, 1959. The merger of the DLW into the E was an end-to-end combination for the DLW in respect to Atlantic Coast-Midwest traffic and a consolidation of parallel lines in the East from Buffalo to the New York metropolitan area. Some economies available from the latter had already been achieved by combining passenger station facilities in Hoboken and some joint track use in south central New York State. A consultant's reported suggested economies of some \$13½ million annually after five years. There was no opposition from users, but the parallel NYCStL, W, and LV did protest for fear of losing existing shares of traffic interchanged at the Buffalo gateway. ICC approval came in September 1960 and the merger became effective in October. The ICC decision was based on the expectancy of helping the financial problems of the two companies and the lack of shipper opposition. The ICC disposed of the other railroads' opposition on the grounds that their possible losses were "all part of the risks in business." The merger involved exchange of one EL share for one DLW and one and a quarter EL for one Erie. Some DLW stockholders did protest their relative proposed share in the merged company, but to no avail.[16]

This merger resulted in a drastic increase in the transportation expense ratio of the combined roads, from a 48 percent average in premerger 1958/59 to a range of 50 to 52 percent in the four years 1960 through 1963. The downturns in the East's traffic over this span of years generally led to deferral of repairs so that their repair expense ratio trends are dominated by that aspect rather than the merger. As far as freight revenues were concerned, the EL's share of regional other-than-coal revenue was not significantly affected from premerger to 1965 by the EL merger, but coal revenue declined significantly. Pre-income tax nroi of the combined E and DLW had dropped to zero the year before merger, continued to decline to a maximum deficit in 1961, becoming half as much deficit for the following two years.

The most nearly comparable system, the NYC, on the other hand, maintained a nearly constant transport expense ratio despite a revenue loss pattern similar to the E-DLW. It too had its repair expense ratios dominated by the extensive deferral. Its pre-income tax nroi reached a low close to zero in 1961 but recovered steadily thereafter without any pause like the EL's. The EL's credit rating of its mortgage bonds was reduced one grade a year after the merger due to deterioration of earning power and working capital and delayed merger benefits. The parallel NYC ratings were not changed.[17]

The Erie management members initially dominated that of the merged system. Following the poor performance in 1963, two and a half years after the merger, the directors took the unusual step of replacing top management. Thereafter, major organizational changes were put into effect and the EL transport and general expense and pre-income tax nroi ratios improved sharply.[18] The average 1964–1966 pre-income tax nroi percent of revenue rose to nearly the level of 1956–1958. This, however, was a significantly less favorable achievement than the corresponding near 50 percent increase in the nonmerging NYC's ratio over the corresponding years.

Post-1959 Merger Proposals—Eastern

The latter phase of eastern acquisitions, began with studies in the late 1950s, differed from the previous ones in that fewer were growth oriented and many were directed toward solving the financial and other problems arising from the inheritance of weak financial structures, the decline in freight traffic resulting from decline in coal use, shift in industry products and location, competition from other modes of transport, and rising losses from the passenger train services.

In respect to New England roads whose earning power had been the most seriously affected, a 1960 J. G. White consultant's study of merger possibilities concluded that none were feasible.[19]

In the heart of the East, in early 1960, the NYC entered into discussions with the CO and BO looking toward the possibility of a two-party eastern railroad pattern made up of an already existing P-NW family and a combination of the CO, BO, and NYC. The NW takeover of the V had been a move that, some thought, doomed the chances for a three-system arrangement for the East because it removed the possibility of a third one built around the strength of a Pocahontas road with profitable coal traffic. At about the same time, both the NW and the CO started looking for partners in the creation of major eastern systems. The NW entered into talks with the NYCStL and the CO did so with the BO. The CO rejected the NYC's desire to join in control of the BO. The NYC, losing out to the CO, turned to the P for renewed discussion of merger. When the P-NYC (PC) merger proposal was activated the NY and CO-BO reacted by proposing their own merger. In opposition, the PC argued then that the East should have a three-way system for fair balance.[20]

Chesapeake and Ohio-Baltimore and Ohio

In May 1960 the CO made an exchange offer of one CO common share for one BO preferred and for one and three-quarters BO common. This was conditioned on obtaining 80 percent of the shares so as to obtain the tax advantage

Principal Lines: Chesapeake and Ohio, Baltimore and Ohio, 1963

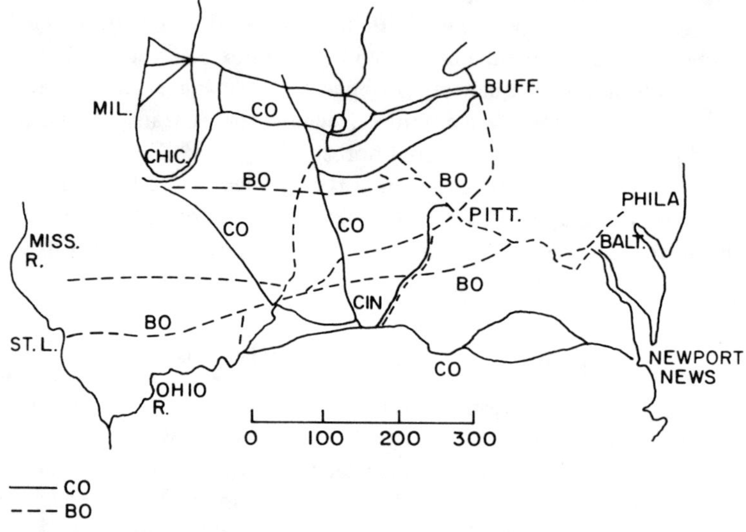

for the CO of BO losses. This triggered a competitive struggle between the CO and NYC for control of the BO. It started with a NYC counter exchange offer. The CO in June also made direct purchases of BO stock aggregating some 19 percent of the voting stock. The NYC and affiliated interests in turn purchased some 20 percent and offered one and a half shares of common plus $6 for each share of BO. By mid-December 1960, holders of 50-odd percent of the BO had assented to the CO offer. By January 1962 the NYC withdrew. Later in 1964 the CO increased its BO holdings to some 90 percent by acquiring the NYC and related holdings. The CO made it clear that the degree of its affiliation with the BO depended upon the latter's improved performance, with actual merger to be deferred. The CO did not want to take on the possible risks with the BO debt.

The CO-BO affiliation brought together a depressed eastern system extending from Philadelphia through Baltimore 840 miles to Chicago and 1,015 miles to St. Louis, and a strong Pocahontas one extending from Hampton Roads through Cincinnati to Chicago, 921 miles, and to Detroit, 829 miles. The BO had affiliates that extended it to the New York City area. The addition of the BO plus these affiliates would increase the CO 1960 ton-miles by 112 percent, and of the BO alone, by 86 percent. The CO plus BO employment amounted to 58,000.

With acquisition of control the CO moved into management and proceeded to improve the BO equipment inventory and upgrade other facilities. The estimated savings just from coordination amounted to $13 million, and following the expenditure for improvements of $232 million were to reach $45 million annually after five years. The ICC approved the control in December 1962 on the grounds that it would provide the BO much-needed assistance in restoring its properties, diversify CO traffic, and give the CO an opportunity to invest its surplus funds in another carrier with growth potential. The ICC also concluded that the CO and BO were complementary and there would be no lessening of competition, and that the unified system would neither develop "overwhelming strength" nor cause the NYC "position to deteriorate to any appreciable extent." Labor objections to employee protective provisions and consequent court proceedings reaching to the Supreme Court delayed the effective data of approval. Coordination of management began in early 1964.[21]

The CO-BO unification came as the freight traffic in the East and Pocahontas region started upward from the trough of 1960/61. Freight revenue was to increase steadily to 1972. However, the average transportation ratios of the combined two roads showed no improvement from the preunification year 1963 through 1970. Further, the general and superintendence expense ratios rose almost continually after 1963. Pre-income tax nroi rose above preunification levels temporarily in 1965 and 1964 but dropped back subsequently to levels lower than preunification. The ratio of pre-income tax nroi to revenue declined to 7½ percent five years after unification from 10 percent earlier. None of these trends indicated significant gains, rather some deterioration after unification.

The CO's moves brought a *Moody's* warning in 1960 and 1961 that "a consolidated CO would not be as strong financially as the CO was individually." The CO equipment trusts and senior general mortgage bond ratings were reduced one grade.[22] The CO common dividend rate remained unchanged from 1957 through 1970; the original CO stockholders did not gain from the unification. On the other hand, the BO common shareholders moved from a 1958/59 $1.50 to none in 1961. With unification, unstable to nonexistent dividends after exchange for CO shares became a steady $2.29 one through 1970.

Norfolk and Western-New York, Chicago, and St. Louis-Wabash-Pittsburgh and West Virginia

In early 1960 the Norfolk and Western (NW) announced it was considering unification of the New York, Chicago, and St. Louis (NYCStL), Wabash (W), Pittsburgh and West Virginia (PWV), and Akron, Canton, and Youngstown (ACY) with the NW. To counter EL objections in October 1961, the NW entered into an agreement with the EL to negotiate some form of ultimate affiliation with it. Further, the NYCStL was to participate in a joint yard with the EL at Buffalo.

The NW proposed merger with the NYCStL by exchange of 0.45 NW common for 1 NYCStL. The W was to be leased for eight years with a base rental of $8½ million plus, during the first six years, $1.35 million annually for every $1 the NW common dividend exceeded $5, the current rate. After the eight years the NW was to merge with the W.

The NW was to purchase the ACY stock for $6.5 million and take over the PWV operation, paying $0.9 million annual rent. In addition, the P was to sell its line between Columbus and Sandusky, some 108 miles, to the NW for $27 million, retaining trackage rights. This was to provide the missing link to tie the NW to the NYCStL. The P system held one-third of the voting stock of NW along with 99½ percent of the W common.

The ICC found broad evidence that the P had the power to control the NW. This together with the P providing the necessary rail link led to their conclusion that the P must have approved the unification plan. P divestiture of NW stock was required by the ICC. This unification joined a financially very strong Pocahontas coal system of 663 miles between Norfolk and Columbus with what had been in preceding years the two financially strongest eastern roads, the NYCStL extending 524 miles between Chicago and Buffalo and the W, some 940 miles between Buffalo and Kansas City, tapping western traffic at Des Moines and Omaha as well as Kansas City. The PWV provided access to Pittsburgh and to the WM with its Baltimore facilities. The ACY tapped the industries of Akron and was a segment in a through east-west route. The unified system all told provided a network of great and extensive strategic strength. The NW would obtain a more diversified type of traffic, and the other constituents would participate in valuable coal traffic. The ultimate annual savings were estimated to be $27 million. In 1960 the NW ton-miles were 22½ billion, the NYCStL, 10 billion, the W, 6½ billion, and the two smaller roads together ¾ billion, adding 77 percent to the NW ton-miles. The combined employment amounted to some 36,000.

Principal Lines: Norfolk and Western—Virginian, 1959; Norfolk and Western—New York, Chicago, and St. Louis—Wabash—Pittsburgh and West Virginia, 1964

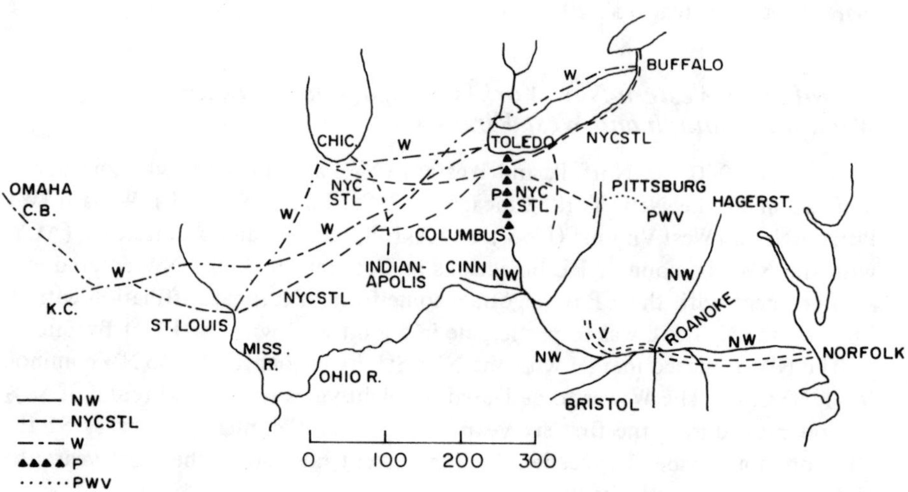

The merger plan subject to the P divestiture of its NW stock had been given "virtually universal approval by shippers." They offered no opposition given NW acceptance of the usual protective conditions to keep open all joint traffic routes with other roads. ICC general approval was given in June 1964; the merger and leases were effective in October 1964. The EL, DH, and BM, however, in view of likely diversions of their traffic that would result from this and various other eastern mergers being proposed, requested the ICC to require inclusion in the NW family or if not, in the PC.

The EL's position continued to pose a problem. Both its components, the Erie and DLW, had been weak just prior to their merger and it continued to have serious problems, which might prove burdensome. All of this caused the NW to draw back from affiliation unless the risks were reduced by EL reorganization and financial restructuring. The DH, on the other hand, had a strong capital structure and a stable financial record but was vulnerable to traffic diversion by a merged P-NYC system. The BM was even weaker than the EL. However, the NW did not argue for the alternative of inclusion of the three in the PC system.

In response to the statutory guideline of considering "the effect upon the public interest of the inclusion, or failure to include, other railroads," the ICC in a 1967 supplementary decision did require the unified NW system, through a holding company, to offer to acquire the EL, DH, and BM with specified conditions and stock exchange ratios. Each in turn was given the opportunity of rejecting these acquisition terms. By mid-1968 both the EL and DH had agreed to the terms and were taken into the NW family via the Dereco holding company. The BM management and stockholders rejected the terms and remained independent. The 1966 EL plus DH ton-miles amounted to 35 percent of the NW system's. The final NW system extended from the New York port area to Buffalo and on west to Detroit, Chicago, and St. Louis, and the Missouri River gateways. It connected Norfolk with this network and by the DH extended it north to Canada and to a BM New England connection. From the original NW stockholders' point of view, the original merger of the NYCStL and the subsequent acquisition of the EL and DH were at the cost of a 35 percent increase in NW common share outstanding.[23]

The NW unification resulted in a modest deterioration in the transportation ratio of the combined systems. For several premerger years it had ranged from 33½ percent to 35 percent while five years later it was from 36 percent to 37 percent. General and superintendence expense ratios also increased slightly instead of decreasing as might be expected by then. The NW system had earlier shown more rapid increase in coal revenue than the CO, and this continued to be the case after unification though at a lesser relative rate. Factors related to the different types of coal in mines located on the two systems as they related to demand, particularly foreign, had more to do with relative rates of increase in revenue than did changes due to unification.

As was the case of the CO-BO, credit-rating agencies called attention to possible weakening of NW credit with unification. On the other hand, the ratings of the bonds of acquired roads were initially increased. Then three years after the NW unification all of the NW family debt was downgraded one step because of "unfavorable operating results" and a 40 percent increase in fixed and contingent charges.

In the years before the NW unification, dividends had increased steadily from $4.00 in 1957 to $6.00 in 1963 and $7.00 in 1964, the earlier NW-V merger having been a factor. After the later 1964 unification, dividends fell back in the first year to $6.50 and to $6.00 from then to 1969, five years after unification. In terms of financial performance, these results did not represent any gain from the unification.[24]

Pennsylvania-New York Central-New York, New Haven, and Hartford

In October 1961 the NYC advised the P that it was ready to resume merger negotiations. Agreement on terms was reached in mid-January 1962 and application for ICC approval filed in March. The merged company was to issue 1 share for 1 of P and 1.3 for 1 of NYC. As with the NW merger case, the P was to dispose of its NW holdings in a reasonable time. The NYC and P expressed opposition to inclusion of other carriers in their merged system, though possible inclusion of the NYNH&H under limiting conditions was recognized as a possibility.

Principal Lines: Pennsylvania, New York Central, 1968

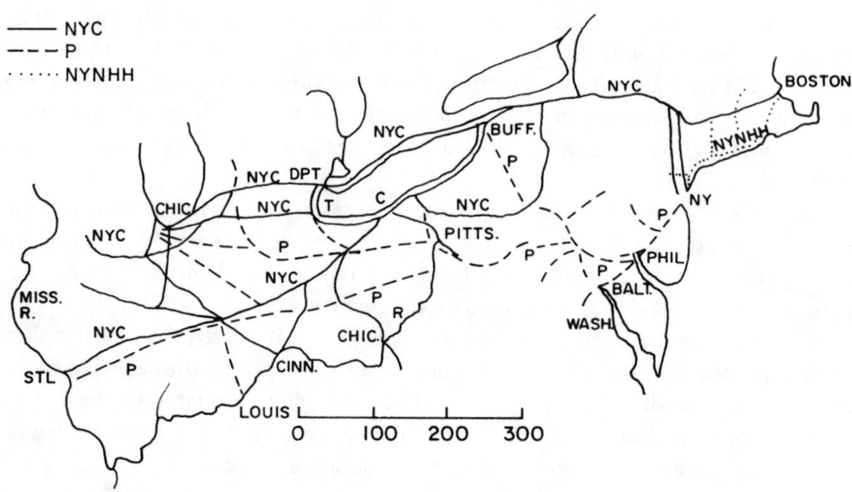

In contrast to the two just reviewed mergers, the P-NYC's objectives were not growth, but to preserve and strengthen the two systems, avert further deterioration of plant, avoid bankruptcy, and improve service. It was the NYC that came to the P, asking for reopening of negotiations after the NYC had failed to obtain what it at the time preferred, affiliation with the CO. It was the NYC fear that with the build-up of the NW-NYCStL-W and the CO-BO systems it could not remain competitively viable that led to its affiliation request. At this point the only thing for the NYC to do was to agree to merge with the P, which was something attainable. This was Justice William Douglas's conclusion about unification that "the making of mergers was based on 'attainable alliances' rather than any truly balanced competitive basis."[25]

On the P's side it had wanted to take over the NYC earlier and was still quite ready to do so. In this sense, there was an element of growth involved—the P, as one of two traditional competitors, would be increasing its operations by takeover of the other. It was a P-based company that was offering to exchange its shares for the NYC's. The merged PC would have 73 percent more ton-miles and 79 percent more employees than the P alone. The combined system would have 120,000 employees, more than double the number of either of the other two unified systems under consideration in the East. It was estimated that ultimate annual savings would amount to $80 million and that freight service would be greatly improved.

Initially, the Railway Labor Executives' Association opposed the merger. In response, in May 1962 the P and NYC presidents reached an agreement with most unions that attrition would be the means of eliminating redundant employees and that there would be no layoffs due to any cause unless there was a 5 percent or greater decline in revenue in any thirty-day period. The NYC and P thus removed the opposition as the association then took a neutral position on the merger. Other resistance was based on reduction in competition and, in particular areas, on lowering of levels of train service. Other rail systems objected because of worry as to diversion of traffic. This was countered by provisions to insure maintenance of all existing interchange and joint tariff routings together with the requirement of reciprocal switching for the benefit of competitors in the Pittsburgh terminal region.

An important overall aspect in consideration of the merger was the unquestioned reduction in competition between railroads. The ICC argued that this loss would be balanced in the overall public interest by the better service expected from merger and by the creation of a more viable rail transport system than would be possible with a continuing oversupply of rail facilities. To meet the worries of the ICC, approval was in the end conditioned on including the NYNH&H, in the merged system giving certain other roads the rights to be considered for inclusion either in this or the NW merger and to ask for indemnification for losses. Ultimately the P-NYC merger was initially approved by the ICC in April 1966, and again after reconsideration in September. Supreme Court confirmation came in March 1967 and consummation finally in February 1968.[26]

The results of the P-NYC-NYNH&H merger had two phases, first to mid-1970 with decisions based on usual private corporate objectives, thereafter in bankruptcy under control of the Court with quite different rules for decision making. Just prior to merger and for some time after, the critical element of expenses, measured by the freight transport expense ratio, got out of hand. In the premerger years 1964 through 1966 that ratio ranged from 44 to 45 percent of revenue. After merger it rose to 46 percent in 1968 and reached 50 percent in 1970. Even after bankruptcy with added pressure for control of expenses the ratio remained well above premerger levels, some 3 percent points. The general expense ratio also increased drastically, from 4.4 percent in 1965/66 to 6.4 percent in 1970. The superintendence ratio in turn increased from 3.7 percent to 4.3 percent. Even after several years under bankruptcy trustees, these latter two ratios remained significantly higher than before merger, 4.8 and 4.1 percent respectively. (These postmerger ratios do not include the $112 million extra labor costs which were arising from compliance with the labor contract agreed to in 1964 and charged to surplus.)

The combined P-NYC-NYNH&H share of eastern (the CO and NW excluded) region freight revenue had increased in the early 1960s slightly more than had the remainder systems. With the traffic decline from the 1966 to 1967 economic downturn the combined PC roads lost 3 percent, the others only 2½ percent. During the subsequent recovery years to 1970 the PC gained only 9 percent; the remaining East, 16½ percent. Thereafter, with the continued regional revenue growth to 1972, the PC recovered some of its share, reaching 39 percent compared to the other roads' 33 percent.

The loss with merger in control over of important elements of expense and in regional share of traffic and revenue together with the 1967 slowdown resulted in drastic deterioration in pre-income tax nroi. For the combined PC roads there had been a significant recovery after 1961 and again from 1964 to 1966 from 74 to $108 million. The 1967 decline and premerger problems brought a $136 million deficit; by 1970 the deficit was $212 million. With transfer to trustees and drastic steps to cut expenses the deficit was cut to $87 million by 1973.

With these results and the breakdown of other financial factors the merger resulted in the PC credit ratings falling from A and Ba for equipment and senior mortgage debt respectively to Caa and Ca. The payouts of dividends by the two principal systems in the merger had been gradually increased from the low years of the early 1960s to $55 million in 1966. Despite the deficits of 1967 and subsequent years, the dividends were continued at that level through 1968, somewhat diminished in early 1969 and terminated in the fall of 1969. The PC operating and financial results were catastrophic.

The nearest to comparable system in the eastern region was the BO. Its freight transportation expense ratio did not rise after 1966, staying with the range of 39 to 40½ percent through 1973. Further, its pretax nroi rose gradually from 1967 through 1973. Because of the BO's affiliation with the CO its credit and dividend performance cannot be used for comparison except to say that the BO fared better than any of the PC merged components.

Chesapeake and Ohio-Chicago, South Shore, and South Bend

In early 1965 the CO proposed to purchase control of the Chicago, South Shore, and South Bend (CSSB), an electric interurban line from south of Chicago some ninety miles to South Bend, Indiana, along the southern shore of Lake Michigan. This route would provide the CO access to certain steel plants, particularly the new Burns Harbor facilities of the Bethlehem Steel Corporation. The Monon had acquired 20 percent of CSSB shares for $25.00 a share in 1964 without ICC approval and against the CSSB's opposition. The latter challenged the M purchase as unlawful. In March 1965 the CO applied for ICC permission for purchase of CSSB shares at $42.50 per share, roughly its market price at the time. Thus 100 percent ownership of the stock would cost $13 million. The M protested the CO proposal and defended its purchases, but finally sold its holdings after the ICC approved the CO purchase.[27]

Chesapeake and Ohio, Baltimore and Ohio-Western Maryland

In 1964 the unified CO-BO system proposed to the ICC the taking control of the WM. The first step was acquiring control by removal of the independent trusteeing requirement placed many years before on the 43 percent of stock acquired by the BO. Merger was the ultimate aim.

The WM extended from Connellsville to Baltimore, 175 miles, and to Shippensburg, Pennsylvania, 202 miles. It was a segment in the "alphabet" and "Pittsburgh Dispatch" (Central States Dispatch) east-west through routes. The WM was parallel to the BO across the Allegheny Mountains and with merger this part of the WM would be abandoned. Savings were estimated at $6 million annually. The ability of a small road like the WM to continue successfully in a field of larger ones was questioned, although the WM had done well financially. An opposing commissioner argued that the WM was like the Western Pacific in relation to the Southern Pacific and was able to provide "viable competition" via its traditional role in connection with the two through routes. In 1967 the ICC approved the CO-BO control and the merger was effected in 1975.[28]

Norfolk and Western-Chesapeake and Ohio, Baltimore and Ohio

As a counter to the P-NYC merger, in August 1965 the NW and CO systems made plans themselves to merge and create a system somewhat comparable in size to the PC. The new system would be prepared to include the EL, DH, BM, CNJ, and R subject to two conditions: first that no subsequent substantial adverse financial changes afflict the five smaller roads, and, second, that it be able to obtain certain tax advantages from their past deficits. The stock exchange basis would be three-quarters of a share of NW common for one share CO. Some $50 million ultimate annual savings were contemplated. Application for this merger was filed with the ICC in October 1965. The P-NYC and then PC in opposition argued that the existing two systems, NW and CO-BO, each had a competitive advantage over the PC, particularly because each had important profitable coal traffic. With the PC bankruptcy in June 1970, any threat of that system to NW and CO disappeared and in March 1971 the CO-NW merger proposal was withdrawn.[29]

Post-1959 Merger Proposals—Southern

Because so much of the railroad network of the South had been aligned into the major regional systems prior to 1960, acquisition activity was limited thereafter. The Central of Georgia, having been divorced from proposed StLSF control, was bought by the S. Studies were made of a possible partnership of the StLSF itself with the S and also with the ATSF, but nothing came of either. Two major proposals sought to merge lines, the ACL with the SAL and the IC with the GMO. Both were ultimately consummated. The LN obtained access to the Chicago and northern Indiana area in two moves. Finally the LN was brought fully within the SCL family by exchanging its stock for the SCL Industries Company stock. The last was done without involving the ICC because the acquiring company was not a railroad.

Southern-Central Georgia

When the CG stockholdings of the StLSF became available as a result of the ICC divestiture requirement, the Southern (S) in August 1960 contracted to buy them, subject to ICC approval, for what the StLSF had paid for them. The CG would provide the S with more intensive coverage of southern Georgia and Alabama and access to Savannah. Both the SAL and the IC opposed the acquisition as damaging their ability to attract traffic in connection with the CG as a neutral. However, the ICC felt the interests of the two would be protected by the usual requirements of preserving existing through rates and routes. The ICC found the S and CG to be largely complementary so competition would not be seriously affected, and that there would be some $6 million annual savings. Control of the S-CG was approved in November 1962. The CG ton-miles amounted to 15 percent of those of the S system in 1963. This merger was accompanied by ICC approval of the union demands for the strictest yet attrition requirement that labor should be protected even against any affects of new technology after the merger.[30]

Atlantic Coast Line-Seaboard Airline

Studies concerning an ACL-SAL merger were initiated in 1959 and a proposal for merger was submitted to the ICC in July 1960. The two systems ran roughly parallel south from Richmond to Florida through Jacksonville. The ACL continued on through the central and western parts of the state to Tampa, 919 miles, and the SAL similarly, 850 miles to Tampa and still further to Miami, totaling 1,046 miles. Both had lines extending westward to Atlanta, Birmingham, and Montgomery. The two were of roughly the same size, with some 13,000 em-

Principal Lines:
Illinois Central—
Gulf Mobil and Ohio, 1972;
Gulf Mobil and Ohio—
Alton, 1947

Principal Lines:
Atlantic Coast Line—
Seaboard Airline, 1967;
Southern—Central
Georgia, 1963

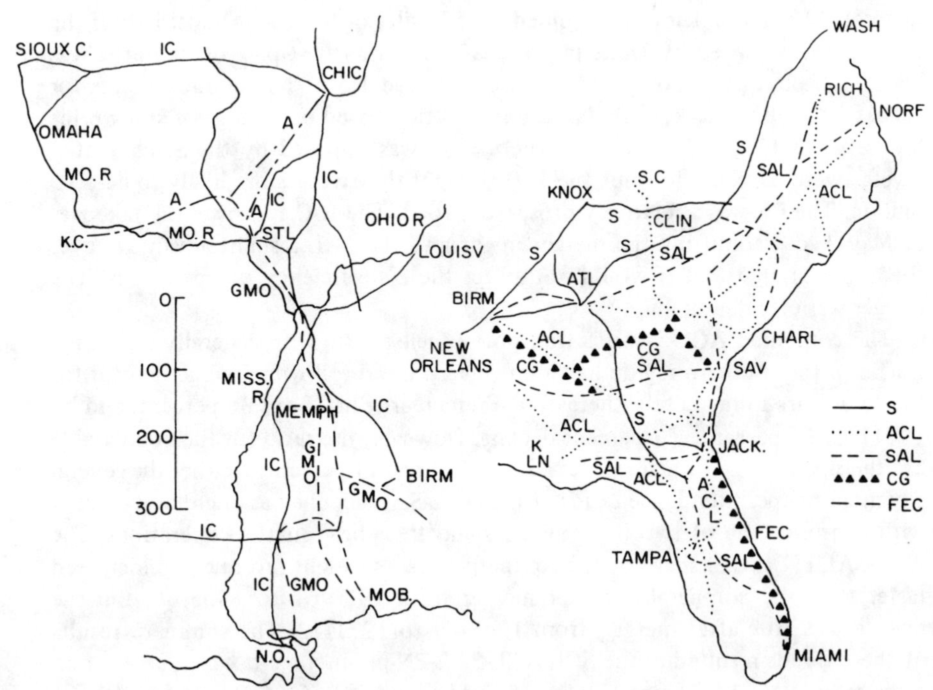

ployees each. The proposed common stock exchange ratio for merger was 1.42 ACL common shares to 1 SAL. The main thrust of the argument for the merger was that the underutilization of their lines and duplication of facilities would be eliminated and that improved service could be provided by use of the best facilities of each in a combined system. The annual savings estimated by the roads was $39 million after five years. The ICC concluded $20 million was more likely. The proposal had the general approval of regional bodies and shippers; only Georgia took a neutral stand. Opposition came from major paper companies. It was shown that competition would be eliminated in respect to approximately a third of the traffic involved. An extensive public relations program was carried on by the ACL and SCL to gain shipper and community support. A dissenting opinion argued that "it is competition not the ICC which is the prime regulator of railroad rates" and that the decision "disparaged competition and exalted regulation." Lengthy court review at the request of competing carriers delayed final effective approval and the merger did not take place until July 1967. In 1966 the SAL ton-miles were 86 percent of the ACL.[31]

Seaboard Coast Line-Piedmont and Northern

In 1967 the SCL applied for permission to merge with the PN, which extended in two unconnected segments diagonally across central North and South Carolina, in total, 112 miles. They were joined by 53 miles of S track. Almost half of the PN stock was owned by Duke interests and an important part of its traffic was coal for Duke Power Company. The SCL offered 1.5 of its common shares for 1 PN share so the market value of the transaction based on a range of stock price lay between 11 and $17 million. The merger was opposed by the S. Estimated savings were $1.5 million but the ICC thought they were more likely to be $0.5 million. The PN was a relatively prosperous road. The ICC approved the takeover in May 1969, admitting the merger might give the SCL a slight advantage over the S but argued that it would not affect the S's efficiency or operations. The merger was effected in July.[32]

The combined ACL-SAL-PN transport expense ratio with generally increasing traffic in the southern region had a downward trend following merger except for the two years immediately thereafter. Premerger it had been 38 percent, and by 1971/72, 35 percent, a 7 percent decline. However, the ratio for the comparable Southern system in the same interval had declined 11 percent. Neither the general expense or superintendence ratios of the ACL-SAL declined as might be expected with consolidation of two managements and their headquarters operations. The ACL-SAL-PN (SCL) share of the southern region's freight revenue had increased faster than the comparable S's premerger from 1960/61 to 1965/66. But the reverse was true after merger, from 1968/69 to 1971/72. The summary results of these trends resulted in the SCL-ACL-SAL-PN pre-income tax nroi proportion of revenue in 1971/72 being 1 percent point less than, 1965/66, premerger, 10 percent compared to 11 percent. During the immediate postmerger years it had declined to 7 percent. On the other hand, the S's ratio increased from 15 percent to 18½ percent, suggesting that with the South's traffic growth the minimum expectation should be improvement in the ratio not the merged system's slight decline.

The ACL-SAL credit ratings showed a one-step improvement for ACL equipment trusts directly upon merger. However, in August 1969 all equipment trust ratings were reduced one grade as a result of postmerger erosion of working capital, increase in equipment rentals, and lower coverage of fixed charges.[33] In contrast, the S credit ratings did not change. Common stockholder returns of the original ACL had been $2.00 annually for premerger years through 1962 and then gradually increased to $4.00 just before merger. Subsequently, and with conversion to SCL Industries shares, the returns dropped back to $3.12 for 1971/72. The SAL dividends had been $2.00 but in the slowdown of the early 1960s were cut back to $1.60, increasing to $1.80 just before the merger. Then with the merger and conversion to SCL Industries they became $2.20 for 1971/72. There was a long-term substantial 56 percent gain for the ACL and 10 percent for the SAL.

The ACL-SAL merger resulted in two years of seriously worsened performance followed by recovery but to a level of regional revenue share and pre-income tax nroi still below their premerger ones. But dividend returns for the ACL shares in particular achieved higher levels.

Southern-Norfolk and Southern

In early 1972 the S reached an acquisition agreement with the NS. The NS operated from the Norfolk area across North Carolina to Charlotte, 398 miles. It had come out of receivership in 1942 and had been able to pay dividends from 1948 through 1957 but had deficits most years thereafter. The S offered 0.7 share of a $3 preferred (convertible into 1 share of S at $52) for each NS share. This amounted to on the order of $20 million value for the NS. The acquisition was approved by the ICC in November 1973 and consummated in 1974.[34]

Illinois Central-Gulf Mobile and Ohio

During the 1950s the CBQ had held 9 percent of the voting stock of the GMO, disposing of it in 1961. In 1962 the CNW acquired 15 percent of the GMO common stock. This led to a counterstudy of an IC merger with the GMO. The GMO was one of the country's financially strong roads. It paralleled the IC from Chicago to the Gulf of Mexico, 1,055 miles to New Orleans for the GMO compared to 921 miles for the IC. Both reached Birmingham. The GMO went to Mobile, 929 miles from Chicago, and the IC to Gulfport, 898 miles. Both went west from Chicago to the Missouri River—the IC to Omaha, 515 miles; the GMO to Kansas City, 488 miles. Application for merger approval was made in May 1968. The IC proposed giving the GMO common 0.75 of a share of Illinois Central Industry (ICI) preferred, convertible into 3 ICI common.

The MP and KCS were active protestants, fearing significant diversion of traffic. The protestants also objected to the UP's 23½ percent holdings of the IC Industries stock as giving the UP influence over the merged ICG policies and thus possibly undue competitive strength. Savings were thought by the ICC to be $12 million annually. It was argued that the increasing size of adjoining carriers as a result of recent unifications, in particular the LN-CEI combination, which was a strong competitor to the GMO, made the merger desirable. The ICC estimated that not more than 10 percent of the combined traffic of the IC and GMO was competitive. The ICC gave approval in December 1971, conditioned on UP divestiture within ten years of its IC Indiana holdings and on the merged systems takeover of three small roads that would be particularly hard hit by diversion. After MP and KSC appeals and final court affirmation, the merger was consummated in August 1972. The 1971 GMO ton-miles added 36 percent to the IC's.[35]

Louisville and Nashville-Chicago and Eastern Illinois, and LN-Monon

Before World War II the LN and S had jointly held a majority of the Chicago, Indianapolis, and Louisville stock (CIL), later called the Monon (M), giving them

Principal Lines: Missouri Pacific—Chicago and Eastern Illinois, 1967; Louisville and Nashville—Chicago and Eastern Illinois, 1969; Louisville and Nashville—Monon, 1970

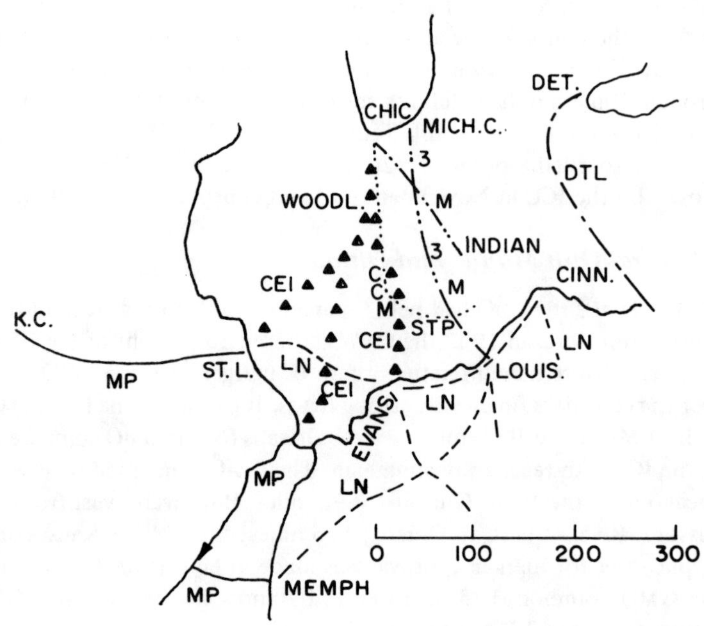

control of an access route to Chicago from the South. This control was lost with the CIL reorganization during the war. The LN had also participated in a joint north-south route with the Chicago and Eastern Illinois (CEI). Beginning in 1962 in conjunction with the MP acquisition of the CEI, the LN was a participant in seeking control of the CEI. The LN in June 1969 finally acquired outright, for cash and CEI securities that the LN owned, the southeastern branch of the CEI from Evansville to Woodland, Illinois, and trackage rights north from there to Chicago, totaling 287 miles. The ton-miles involved were not published.

In September 1968 the LN applied for merger with the M, which extended from Chicago to Louisville, 324 miles, with branches to Michigan City and Indianapolis. The M had been financially weak and unable to modernize its facilities. The proposed purchase arrangement was an exchange of LN convertible preferred shares for M common, providing ultimate conversion into one LN common for three M. This was equivalent to 20 to $44 million in market value range in 1971. Estimated savings after five years were $2½ million annually. The M ton-miles in 1969 were 4 percent of the LN. The DTI opposed the merger for fear of diversion of its interchange traffic with southern roads at Cincinnati. The Wabash Valley Association objected because it would lead to operation by the LN of what had been two competitive routes through Indiana. There was the possibility of reduction of service on the CEI, one running through Terre Haute, Indiana, to Evansville. The association wanted a S acquisition of the M to preserve competition. The CMStP, which operated a branch south from Chicago to Terre Haute, asked that its route be strengthened against the LN's competition by being granted trackage rights south of Terre Haute to the Ohio River gateway of Louisville. The ICC approved the LN-M merger in September 1970 with the provision that the LN maintain the same level of service and maintenance on the M route as on the CEI, and that the CMStP be given the trackage rights over the M that it had requested. This would introduce a new competitive route from Chicago across Indiana through Terre Haute to the South. The merger was consummated in September 1970.[36]

Post-1959 Merger Proposals—Western

Beginning with 1959 and continuing through 1964, numerous possibilities for merger of midwestern systems, large and small, were studied by carriers and their consultants. First off, combinations both of the CNW with the CRI and of the CNW with the CMStP were considered. Both were shelved by the end of 1960. After earlier interest in joining with the CMStP and then in merging with the TPW, the MStL in 1960 agreed to merge with the CNW. In June 1962, the SP and CRI initiated a study, and the UP joined in it in September. In May 1963 they agreed on a plan for the UP to take over the CRI and sell its southern lines including the Tucumcari-Kansas City segment of the "Golden State" transcontinental route to the SP. In June 1963 the CNW countered with a merger offer to the CRI. At the same time, the CNW resumed negotiations with the CMStP resulting in early 1965 in agreement on merger terms and filing an application with the ICC that was to be withdrawn later. In the meantime, in June 1964, the CNW extended a merger offer to the CGW. In October 1965 the CNW modified its intentions in respect to the CRI by agreeing to sell to the ATSF the CRI network south of Herington, Kansas, excluding the Tucumcari line. This brought major central and southern systems west of Chicago into the CNW, UP-CRI merger discussion. In respect to rail routes east of all this, the ATSF and the StLSF in 1964 initiated a merger study, but, not being able to agree on terms, dropped it in 1965. MP merger talks with the ATSF were deferred. Throughout these years the GN, NP, CBQ, and their affiliates were also carrying on studies of their possible unification and filed with the ICC in February 1961. In the far west, in April 1960, the SP took steps toward control of the WP and the ATSF counterfiled in October. Both were denied control by the ICC in 1965.

Principal Lines: Chicago and Northwestern—Minneapolis and St. Louis, 1960; Chicago Great Western, 1968; Atchinson and Sante Fe, Pennsylvania—Toledo Peoria and Western, 1960

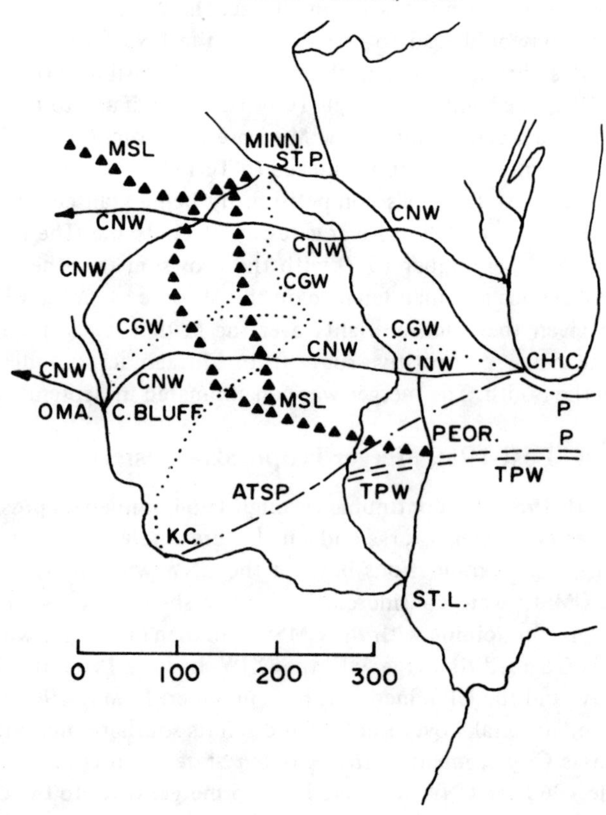

Chicago Northwestern-Minneapolis and St. Louis

The MStL extended from the Twin Cities across Iowa down to Peoria, Illinois, 686 miles. After coming out of receivership in 1943, it became a viable operation paying dividends every year through 1960. It was not a segment in any major joint long-haul route nor did it have control of any particularly desirable traffic. Its management was convinced it had to merge to assure its long-run prospects. It first tried to induce a large system to take it on, then tried to join with a road more its size, the TPW, to form a small system with better than the independent bargaining power. It finallly was offered a merger arrangement with the CNW in 1960. The then chairman of the CNW, Ben Heineman, had been an active director of the MStL from 1954 to 1956. The proposal was presented to the ICC in May. The MStL stockholders would get $25.00 of first mortgage MStL 6 percent bonds assumed by the CNW for each MStL, par $25.00 common share, which had been paying $1.40 annually for several years. In effect, the exchanged bonds that the CNW would assume plus $3½ million cash to the company itself made the purchase price about $21 million with minimal cash required. Annual savings were estimated to be $3 million. No evidence in opposition was presented and the ICC approval in October 1960. The MStL ton-miles in 1959 were 13 percent of the CNW. There were also $3 million of tax benefits from the merger, which led the MStL corporate shell to be spun off as the basis for a conglomerate.[37]

Southern Pacific, Atchison, Topeka, and Santa Fe-Western Pacific

From April to September 1960 the SP system, through a subsidiary, acquired almost 10 percent of WP stock with a view to control. In response, in October the ATSF, through a subsidiary, bought 20 percent. The GN and UP systems also each acquired 10 percent of holdings. The SP applied for ICC approval of control of the WP in October 1960, and an ATSF control application followed shortly afterward. The WP expressed the desire to remain independent. The WP in general paralleled the SP. Both extended from the San Francisco Bay area to Salt Lake-Ogden, 924 miles and 782 miles, respectively, with a 182-mile section of joint double track. The WP was also a 299-mile part of a north-south "inside gateway" route connecting with the GN on the north and the ATSF to the south. This competed with the SP's southern California-Pacific Northwest route, which was nearer the coast.

The SP move involved its increased control over traffic along two important routes and elimination of an independent rate-making road in the far west. Savings were estimated at $10 million annually for SP control, but it was shown much of this could be attained by coordination. In fact, by 1963 an additional 152 miles of WP-SP double track coordination had been put in operation. The SP control of the WP obviously threatened the less strategically located Denver and Rio

Grande along the central transcontinental route and the Great Northern along the Pacific Coast north-south traffic routes. The competitors in the latter, the ATSF and GN, between them as a defensive measure acquired almost 30 percent of WP stock in order to have some say in WP policy. The ICC in January 1965 decided against control of the WP by either applicant. In particular, the ICC concluded the SP control would terminate the vigorous competition between the routes between central and northern California and the state of Washington, and between the two central U.S. routes between California and the East. Further, no improvements in service in either case were forecast with the merger. The ICC also pointed out that the WP was a prosperous carrier and that most of the proposed savings could be accomplished without control.[38]

Great Northern-Northern Pacific-Chicago, Burlington, and Quincy.

Following studies started in the middle 1950s the GN, NP, and CBQ proposed merger in February 1961. Since the turn of the century there had been a community of interest between CBQ and the other two because the latter two had acquired most of the CBQ stock in 1901 and their presidents had been CBQ board members ever since. A past history of attempts at a similar merger, most recently in 1930, made this proposal hardly a surprise. The NP and GN were roughly parallel from the Twin Cities to Seattle, 1,784 and 1,892 miles, respectively, and reached Portland via a jointly controlled subsidiary. The CBQ joined the two at the Twin Cities with a line to Chicago, 430 miles, and extended west from Chicago to Denver, 1,034 miles, and to the vicinity of Billings, Montana, 1,392 miles, where it also connected with the northern lines. The CBQ and subsidiaries also provided a north-south route from Billings, Montana, to Houston and Galveston, via Denver, 1,807 miles.

The merger did not involve growth of the GN, NP, and CBQ family of roads by taking over other roads but was rather a family consolidation. The anticipated gains were by way of improved service and ultimate annual savings estimated by the studies at $45 million, but thought by the ICC to be nearer $25½ million. The active competition between the GN and NP would be eliminated, leaving the Northwest's east-west traffic served by the merged system, by a weak parallel competitor, the CMStPP, and by Union Pacific branches north into Idaho, Washington, Oregon, and Montana. The CMStPP and CNW, as the key Midwest competitors of the merged system, were fearful of its strengthened position and asked for improved participation in joint rates and routings and additional interchange gateways to give them wider access to traffic. Finally, the CMStPP wanted track rights to Portland, Oregon. The proposed merged system in 1969 terms would have 43 billion ton-miles, two and a quarter times the GN, and a total of some 50,000 employees.

Principal Lines: Great Northern—Northern Pacific—Chicago, Burlington and Quincy (CS), 1967

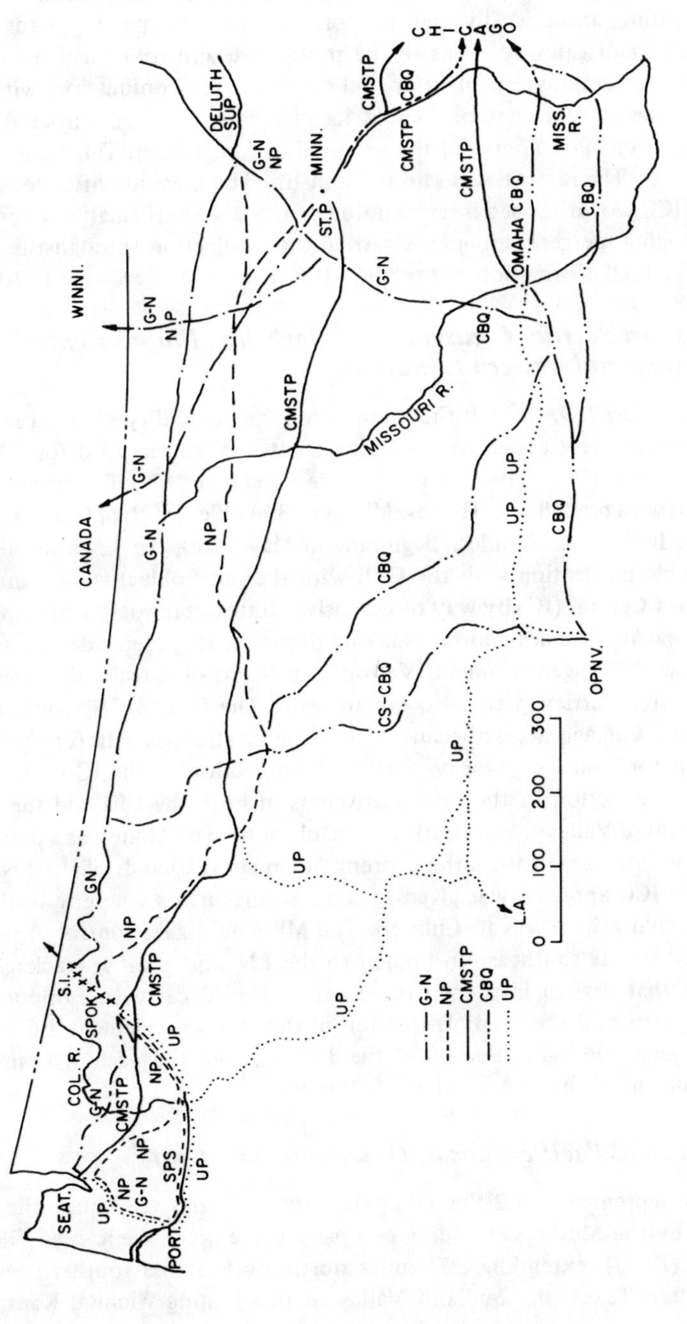

The initial ICC decision in March 1966 was adverse, with five commissioners dissenting, an unusually high proportion. Then the merging roads offered better routing and gateway terms to the protestants and voluntarily agreed to attrition terms for employee protection. On rehearing, the commission, with in the meantime the replacement of two of its members who had earlier disapproved, in November 1967 approved the proposal for the merger. This time there were two dissents. The reversal was said to be justified by these modifications together with the ICC's own revised interpretation of the law as affirmatively fostering and encouraging merger. Opponents carried their objection through the appeals courts with a final affirmation of the 1967 ICC decision in February 1970.[39]

Missouri Pacific, Louisville and Nashville, Illinois Central-Chicago and Eastern Illinois

In mid-1959, the MP first considered the possibility of acquiring the CEI as a means of direct access to the Chicago gateway and applied for ICC approval in September 1961. The CEI main route extended 287 miles from Chicago to St. Louis with branches to Thebes, Missouri, 394 miles south of Chicago, and to Evansville, Indiana, 287 miles. Beginning in May 1960, the LN also began exploring possible unification with the CEI, with the same objective. In January 1962 the Illinois Central (IC) by way of defensive strategy proposed acquiring CEI control but leaving its sales and rate-making departments independent. Savings of some $4½ million were claimed. Various joint-control possibilities among the three interested carriers were also put forward. The IC and CNW opposed giving the MP the Chicago access because it provided a strategic gain for the MP in competition for Chicago gateway traffic. The objection to the IC proposal was based on its reduction in the competitiveness of both the CEI and the joint CEI-LN Mississippi Valley north-south long-haul route. The Monon as a parallel line to the CEI worried about the latter's strengthening in the hands of the LN. In February 1965, ICC approval was given to joint arrangements whereby both the MP and LN could gain access to Chicago. The MP would gain control of the CEI, which would sell its southeastern branch to the LN, and grant it trackage rights north from that branch into the Chicago area. The IC carried its opposition through the courts and the final affirmation of the joint arrangement did not come until February 1967. In June 1969 the LN acquired the eastern branch and some equipment of the CEI for about $40 million.[40]

Texas and Pacific-Kansas, Oklahoma, and Gulf

In September 1962 the TP applied for authority to acquire the small system held by the Muskogee holding company made up of the Kansas, Oklahoma, and Gulf (KOG), extending 203 miles north-south across southern Oklahoma and northern Texas; the Midland Valley, with a joining Wichita, Kansas, with Fort

Smith, Arkansas, 322 miles; and the Oklahoma-Ada-Atoka, a 133-mile east-west line in Oklahoma. From 1926 to 1961 the 203-mile segment has been part of a Kansas City to Texas route in conjunction with the MP, but because of its deteriorating condition had been given up by the latter in favor of a longer route via Little Rock. The Muskogee system had in 1962 just abandoned some 100 miles of line and, though covering its fixed charges, had meager future prospects. It did not have the resources to improve its line to meet modern standards of clearances and heavier track. The TP proposed to purchase the system for $9½ million and sell the 133-mile segment to the ATSF for $1 million. The KOG line would be upgraded and reinstated as part of the MP-TP route south from Kansas City. The competing parallel MKT initially opposed the acquisition but withdrew after being granted some 26 miles of trackage rights over the KOG. The ICC approved the control in June 1964 as improving southwestern rail service in the public interest without undue diversion from any protesting carrier.[41]

Chicago Northwestern-Chicago Great Western

The CGW had discussed merger with various midwestern lines. A proposal in respect to the Soo was terminated in November 1963. In May 1964 the CNW suggested a merger, the terms of which were agreeable, and application for approval by the ICC was filed in November 1964. The CGW operated east-west from Chicago to Omaha, 509 miles, and north-south from St. Paul to Kansas City, 539 miles. The CGW network lay in the heart of the CNW's. The CGW ton-miles in 1964 were 18 percent of the CNW. The CGW earnings had been enough to pay dividends most of the time since 1953 but in the 1960s not enough to keep up with modernization of its equipment and plant. This was one reason for being interested in a larger partner; its lack of bargaining strength was the other. The CNW plan proposed an exchange of 0.7 share of its common for 1 CGW plus $7.38 in cash. Annual savings from the merger were estimated to reach $5 million after five years. The Soo objected because of likely diversion of traffic and the merger approval in April 1967 was conditioned on giving the Soo access to one of the shippers located in an industrial area the CGW had developed. The merger was consummated in July 1968.[42]

Union Pacific, Chicago Northwestern-Chicago, Rock Island, and Pacific

The most extensive of western merger proposals submitted to the ICC grew out of a joint Southern Pacific (SP), Union Pacific (UP) study begun in June 1962 concerning their possible acquisition of the Chicago, Rock Island, and Pacific (CRI). The UP made a merger offer in May 1963 and the Chicago Northwestern (CNW) a counter one in June. The CRI was a traditionally weak road reaching from the Twin Cities and Chicago to Colorado, New Mexico, and down to the Gulf. It

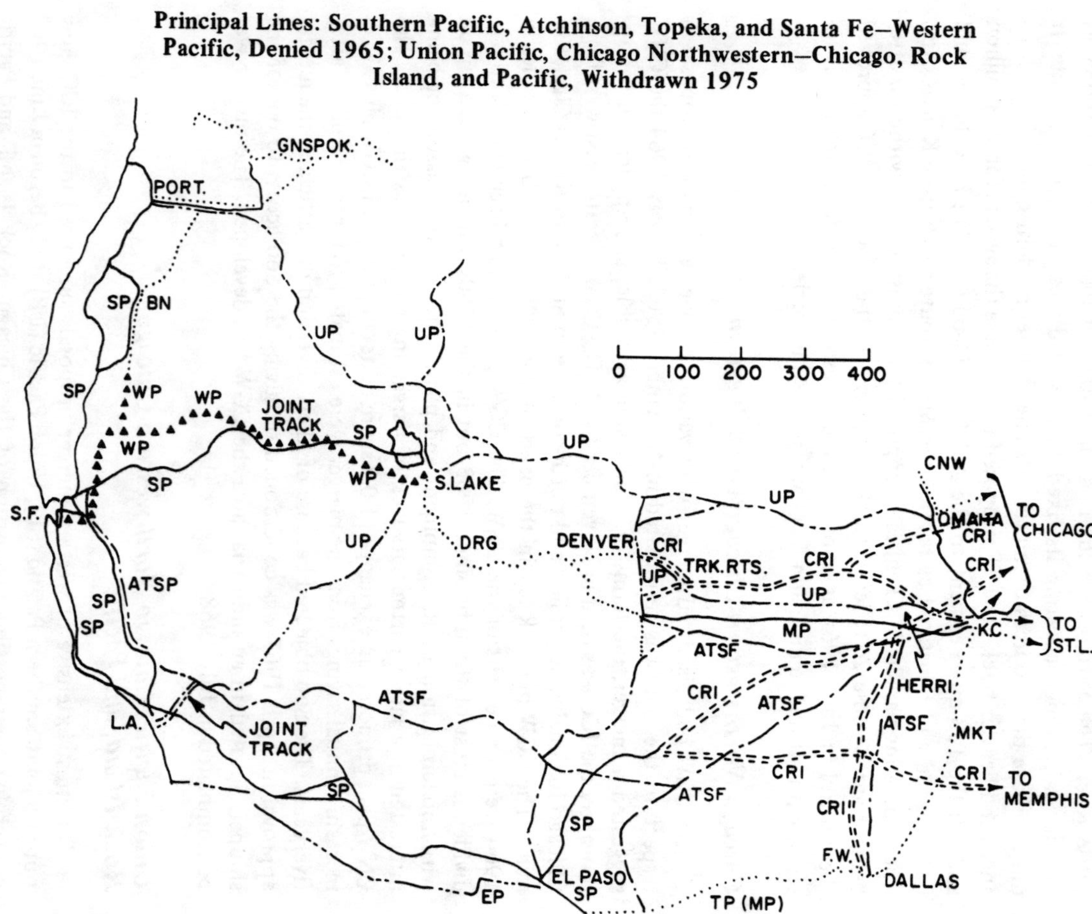

Principal Lines: Southern Pacific, Atchinson, Topeka, and Santa Fe—Western Pacific, Denied 1965; Union Pacific, Chicago Northwestern—Chicago, Rock Island, and Pacific, Withdrawn 1975
GNSPOK.
PORT.
SP BN
UP
UP
0 100 200 300 400
SP
WP
WP
JOINT TRACK
SP
UP
WP
WP
SP
UP
CNW
S.LAKE
UP
OMAHA
CRI
TO CHICAGO
S.F.
UP
DRG
DENVER
CRI
CRI
ATSP
TRK.RTS.
CRI
UP
UP
SP
SP
MP
KC
TO ST.L.
ATSF
HERRI
CRI
ATSF
ATSF
MKT
L.A.
JOINT TRACK
ATSF
CRI
CRI
TO MEMPHIS
SP
ATSF
CRI
SP
F.W.
EL PASO
EP
SP
TP (MP)
DALLAS

had gone into bankruptcy in 1933 and was reorganized in 1947. Thereafter it had staged a comeback through the fifties only to fall back in the following years. It was able, however, to declare dividends from 1948 through 1965. The CNW after its reorganization in 1944 had not been as successful as the CRI. Its management was taken over by Ben Heineman in 1956, and with considerable success in controlling costs it had been able to declare small dividends in 1964 through 1966. On the other hand, the UP was one of the financially strongest systems in the country.

The CRI had long been a partner in the transcontinental "Golden State Route" made up of the SP, 1,216 miles, from California to Tucumcari, New Mexico, thence via the CRI, 1,108 miles, to Chicago and 891 miles to St. Louis. The UP extended from Los Angeles and Portland, Oregon, to Omaha and Council Bluffs, Iowa, around 1,800 miles, but depended upon independent connections east to Chicago, some 500 miles. One of these connections was the CRI, another, the CNW, and a third, the Illinois Central (IC) in which the UP family had a 23 percent stockholding. The CRI had other routes that would be of strategic value to still other western roads. Its Colorado-Kanas City route would give the DRG a much-desired access to a Missouri River gateway, and its Kansas City-St. Louis line would give the ATSF its long-wanted entrance to St. Louis. The CRI line from northwestern Texas to Memphis would provide a western road a direct connection with southeastern roads. These various segments of the CRI had more value as strategic additions to other systems than as components of the CRI itself.

The UP May 1963 merger proposal was to exchange 0.718 of its common for 1 CRI common share and to sell to the SP for $120 million the 3,524 miles of the CRI south and southwest of Kansas City, including the Tucumcari line. In June 1963 the CNW counteroffer was 0.2778 CNW common, $30.00 of 6 percent income bonds and $5.00 for each CRI share. In May 1964 the UP improved its proposal to a share of a $1.80 UP preferred, convertible into 0.85 shares UP common, plus a contingent cash payment based on CRI common and UP preferred dividend differences (around $4.50 per share). A battle developed between the UP and CNW for CRI stockholder acceptance of their respective offers with the UP finally winning in January 1965. Both had earler applied for ICC approval of their respective proposals. The CNW plan involved an agreement with the ATSF for it to buy the CRI lines south of Herington, Kansas, excepting the Tucumcari line but including the Memphis route, for $100 million. In light of the CNW and DRG fears of traffic diversion consequent upon the UP and SP takeover of the CRI, the UP in May 1968 offered to make up CNW revenue losses above a designated level for seven years following merger. In addition, the UP approached the DRG with respect to possible sale to it of the CRI lines between Colorado and Kansas City. The UP suggested $32 million as the price; the DRG, $16 million. The difference could not be resolved and no agreement was reached.

With the stakes in realigned control of routes consequent to acquisition of the various CRI segments so high and with the probable changes in western patterns of traffic so great and widespread, the great number of roads heard, and the quantity of evidence presented, the length of proceedings exceeded all other ICC cases. The examiners' report was not finally handed down until February 1973. The ICC decision was rendered in December 1974. It amounted to a complete rearrangement of the central western and southwestern railroad networks. It allocated the Tucumcari segment of the CRI to the SP, the Amarillo-Memphis one to the ATSF, the Colorado-Omaha to the DRG, and the Missouri River-Chicago to the UP. All this was subject to extensive conditions, among them that the ATSF take on the MKT. However, the CRI went into bankruptcy in March 1975. The UP and ATSF requested and obtained dismissal of the merger case. In this connection the ICC noted in its annual report that unifications were voluntary and not mandatory. The ICC proposed restructuring of the central western and southwestern rail network collapsed, an anticlimactic conclusion to the ICC's most ambitious undertaking in the postwar years.[43]

Missouri Pacific-Atchison, Topeka, and Santa Fe

In May 1966 the MP and its parent applied to acquire control of the ATSF. The MP had purchased for $34 million almost 3 million ATSF preferred shares, 8 percent of voting stock. The ATSF was strongly opposed and suggested that the purpose was to force the ICC to "master plan" the rail systems of the West. No action was taken on the case and the application was withdrawn in July 1968.[44]

* * *

This history of major post-World War II acquisition proposals reveals the preoccupation of the U.S. railroad systems with possible improvement in their strategic strengths as well as other possible gains. On the other hand, some systems had weaknesses, which led to interest in their possible takeovers, if given favorable offer terms. A significant amount of managements' and their staffs' thoughts and energies were devoted to consideration of the many angles of all this, first in an exploratory way and then in the pursuit of all-around approval of a final proposal. This later involved obtaining agreement between all the financial interests involved, labor agreements, and then the winning of regulatory approval at the hands of both the ICC and courts. The railroads involved in all this were not just the principals but also those even remotely affected. Thus most all systems had to devote attention to the mergers in the later stages of the acquisition movement. The opportunity cost of this was undoubtedly high—the diversion of thought and energy from innovation, from marketing, and improved labor relations alone was substantial. Nor could it all be charged to regulatory requirements because it impacted on private property rights of external systems that demanded the full legal protection of those rights quite aside from regulatory constraints.

RESULTS OF UNIFICATION AND MERGER GROWTH OF SYSTEM SIZE AND REDUCTION OF COMPETITION

Of the major consumated acquisitions, two (the EL and PC) were primarily aimed at solving serious financial problems. In the course of this objective both involved combining parallel and thus competitive routes. The resultant systems represented substantial growth; the Erie added 39 percent to its ton-miles; the other, the P, added 85 percent. In contrast, more combinations emphasized growth by acquiring systems some of which were not directly competitive. The GMO obtained a 53 percent addition, the CO, 81 percent, the NW added 67 percent with the NYCStL, W & PMV, and the ACL 86 percent with the SAL. The BN was rather a consolidation of what were already a closely related family of traffic and, therefore, its constituents are not counted as additions.

Over twenty-five years, the proportion of various regions' traffic removed from competition by these ton-miles acquisitions was nearly one-half in the east and some fifth in the South. For the West the BN merger effects are difficult to count because of the above noted intercompany relationships that were essentially just formalized without being actual additions, except for the NP, GN combination. The western reductions with this were only 7 percent.

In more particular terms in the East competition between the two largest and key traditional competitors, the P and the NYC, was eliminated and, in addition, the strategic strength of some of the remaining smaller systems was seriously compromised. In the South large areas lost one competitor out of a previous two or three. The merging of the two strongest of the three northern transmountain systems, the GN, NP and CMStP sharply reduced competition in an extensive part of the north Rocky Mountain and Pacific Northwest regions. The acquisition by one of the southern systems, the LN, of two competing routes connecting the South with the Midwest was hardly balanced by giving trackage rights over one of them to a weak western road, the CMStP, so it could connect with the other major southern system, the S. It is clear that rail competition was markedly reduced.

An assumption was that all this resulted in the remaining systems becoming more effective competition of water and highway carriers and in this way met the test of being in the public interest. The possibility that three major systems in the Southeast, with three rather than two marketing forces going after traffic and three rather than two operations trying to excel in service, for instance, might actually provide greater competition than two was not considered.

Measurable Consequences of Unification

Previous Analysis of Unification Economies

A statistical analysis of the effects railroad system size or scale of operations for the major systems (those with over 2,000 employees) in railroad industry in the mid-1950s had concluded that the largest systems (over 20,000 employees) did significantly less well in respect to rate of return and proportion of revenue going to net railway operating income before income taxes than the middle-sized ones (5,000 to 20,000 employees). This conclusion was after taking into account the economies of route traffic density and the burdens of passenger operations. This was confirmed in a later similar analysis in 1967 of the performance of nineteen major western roads with the conclusion "that cost savings arguments for large railroad mergers have to be very largely discounted."[45]

A 1969 statistical study covered nine post-1955 mergers including in contrast to the sample for this study, three which involved prior control by the acquiring system and three where the acquired roads were much smaller relative to the principal than this study's 25 percent acquired road proportion minimum limit. The conclusions were that "there were difficulties in achieving merger savings" and that "large, more recent and more complex mergers have produced the least favorable results." In particular it was pointed out that the smaller NW-V merger results were favorable and the large NW-NYCStL-W, were particularly poor.[46]

Overview of Measures of Merger and Unification—
Eight Systems, 1947–1972

With savings an important objective of unification the performance of overhead expenses are important. Of them (a) "general" items (covering general officers and staff, and legal and accounting functions) and (b) "superintendence" (covering other departmental officers on down through supervisory personnel), are categories of expenses, changes in which should measure any gains from unification.

Maintenance items are variable expenses but subject to distortion by prior and/or current over- and undermaintenance so that their trends can be dominated by factors other than unification. It is impossible to take these into account so maintenance is not considered. Transportation expenses are strictly current ones and any changes provide an important index of merger results. As a potential factor in growth trends changes in share of a system's regional traffic or share relative to competitor's are another index of results. Finally the net revenues and all categories of expense are reflected in pre-income tax (nroi) and provide a summary measure of current results. Achievement of hoped for improved access to capital markets is reflected in changes in credit ratings, and of benefits gained for stockholders, in improved dividend payments.

Overhead Expense

In respect to the overhead type of expenses, the "general" category showed reductions in ratio relative to revenue in only two of the eight cases. These two were among the small- and medium-scale unifications, the NW-V and the E-DLW. For the latter a change in management after an initial two years of increase in the ratio was followed by great reduction. If the new management had been in place premerger the earlier ratios would surely have been significantly lower, so no reduction would likely be shown as a result of merger. On the other hand, for the three largest-scale mergers there were substantial long-run increases in the "general" expense ratios. In respect to the "superintendence" expense/operating expense ratio, there was only one instance of significant reduction, the E-DLW, again with the aforementioned significant management change involved, making any merger responsibility doubtful. On the other hand, major increases occurred for the three largest-scale mergers (NW-W-NYCStL, CO-BO, and PC).

Traffic Expense

In respect to traffic expense, the ratios to revenue increased with the smaller-scale and pre-1960 cases, and for all subsequent cases decreased. Traffic expense is the smallest of the functional expense categories and therefore not a potential source of important savings. However, its reduction may be related to the failure, to be noted hereafter, to achieve greater shares of the rail market in which the combined systems competed.

Transportation Expense

In respect to the transportation expense ratios, there were significant reductions in two of the three pre-1960 cases, but in the two there were concurrent dieselization programs with their contribution to improving train productivity. On the other hand, the transportation ratios increased with unification in two of the large-scale post-1960 cases (NW-W-NYCStL and P-NYC) and showed no change in another (CO-BO). Only in one case (SCL), with the rapidly growing traffic of the South, was there improvement in the transportation ratio. But in that case the comparable nonmerging system (S) with similar traffic growth showed superior improvement.

Share of Freight Traffic

Increased market share of traffic was a hoped for result of merger or unification and can be measured in changes in the proportion of a region's traffic or as compared to a competing system's traffic. Coal traffic has to be considered separately because its distribution between regions and between carriers was greatly influenced by shifts in coal from use as "steam" coal by utilities and industry to a combination of primarily metallurgical use and exportation. This was an external factor favoring systems with on-line coal mines producing coal suitable for the latter uses. Along with depletion this has resulted, for instance, in the PC's 1973 bituminous coal revenue dropping to 14 percent less than the PC constituents' revenue in 1953, whereas the NW's 1973 revenue was 79 percent greater than its preunification constituents' in 1953. Coal traffic gains following the NW-V merger and subsequent broader merger were primarily a matter of the external factors.

For other-than-coal traffic or for total traffic for minor coal carriers revenue growth of unified systems related to preunification constituants has been followed by increased market shares in only three cases, the GMO-A, NYCStL-WLE, and CO-BO. In the WLE case, strengthening of management just before unification was a factor concurrent with the unification. On the other hand, 'the largest-scale merger, the PC, was immediately followed by a sharp decline in share for three years, almost 2 percentage points out of 40 percent and even by the fifth year still a significant loss. This in turn must have accounted for changing shares of the other roads in this region.

Proportion of Pre Tax NROI Income to Revenue

In respect to effects on nroi pre-income tax as a proportion of operating revenues, the results of merger must be interpreted in light of general regional trends as well as two instances (the GMO-A and NW-V) of concurrent dieselization. The three pre-1960 cases showed significant gains. The other, the NYCStL-WLE itself showed no change, but relative to other systems in the region this was in effect a gain. The four large-scale post-1960 cases all showed declines, that of P-NYC-NYNH&H being the most severe. This was despite the fact that in the 1960s traffic was increasing all around.

Credit Ratings

The hope that unification might improve access to capital markets was not generally fulfilled, even with concurrent nonmerger improvement factors present. Only for the three smaller-scale mergers were *Moody's* acquiring road debt ratings not reduced and for only one, the GMO-A, was it raised. In six of the eight cases *Moody's* had warned of possible downgrading of the acquiring systems' debt ratings with acquisition. Within one to three years, ratings of either the equipment or senior mortgage debt or both were in fact reduced one notch and in one case more. On the other hand, excluding the cases where systems were in financial straights to begin with, the debt ratings for the securities of the smaller acquired systems were generally improved. However, it was the debt of the acquiring or principal systems that would be the future source for new capital and it was their ratings that were generally not improved and occasionally subjected to reduction.

Stockholders' Position and Returns

From the stockholder point of view there were both immediate and long-run effects associated with merger or acquisition. The immediate were in a sense side effects in that they related and to the hope of enhancing the image of merger. The pre-1960 cases did not noticeably involve this phase. The 1964 NS case was preceded by NW dividend increase that had a basis in rising net income, though in the year following unification and merger the dividend was reduced slightly, although combined net income continued to rise. In the SCL case, dividends were increased the year before merger and continued at a higher level for one partner and a reduced level for the other followed by no down adjustment for the following two years despite declining net. The 1968 PC merger was preceded by maintenance of peak dividends in 1967 despite sharp declines in net income of both the NYC and P. These dividends were continued postmerger for over a year despite the net turning to deficits, to be explained only by a desire to maintain a favorable image for the merger. In the SCL case such a policy contributed in part to a later reduction in debt rating, and in the PC case, to bankruptcy.

The longer-run effects, after five years, which represent a major objective of acquisition and merger, would hopefully be stabilization and growth of returns for stockholders. Of the earlier cases both the GMO-A and NW-V provided significant gains in these terms. The improvement in the NYCStL-WLE combination must be credited to a major degree to the premerger installed new management, so any merger effects were not clear. With the CO-PM merger there was an initial sharp decline involving significant drop in coal traffic. Decline in CO dividend rates was followed by a comeback to premerger levels ten years later.

The long-run effects of the big NW acquisition and the ACL-SAL merger are difficult to assess because both their operations were in regions of general revenue growth. The NW dividend rate was reduced 7 percent immediately after merger and 8 percent again two years after. The SCL rate remained level three and a half years after. It was then increased, but because of original stockholder participation being shifted to holding company stock the gain was not passed on to the original holders. The long-run results in the PC case were not only no dividends but also loss of value in bankruptcy. Overall, except for the smaller-scale earlier mergers, there is no convincing evidence of significant gains for the stockholders of the acquiring systems.

On the other hand, stockholders of some of the acquired roads seemed to have gained. Those of the PM received returns better and more stable than the PM alone could have paid. The WLE had their second-highest dividend rate guaranteed for the future. The V stockholders received an immediate rise in dividends and subsequent substantial increases until the 1964 NW larger merger. The BO acquisition by the CO resulted in the former's stockholders receiving stable dividends at a rate almost as high as the next to highest in a series of unstable dividends in the 1950s.

Basic gains from unification or merger were the exception rather than the rule. Cases involving smaller acquired systems in the earlier years provided the successes; the larger-scale later ones provided major disappointments.

Merger Effects on Service

The lack of quality of service data from year to year for the railroads relating, for instance, to elapsed time of car movement shipper to consignee or even actual train transit times makes only limited assessment of merger effects on service possible. The only items available for comparison are the schedules of the limited few railroads published in the *Official Guide of the Railways—of the U.S.* No information is available about the actual adherence to the schedules or the time taken for terminal handling.

In the case of the Seaboard Coast Line merger there was no significant change. Basic schedules, for instance, from Florida points to Philadelphia, New York, and Midwest cities showed only minor adjustments of an hour, more or less. From points in Alabama and Georgia the same was true. Comparison of Wabash premerger schedules with the comparable ones postmerger on the Norfolk and Western (NW) between Buffalo, Detroit, Chicago, east St. Louis, and Kansas City similarly show no significant change. There was a reduction in trains along the Detroit-east Buffalo route.

With the Penn Central merger, schedules likewise were little changed except for the route between southern New England and the South. In this case, the rerouting of trains circuitously through Selkirk (near Albany, New York) doubled the best schedule times between the west shore of the Hudson River in the port of New York and, for instance, Boston. In addition, the PC merger resulted immediately in a period of extreme deterioration of actual car movement time due to almost all imaginable causes, from inadequate capacity of newly used routes to just plain losing track of cars. [47]

A different type of service decline came where a major road took over smaller competitive parallel lines. What had been a main line for the small predecessor became a secondary one with de-emphasis of standards of maintenance and reduced quality of train service. Shippers who had been on the Chicago-Great Western complained of this upon its takeover by the Chicago and Northwestern. [48]

By the mid-1960s freight schedules had been reduced as far as subtraction of twenty-four-hour units of time could be carried out, and "run-through" trains eliminating interchange yarding delays came into wide use so there were few chances for schedule improvements. More likely were negative actions taken by way of consolidating services, economizing to the extent of choosing routings, and yarding patterns that sacrificed transit times.

* * *

Under the provisions of the 1940 legislation, initiative for restructuring of the country's railroad network by acquisition of control and unification was left in the hands of the country's individual systems as they saw fit to strengthen their positions.

The allowed acquisitions were for the most part basically along the lines that petitioning carriers asked for, permitting important strategic gains, though tempered by conditions aimed at preventing the undoing of remaining independent systems. In some few cases, this involved major modifications. Where there were

252

conflicting objectives between competing proposals the ICC had to arbitrate as between claims. The requirements that all parties be duly heard in accordance with both regulatory and plain legal process led to some long delays, substantial railroad staff involvement and expenditure of millions of dollars in consultant and legal fees. Before the two most complicated and controversial proposals were finally consummated as much as six and nine years elapsed.

The analysis of the results of major unifications after the five-year maturation period shows that most of the forecast gains were not achieved. Most important of all, railroad competition was greatly reduced. Not only were the number of systems reduced but some of the weaker systems in the East and Northwest were further weakened so as to markedly cut their competitive roles.

13

Financial Performance of the Railroads

The financial performance of the railroads in the postwar quarter of a century was deeply involved with continuously rising material prices, wage rates, and fringe benefits; increasing intermodal competition; and major fare, rate, and division adjustments. The problem has been balancing of revenues and costs by increasing productivity, by reductions in, and even the elimination of, some services, and by improvement of others. Financially, taxes, rents, and debt requirements, interest, sinking fund payments, and security issue maturities were obligations, many from the past, that had to be met from the balance of revenue and expenses, short of bankruptcy. On the other hand, there was discretionary control of the expenditures for maintenance, early retirement of debt, investment in new facilities, and dividends. The balancing focused on levels of repair of road and equipment and of a viable working capital position. Underlying much of this was the system security structure inherited from the past, but for most systems subjected to change just before or during the early years of the period under review.

There were some important elements common to all the railroads in much of this. These were the country-wide general terms of wages and benefits, price levels of capital goods and material items, and the state of capital markets. Equally in common were federal regulatory constraints and the nationwide spread of highway and air competition. On the other hand, the nature of traffic, prices for transport services, and the extent of waterway competition were elements that varied widely from region to region. There were also local regulatory constraints that variously affected that part of traffic that was intrastate.

Measures of overall financial performance are available in the income accounts of the railroads. One is net railway operating income (nroi), which shows the balance left of revenue after operating expenses, taxes, and equipment rents. Another is net income, which takes into account other rents, interest, and miscellaneous income and expenses. Cash and working capital are items that involve the liquidity of the corporate entities. Then there are dividends, which reflect the judgment of management and directors in respect to level of working capital, one use of internally generated funds, and stockholder interests. The individual system appraisal is supplemented by review of outside appraisal in the form of credit ratings. *Moody's* bond-rating changes are used in this connection.[1]

254

HISTORICAL BACKGROUND

The prewar depression and the war had substantial impact upon the subsequent financial affairs of the railroads as is evidenced in Table 30. From 1929 to 1932 the revenues in all regions but the Pocahontas had dropped precipitously, roughly by one-half. Net income for each of the three major regions had turned negative, beginning with 1931 in the South and 1932 in the East and West. For the West it remained negative until 1940; for the East, until 1935; and the South, 1936. By 1940 some two-fifths of current interest requirements in the West were not being met, one-fifth in the South, and one-eighth in the East. By 1932 dividends had been cut by over 90 percent in the East, 80 percent in the West, and practically eliminated in the South. Eight of the seventeen major independent western roads and four of the fifteen eastern had been placed in bankruptcy or receivership along with two in the South. Only the three Pocahontas region roads, the Norfolk and Western (NW), Chesapeake and Ohio (CO), and Virginian (V), held their own.

Then with the war, increases in much traffic, industrial production going to three shifts and seven days a week, the imposition of minimum carloadings, and restrictions on passenger train-mile increases together resulted in highest ever load factors. As a result, net income rose sharply. At the peak in 1942 southern and western net income exceeded any previous levels. Dividends were not increased

TABLE 30

Peak and Low Year Net Income After Taxes and Dividends

(Class I RRs 1929 to 1946)

(Millions)

	East		Pocahontas		South		West	
	Net Inc.	Divs.	Net Inc.	Divs.	Net Inc.	Divs.	Net Inc.	Divs.
1929	$405	$223	$82	$37	$73	$49	$337	$182
1930				40				
1932	−48	21	43	36	−49	1	−86	36
1942	304	68	65	48	126	21	407	65
1945	134	73	47	51	49	26	244	96

(Source: ICC, *SRUS*, Table 55 or 158; *TSUS*, Table 158.)

commensurately, the wartime peak dividends for the South and West being only about one-half of their peak in 1929, and for the East, one-third. Only for the Pocahontas region were they greater, up by a fifth from the predepression peak in 1930. After 1942 or 1943 net incomes for all but the Pocahontas region dropped sharply.

The impact of the depression on railroad finances had led to direct government help by way of loans for maintenance and rehabilitation. In 1932 the Reconstruction Finance Corporation (RFC) had been created to enable the railroads to obtain capital funds under circumstances such that ordinary issue of securities would have been impossible. The RFC provided guarantees, standby support of issues, and actual purchase of securities and direct loans. By the end of 1949 there had been loans and purchases totaling $849 million, of which $398 million were then still outstanding. By this date other government arrangements for maintenance, etc., had provided the railroads $201 million, of which all but $10 million had been repaid. The improved income of the war years had been channeled into the repayments of both types of aid. In parallel with this, the federal bankruptcy laws were amended in 1933 and 1935 to facilitate reorganizing railroad corporate financial structures and in 1939 and 1942 to provide for "readjustments" short of bankruptcy.[2]

As a consequence of the depression experience the improvement of the financial structures of the railroads was a principal preoccupation of management, trustees, courts, and the ICC in the 1940s. With the success of the wartime operation for the first time in many years railroads, with few exceptions, were in an ample financial position, and financial markets were ready to provide funds on the most favorable terms. There was every incentive to proceed actively toward rearranging financial structures in order that they be more viable in the future. The big element of uncertainty lay in estimating the relation of what was happening in the 1940s to what might happen in the future in respect to traffic, revenue, expenses, and net income. This raised questions as to timing, whether to wait on the restructuring until a better view of the future unfolded or act immediately to take advantage of the known favorable factors. In the main, the latter way prevailed; the receiverships and trusteeships of the 1930s were largely dissolved by 1949. The Missouri Pacific (MP) was the only major system not out of bankruptcy by then. This was because of special ownership and control problems without which the MP too would probably have been restored to normal. The marginal securities were written down and the claimants for unpaid interest and principal value of debt were given some cash and a variety of scaled down new securities, which carried the low interest rates then current. From 1944 through 1948 major reorganizations reduced the par value of bonds outstanding in the West by 19 percent, and in the South by 7 percent, but made little change in the East, only 1 percent.

The changes in the *Moody's* ratings of general first mortgage bonds provided a specific measure of the effect of all this. These ratings (as shown in Table 31) had particular significance because they affected the potential borrowing terms for the railroads. Divisional mortgage bonds, which generally had higher ratings because of prior rights and liens on specially profitable route segments, are disregarded because they were not open-ended and are being eliminated because they are not available for additional financing. General mortgage bonds were the vehicle for nonequipment financing. From 1940 to 1949 the ratings of the senior issues of this type for all the major roads (independent companies with over $25 million annual revenue in 1960) improved sufficiently to eliminate all "Caa" to "C," "poor-standing," or lower-rated bonds. The greatest gains were in the South and West, the latter reflecting particularly the consummation of six reorganization plans. The generally poorer relative standing of the eastern roads is evident. The top ratings in both 1940 and 1949 for the Pocahontas, principal coal carriers, stand out. It was significant that nearly half of the western road 1950 ratings ranged from "A," "higher medium, with many favorable investment attributes," to "Aaa," "best quality."

As a result of trends in capital markets, generally interest rates had declined beginning in 1934, and after a slight upturn in the first years of the war they turned down to an alltime low. The average yield for railroad bonds, Moody rated "A,"

TABLE 31

Number of Independent Major Railroads Whose Senior
General Mortgage Bonds Fall in Each of Moody's *Rating Categories*

	East		Pocahontas		South		West	
Medium year:	1941	1950	1941	1950	1941	1950	1941	1950
Grade								
Aaa "best"			1	2			1	2
Aa, "high"	1		2	1			2	1
A, "higher medium"	1	4				1		4
Baa, "lower medium"	3	3			4	5	4	4
Ba	6	8			2	1	2	4
B	1	1				1	1	1
Caa, "poor"	2					1	2	
Ca	1					1	4	
C, "lowest"								

(Ratings based on data for the year previous to manual year.)
(Source: *Moody's Railroads,* 1941 and 1950.)

"higher medium grade," had been 5.0 percent at the end of 1929. By 1940 it was down to 3.9 percent, by the end of 1945, 3.0 percent, and three years later, 3.3 percent. The very low rate of interest led to widespread refinancing of the outstanding high nominal rate of interest, callable railroad bonds. Railroad issues accounted for 14.5 percent of all newly issued bonds in the U. S.'in 1944 and 9.0 percent in 1945 compared to from 2 to 8 percent in the five prior years.

New bonds were issued to refund or redeem older ones in the western region to an amount equal to 29 percent of the par value of the total outstanding at the end of 1940. For the Pocahontas region the proportion was 22 percent; for the East, 18 percent; and the South, 10 percent. As previously mentioned, the bonds issued in course of reorganizations during this period carried the then current low interest rates.

Interest accruals dropped sharply in all but the Pocahontas region as a result of these developments. Comparing 1940, before the reorganizations, with 1949 indicates the change. (See Table 32.)

It should be noted that interest accruals rather than actual payments are considered in this comparison. This is because even though during bankruptcy a large share of fixed bond interest payments were omitted, in general they were ultimately recognized in cash and/or in securities paid out in the process of reorganization. The western roads had effected the greatest proportionate interest reduction, by one-half. The southern were reduced by over a third, and the Pocahontas', the least. The relatively low reduction for the eastern roads was an indication of the severity of their overall problem even during the prosperous war years.

TABLE 32

*Interest Accruals on Debt Other than Equipment Obligations**

(Class I RRs and Lessors)

	East	Pocahontas	South	West
1940	$213	$13	$72	$246
1949	149	13	45	122
Change 1940 to 1949	–30%		–38%	–50%

(Source: ICC, *SRUS*, Tables 148, 158, 162.)

*Estimated from data for total interest by subtracting estimated equipment obligation interest calculated from estimated average interest rate applying during previous ten years, 2.4 percent for 1940 and 2.3 percent for 1949. The interest charges for equipment are so small a part of the total that possible error in their estimate would not significantly affect the percent of change.

TABLE 33

Total Interest Accrual Proportion of Operating Revenue
Plus Net of Other Income and Expense

(Class I RRs and Lessors)

	East	Pocahontas	South	West	U.S.
1940	11%	5%	13%	15%	12½%
1949	5	3	4	4	4

(Source: ICC, *SRUS,* Tables 148, 158, 162.)

Of significance were the declines in the proportion of total interest, including that on the increased equipment obligations, to gross income (operating revenue plus the net of other income and expenses), as shown in Table 33. This decrease reflects the combined effects of general inflationary revenue increases and the just discussed net interest reductions. Concurrently, railroad labor costs increased from 46 percent of operating revenue in 1940 to 49 percent in 1950. Dividend payments declined from 3.6 percent to 3.2 percent of gross.

While the interest proportion in 1940 was highest in the West, by 1950 it became the lowest, Pocahontas excluded. The reverse was true for the East. For the West the share in 1950 was only 22 percent of what it had been in 1940; in the South, 29 percent; and the East, 40 percent. The Pocahontas roads were unique with a lower than other region share at both points of time.

With the help of the favorable capital market conditions in the country and new statutory bankruptcy and readjustment provisions, and in response to the depression demonstrated need for write-downs of securities, the railroad and investment banking leaders together were able to largely restructure the finances of the railroad industry. The ICC regulation calling for competitive bidding was an important new competitive element in the finance picture. The exceptions were the systems where original financing had not provided for readjustment as economic conditions changed. An overall of these and the country's high rate of inflation, and low level interest in general reduced to the point where it took only a minor part of gross income.

POST-1949

The special wartime phase of U.S. railroad finance gave way to new postwar patterns of capital expenditures and financial transactions. The analysis of these can be facilitated by reviewing the performance of the railroads in three distinctly different phases. The first covers the postwar adjustments from 1949, following the closing out of the bankruptcies, on through the rising level of economic activity to the end of 1957; the second, the subsequent depressed period for many of the railroads, 1958 through 1962; and the third, the generally resurgent period, 1963 through 1972.

Institutional Aspects of Financing

Throughout the three phases certain common institutional aspects of railroad finance played an important role. For one, in the high rates of income tax, in 1950, for instance, averaging 43 percent of net income, made issuance of debt rather than stock the favored means of raising capital from the stockholders' and thus management's point of view. Interest on debt was deducted before determining net income upon which the taxes were based so that there was more net available to stockholders than if the equivalent amount was to be raised by sale of stock shares. Further, in the South and West the acceptability of debt issue had been improved by the reduction of the ratios of debt to stock as a result of the reorganizations and bond retirements just mentioned. For western roads, for instance, the long-term debt account had been twice the stock account in 1940; by 1950 the two were about equal.

The issuance of fixed interest debt could take either of two general forms, bonds or equipment obligations. Bonds were usually secured by a lien on the fixed property of a railroad, either directly as with mortgage bonds or indirectly as with collateral trust bonds with their collateral being mortgage bonds. Usually, the provisions of system general mortgage issues provided that additional amounts could be issued to the extent of 65 percent of the expenditures for additions and betterments to the properties upon which the issues had a lien. In the postwar years maturities of twenty-five to forty years and sinking fund payments of ½ percent to 1 percent annually were usual. Such issues were potentially available as a means of obtaining external financing for the companies with the better credit ratings, for first mortgage bonds, *Moody's* "A" or better, or sometimes even with "Baa."

The other general debt category covered equipment obligations of which there were two types. Both were secured by the particular units of equipment for the purchase of which the money was obtained. One type, equipment trust certificates, had been in use for a long time. They had serial maturities, usually an equal amount each year for fifteen years. There was an accompanying cash down payment, for the most part of 20 percent of the purchase price of the equipment. The other type was the newly popular conditional sales agreement, which had first been offered by banks just before and during the war and which became a widely used debt instrument thereafter. It was more flexible as to term and down payment amounts. There was less or no initial down payment required and shorter periods to maturity than with the equipment trusts. Interest for conditional sales agreements was generally two- or three-tenths of a percentage point higher than for the trusts. The financially more conservative equipment trust conditions led to their higher *Moody's* ratings, usually by one grade, than for first mortgage bonds. The sales agreement notes not being sold to the public were not given published credit ratings.

Equipment debt provided a ready and advantageous way of acquiring external funds under almost any condition. For companies with lower credit ratings, interest rates were substantially lower than for the mortgage bonds. In 1965, for instance, a "Baa" rated thirty-year first mortgage bond issued by the Northern Pacific carried a 4.1 percent interest rate. A concurrent equipment trust was sold with a 2.75 percent rate, the general level available for western roads that year. In 1958, when interest rates were higher, a "Baa" rated twenty-five-year bond for one company had a 5.6 percent cost; an "A," a twenty-year one, for another company, 4.3 percent. Both companies paid 3.5 percent on equipment trusts with common terms. Companies that were then not in a favorable position to sell new bond issues could almost always borrow on equipment obligations, leaving such internal funds as were available for roadway investment. Equipment debt was thus the preferred method for raising outside capital. It provided the easiest procedures and the lowest interest charges of any means and was possible for all systems almost regardless of credit standing.

The postwar period also saw a completely new means of applying outside capital to the financing of equipment for railroad use. This was the purchase and ownership of equipment by financial institutions such as insurance and general credit companies, and even by groups of individual investors and their leasing of it to the railroads. It was the institutions' interest in tax shelters that provided their principal incentive. From the railroad point of view, if it did not have net income against which to offset credit against taxes it could get the advantage by allowing ownership of equipment to be in profitable financial institutions' hands. The latter would take the credits and pass some of the gains on in the form of lower effective interest rates. Further, the railroads were relieved of providing cash for initial down payments. With the introduction of accelerated depreciation and investment tax credits the advantages of lease rentals were greatly increased during the 1960s. Again ease of procedure, lowest of interest or its equivalent embodied in rental charges, and general availability were dominant factors as against mortgage debt or stock issue.

Quarter Century of the Financing

1948–1957

The important financial problem of the railroads in the first decade after the war was the finding of some $13 billion for investment in new facilities. In addition, on the order of $1 billion was sought for meeting of debt maturities and retiring or replacing debt to obtain lower interest charges for those systems not having benefited from the reorganization security restructuring.

The environment in which financial decisions were made was one of general optimism after the 1950 upturn canceled the effects of the 1949 low year. Freight traffic had leveled off after the war well above any previous peacetime highs, and initially passenger traffic was about at the level it had been in the late 1920s. As previously indicated, there had been the marked improvement in the credit standing of the railroads through the war and reorganization phase, though this was to be followed by some deterioration. This grew out of the difficulty of matching increased expenses with continuing wage and material price increases, the five-day work week, and limitation of rate and fare increases because of competition and relocating of industry.

The *Moody's* senior general mortgage bond ratings for five eastern roads—the NYC, P, BM, NYNH&H, and Reading—were reduced one grade. On the other hand, ratings for two smaller ones, the Delaware and Hudson and Western Maryland, were lifted one. In the South and West general economic growth and possibly better management countered the continuously increasing wages, etc., and competition, so that only a few special cases did credit ratings drop, and for six—the S, GMO, CG, DRG, KCS, and MP—they increased. The exceptions were among the traditionally weak—the CNW and CRI.

The capital markets were ready to supply funds, though the unusually low interest rates of the latter 1940s were no longer available. In the case of the railroads, nominal equipment trust interest rates increased from an average of 2.0 percent in 1947 to 3.8 percent in 1957, and yields on "A" rated railroad bonds from an average of 3.5 percent in 1947 to 4.0 percent in early 1957 and 4.5 percent at the end of that year. The corresponding increase in cost of labor inputs over the same period is measured by the average hourly wage rates of $1.20 in 1947 and $2.32 in 1957, almost twofold.

For 1947 through 1957 the sale of bonds and equipment obligations is presented by regions in Table 34. The published statements as to purpose of an issue are the basis for assigning issues to the category of being used for new facility investment. Issues to restore working capital depleted by prior investment expenditures are included.

It should be noted that there were large issues of bonds sold during this period for the purpose of refunding or redeeming outstanding bonds and an occasional one for acquiring other companies. It is obvious the equipment obligations were almost the sole source of outside funds for investment in additions and betterments. The amount raised by this means was large. For two consecutive years, 1951 and 1952, the East alone obtained over $300 million annually and in 1949 and 1952 the West, over $200 million. For the country as a whole the period total was $5 billion of gross external funds against the gross investment of $13 billion.

TABLE 34

Estimated Debt Issued for New Facilities, 1948–1957
(Billions)

	East	Pocahontas	South	West
Bonds		neg.	neg.	$0.1
Equipment Obligations	$2.2	$0.4	$0.9	$1.7

(For 1948 through 1951 conditional sales agreement capital amounts were not compiled by the ICC and are estimated as being 89 percent of the cost of equipment purchased through such agreements.)

(Source: ICC, *SRUS, TSUS,* Tables 138, 139, 146, 146A, 147A; by calculation.)

The net rather than gross flows of finance capital present a different picture because of the large amounts returned by the railroads to the capital markets by way of sinking fund purchases, bond redemptions, and payment of equipment debt installments. Throughout the 1947–1957 phase, annual bond plus note retirements exceeded new issues in all regions and years, except in the Pocahontas. Even equipment installments exceeded new equipment debt for two or three years in the mid-fifties, except in the West. For this phase as a whole the decline in outstanding bonds and notes (excluding debentures and income bonds, issued in exchange for preferred stock) ranged from 16 percent in the East to 11 percent in the West. In this case, 1948 is taken as the initial year to avoid the effect of the debt reduction in the last but one of the major reorganizations.

From 1947 through 1958 the net outside funds obtained by equipment debt were some $0.8 billion in the East, $0.7 billion in the West, $0.4 in the South, and $0.2 in the Pocahontas region, some $2 billion for the country as a whole.

1958–1962

The 1957/58 downturn in railroad traffic inaugurated a new phase in railroad finances. Eastern revenues declined by 13½ percent; Pocahontas, 18 percent; southern, 7 percent; and western, 3½ percent. Adjustment of expenditures to match loss of revenues had to be the major preoccupation of managements. Maintenance expenditures were sharply reduced. Investment outlays were even more drastically cut as it discussed elsewhere. The contractually obligated payments for sinking fund requirements and equipment obligation installments had to be continued.

Between 1955 and 1962 common stock dividends were cut by 58 percent in the East and 23 percent in the South, but increased 3 percent in the West and 20 percent in the Pocahontas region. Interest rates rose on the average for equipment trusts from 3.75 percent in 1958 to 4.13 percent in 1962. Despite these negative trends hourly wages continued to increase, from $2.26 average at year end, 1958, to $2.72 in 1962, up 20 percent.

The credit ratings of the largest eastern road, the Pennsylvania (P), the newly merged Erie-Lackawana (EL), and five smaller roads were all lowered one grade. The CO was demoted from Aa to A. On the other hand, bond ratings for the southern roads and all but five of the western remained unchanged. Of the five, three were raised one grade. Again, two traditionally weak ones were reduced, one grade. The minor revenue declines in the South and West were not sufficiently great to have the across-the-board impact on credit standings that the major drop in the East had.

New equipment issues were sharply curtailed, but significantly less in the West than in the other regions, as its needs for new and added equipment continued. In 1958 two mortgage issues totaling $38 million were sold largely for additions and betterments, one of $23 million to meet a maturity.

In response in part to the railroads' financial problems, provisions of the Transportation Act of 1958 offered government guarantees of up to $500 million for borrowing by roads otherwise unable to obtain necessary funds on reasonable terms. Not as many applications as were expected were forthcoming in the first years; only $53 million were approved by mid-1960. Even with extension of the aid two years, the final total came only to $241 million by 1963. Only a few relatively small requests were denied. Most of the guaranteed issues were related to rehabilitation as well as to capital improvements. Eighty-three percent of the aid was for eastern roads, reflecting the downturn's dominant impact in the East.[3]

During the latter part of this phase the only important bond and note issues sold publicly, $75 million worth, were for redemption and acquisition of other company stocks. Gross borrowing for this five-year phase amounted to a somewhat greater proportion of investment in facilities than in the previous phase. Except for the East, with the issuance of the guaranteed debt, equipment issues were almost the entire source of outside capital funds for new facilities. (See Table 35.)

TABLE 35

Estimated Debt Issued for New Facilities, 1958–1962

(Billions)

	East	Pocahontas	South	West
Bonds and Notes Issued	$0.1	neg.	$0.1	$ .04
Equipment Obligations	0.4	0.1	0.3	0.6
Total	0.5	0.1	0.4	0.7

In respect to net flows of outside capital for both the eastern and western roads, the retirement of both bond debt and equipment obligations exceeded new issues. For the East in particular, retirement of outstanding debt exceeded new issues by over half a billion dollars. This added to the nearly one billion for fixed facility additions and betterments meant that $2 billion had to be supplied internally. A significant amount of this was covered by cash from sales of assets and reduction in working capital. In the case of the West, there was $0.3 billion of debt retirement and $2 billion covered by internal sources and only minor reduction in working capital, again reflecting the relatively lighter impact of the downturn in the West. For the other two regions there was a net inflow of outside capital, minor for the southern roads, but for the Pocahontas, enough to cover almost a quarter of their gross investment.

During this phase, 1958 through 1962, leasing of equipment became a major factor in the East because of the deteriorating financial position of its roads. Estimating leased equipment investment at the average prices applying for all new units suggests that some half a billion dollars of external funds for equipment purchase were in effect made available to the eastern railroads in this way. This was somewhat more than was obtained through usual equipment debt financing. Other regions' leasing had not yet become important.

1963-1972

The analysis for this last period is difficult since data comparisons can be only approximate because of the security and accounting adjustments that accompanied the large-scale mergers. Because of the vastly different characteristics of the eastern systems and those that are basically Pocahontas (the NW merger brought some eastern ones into the latter regional category), they are considered separately so far as possible. For comparison, the figures of the New York, Chicago, and St. Louis (NYCStL), Wabash (W), and Pittsburgh and West Virginia (PMV), all now becoming part of the NW, are not included in the eastern region, and the earlier Pocahontas region figures are expanded to include them. There was no shift in roads in the southern and western regions.

The 1963 through 1972 period was characterized, except for the downturn year of 1967, by continuous increase in revenue ton-miles for the South and West, and in freight revenues for all regions. Freight revenue gains over the ten years were least for the contracted East, for the NYCStL, W, and PWV, 33 percent, and most for the South, 79 percent. The changes in net income before income taxes had a regionally different pattern than revenue. From 1963 through 1966 the trend in all regions was upward, dramatically so for the East, where there initially had been practically no net income. With the 1967 downturn there was only a mild decline for the southern and Pocahontas regions, but drastic deterioration for both the East and West. Thereafter the East continued down to a series of deep deficits. The western and the enlarged Pocahontas group, including the

NYCStL, W, and PWV, operating income before taxes recovered but neither quite reached the 1965/66 levels. The southern roads' however did, with 1972 40 percent above 1966.

From 1963 to 1968 interest rates rose gradually, annual averages for equipment trusts from 4.3 percent to 5.5 percent. Thereafter, in line with general trends, there was a sharp jump to 8.5 percent in 1970, and then a slight decline, to 7.2 percent in 1972. Average hourly pay had increased from $2.72 at the end of 1962 to $5.30 in December 1972, up 95 percent.

During the 1963–1972 phase the credit ratings of most of the eastern roads deteriorated seriously. All but the Maine Central dropped to one of the C ratings or from Caa to a still lower one. Of the Pocahontas roads, the NW went from Aaa to Aa while the CO remained A. There were no changes for the southern roads. Of the western roads, one, the Denver and Rio Grande (DRG), rose from A to Aa, and the CBQ upon merger with the BN, from Baa to A. The ATSF and Union Pacific were down from Aaa to Aa, CRI from Baa to Ba, and the Missouri Kansas and Texas from Ba to B. There were no changes in the ratings of the other western roads.

During this period the demands for outside capital to meet bond maturities were below those for the refinancing of the 1950s. Only a few publicly held issues came due between 1963 and 1965, in total $90 million. These were refinanced by four A rated new issues, three for southern roads, and one for a small eastern one. Interest rates ranged from 4½ percent to 4⅞ percent, roughly the same as those for new utility and industrial bonds. There followed an interlude with few maturities, such as there were being met out of internal funds. The next requirement for outside funds for maturities was in late 1969, met by a $21 million, nine-year, 7¾ percent first mortgage bond, this interest rate comparable to that for other industry at the time. This was followed by a $48 million Baltimore and Ohio (BO) maturity met in part by an A rated $27 million seven-year collateral issue carrying an 11 percent coupon, in line with generally increasing interest rates.

From December 1970 to April 1972 three issues, all rated A by *Moody's,* were sold to cover further maturities. A total of $155 million was involved with interest rates ranging from 7¾ percent for one with a six-and-a-half-year term to 8½ percent for a twenty-five-year one. The average interest rates for new issues for all types of corporations in the U.S. ranged from 8.0 percent in 1969 to 8.9 percent in 1970 to 7.8 percent and 7.5 percent in 1971 and 1972. Finally, in 1972 the BO sold $55 million, 6½ percent, twenty-five-year first mortgage bonds exchangeable into stock to meet further debt retirements.

In addition, during this phase there were two issues sold for general corporate purposes. One, in 1963, was in the South of $22 million SAL 7⅝ percent twenty-five-year mortgage bonds. Another, in 1972, was for the western, $65 million BN 5¼ percent twenty-year convertible debentures. The latter along with the just

Outstanding and Funded Debt and Equipment Obligations and Net Lease Rent Payments to Insurance Companies, etc.—Class I Railroads and Lessors to Them

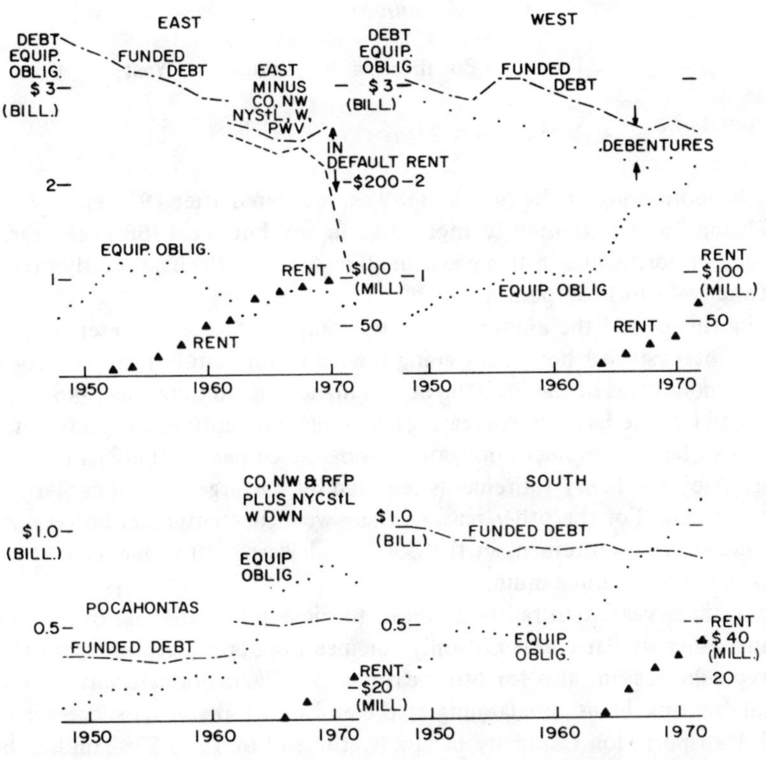

mentioned "exhangeable" bonds were the first recent sales to the public of this type of security for railroads. Both avoided the high interest rates of the 1970s by offering future claims upon future profits. Previously convertible issues had only been issued in conjunction with corporate reorganizations and those in the 1940s. There also were annual issues by the NW in exchange for the P holdings of NW stock, which had to be divested in connection with the NW merger.

During this phase as in the two earlier ones the main railroad source of outside funds for investment in facilities was the equipment trust and conditional sales agreement debt. In all regions the level of annual new issues increased rapidly after 1962 reaching a peak in 1966. Rising traffic and needs for improved equipment accounted for this. Thereafter in the East and Pocahontas regions there was a general decline to 1972. (See Table 36.) In the East there was an increasing use of lease-rental equipment, which accounted for some of this decline. Railroad

TABLE 36

Equipment Debt Issues, 1963–1972
(Billions)

	East	Pocahontas	South	West	U.S.
New Issues	$1.2	$1.2	$1.6	$3.0	$7.0

equipment-borrowing in the South and West recovered after 1966 and 1967 and in 1971 and 1972 amounted to more than in any but the 1966 peak year. The magnitude of borrowings in this phase in all regions but the East greatly exceeded that of the 1948 to 1957 period.

During this period the amount raised by equipment issues represents substantially the total railroad borrowing going toward investment in facilities. The percent this amount was of the investment was higher than during the 1948 to 1957 period in all but the East, where leasing again made the difference. As to net flow of capital so far as equipment obligations were concerned, in the East new issues were offset by the heavy retirements required by the large scale of earlier 1947–1958 borrowing. For the other reasons there were substantial net inflows. As to other funded debt, retirement in the South and West led to roughly 10 percent declines in the totals outstanding.

During these years two railroads began to make substantial use of short-term bank and other similar credit not only for meeting bond maturities and investment expenditures but also for other cash needs. The major case was the P with $37 million bank loans outstanding at the end of 1966 and its successor Penn Central Transportation Company having by the end of 1970 $382 million bank loans, $83 million commercial paper notes plus $50 million of Eurodollar credits. These were involved with merger related extra expenditures and dividends, which exceeded current income. The other system, the Union Pacific, at the end of 1970 had $150 million of bank credit outstanding, in this case it being associated with development of coal and oil resources.[4]

Of major importance during this period was outside financial institutions' own investment in equipment for rental to the railroads. This amounted to around 3 to $4 billion, estimated as previously noted. The eastern roads were involved with over half of this type of capital investment and the dollar amounts were in excess of what they obtained from their own issues of equipment debt. For the other regions, the proportion was only from a quarter to a fifth. Substantial additional investment was also made for cars leased to shippers. This latter period's experience demonstrated the railroads' and financial institutions' ability to adopt new ways of meeting investment needs under adverse conditions. The surprising thing was the ease with which a seriously ailing large system could get its credit extended.

PASSENGER AND ALLIED SERVICES LOSSES

The financial performance of railroad systems has been affected to widely different degrees by the extent and various characteristics of their passenger and allied services. Most of the systems in the densely populated East have been traditionally involved in higher proportions of passenger to freight services than in the rest of the country. In addition, most of those systems serving the large older metropolitan districts—New York, Philadelphia, Boston, and Chicago—have had extensive suburban operations saddling them with short-haul peaking commuter traffic, which involved unit costs higher than the more day-around long-haul intercity traffic.

In the postwar years these passenger operations have generally been operated at a loss, the extent of which has been difficult to assess because of the substantial proportions of incurred costs being in common with freight operations. As indicated in the section on passenger services, the attribution of costs between the two is bound to be based on some arbitrary basis and therefore subject to debate. For reasons given earlier, the ICC basis is used, though it may underestimate the real passenger responsibility.

The practically available means of estimating overall financial burdens is the subtraction of the passenger net railway operating income (nroi) from the freight nroi before income taxes. (These data have only been published for individual roads since 1953.) This does not take into account interest charges for capital investment in passenger facilities, but no such data have been collected and published.

The effects of the passenger burden are not only a matter of their incidence at any given point in time but also the extent to which they have been able to be controlled by management over the years. Since the recession year 1954 was the first year of availability of individual system data, the following year with more normal freight traffic is taken as the initial year for analysis. Nineteen sixty-six is the last year in which some of the most important systems were still separate. The two dates determine then the span of years for analysis of the degree of control of passenger burden over time.

In 1955 there were three systems with extraordinarily high ratios of passenger nroi deficits to freight positive nroi plus income tax returns, the BM, NYNH&H, and CNW. Two were in the East and one in the Chicago area, all three with heavy suburban services. The deficits in all three cases amounted to over 60 percent of the freight nroi. All three were systems whose financial futures were to be poor. At the other extreme, in the same year there were ten systems with the passenger deficits absorbing less than 20 percent of freight nroi plus income taxes. Two were medium-sized eastern systems, the DH and NYCStL; three were the Pocahontas roads; one was in the South, the S; and the remaining four were small or medium-sized systems in the West, the CGW, DRG, KCS, and StLSW. They were all to have a favorable future financial performance.

In the years after 1955 with the decline in passenger demand the degree to which passenger train-miles and passenger losses were reduced varied widely. Several medium and small western roads were the most aggressive, with two eliminating the service entirely, the CGW and StLSW, and two others, the Soo and the StLSF, cutting back by more than 70 percent. Region considered, the overall performance of all four was above average. On the other hand, two other smaller western roads were the slowest to cut back, the DRG and KCS system, with only 23 and 26 percent reductions. The performance of the former was excellent and the latter above average. The southern roads reduced passenger train-miles around 20 percent, with one exception, the SAL, only 9 percent. They too remained prosperous with the help of their strong freight traffic growth. The financial pressures to reduce were greatest in the East, but the metropolitan area roads had substantial suburban train-miles, which could only be cut back slightly or not at all. On the other hand, their heavy intercity train-miles provided the opportunity. The maximum was a 60 percent reduction for the NYC, and the least, 40 percent, for the NYNH&H. A combination of this last low rate of cutback and loss of freight traffic accounted for the latter's poor performance and early bankruptcy. The combined only mid-range of intercity cutbacks and the heavy commuter losses of the NYC and P certainly contributed greatly to their financial collapse as the Penn Central.

The traditional suburban commuter services of some of the eastern roads, particularly the EL, NYC, and P, proved to be a significant burden on the freight earnings and an important factor in their financial problems. On the other hand, some of the western roads could continue to carry passenger losses because they were minor compared to substantial freight nroi. This enabled some systems to continue satisfactory financial performances in spite of such losses.

MAINTENANCE AND REPAIRS

A distinct and important element in the financial performance of the railroads is the variability in expenditures for maintaining fixed facilities and equipment. The combined accounts for maintenance amounted to a third or somewhat less of operating revenues. Accruals for depreciation are a stable part of the maintenance expense. Since they accrue principally in respect to equipment they have been gradually increasing over the years as the railroad investment in equipment has increased. Retirements are another noncash component of maintenance, but are of a minor proportion and irregular. The remainder is the actual cash expenditure for labor and materials to repair the varied facilities used in railroad operations. For the most part, this has ranged from 22 percent to 28 percent of operating revenues.

Repair expenditures have shown considerable flexibility. This is possible because structures, track, and equipment normally have a reservoir of service life in their parts and a range in possible standards of quality. Thus repairs have the possibility at managements' discretion of being made in excess of normal requirements or short of that, this being referred to as "deferred." This last can be carried to a drastic extent in the short run and has in some cases been carried out over surprisingly long periods when considerable deterioration in condition is accepted. For equipment the possibilities are more limited than for structures since failure to maintain standards can result with the former in more immediate and critical failures than with the latter. For instance, failure to keep running gear of cars in good repair can lead to derailments, while postponing tie replacement, up to a point, does not cause service failures or can be compensated for by reducing speeds.

The long run trends of repair expenditures have been affected both by improvements in almost all types of railroad facilities and in techniques of repair. Heavier and welded rail have meant longer rail life; diesel locomotives have required less repair effort than steam. A wide range of improved track maintenance and shop tools and machines have lowered the repair labor required. These gains have opposed the constantly rising unit labor and material prices. Underlying these factors have been the changing levels of freight and the continuous decline of passenger train services with their effects on need for repairs and on the minimum standards for the condition of facilities.

There were substantial differences between railroads in the extent to which advantage was taken of the potential flexibility in repair expenditures. Differences in earning power and adequacy of cash flow made for significant variations. Several other variables have been significant. One is the past degree of maintenance, previously well- or overmaintained facilities providing more leeway. Management attitudes toward acceptable quality of track and equipment are a related factor. Management and director interest in maintaining dividends with declining revenue or just increasing dividends as a show of improved performance is another influence on repair expenditures.

The effect of all these factors in combination can be reviewed as they varied between regions and individual systems. The graphs on page 272 portray the regional differences. The comparisons are between average biennium (rather than one-year to avoid chance irregularities) expenditures at five points five years apart in the twenty-five years covered by this study beginning after the immediate postwar levels of repair. The first two points represent bienniums with prosperous levels of revenue; the next, 1961/62, one with the lowest revenues; and the last two encompass the subsequent revival of revenues.

For the three major regions, between the first two points in time there was little change in revenue level. The eastern region was unique with a sharp decline in repairs resulting largely from greater pressure from relatively heavy financial obligations (basic labor and material prices were the same for all regions) and increased share of revenues going for transport expenses than in the South and West. In the next five years to the low-revenue biennium, 1961/62, the East's decline was by far the greatest. Repairs were decreased sharply all around. Over the two five-year periods, the eastern repair reduction was substantially greater than the other

Biennium Annual Average Operating Revenue and Way and Structure and Equipment Repair Expenditure—By Regions
(Billions)

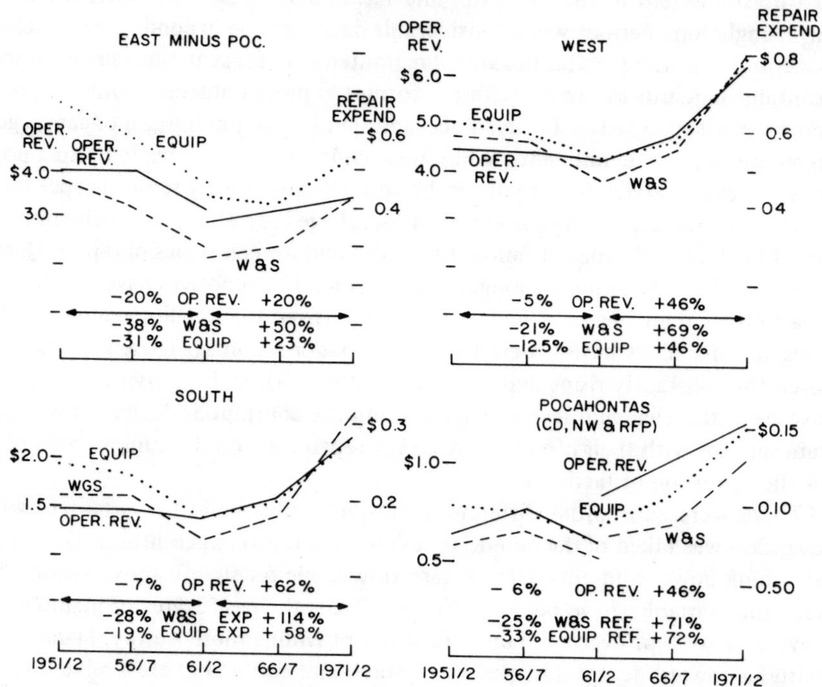

(Source: ICC, *Statistics of Rys. in U.S., 1951, 1952*; *Transport Statistics in the U.S.*)

(1961/62 to 1971/72 comparative data based on Pocahontas region roads to include NYCStL, W, and PWV figures for 1961/62 and CO, NW, and RFP together constituting a Pocahontas group for 1966/67 and 1971/72.)

regions. Revenue changes were a major factor in degree of repairs and, for the most part, both ups and downs of repair expenditures were at rates in excess of those of revenues. Repairs in a sense can be said to be more "variable" than revenues.

Coming out of the low point, for the third five-year period to 1966/67, repair expenditures in the South, West, and Pocahontas regions were increased at significantly greater rates than in the East. The latter's revenues failed to increase relatively as much as for the other regions. Yet in the face of this, eastern dividend payments were increased fourfold compared to only +26 percent for the South and +34 percent for the West.

From 1966/67 to 1971/72 revenues jumped sharply in all regions but the East. All faced the need to increase the extent of repairs. All were faced with the same accelerating increases in unit material and labor costs. The eastern roads were burdened with serious past neglect of repairs and increased their expenditure in relation to revenue to a much greater extent than roads in the other regions. In part, this was made possible by the bankruptcy of a major number of roads in the East, which spared them the payment of some $80 million annually in bond interest and eliminated that for dividends.

The long-run regional trends in repair expenditures also reflect the long-run changes in traffic volumes. This basic factor can be measured roughly by combined passenger and freight gross-ton-mile (gtm) changes. From 1951/52 to 1971/72 the eastern roads* had a 23 percent decline in gtm, and the Pocahontas,† some 10 percent. On the other hand, for the southern system combined gtm's increased 25 percent, and the western, 10 percent.

The difference between individual system trends of repairs can be most directly portrayed, free of unit expense inflation, in terms of physical units replaced annually. Track miles of new rail led in replacement of old is the most usable for this purpose of the few items for which data are available. New rail is generally laid in the most heavily traveled and important lines. The typical life of rail is first in such use, then transferred to secondary lines, and finally to tertiary or branch lines and yards, all adding up to a life on the order of fifty years. During recent years on a number of railroads with declining passenger service many miles of second and other multiple tracks have been abandoned so that large amounts of second-hand rail have been made available and reduced the need for new rail. In addition, heavier and otherwise improved rail has over the years decreased the need for replacement. Further, the extent of replacement with new rail has been related to the general decrease in passenger service and the variation in trends of freight traffic, together measured by the changes in combined gross ton-miles. The graphs on page 466 show for a sample of systems of different types the contrasting trends in new rail laid.

In the West three large prosperous roads with generally increasing freight traffic made sharp reductions in new rail laid in the poor years 1960/62 but by 1970/72 were laying new rail to the extent of 70 percent to 94 percent of the average laid in the good years of the 1950s. A smaller western system, the DRG, not shown, made a reduction of a third in the poor years and by 1970/72 was equaling its good 1950s record. On the other hand, two weaker large western systems cut their annual new rail by 80 percent plus in the 1960/62 period, but by the 1970/72 were still more than 70 percent below the 1950s level. One of these systems had a 20 percent gain in gross ton-miles, the other a nearly 10 percent decline. A smaller weak road, the MKT, not shown on the graph, presented the extreme case of near zero replacement in the latter years except when government guaranteed loans were available.

The eastern roads followed a somewhat different course, cutting back sharply even in the high-revenue years 1955 to 1957. By the early and mid-1960s the miles

*To make the regional comparison possible the 1951/52 gtm for the East excludes the roads which were later part of the merged NW.
†In 1951/52 includes the roads later part of the merged NW system and in 1971/72 comprises the CO, NW, and RFP.

Triennium Average Annual System New Rail Track-Miles Laid in Replacement; Combined Passenger plus Freight Annual GTM, Initial and Final Periods

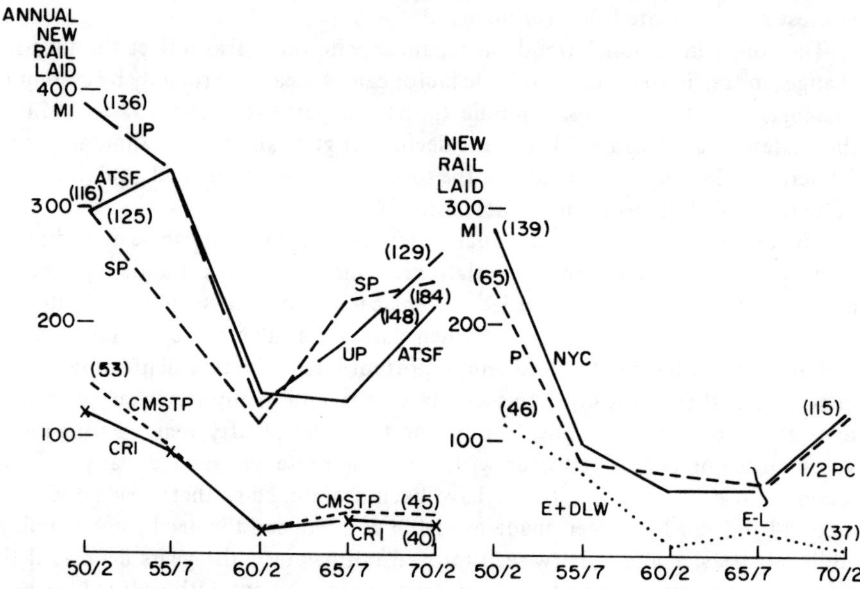

(Source: *Moody's Transportation Manual*; ICC, Stat. Rys. U.S. and *Transp. Stat. U.S.*; by calculation.)

laid by the combined NYC and P dropped to only 21 percent of that laid in the 1950 to 1952 period. By the 1970 to 1972 period the bankrupt successor PC, without bond interest charges and no dividends laid 48 percent of the earlier amount, with a gtm decline of 24 percent. The Erie-DLW was representative of some of the smaller hard-pressed eastern systems that by the 1960s essentially discontinued laying new rail. The CNJ, BM, and LV, not shown, were other examples of this.

Over the twenty-five years reviewed in this study expenditures for repairs have demonstrated a considerable range of controllability. This was on top of generally increasing productivity in repair efforts. Considering the three major regions, coming out of the wartime operation, regional averages of repairs to revenue ranged from 29 percent to 30 percent. By 1956/57 the eastern roads had reduced this share by 4 percent points, with the emphasis on cutting back on way and structures. The western and southern region reductions were only 2 percent points. By the low point in revenues, 1961/62, the roads in the East and South were spending 23½ percent, and in the West, 24 percent. From that point to the mid-sixties their shares declined still further to 22 percent. Over the same period there was little change in the other two regions. The continuing adverse financial position of most eastern roads along with the maintenance of dividend payments by the two largest roads resulted in maximum pressure to put off repairs. Deferred maintenance built up to the extent that it represented severe running down of the capital assets, both road and equipment. On the other hand, with greater increases in traffic and more favorable general financial performance the southern roads avoided such deterioration. In the West, with generally favorable conditions, the strong roads maintained workable levels of maintenance, but the weaker ones were not able to restore their repair levels and like the eastern ones were running down their properties.

CASH AND WORKING CAPITAL

Another aspect of the financial history of the railroad industry has involved up and downs of cash and working capital. Regional differences were significant and to a great extent reflected the regional variations in levels of net income. For all regions cash items (cash plus "temporary cash investment" plus in one instance "loans and bills receivable") fell sharply relative to cash flow. In absolute terms, the cash items fell in all but the Pocahontas region. Table 37 shows the percent decline was greater for the eastern roads than the others from the early 1950s to 1960s, and for the eastern and western from the early 1960s to 1971/72.

The eastern roads' greater declines resulted basically from their difficulties beginning with the recession of 1957-1958 in making both ends meet. The Pocahontas roads' initial gain and later stability reflected their high proportion of generally renumerative coal traffic.

Table 38 shows working capital, as measured by the net of current assets and liabilities, fell in all regions more drastically than the cash items. Again the eastern roads had the most serious decline, to near zero in the early 1960s and a negative value in 1969.

TABLE 37

Magnitude of Year-End Cash plus Temporary Cash Investments
(Millions)

	East*	Pocahontas†	South	West
Early 1950s	$500±	$100±	$300±	$950±
Early 1960s	300±	200±	250±	900±
1971/72	140±	170±	200±	650±

*Minus roads merging with NW.
†Plus roads merging with NW.

TABLE 38

Magnitude of Year-End Working Capital

(Millions)

	East*	Pocahontas†	South	West
Early 1950s	$350±	$110±	$250±	$800±
Early 1960s	65±	200	200	600
1971/72	40±	100±	160±	300±

*Minus roads merging with NW.
†Plus roads merging with NW.

The western roads came next in rate of decline. The Pocahontas roads at the other extreme gained to the early 1960s and overall held their own. In all regions, increases in "accrued accounts payable" exceeded the declines in working capital. "Audited accounts and wages payable" in the three major regions declined from the early 1950s to 1971/72 and for the Pocahontas remained roughly the same. A major offsetting item, except for the Pocahontas region, was the decrease in "accrued taxes payable" as a result of declining income taxes.

These declines in liquidity were a factor in the downgrading of bond ratings. The rating agencies feared that without a sufficient cushion of cash and working capital short-run downward fluctuations of revenue or loss of control of expenses could too readily push management beyond the point of being able to meet interest and other contractual requirements.

DIVIDENDS

An end result of financial performance are common stock dividends, the residual after management's balancing revenues and expenses, provisions for investment in road and equipment, passenger deficits, level of repairs, and working capital needs. Dividends are also the ultimate measure of difference in the performance of individual systems.

Immediately before the war, in spite of improving economic conditions in the country, the toll taken by the depression was still apparent in the dividend payments for systems in all regions but the Pocahontas. For the larger systems common dividends were paid out by only one in the East, the Pennsylvania (P), responding to a tradition of never missing an annual declaration; by all three Pocahontas major coal roads; by two in the South, the Louisville and Nashville (LN) and the Atlantic Coast Line (ACL); and four of the western six, which were not involved in reorganization, the Santa Fe (ATSF), Great Northern (GN), Burlington (CBQ), and Union Pacific (UP).

Following the successful wartime performance, the reorganizations, and immediate postwar adjustments of financial structures the dividend picture was radically altered. In the East the NYC, E, and Delaware Lackawana and Western (DLW) resumed dividends. Due to long-accumulated arrears on its preferred the successful New York, Chicago, and St. Louis did not immediately. On the other hand, the New England and a number of other eastern roads failed to do so basically because of adverse trends in their traffic make-up. In the South all but the Central of Georgia (CG) were paying dividends as were all but three in the West. Two of these were the small Chicago Great Western and the traditionally troubled Missouri, Kansas, and Texas; the other was the Missouri Pacific, which was still to be reorganized.

Thereafter in the East a relatively stable level of traffic, 1954 excepted, was followed by a decline bargaining in 1957/58 that reached lows in 1961/62. There was a sharp differentiation between the performance of systems through those years. Two major systems, the NYCStL and Wabash (W) maintained a steady level of dividends until their takeover in 1964. The BO started payments in 1952, maintained them at top level through 1957, and in declining amounts until 1962, when exchange into CO shares was offered. The two largest systems, the NYC and P, had to reduce their payments in 1954 and, thereafter rose to a peak in 1957. They then dropped them to minimal amounts, nothing for the NYC for 1961 and 1962. The remaining New York-Chicago system, the E, and its merger partner the DLW paid dividends through 1957 but none thereafter. On the other hand, three among the smaller eastern systems initiated payments in the 1950s and continued them through the 1960s. The three were without significant passenger burdens, finally eliminating their passenger trains, and without management problems.

With the rise in freight traffic after 1962 the two largest eastern systems started because of merger considerations what seemed to partake of a competitive battle to keep up with each other's dividend increases, despite the development of the serious financial problems noted. They ended up finding themselves as a merged system falling into bankruptcy in 1970. The varied problems overtaking the eastern systems led almost all of them to stop dividend payments.

The Pocahontas roads with their heavy coal traffic were able to maintain dividends throughout the whole period covered. The CO reached a peak in 1957, a level continued through 1970, when a 12½ percent cutback followed the decline in traffic. The NW dividend rate was increased gradually to a peak coincidental with its second merger in 1964. Thereafter the rate was reduced in stages, down by a total of 29 percent by 1972.

The dividend performance of the southern roads reflects the general growth of the region particularly in its eastern sections. The Southern, ACL, and SAL increased payouts sharply through 1957. With minor setback in freight revenue, the latter two cut back their dividends while the S maintained its, despite a slightly greater loss than the other two. The other two larger systems also increased their

Common Stock Cash Dividend Payments to System Affiliates

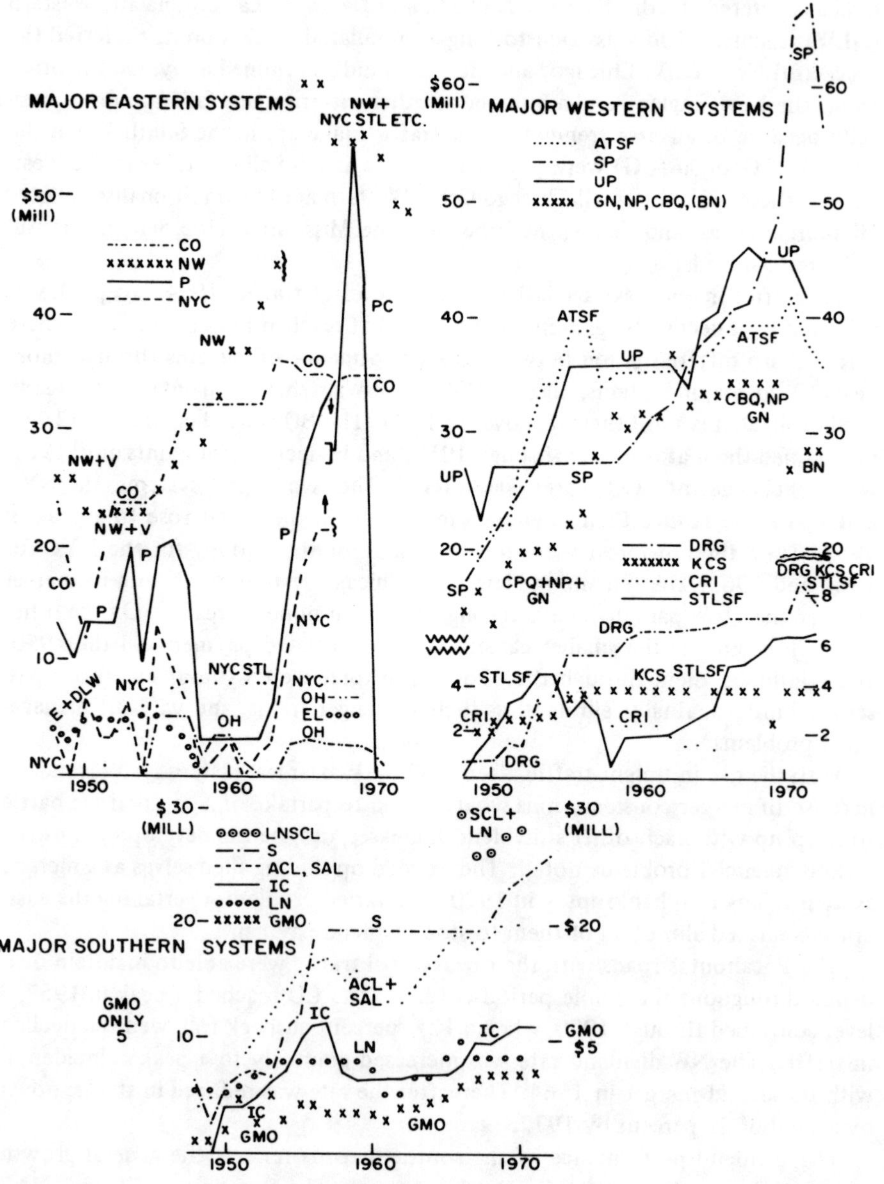

Source: Moody's *Transportation Manual* (by calculation).

dividends to a peak in the mid-fifties, cut back during the subsequent decline, and increased them again, but generally not significantly above the top levels attained earlier. The smaller GMO system had a somewhat erratic dividend course during the 1950s, a slight decline to 1961, and then for three years prior to merger with the IC to a level 50 percent above the high of the fifties. The prosperous environment of the South, though not uniformly distributed, provided successful financial performance, which was reflected in substantial dividend increases for a majority of the systems.

In the West, with a growing level of activity except in the prairie states, dividends increased steadily for the larger carriers up to 1970 when the greatly increased labor costs started to take their toll as elsewhere, and cutbacks were initiated. However, three of the smaller carriers—the DRG, KCS, and StLSF—were able to pay out as much in 1971 and 1972 as they had in any other years. The traditionally weak roads, however, stopped their payments in the mid-1960s.

These system differences in performance over the whole period under review are highlighted by contrasting rates of increase or lack thereof in public common dividend public payments. Reflecting the lack of major increase in economic activity for their region from the early years 1948–1950 to 1970–1972, there was no long-term growth for any eastern system. There were interim peak payments in 1957 and again between 1966 and 1968, but by 1971/72 no independent system made public dividend payments.

In the Pocahontas region the CO doubled its payments from 1948–1950 to 1970 but fell back to one and a half times by 1971/72. Its affiliation with the BO certainly was a restraint on availability of cash for dividends. In the case of the NW, including the payments made by its acquired lines in the years prior to merger, growth was 2-fold by 1969 but fell back to 1.8-fold for 1971/72. For the NW, despite its merger with what had been the most prosperous eastern roads, the increase in dividends was little more than that of the CO.

The southern roads, with high economic activity growth, had the maximum growth of dividend payments in the range of from 1½ fold for the LN alone to almost 3 fold for the sum of the ACL, SAL, and LN from 1948–1950 to the unified group in 1972 and for the IC from 1950; to 5 for the S and 6 for the GMO.

In the West the four large systems, ATSF, BN, SP, and UP, increased their payouts over the same years from 1½-fold for the BN to 3-fold for the SP. The increases for three smaller systems ranged from 2½-fold for the KCS system to 11-fold for the DRG. It may be noted as an aside that the growth for the Canadian Pacific controlled Soo was 5½-fold. On the other hand, five systems ended up with no payout, four having paid some dividends and one, the MKT, none. No ratio can be computed for the MP because it was still in bankruptcy in 1948–1950. Its first dividend was in 1956 and the 1970–1972 annual payments were roughly double those of the latter 1950s' annual rate.

From a longer run view it may be noted that southern roads common dividend payments rose to one to two and a half times what they had been in 1928/29. For the West the combined constituents of the BN paid out one-third again as much as its predecesors had earlier, while the three large nonmerging systems paid out from two to three times as much in 1970–1972 as they had in 1928/29. It should be noted that they were in regions with greater economic growth than the BN. The small successful western road had been without payments in one or both of the years 1928 and 1929.[5]

* * *

The U.S. railroads, as a result of the reorganizations during the 1940s, retirement and refunding of bonds at low interest rates, and general rate increases, entered the postwar years with greatly reduced interest accruals. For the western and southern roads the ratios of interest to operating revenue were only a quarter of what they had been, and for the eastern, 40 percent. From this position, the main achievement of the first postwar decade to the 1958 downturn was the raising of capital funds sufficient to provide investment of some $13 billion in new facilities, nearly completing the replacement of steam locomotives by diesel-electrics, modernizing the passenger car stock, and replacing almost one-half of the freight car fleet. To renew in such a short time a large part of the capital stock of a capital-intensive industry was a feat not matched by other such industries in the country.

The next phase, the five years 1958 to 1962, was one of sharply reduced freight traffic in the eastern and Pocahontas regions, revenue down 20 percent and 25 percent respectively, but for the South and West off only 8 percent and 5 percent. Investment in additions and betterments were sharply reduced, and the increase in equipment obligations outstanding leveled off for all regions except the East. There increased dependence on noncarrier sources of financing for equipment by means of leasing from insurance and other financial institutions resulted in declining balances of railroad obligations but continuous increase of effective interest and related rental costs.

During this depressed phase dividends were maintained in the West and the Pocahontas region, lowered in the South, except for the top performing S and GMO, and sharply reduced or eliminated for the major roads in the East—the P, NYC, BO, and EL. The pressure to cut costs led to deferred way and structure maintenance generally, least, however, for the West. For the East this had been preceded by significant reduction in previous years. Cumulatively the extent led to serious deterioration of facilities.

The final decade through 1972 saw a major revival with the upturn in freight traffic after 1962. Beginning in 1958 there had been experimentation with increased capacity and new types of freight car designs, which became generally accepted by 1962. They were of sufficient economic value to prompt their purchase to replace the older equipment. In addition, accelerated depreciation and investment incentives with new railroad income tax provisions gave added stimulus for investment in equipment generally.

This led to expanded use of lease-rental financing in this final phase bringing in as much as $1 billion in the peak year from outside private financial capital. For freight cars, the principal item, by the end of 1972 there were $5 billion gross investment by this means in so-called "private-line" freight cars leased to the railroads. At the same time the railroads' investment though sale of their own debt amounted to $11½ billion.

The upturn in freight traffic together with the better control of passenger service in line with the declining demand combined to improve nroi and net income. For the eastern systems the improvement seemed spectacular because several systems had been running deficits.

With a temporary sag in traffic and freight revenues in 1967 and an acceleration in wage rate increases there was, however, a critical reversal in net incomes. It was worst for the eastern lines with nroi down 73 percent; least for the southern, down only 15 percent. There were major differences between regions overall from 1966 through the 1967 sag to 1972. In the East the change was from a $216 nroi to a $140 deficit. The Pocahontas and western region roads' nroi's remained practically the same. Only the South showed a gain, 37 percent. The catastrophic results in the East was to a large extent the result of the PC merger, which covered more than half the region's traffic and operations and adversely affected several of the region's smaller roads. From 1967 to 1972 six Class I eastern systems went bankrupt. In this last phase, during the last two years to 1972, in the South dividend payments to the public were maintained. Following substantial dividend increases several years after 1966, the four largest western systems were forced to cut theirs in 1971 and 1972.

These last years in the quarter century of the railroads' performance saw their financial crisis in the East, which was to lead to relief from the two problems that had gotten out of hand. One was the burden of the passenger and train services, which was transferred to the federal sphere by means of Amtrak. The other was the large segment of eastern systems gone bankrupt and then removed from the private realm for resuscitation by the U.S. Railroad Administration and Conrail.

14

Epilogue

The quarter of a century of postwar railroad performance reflects above all else the influence of the major advances and their diffusion in other-than-rail transport technologies.

The already developed innovation of the internal combustion engine highway vehicles was further refined to give greater reliability, comfort, speed, and capacity. Equally important were the improvements in highway characteristics culminating in thruways permitting continuous high speeds and uninterrupted intercity passage. The attractiveness of the improved highway transport was overwhelming and led to vast investment in vehicles by individuals and business, and in intercity highways funded primarily by user taxes and fees.

The qualities of passenger, express, and mail highway transport compared to rail led to displacement of most of the latter's short- and medium-haul traffic. Advances in rail technology by way of diesel motive power, air conditioning, and streamlining could not match those of highway transport. Further, the inability to find rail innovations that could provide major capital and labor productivity gains precluded economies enabling price reduction, which might significantly counter the highway service advantages.

In turn, advances in air transport technology brought about increases in air transport speed, comfort, and safety. This attracted large capital investment in planes and carrier terminal facilities by private business and individuals. Parallel expenditures were demanded of governments for airport facilities and were paid for by a combination of charges for their use and local government general and government agency revenues. The airways and control of their use was the province of the federal government with expenditures paid for entirely out of general government funds until 1971. The qualities provided by the rapidly expanding air transport displaced much of the middle and most all of long distance intercity rail passenger, express, and mail traffic.

The advances in highway transport also had great impact on freight transport. The greatest advantages were its ubiquitous door-to-door handling of freight using the country's 3½ million-mile network of streets and roads, reinforced in later years by the high-speed unobstructed thruway system. In addition, the detailed control by a driver at all times of the individual vehicle in both line-haul and terminal handling by a responsible individual provided a highly attractive quality of service. In the early part of the postwar years this led to for-hire carriers building up a less-than-truckload service, which in the end displaced the rail less-than-carload and small package traffic. Further advances leading to increased vehicle capacities and the thruway network enabled truck transport to invade the province of rail carload traffic.

The third area of technical advance was in pipeline transport. A breakthrough had come during the war allowing larger diameter pipes and lowered both fluid and gas costs. Capacity increased rapidly thereafter. This struck at the most profitable area of rail transport, that of carrying basic energy in the form of coal. There was a tremendous expansion of oil, gas, and refined petroleum product to transport. A major result was to displace a large volume of rail coal traffic. The pipeline form of transport was totally and privately funded and operated, and its intercity unit costs were generally below rail.

The railroads' response to these changes involved a major reversal in their policies. The wartime and immediate postwar experience had suggested there was still a substantial demand for intercity coach and sleeping car services, despite a long prewar downward trend. As the war ended, an investment decision was made to spend over a billion dollars to bring the passenger car fleet up to the state-of-the-art standards and to give priority over freight in replacing steam with diesel motive power. But after the Korean War it became apparent that this would be of no avail. Thus, after a relatively slow reduction in passenger services with pretty much all basic major intercity services maintained through the early 1960s, there was a sharp curtailment despite regulatory constraints. By 1971, noncommuter passenger-miles had become only one-eleventh of their 1947 level. The federal government in effect was brought in to bail out the private railroads from the burden of the small amount of remaining intercity passenger services. Beginning somewhat earlier, the state and local governments took on part of the commuter expenses. But it remained, however, that a number of the railroads still bore a not insignificant burden of costs associated with the passenger services operated or subsidized by others.

The developments in respect to less-than-carload freight services followed a somewhat similar scenario. The demand for these services had declined rapidly before the war and, after a build-up during it, started downward again. The railroads initially sought to oppose the losses to the trucks with further provision of pick-up and delivery service and special trains for lcl merchandise traffic along dense traffic routes. This, however, added costs to those already in excess of revenues. Economizing steps by way of closing smaller stations to such traffic, pooling of competitive line-haul handling, more efficient terminal handling, and incentive rates to increase shipment weights were insufficient to turn around mounting deficits.

Basically, lcl traffic per-car loadings, around 5 tons in 1957 for instance, were so low as to eliminate possible use of the railroads' potential in carrying such freight with effective use of their resources. Again, despite the formalities of regulatory constraints, most railroads were well out of the lcl business by the early 1960s.

In respect to this withdrawal of resources from two services that could not be made to meet marginal costs, automobiles and trucks may be credited with not only having been the cause of it but also having fortunately bailed out the railroads by taking over the two types of traffic. Without that the railroads with the rapidly increasing wage rates applied to their two most labor-intensive services would have incurred deficits surely fatal to their continuance as private enterprise.

Following external technological change labor costs, wages and benefits, taking some half of railroad revenue, were the next most significant element in railroad performance. Railroad unions, with dominant control in contract bargaining because of their political strength and their critical strike threat of stopping services essential to the country, pressed for and obtained increases that were among the highest for any industry. The increases, for instance, were neck and neck with the automobile industry, which was a relatively young and growing industry with both possibility of all-around increased productivity and seemingly insatiable demand to absorb the increasing costs. This was not the situation for the mature railroad industry.

Further, the union contract working-condition rules were allowed little modification in response to the changing technology of railroading. For instance, the requirement of a fireman on a locomotive in freight train service was based on the need for them with steam motive power and was not lifted from manning requirements for diesels until some twenty years after diesels had first become widely used. Another instance was the continuance of 100 miles as the standard of a basic day's pay in freight service, though the 100 miles was established in the 1880s with old unrefined steam power and without modern signaling and communication facilities. Thus, despite the fact that 200 miles could in recent years easily be covered by through freights in well under eight hours, the crews would be paid two days' basic pay for such a run, or if confined to the original 100 miles, make the run in just a few hours but get a full day's pay. This, with retention in many cases of the influence of old steam days' spacing of points for engine crew changes, results in eighteen crews for a Chicago to Los Angeles run of some sixty hours.

The final straw was the 46 percent wage rate increase demanded and finally obtained effective 1970 through mid-1973, which was reflected in rates increased for all commodities and in all regions. Railroads' continuously increasing unit labor costs could only lead to decreasing margins of revenue over expenses. Despite the withdrawal from the two branches of service with great deficits and increased carload freight service productivity, the pressure on the carload freight revenues was great enough to lead in some regions to maintenance deferral to the point of erosion of roadway and equipment conditions below acceptable operating standards. In some cases, it also led to reduced or even elimination of returns on capital investment.

The railroads have seen their technological advances emphasize longer, heavier, and faster trains with the more reliable operation of the stronger locomotives, cars with roller bearings, etc. No industry has completely turned over its inventory of the main elements of production in as few years as the railroads have with the substitution of diesel for steam motive power. Few innovations in any industry have provided as great gains for both labor- and capital productivity.

Of equal impact on production were the somewhat later technological advances in the direction of increased car capacity and better protection of their contents. This again required large amounts of capital. Innovations by way of financing by lease rentals and of shipper investment in cars were brought into use to meet the increasing needs. Less spectacular were the widespread development and investment in improved maintenance machines, communication facilities, train control systems, etc.

The improvements in service and productivity in the course of all this have largely been in respect to line-haul, heavier trains and shortened scheduled elapsed times. The terminal handling time for shipments was in general not improved and still had a vexing degree of variability (unit trains were the exception). The average utilization of freight cars was likewise not improved. This has involved high proportions of empty movement, irregularity of demand, and unbalanced flows of commerce, all making for difficulty in matching "made-empties" with shipper requests for cars for loading. These were factors in addition to basic difficulties in terminal switching of both loaded and empty cars.

Financially, the railroads started out the postwar years by completing the joint efforts of managements, financial institutions, the courts, and the ICC to improve the financial security structures and reduce the fixed charges of the numerous systems that had been in bankruptcy. There was also a widespread exchange or refunding of high interest rate bonds to take advantage of the low interest rates into the 1950s. Interest as a share of revenue was for the country as a whole cut to 4 percent. On the other hand, throughout the years equipment debt obligations were issued in large quantities. This was to provide essentially the only source of outside funds for investment in facilities, except for lease-rental arrangements, which became significant in the later years. With these various means of raising funds the effective interest payments became in more recent years a somewhat higher share of revenue. Considering the low average rate of return on overall investment, the relative ease of attracting capital by these means was astonishing. The marginal expected returns from investment in improved equipment far exceeded the average return on total investment.

The financial problems of what had long been the weaker systems largely remained. Mergers did not solve them, for instance, in the case of the Erie-DLW and the New York Central-Pennsylvania-NYNH&H. For nonmerging systems, like the CMStP, EL, and DH, their problems were exacerbated. Mergers produced little of the gains heralded in merger advocacy and some serious adverse results. Service improvements were limited and there often had been serious deterioration immediately following some mergers, particularly the NYC-P. In southern New England the damage was permanent. Mergers reduced interrailroad competition in large areas of the country, the NYC-P in the North, the ACL-SAL in the South, the IC-GMO in the middle of the country, and the GN-NP-CGQ in the plains states and the Northwest.

All told, the postwar twenty-five years saw sharp regional differences in railway performance. In the East systems faced a combination of slow economic growth, heavy burden of passenger service, greater than other region managerial and organizational problems, limits on ability to control labor productivity, merger failures, and financial problems that forced deferral of maintenance to the point of serious erosion in condition of facilities.

In the Pocahontas region, South, and West the railroad systems were favored with varying degrees of significant regional economic growth, less than eastern passenger burdens, mostly normal and some top managements, ability to improve labor productivity, and sufficient leeway to maintain their properties reasonably well. There were in the West exceptions by way of the few traditionally marginal systems that were not able to keep up.

Eastern and southern systems were subject to the same levels of truck competition with quite similar length hauls for commodities subject to that intermodal competition. Western systems with longer hauls faced less truck competition, except that their relatively greater share of agriculture exempt commodities subjected them to a particularly strong segment of truck competition. The degrees of water competition varied regionally and had impact on a different array of commodities and local route patterns than did trucks so as to make difficult any regional relative assessment.

With the western weak system exceptions, all but the eastern systems performed as viable private enterprises. Returns on investment were not equal to those of rapidly growing firms with products in great demand but never the less were able to attract capital at a degree that enabled them to modernize their inventory of equipment at a surprising rate for such a capital-intensive industry.

Notes

2. The Organization of the Railroad Industry

1. All data, except as otherwise noted are from ICC, *Statistics of Railways in the U.S.* (SRUS); ICC, *Transport Statistics in the U.S. (TSUS)*; appropriate years.

2. Class I railroads and terminal companies 1945-1955 were those with annual operating revenues of over $1 million; 1956-1963, over $3 million; 1965-, over $5 million.

The Major Class I Line-Haul Companies and the Abbreviations Used for Them

A. Independent at Some Stage from 1947-1972:

New England:
Bangor and Aroostook (BA)
Boston and Maine (BM)
Maine Central (MC)
New York, New Haven, and
    Hartford (NYNH&H)

Atlantic Coast-Chicago, St. Louis:
Alton (A)
Baltimore and Ohio (BO)
Chicago and Eastern Illinois (CEI)
Chicago, Indianapolis, and Louisville (CIL),
    Monon (M)
Delaware and Hudson (DH)
Delaware Lackawana and Western (DLW)
Erie (E)
Lehigh and New England (LNE)
Lehigh Valley (LV)*
New York, Chicago, and St. Louis
    (NYCStL)
New York Central (NYC)
New York, Ontario, and Western (NYOW)
Pennsylvania (P)
Pittsburgh and West Virginia (PWV)
Wabash (W)*
Western Maryland (WM)*

Pocahontas:
Chesapeake and Ohio (CO)
Norfolk and Western (NW)
Virginian (V)

Southern:
Atlantic Coast Line (ACL)
Central of Georgia (CG)
Florida East Coast (FEC)
Gulf Mobile and Ohio (GMO)
Illinois Central (IC)
Norfolk and Southern (NS)
Seaboard Airline (SAL)
Southern (S)

Western:
Atchison, Topeka, and Santa Fe
    (ATSF)
Chicago and Great Western (CGW)
Chicago, Milwaukee, St. Paul, and
    Pacific (CMStPP)
Chicago and Northwestern (CNW)
Chicago, Rock Island, and Pacific
    (CRI)
Denver and Rio Grande Western (DRG)
Great Northern (GN)
Kansas City Southern (KCS)
Kansas, Oklahoma, and Gulf (KOG)
Minneapolis and St. Louis (MStL)
Missouri, Kansas, and Texas (MKT)
Missouri Pacific (MP)
Spokane International (SI)
Southern Pacific (SP)
Toledo, Peoria, and Western (TPW)
Union Pacific (UP)
Western Pacific (WP)

*Controlling stock in hands of trustees.

B. Controlled by industry:

    Bessemer and Lake Erie (BLE), U.S. Steel
    Duluth, Mesabi, and Iron Range (DMI), U.S. Steel
    Lake Superior and Ishpening (LSI), Cleveland Cliffs Iron
    Piedmont and Northern (PN), Duke Power

C. Controlled by Canadian railroads:

Soo
Grand Trunk Western (GTW)
Duluth, Winnepeg, and Pacific (DWP)

3. *The Great Railway Crisis—An Administrative History of the United States Railway Association,* Prepared by John C. Harr, Nat. Acad. of Pub. Administration (1978), pp. 738-41.
4. *The Value Line, Investment Survey,* vol. XXXI, April 30, 1976, p. 649.
5. 388 ICC 513 (1969).
6. 166 US 290 (1897); 171 US 505 (1898).
7. 77 ICC 252 (1923).
8. *RA,* v. 98, 1/26/1935, p. 113.

3. Environment Surrounding the Railroads

1. Except as otherwise noted, figures in this section come from: U.S. Dept. of Commerce, *Sur. of Curr. Bus.,* v. 54, #4, April, 1974, pp. 34-45 (by calculation).
2. *OBERS, Projections, Regional Economic Activity in the U.S., Vol. 1, Concepts, Methodology—,* U.S. Water Resources Council, Washington, D.C., (1974), pp. 4, 11-35.
3. The data for this section, except as otherwise noted, are from DOT, FHA, *Highway Statistics, Summary to 1965,* annually 1965-1972. ICC, *TSUS,* 1972, Part 7, Tables 2, 37, ICC, *Statistics of Class I Motor Carriers, 1946, 1947,* Tables 9, 20, 31, 42, 46, Nat. Assoc. Motor Bus Owners, *Bus Facts,* appropriate years.
4. House Doc. #124, 89th Cong., 1 Ses., 1965, *Supplementary Report of the Highway Cost Allocation Study.*
5. ICC, *SRUS,* Tables 175, 1946-1953; *TSUS,* Part 6, 1954-1972; Fed. Power Commission, *Natural Gas Investigation,* N.L. Smith and H. Wimberly (1948), p. 239; ——, *Annual Report,* 1972; ——, *Natural Gas Survey,* (1973), v. III, pp. 102, 126, 133.
6. Except as otherwise noted, the sources of data for this section are: Dept. of Army, Corps of Engineers, *Annual Report of the Chief of Engineers,* 1946, Part 1, vol. 1, pp. 1, 19; ——, *Civil Works Activities,* 1965, vol. 1, p. 4; Dept. of Comm., Bur. of Census, *Census of Governments,* vol. 4, #5, *Compendium of Government Finances,* (F.U.), Tables 8 and 10.
7. DOT, Off. of Transp. Planning and Analysis, *Estimated Expenditures on Domestic Transportation Capital Improvement and Operating Programs* (1974), p. xii.
8. Data for this section, unless otherwise noted, are from: CAB, *Annual Report,* 1947: ——, Bur. Accts and Statistics, *Handbook of Airline Statistics,* appropriate years: DOC, Bur. of Census, *Census of Government,* 1972, v. 4, #5, *Historical Statistics,* Table 4; v. 6, #4, *Compendium of Gov. Finance,* Tables 3 and 8.
9. DOT, *Airport and Airway Cost Allocation Study, Federal Costs,* (1973), Part 1; J.J. Warford, *Public Policy toward General Aviation,* (Washington, D.C., 1971).
10. K. T. Healy, *The Economics of Transportation in America,* pp. 374-443 (New York, 1940).
11. *RA,* v. 140, May 14, 1956, pp. 11-12.
12. 372 US 744 (1963).
13. *RA,* v. 166, 2/3/1969, p. 25; ——, v. 171, 8/9/1971, p. 44B.
14. The data used in this section is from ICC, 60th-86th *Annual Report* of ICC, (1946-1976), except as otherwise noted.
15. 293 ICC 93 (1954); 322 ICC 301 (1964).
16. 321 ICC 238 (1963); 337 ICC 298 (1970).
17. 345 I, II, III ICC 1.
18. ICC, 60th-86th *Annual Reports,* ICC (1946-1972), Tables of Construction and Abandonment Proceedings; ICC, 83rd *Annual Report,* 1969, p. 14 (by calculation).
19. 245 ICC 57 (1941).
20. 372 US 744, 759 (1963).

21. 235 ICC 723, 734–42 (1940); 199 Fed. Suppl. 635 (1961); 372 US 744, 759–60 (1960).

22. 392 US 571, 595 (1968).

23. ICC, BE, Interagency Rate Adjustments, Rail and Motor, Wash., D.C. (1956), pp. 216–20; 280 ICC 681 (1951); 309 ICC 347 (1960).

24. 329 ICC 824.

25. ICC, 78th *Annual Report* of ICC (1964), p. 23; 81st, p. 19; 82nd, p. 23.

26. H. B. Vanderblue and K. F. Burgess, *Railroads-Rates-Service-Management* (New York, 1924). James C. Nelson, *Railroad Transportation and Public Policy* (Washington, D.C., 1959).

27. Ann F. Freidlander, *The Dilemma of Freight Transport Regulation* (Washington, D.C., 1969).

28. Bell J., of Ec., vol. 12, Spring '81; R.C. Levin, *Railroad Rates, Profitability, and Welfare under Deregulation,* C. Winston, *The Welfare Effects of ICC Regulation Revisited.*

4. Passenger Service, Fares, and Operation

1. The data used in this chapter, except as otherwise noted, is directly or by calculation from the appropriate year: ICC, SRUS, TSUS. ——, *Comparative State. Oper. Averages, Series 200* (up to 1950); M or Q 213 *Pass. Train Performance of Class I Steam Rys.* (to 1964); M or Q 220 *Rev. Traffic Stat. of Class I Steam Rys.*; M or Q 250 *Pass. Traffic Stat. (other than commutation) of Class I Steam Rys.* (to 1964); A 300 *Wage Statistics Class I Steam Rys.*; A 750 *Rev., Exp., Other Income and Statistics, Class I Motor Carriers*; ——, 43rd-75th *Annual Report,* 1929-1971; U.S. Dept. of Comm. Bur. of Public Rds., *Highway Statistics*; CAB, Bur. of Accts. and Stat., *Handbook of Airline Statistics*; U.S. Dept. of Comm., Bur. of Census, *Stat. Abstract of U.S.,* Tables, Population, Personal Income, by States; Automobile Manufacturers Assoc., *Automobile Facts and Figures*; Natl. Assoc. of Motor Bus Operators, *Bus Facts.*

2. 182 ICC 263 (1932), pp. 394-96; 219 ICC 174 (1936), pp. 190-95, 201, 206, 256; *Railway Age,* Jan. 1, 1927, p. 61, Jan. 5, 1929, p. 106, Jan. 30, 1930, pp. 102-3, Jan. 3, 1931, p. 107.

3. *The Official Guide of the Railways,* Sept. 1929, Sept. 1939.

4. 214 ICC 174 (1936).

5. ICC, Bur. of Statistics, Statement #4129, B. Aitchison, *Preliminary Examination of Factors Affecting the Demand for Rail Passenger Travel* (Wash., D.C., 1941).

6. Fed. Coord. of Trans., *Passenger Traffic Report* (Wash., D.C., 1935), pp. 242-47.

7. ICC, Bur. of T. E. & S., #577, *A Brief History of the Separation of Railroad Operating Expense Between Freight and Passenger Services* (Wash., D.C., 1957); Research Committee of the Aeronautical Research Foundation, John R. Meyer, Chairman, *Avoidable Costs of Passenger Train Service* (Cambridge, 1957), pp. 7, 8, and 35.

8. 266 ICC 537 (1946).

9. 268 ICC 303 (1947); 268 ICC 457 (1947); 269 ICC 240 (1947); 269 ICC 281 (1947); 269 ICC 632 (1948); 272 ICC 67 (1948); 276 ICC 433 (1949).

5. Baggage, Mail, and Express Services

1. Unless otherwise indicated, the data for this section is directly or by calculation from ICC, SRUS, TSUS, *Annual Report on Statistics of Railways in the U.S.,* Tables 158, 168, 169, appropriate year; *Ann. Rpt. on Transport Statistics in the U.S.,* Tables A1, 168, Part 3 or Part 1, Sec. F.; Post Off. Dept., *Ann. Rpt. of the Postmaster General of the U.S.*; ——, *Cost Ascertainment Report,* appropriate years.

2. 283 ICC 503 (1951), p. 561-64.

3. 323 ICC 468 (1964), 494; 326 ICC 594 (1965).

4. 308 ICC 545 (1959).

5. *Moody's Transport. Manual, 1963,* pp. 958-59, *1971,* p. 209; 323 ICC 1 (1964), 22; 325 ICC 285 (1963), 311.

6. 323 ICC 468 (1964); 328 ICC 594 (1965).

7. ICC Bur. of Eco., *Transport Economics,* Jan. 1973, pp. 5-8.

6. Pricing of Carload Freight Services

1. 262 ICC 447, 695 (1945).

2. 284 ICC 167 (1953); 344 US 905 (1952); 297 ICC 143 (1955); 306 ICC 737 (1959).

3. 248 ICC 545 (1942); 255 ICC 357 (1943); 256 ICC 502 (1943).

4. 264 ICC 695 (1946); 266 ICC 537 (1946); 269 ICC 33 (1947); 270 ICC 463 (1948); 276 ICC 9 (1949); 284 ICC 589, 591 (1952); 281 ICC 557 (1951).

5. ICC, Bur. of Transp., Ec. & Statistics, #R1-1 (Aug. 1959). The ICC index based on 1950=100. It extended back to 1947 for which year it was 87. The increases from 6/20/1946 to 1947 were 19 percent. By backward extrapolation the 1946 index is estimated as 67.

6. 298 ICC 279 (1956); 299 ICC 429 (1956); 299 ICC 557 (1957); 300 ICC 633 (1957); 302 ICC 665 (1958); 304 ICC 289 (1958); 313 ICC 373 (1961).

7. 300 ICC 633, 664 (1957).

8. 332 ICC 280 (1968); 332 ICC 714 (1969); 337 ICC 436 (1970); 339 ICC 125 (1971); 341 ICC 288 (1972).

9. 262 ICC 447 (1945); 281 ICC 213 (1951); 284 ICC 589 (1952); 296 ICC 555 (1955); 298 ICC 279 (1956).

10. *RA,* v. 143, July 22, 1957, p. 13; 308 ICC 439 (1959); 372 US 744 (1963).

11. 335 ICC 798, 841, 847, 858 (1970).

12. 337 ICC 436 (1970).

13. 196 ICC 127 (1933); 216 ICC 435 (1936); 219 ICC 245 (1936); 293 ICC 93 (1954).

14. 296 ICC 219 (1935); *TW,* v. 95, 4/9/55, p. 36.

15. *RA,* v. 136, 4/19/54, p. 11; v. 141, 12/10/56, p. 7; v. 142, 4/8/57, p. 10; v. 144, 1/13/58, p. 16.

16. *RA,* v. 147, 11/30/59, p. 55; 322 ICC 301, 307-12 (1964); 337 ICC 557, 560 (1970).

17. 11 ICC 382, 403 (1905).

18. The author was informed of this by the traffic vice-president of the road involved.

19. 243 ICC 589 (1941).

20. 235 ICC 485 (1939).

21. 243 ICC 589 (1941); P. W. MacAvoy and J. Sloss, *Regulation of Transport Innovation* (New York, 1967), p. 22.

22. 270 ICC 584 (1948); 273 ICC 736 (1949); 280 ICC 585 (1951); 299 ICC 409 (1956).

23. Pittsburgh Consolidation Coal Co.—Internal Memo, 6/1/55, *Volume Rates on Bituminous Fine Coal;* 294 ICC 233 (1955); 296 ICC 489 (1955).

24. *RA,* v. 138, 3/7/55, p. 9.

25. 304 ICC 769 (1958); 306 ICC 195 (1959); 308 ICC 99 (1959); 308 ICC 673 (1959).

26. *Business Week,* 3/9/1963, p. 34.

27. 318 ICC 641 (1963); 321 ICC 582 (1963); 325 ICC 752 (1965).

28. 335 ICC 111 (1969); 339 ICC 579 (1971).

29. 313 ICC 247 (1961).

30. 306 ICC 195 (1959); 306 ICC 703 (1959); 308 ICC 99 (1959); 308 ICC 217 (1959); 318 ICC 217 (1962); 325 ICC 752 (1965).

31. For a general review of these developments in respect to coal rates see MacAvoy and Sloss, sufra.

32. Letter from the president of the ATSF to (author), 5/24/67.

33. *RA,* v. 164, 1/29/68, p. 22.

34. *Min. Yr. Bk.,* 1950, pp. 613 ff.; 1961, p. 113; 1972,; v. II, p. 135; 1973, v. II, p. 126.

35. 302 ICC 665, 690 (1958).

36. 291 ICC 527 (1954); 299 ICC 195 (1956); 300 ICC 102 (1957); 314 ICC 149 (1961); 321 ICC 473 (1964); 355 US 175 (1957); 373 US 372 (1963).

37. 302 ICC 109 (1957); 314 ICC 149 (1961).

38. ICC, I & S, #6742, Statement and Exhibits, A.L. Graburn, Mrg. Coal Traffic, P.

39. 246 ICC 679 (1950); 313 ICC 549, 553-57 (1961); 323 ICC 146 (1963).

40. The Cleveland-Cliffs Co., *Cliffs, Iron Ore Analyses*, 1968, p. 35, 345 ICC 548, 675, 698 (1976).

41. 323 ICC 746 (1965); 345 ICC 548, 682/684 (1976).

42. MYB, 1950, v. 1, p. 633; 1973, v. 1, p. 614; *Cliffs, Iron Ore Anal.*, 1968, pp. 35-39; 345 ICC 548, 675, 682, 684, 841 (1976) (by calculation).

43. 332 ICC 166 (1968).

44. 286 ICC 203, 226 (1952); 291 ICC 93 (1953); 345 ICC 548, 677, 687, 696, 758, 774 (1976).

45. 276 ICC 221, 238 (1949); 287 ICC 315, 337 (1952); letter to author, 3/7/56, from ass't. frt. traff. mgr, WP; 345 ICC 548, 696-98 (1976).

46. *Moody's Indust.*, 1968, p. 722; 345 ICC 548, 698 (1946).

47. In 1953 the unreasonableness of some 1948 iron ore freight changes was claimed by the *Youngstown Sheet and Tube*, but this related to the interpretation of the general increases of that period as they were applied to the iron ore rates. 291 ICC 122 (1953).

48. 276 ICC 679 (1950); 332 ICC 166 (1968); 291 ICC 93 (1953); 291 ICC 527 (1954); 302 ICC 109 (1957); 323 ICC 746 (1965); 321 ICC 473 (1964); 274 ICC 439 (1949); 273 ICC 749 (1949); 287 ICC 315 (1952).

49. ICC, *Frt. Commodity Statistics*, 1950, for mentioned railroads; 345 ICC 548, 802-16 (1976).

50. 350 ICC 228, 260 (1974).

51. 335 ICC 798, 804-8 (1970).

52. 237 ICC 245 (1940).

53. Ex Parte 62 through 223, *Increased Rates Cases*, cited earlier.

54. 266 ICC 627 (1946); T. C. Bingham and M. J. Roberts, *Citrus Fruit Rates* (Gainsville) (1950), p. 66.

55. 284 ICC 589, 633 (1952).

56. 272 ICC 648 (1958); 347 US 645 (1954); 304 ICC 374 289 (1958).

57. 318 ICC 469 (1962); 321 ICC 738 (1964).

58. 329 ICC 854 (1967); 332 ICC 714, 759 (1969); 337 ICC 436, 447 (1970); 339 ICC 125, 267, 283 (1971); 341 ICC 290, 448 (1972).

59. 332 ICC 136, 151-52 (1967); 340 ICC 470 (1972).

60. ICC, Bur. of Eco. & Stat., *Carload Waybill Statistics, 1960, TD1*, p. 14; DOT, FRA, Off. Eco., *Carload Waybill Statistics, 1972, TD1*, p. 12.

61. *RA*, v. 149, 8/29/60, p. 17, v. 150, 4/24/61, p. 32-36 (by calculation); 341 ICC 290, 443 (1972).

62. 341 ICC 622 (1972).

63. 350 ICC 228 (1974).

64. *USSA*, 90th ed., Table #1114, 96th ed., Tables #1262, 1269.

65. 276 ICC 621 (1949); 281 ICC 793 (1951).

66. 123 ICC 203 (1927); 227 ICC 494 (1938); 246 ICC 253 (1941).

67. 123 ICC 203 (1927); 227 ICC 285 (1938); 227 ICC 439 (1938); 227 ICC 494 (1938); 246 ICC 253 (1941).

68. Data for following sections are from: ICC, *Carload Waybill Statistics*, Mileage Block Distribution, State-to-State Distribution, Territorial Distribution, appropriate years; DOT, *Carload Waybill Statistics*, Territorial Distribution, 1972 (by calculation).

69. 339 ICC 125, 257 (1971); 341 ICC 290, 468-9 (1972).

70. ICC, *Class I RR, Commodity Statistics*, 1966, 1972; ICC, *Class I Motor Carrier* (Common and Contract), *Commodity Statistics*, 1966, 1972.

71. 276 ICC 621 (1949); 281 ICC 793 (1951).

72. 299 ICC 255 (1956).

73. ICC, B. T. E. & S., *Carload Waybill Analyses*, 1950, *#5131*, B. E. *Carload Waybill Statistics*, 1963 and 1964, *TD1*; DOT, FRA, OE, *Carload Waybill Statistics*, 1972, *TD1*.

74. MacAvoy and Sloss, *sufra*, pp. 21-35.

75. DOC, *1963 Census of Transp.*, vol. III, Pt. 1, Table 2, *1972 Census of Transp.*, vol. III, Pt. 1.

76. 308 ICC 247 (1959); 310 ICC 521 (1960); 173 Fed. Suppl. 397 (1959).

77. ICC Act., Sect. 15 (6).

78. 234 ICC 175 (1939); 287 ICC 479 (1953).

79. 325 ICC 1 (1965); 393 US 87 (1968); 337 ICC 74 (1970).

80. 269 ICC 265 (1948); 316 ICC 351 (1962).

81. 203 ICC 299 (1934); 321 ICC 17 (1963); 322 ICC 491 (1963); 238 Fed. Suppl. 528 (1965); 387 U.S. 326 (1967).

7. Less-than-Carload Freight—Service and Pricing

1. Fed. Coord. of Transp., *Merchandise Traffic Report* (Wash., D.C., 1934); ICC *SRUS*, Table 50, appropriate years, Commodity Statutes, Class I Railroads, appropriate years.

2. 262 ICC 447 (1945), p. 585.

3. Exhibit, Docket: *Analysis of Rail LCL Traffic by Territory* (Wash., D.C., April 1948), pp. 23, 120.

4. 273 ICC 57 (1948); 283 ICC 171 (1951); 284 ICC 551 (1952), pp. 553, 557-58; 288 ICC 555 (1953), p. 564; 306 ICC 539 (1959); *TW*, v. 130, 5/27/60, p. 10.

5. *RA*, v. 127, 7/16/49, p. 16; 283 ICC 171 (1951); *TW*, v. 132, 10/21/1967, pp. 35-36.

8. Freight Operations

1. Fed. Coord. of Transport., Section of Transport Services, *Freight Traffic Report*, (DC 1935), vol. III, pp. 172, 220.

2. Unless otherwise indicated, data for this section are from: ICC, Bur. of Accts., Statements #1-50, 6-57, 3-62, 6-69, ISC-72; ——, *SRUS*, appropriate years, Tables 55A, 158, 165, *TSUS*, Tables 55A, 162; ——, *M&Q 210, M&Q 240, A 300*.

3. *Presidential Railroad Commission Report* (D.C. 1962), pp. 86, 91-92.

4. Data for this section are from the appropriate volume of *Railway Age* and selected "symbol" freight train schedule books.

5. The data for this section are, unless otherwise indicated, directly or by calculation from: ICC, *SRUS*, 1940-1953, Tables 61, 158, *TSUS*, 1954-1972, Tables 61, 162, *Freight Commodity Statistics*, 1947-1972, *Carload Waybill Stat.*, 1946-1966, 1972, *#M&Q 210, M&Q 240, A 300, 100*; AAR, *Year Book of Railroad Facts*.

6. Fed. Coord. of Transp., *Frt. Traffic Report, Pt. III*, pp. 172, 220.

7. *RA*, various issues, 1947-1960, under index heading "Annual Review and Outlook" and "Yards."

8. The data for this section are from ICC, *SRUS*, Table 26, *TSUS*, Table 22; *Railway Age*, various Jan. dates, "Annual Review of Car and Locomotive Orders," by calculation.

9. *RA*, vol. 147, Aug. 24, 1959, p. 32.

10. ICC, *SRUS*, Tables #158, A1, *TSUS*, Tables #159, A1, *Freight Commodity Statistics*, Various Issues.

11. Data for this section, unless otherwise noted, are from: ICC, *SRUS & TSUS*, Tables #21, 23, 24, and Pt. 9, Statement *#Q 240, #100*, Statements *#1-50, 6-57, 3-62, 6-69, ISC-72, TE*, Feb., 1968, p. 7, April 1973, p. 9; AAR, CSD, *CS54-1B, CS8A, Yearbook, RR Facts*.

12. 304 ICC 289, 383 (1958); 311 ICC 373, 426 (1960); 337 ICC 23, 43 (1970); 339 ICC 655 (1971); 340 ICC 83 (1971).

13. 274 ICC 383 (1949); 297 ICC 291 (1955); 300 ICC 577 (1959); 311 ICC 373, 426 (1960); 332 ICC 176 (1968); 396 U.S. (1976).

14. 335 ICC 264, 285 (1969).

15. 335 ICC 264, 289 (1969); 337 ICC 217 (1970); 340 ICCF3 (1971); 343 ICC 360 (1974); ICC *Annual Report*, 83rd, p. 8, 84th, pp. 8-9, 86th, pp. 24-29, 87th, pp. 20-22.

16. *RA*, v. 174, 1/29/73, p. 73.

17. 335 ICC 264, 294 (1969); 337 ICC 183 (1969); 337 ICC 217 (1970); 340 ICC 83 (1971); 343 ICC 360 (197); ICC, 83rd *Ann. Report*, pp. 8, 84th *Ann. Report*, pp. 8-9, 86th *Ann. Report*, pp. 24-29, 87th *Ann. Report*, pp. 20-22.

18. *RA*, v. 174, 1/29/73, p. 73.

9. Labor

1. BLF & E, *The Fireman's Press*, January 1950, p. 13.

2. Railroad Retirement Board, *Quarterly Review*, Jan.-Mar.

3. The sources for this section are: Fed. Coord. of Transp., *Survey of Rules Governing Wage Payments in the Engine and Train Service* (Washington, D.C., 1936); *Report of the Presidential Railroad Commission* (Washington, D.C., 1962); W. D. Hines, *War History of American Railroads* (New Haven, 1928), pp. 152-91.

4. The sources for this section are from the issues of appropriate years: ICC, *SRUS*, 1947-1953, *TSUS*, 1954-1972, M300, A300, 300, *Wage Statistics of Class I Railroads in the United States*; Railroad Retirement Board, *Annual Report*; U.S. Dept. of Labor (B.L.S.) *Handbook of Labor Statistics*, 1973, Bul. 1735, Wash., D.C.

5. The basic sources for this and subsequent sections on wages, unless otherwise noted, are from issues of appropriate years: AAR, *Review of Railway Operations* in–(Wash., D.C.); National Mediation Board, *Annual Report*–(Wash., D.C.); Report to the President by the Emergency Board, No.–(Wash., D.C.); U.S. Railroad Retirement Board, *Annual Report*–(Wash., D.C.), *The Monthly Review, Quarterly Review*; U.S. Dept. of Labor (B.L.S.), *Monthly Labor Review, Current Wage Developments, Handbook of Labor Statistics*, 1973, Bul. 1735 (Wash., D.C.), *Wage Chronology: U.S. Steel–1937-1973*, Bul. 1814; General Motors, *Annual Report*; U.S. Steel Corp., *Annual Report*; ICC, *SRUS*, 1947-1953, *TSUS*, 1954, Statements, M125, Q125, *Selected Income and Balance Sheet Items of Class I Railroads in the United States*, Statements, M300, A300, 300, *Wage Statistics of Class I Railroads in the United States*; U.S. Dept. of Labor, Labor-Management Services Administration, *Railroad Shopcraft* (Wash., D.C.); H. M. Levinson, *Determining Forces in Collective Wage Bargaining* (New York, 1966); R. M. McDonald, *Collective Bargaining in the Automobile Industry* (New Haven, 1963); A. M. Ross, *Trade Unions Policy* (Berkeley, 1956).

6. Sources for this and subsequent sections concerning employee benefits are from: Railroad Retirement Board, *Annual Report*, (Wash., D.C.), *The Monthly Review, Quarterly Review*, (appropriate years); *Social Security*; Feb. 1966, pp. 27-35, "Ten Years of Employer Benefit Plans"; Association of American Railroads–*A Review of Railroad Operations in* (Wash., D.C.); Hse. Doc. 92-350, *The RR Retirement System: Its Coming Crisis* (Wash., D.C., 1972), 93-1345, *Railroad Retirement Act Restructuring* (Wash., D.C., 1974) p. 211.

7. CEA, *Ann. Report*, Jan. 1964, pp. 54-55; Jan 1967, pp. 121-23.

8. *RA*, v. 156, May 25, 1964, p. 7.

9. *RA*, v. 160, March 28, 1966, p. 38; *Locomotive Engineer*, Dec. 22, 1967.

10. *TW*, v. 131, Sept. 23, 1967, pp. 40-51.

11. *The International Teamster*, May 1970, p. 6.

12. W. D. Hines, *War History of American Railroads* (New Haven, 1928), pp. 166-67.

13. ICC, Statements, M300 A300, *Wage Statistics of Class I Railroads.*

10. Management

1. Chester Barnard, *The Functions of the Executive*, (Cambridge, Mass.: Harvard U. Press, 1940), pp. 6, 219-34, 258-59.

2. Personnel changes are from *RA*, "People in the News" section; *Who's Who in Railroading*, Simmonds-Boardman, N.Y., various issues.

3. *RA*, v. 136, Jan. 24, 1954, p. 7.

4. *RA*, v. 148, 2/1/1960, p. 32.

5. U.S. Dept. of Commerce, *Report of Railroad Professional Group on Various Aspects of the New York, New Haven & Hartford Railroad Company's Problems,* submitted by F.B. Whitman, June 28, 1962 (Washington, D.C.), pp. 30, 55.

6. 327 ICC 151, 172 (1966).

7. *RA,* v. 138, Oct., 10, 1955, p. 46.

8. *RA,* v. 156, Feb. 17, 1964, p. 23.

9. *RA,* v. 154, June 6, 1963, p. 7.

10. *Moody's Bond Survey,* v. 44, 5/20/52, p. 443; v. 45, 2/2/53, p. 645, 7/27/53, p. 345; v. 49, 11/30/57, p. 158; v. 52, 6/13/60, p. 467; v. 54, 9/17/62, p. 365.

11. *Dun's Review,* v. 90, Dec. 1960, p. 38; v. 104, Dec. 1974, pp. 43, 46-50.

11. Growth of Railroad Systems—Internal

1. Data for this chapter is by calculation from: ICC, *SRUS* and *TSUS,* appropriate years.

2. ICC, *Examiner's Report, CNW-Control-CRI,* vol. I (1971), pp. 395-96.

3. 287 ICC 611 (1953); 351 ICC 321 (1976).

4. *Moody's Railroads, 1951,* pp. 898, 1020, *Transportation, 1958,* pp. 1015, 1465, *1963,* p. 1255; ICC, *SRUS,* Table 180, *TSUS,* Part 8.

5. CAB 379 (1943).

6. *Moody's Industrials, 1930,* p. 2326.

7. 8 CAB 726 (1947).

8. 4 CAB 104 (1943).

9. 182 ICC 263 (1932); 12 MCC 461 (1939), 26 MCC 529 (1940), 34 MCC 599 (1942).

10. 63 MCC 91 (1954); 364 US 1; 89 ICC 189 (1962); 114 MCC 321 (1972).

11. ICC, *Stat. Class I Motor Carriers,* Tables 30 & 58, *TSUS,* Part 7, Motor Carriers, Tables 29, 29A, 30 (by calc.).

12. *Moody's Transportation Manual, 1954,* p. 219, 1108; 317 ICC 39 (1962); 342 ICC 416 (1972); 342 ICC 666 (1973).

13. Data for this section from *Moody's Transportation Manual,* appropriate year and company compilation; ICC, *TSUS,* Part 6.

12. Growth by Acquisition of Other Railroads and Results of Unification

1. The sources for corporate events and financial data are *Moody's Transportation Manual,* appropriate year and company compilations; for geographic detail and mileages, *The Official Guide—*; for basic statistics, ICC, Bur. of T. S. & E., *Statistics of Railways in the U.S.,* Bur. of Accts., *Annual Report on Transport Statistics in the U.S.* A definitive review of the acquisition process with emphasis on personal motives and involvement is Richard Saunders, *The Railroad Mergers and the Coming of Conrail* (Westport: Ct., 1978).

2. 331 ICC 228, 269 (1967).

3. 267 ICC 295 (1947); 307 ICC 5 (1958).

4. J.H. Lemly, *The Gulf Mobile and Ohio* (Chicago, 1953), pp. 183-91.

5. 261 ICC 343 (1945); 261 ICC 405 (1945); 271 ICC 63 (1948).

6. 267 ICC 163 (1946); 267 ICC 207 (1946); 267 ICC 548 (1947); R. Saunders, *sufra* pp. 65-66.

7. 267 ICC 163 (1946); 267 ICC 401 (1947); *RA,* v. 128, 1/21/50, p. 57, 5/13/50, p. 69.

8. *MBS,* v. 43, 6/25/51, p. 390; v. 44, 5/20/52, p. 443.

9. 261 ICC 239 (1945); 271 ICC 5 (1948); J. Borkin, *Robert R. Young, the Populist of Wall Street* (NY; 1969), pp. 94-131.

10. 295 ICC 131 (1955); 295 ICC 703 (1958); *RA,* v. 146, March 9, 1959; R. Saunders, *supra,* pp. 68-69.

11. Saunders, *supra,* pp. 185-86; J. Borkin, *supra,* p. 222; *RA,* v. 146, Jan. 19, 1959, p. 9, Feb. 2, 1959, p. 832.

12. 295 ICC 563 (1957); 307 ICC 37 (1958); 312 ICC 125 (1960).

13. 224 ICC 181 (1927); 295 ICC 523 (1957); 361 US 173, 361 US 945.

14. 295 ICC 425 (1957); 158 Fed. Suppl. 248.

15. 117 ICC 67 (1926); 307 ICC 401 (1959).

16. 312 ICC 185 (1960); Saunders, *supra*, pp. 95-124.

17. *MBG*, v. 53, 11/20/1961, p. 137.

18. *RA*, v. 154, 5/13/63, p. 36; v. 155, 7/1/63, p. 40.

19. *RA*, v. 148, 5/2/1960, p. 16.

20. *RA*, v. 148, 5/30/60, p. 10; Saunders, *supra*, pp. 126-30, 147, 252-58, 294.

21. 317 ICC 261 284, 291 (1962); 327 ICC 475, 566, 567 (1966). 375 US 216 (   ); Saunders, *supra*, pp. 126-30.

22. *MBS*, v. 52, 5/2/1960, p. 551; v. 53, 3/13/1961, p. 658.

23. 324 ICC 1 (1964); 330 ICC 780 (1967).

24. *MBS*, v. 52, 10/3/1960, pp. 244-45; v. 53, 8/7/1961, p. 346; v. 59, 12/18/1967, pp. 37-38.

25. 386 US 372 440 (1967).

26. 327 ICC 566 (1965); 327 ICC 475 (1966); 328 ICC 304 (1966); 334 ICC 25 (1968); 386 US 372 (1967).

27. 330 ICC 477 (1966).

28. 328 ICC 684 (1967).

29. 336 ICC 899 (1970); *1971 Financial Summary, CO/BO* (Chessie System, Cleveland), p. 8.

30. 295 ICC 563 (1957); 312 ICC 39 (1961); 317 ICC 557 (1962).

31. 320 ICC 122 (1963); 386 US 544 (1967).

32. 334 ICC 378 (1968); ICC 83rd *Ann. Report*, p. 22.

33. *MBS*, v. 61, 8/25/1969, p. 488.

34. (Decision not printed) ICC 88th *Ann. Report* (1974) p. 26-27.

35. 338 ICC 805 (1971); 409 US 1094 (1972).

36. 327 ICC 279 (1965); 338 ICC 134 (1970); 342 ICC 578 (1972).

37. 312 ICC 285 (1960).

38. 327 ICC 387 (1965).

39. 328 ICC 460 (1966); 331 ICC 228 (1967); 396 US 91 (1970).

40. 327 ICC 279 (1965).

41. 324 ICC 309 (1964).

42. 330 ICC 15 (1968).

43. 347 ICC 556 (1974); ICC, 89th *Annual Report*, (1975), p. 17; 90th *Ann. Report* (1976), p. 23.

44. ICC, 82nd *Ann. Report*, p. 64; *Moody's Transp. Manual*, 1967, p. 955.

45. Saunders, *supra*, pp. 264-71.

46. Saunders, *supra*, p. 219, 234.

47. K.T. Healy, *The Effects of Scale in the Railroad Industry* (New Haven, 1961); DOT, *Western Railroad Mergers* (Wash., D.C., 1969).

48. R E Gallamore, *Railroad Mergers: Costs, Competition* (Mimeo, Cambridge, 1969) pp. 275-77.

13. Financial Performance of the Railroads

1. Unless otherwise indicated the sources of data are: ICC, *SRUS, TSUS*; U.S. Dept. of Labor, BLS, *Handbook of Labor Statistics*, 1973, Bul. 1753; Moody's Investors Service, *Moody's Railroads*, 1940-1951, *Moody's Transportation Manual*, 1953-1973.

2. ICC, 57th, *Ann. Report*, pp. 30-34.

3. ICC, 73rd, *Ann. Report*, 1960, p. 76.

4. *Moody's Transp. Manual, 1967*, p. 364; *1971*, pp. 489, 558, 573.

5. From ICC, *SRUS*, 1929, Table 53a and ICC, *TSUS*, 1972, Table 126, by calculation.